SEX IN DEVELOPMENT

SEX IN DEVELOPMENT

. . .

Science, Sexuality,
and Morality in Global
Perspective

. . .

VINCANNE ADAMS *and*
STACY LEIGH PIGG,
editors

. . .

Duke University Press
Durham & London
2005

. . .

©2005 Duke University Press
All rights reserved. Printed in
the United States of America
on acid-free paper ∞
Designed by Amy Ruth
Buchanan. Typeset in Scala
by Keystone Typesetting, Inc.
Library of Congress Cataloging-
in-Publication Data
appear on the last printed
page of this book.

. . .

• • •

To John Norby (from V. A.)

and to Jana Ghimire, *srijana*

(from S. L. P.)

• • •

CONTENTS

• • •

ACKNOWLEDGMENTS

• • •

This volume grew out of a creative spark in a spur-of-the-moment conversation at a conference and, since 1999, a widening circle of colleagues have joined us in discussing the questions we raise in this volume. We owe our first acknowledgments to the contributors who made their work available for this collection and whose patience and responsiveness to our editorial suggestions was outstanding. Although it has taken much longer than either of us anticipated to complete this volume, we deeply appreciate the willingness of the contributors to join in the project and stay to the end. Lively discussions with participants at several conferences were key to the intellectual formation of this work, including the panel "Sex, Science, and the State" (organized by Stacy Pigg, with the participation of Leslie Butt and Lawrence Cohen) at the American Ethnological Society meeting in March 1999; the conference "Sexualities, Masculinities, and Culture in South Asia," organized by Sanjay Srivastava at Deakin University in Melbourne Australia; and the panel "Internationalisation and the Subject of Sex" (organized by Stacy Pigg and Leslie Butt) as well as the plenary sessions at the Third Conference of the International Association for the Study of Sex, Culture, and Society at the University of Melbourne in October 2001. We also wish to recognize here the creative dynamic of our collaboration. For Stacy, Vincanne's uncanny, electrical ability to bridge ideas with a spark of insight has animated this project from the beginning. Always able to go straight to the core, to see the big picture, to turn the perfect phrase, and to pull it all together, her unwavering depth of intellect has held this volume together in numerous practical and ethereal ways. For Vincanne's part, thanks are due to Stacy for her perspicacity, tenacity, and analytical brilliance. More than most collaborators, she seems always to be able to mix the hard and dirty work of painstaking revisions and literature reviews with a commitment to freshness of insight, relevance, and originality. We thank each other for collegiality and friendship; we have benefited enormously from working together on this volume. Thanks are also owed to the three anonymous reviewers who carefully read each chapter and offered extensive and wise suggestions for revision. Kelly Gardiner, Melinda Belcham, and, most important, Denielle Elliott assisted in the preparation of the manuscript—without them we might as yet be checking bibliographic references and wrestling with hidden codes in Microsoft Word. Finally, thanks go to Ken Wissoker who, in numerous conversations at annual meetings, recognized the importance of our analytical commitment to bringing research on sexuality together with thinking about science and the state, and who, always with a gentle but inspirational voice, continued to encourage us to refine the materials.

STACY LEIGH PIGG AND VINCANNE ADAMS

Introduction: The Moral Object of Sex

• • •

Our starting point for this volume is the recognition of the multiple moral investments that people have in sex; our concern is how these investments are shaped by science, medicine, technology, and planning rationalities. Sex is a vehicle for moral objectives, and the "objectification of sex" is a moral act. What, then, are the effects of development projects that objectify sexuality? How does the type of objectivity contained within scientific accounts of the sexual body enter into social life? If sexuality is located in dense webs of socially meaningful moralities, then what are the repercussions of the myriad modernizing projects that claim neutrality and objectivity while placing sexuality within notions of population management, human rights, disease prevention, risk reduction, child survival, and maternal health? How do the sexual and reproductive sciences (in tandem with demography, epidemiology, and the social sciences) attempt to create a universal "normal" sexuality? And how do projects touching on sexual and reproductive health make use of this notion? Sexual practices may be seen as sites for expressing, confirming, or transgressing various existing and/or imported moral codes and, as such, they may be seen as having explicit moral "objectives." However, moralities are also externally constructed by political arrangements, health programs, conceptions of biology and reproduction, and nationalisms.

The chapters in this book address the attempts made to objectify sex and sexuality in the name of health and well-being. Science, medicine, and technology frame sexual acts in apparently amoral biological terms. In so doing they also generate specific procedures for knowing, manipulating, and managing bodies. In scientific discourses pertaining to family planning and AIDS prevention, for example, an implicit set of moral assumptions about the purposes of sexual relations and the nature of the person is concealed in rational projects of social and medical welfare that give the appearance of moral neutrality. Similar effects are produced in contemporary sexual identity politics that advocate the possibility of specific pleasures and erotics without moral blame. Yet, even packaged in these ways the "sexual lessons" learned from development aid and its related postcolonial transnational engagements are clearly not devoid of moral principles and judgments. Morality matters: it is contested, debated, and refigured in and through the interventions that directly or indirectly target people's sexual lives—interventions that themselves mediate concerns about nationalism, geopolitical relations, and post- or neocolonial identity politics.

By focusing on interventions ranging from fertility control to disease prevention and sex education, we, the contributors to this volume, draw attention to the hidden moral trajectory of these rationalizing projects and explore the specific moral eddies created in their wake. What objectives are achieved by moralizing or putatively de-moralizing sexuality? What kind of moral object does sexuality become in these encounters? What moral contestations are set in motion by dehistoricizing sexuality within its myriad international contexts?

Our questions here thus emerge at the intersection of at least three literatures: the cultural analysis of sexuality; the critique of development; and the explorations of biology and nature in science and technology studies. We argue that the analytical tools provided by each of these bodies of work are needed to account for the meanings, visibility, moral articulations, practices, and power of "sexuality" inside and outside the Euro-American West. Cultural and historical studies of sexuality offer much in the way of exploring the complexities of sexual practices and their implications, while social studies of science and of development offer refreshing insights into the often mundane programs that frequently function as the instruments through which neocolonial, nationalist, and identity politics are articulated. We believe that it is necessary to look closely at the actual situated dynamics of these relationships in a way that goes beyond the simplistic notion of a "confrontation" between modern and indigenous values.

In this volume we also propose a symmetrical historicization of sexuality both inside and outside the Western project. As Michel Foucault's argument about the discursive construction of sexuality suggests, and as much social history demonstrates, sexuality as a discursive term is a recent invention in the Euro-American context. The idea of "sexuality" as an autonomous, reified realm of human life emerged within the context of the restructuring of production and reproduction under capitalism and through the emergent medicalization of sexual practices (Jordanova 1995; Ross and Rapp 1997; Weeks 1998). In light of this we need to consider carefully what it means, on the one hand, to seek to explain "sexualities" outside this context and, on the other, to address programs and practices based on the notions of sexuality that arise precisely from this context. In what sense can we speak of sexuality as it exists outside the Euro-American context? How have specific sexualities been produced and transformed within other traditions, other histories? In what specific ways have these sexualities been embedded (or not) in moral concerns? How can we trace the outcomes of the reification and rationalization of sex in health development and social welfare programs, particularly as they relate to other historical sexual formations? To what extent, and in what forms, do internationally circulating frameworks of development and science carry forth a rationalization of sexuality? And how are these reinvested with moral meaning in the course of social practice itself? How do various visions of sexuality circulate in and through political agendas in the family, the village, the nation, and in religion and translocal institutions? Do they generate a morally embedded form of "backtalk" in opposition to capitalism, modernity, and colonialism? And, if so, then what are the implications of this for various social actors?

Not surprisingly, the past few years have witnessed an increasing number of anthropological and historical papers and presentations that speak to these questions. In this introduction, our aim is to show how the fields of sexuality, development, and science might come together in a constructive manner. In tracing the tensions between a sexuality that is universalized and a sexuality that is specific in meaning, practice, and outcome, we show how each of these fields has both uncovered and reproduced these tensions.

Sexuality

In his 1929 preface to Bronislaw Malinowski's *The Sexual Life of Savages*, Havelock Ellis (1932 [1929]: vii) wrote of the importance of ethnological data in building scientific knowledge about the sexual dimensions of human life: "The sexual life of savages has long awaited its natural historian." Ethnological descriptions of "unspoilt people" were to provide the comparative data necessary to achieve a clear picture of where human nature left off and social molding began. As Ellis himself realized, this comparative scientific project was but another stage in the longer history of European fascination with the sexual customs of those who were defined as "other." Moral judgments about the development of civilization were debated in and through "scientific" claims about the sexual behaviors of "native others." Indeed, when Ellis wrote his introduction, sexological publications frequently contained long passages describing sexual practices in non-Western societies. Here the "other" was used as a form of displacement, enabling ethnological accounts to introduce topics that at "home" would be risky and morally fraught.[1]

With the relativist turn in the early twentieth century (Stocking 1987: 199–208), synchronic models emphasizing the internal logic and cohesiveness of separate "cultures" gave rise to a different kind of contrastive rhetoric. R. W. Connell and G. W. Dowsett (1992: 58) write that "after psychoanalysis, ethnography became . . . the most important body of evidence requiring a social theory of sexuality." The first decades of the twentieth century were a time when the scientific investigation of sexuality consolidated numerous fields of academic inquiry. A focus on the "sex instinct" and the "sex drive" was consolidated in and through biological science (particularly through endocrinology and research on the reproductive system), psychological theories of motivation (such as Freud's), and functionalist social science. Experimental laboratory science, clinical case observation, and the scientific study of society all attempted to produce empirical evidence from which general explanations of functions and processes could be built. During this period, distinct "social" and "biological" axes of sexuality were parsed.[2]

Now, almost a century later, many theorists cast a skeptical eye on the universalism and objectivism inherent within this approach to knowledge about sexuality. This skepticism is grounded in an understanding of colonial discourses of difference, in interpretive approaches to the social production of meaning, and in feminist analyses of the gender biases that have informed scientific work on nature and the body.[3] Thus, today, while one wing of research on sexuality still pursues evolutionary and biological questions about molecular-cognitive interactions and sustains an avid interest in the pursuit of universalistic claims about human nature, another wing explores the formations of sexual meanings and arrangements as mutable and contextually dependent specificities in and through which erotic encounters and reproductive consequences are invested with moral significance.

In recent decades two main insights have transformed research on sexuality, prying apart the tightly fused assumptions about how bodies, sexed as male and female vessels containing "universal" sexual instincts, express inherent desires in socially debated forms. First, feminist interrogations of gender have complicated our notions of maleness and femaleness by critically examining the processes that make women and men and that organize gendered spheres of social activity within relations of power (Ortner and Whitehead 1981; di Leonardo 1991; Rosaldo and Lamphere 1974; Ragoné and Twine 2000; Reiter 1975). A rich body of ethnographic and historical research shows how the gendering of persons is knit into the organization of kinship and procreation, productive and reproductive relations, and class (e.g., Findlay 1999; Kelly 1997; Lancaster 1995; Rubin 1975; Walkowitz 1980; Weston 1996; White 1990). Feminist analysis has exposed the naturalizing assumptions that undergird normative masculinity and femininity, and it has shown how these assumptions have been woven into colonialist endeavors (Fausto-Sterling 1985; Haraway 1998; Jordanova 1989; Keller 1995; Martin 1986). And queer theory has further disarticulated the presumed natural relation between sexed bodies, gender, and desire (Butler 1989; Patton 1985; Rubin 1984). Developed within the contexts of both activism and social science inquiry, these arguments have made it possible to conceptualize sexuality and erotic desire independently of gender and to think of a sexuality unmoored from a heterosexual matrix—a position that enables us to question the distinctive naturalisms of Western folk and scientific thought (Butler 1989; Morris 1995; Rubin 1984; Weston 1993).

Second, theories of sex and society have shifted from models stressing the social regulation of sexuality to those stressing the social production of sexuality (Vance 1991). The analytical perspective of social constructionism has enabled us to examine, in any given time and place, the intersecting factors that account for the apparent solidity of foundational ideas. Constructionism illustrates how sexuality exists within the articulation of economic, social, and political structures and within the systems of meaning and representation they sustain. With its emphasis on historical change and context, constructionism is wary of universalizing explanations of sexual meaning, motives, and practices. From a constructionist perspective, all sexualities are local.

In contrast to theories that assume that a natural history of human sexual capacities is the bedrock on which comparative accounts of social regulation is anchored, contemporary works—following insights from feminist research— ask how the proliferation of modes of speaking and writing about sexuality were and are imbricated in managing complex differentials of power and in effecting dispersed means of social control, particularly through forms of self-revelation and monitoring. Much of this literature builds on the work of Foucault, who stepped outside the sexological framework to link the development of the sexual sciences themselves to the management of populations.

But even Foucault separates "a medicine of sex" from "a biology of reproduction," treating them as distinct streams (Foucault 1978: 54–55, discussed in Clarke 1998: 18).

This analytic distinction between a biologically reproductive "sex" and a culturally constructed "sexuality" continues to hold currency in some sexuality literature, particularly when it is embedded in an often implicit separation between "the West" and "the rest." Sadly, this nested distinction continues to organize how this literature is read, thereby stunting what we believe to be its most interesting comparative questions. Ironically, the persistence of this dichotomy can be explained by what we now know about the emergence of sexuality as a distinct, nameable, autonomous domain in the modern West. After all, the proposition that sexuality is socially constructed requires a concept of sexuality from which to launch an exploration of its context-dependent constitution.[4]

In social analyses of sexuality, too often the history of Western sexualities takes center stage against a rhetorically constructed backdrop of "other cultures." Thus, contrastive cases—the berdache; ritual homosexuality in Melanesia; the active and the passive partner in Latin America, and so on—are used to present "alien" forms in contrast to Western "commonsense" forms. In order for "other cultures" to function as the contrastive background that makes "our own culture" visible, these lifeworlds are often dehistoricized so as to maximize a sense of difference (pace Weston 1993; Manderson and Jolly 1997).[5] Sexual practices are seen as offering potent symbolic markers of difference precisely because, as Foucault has argued, the concept of sexuality itself condenses core beliefs about the nature and/or constitution of self, identity, culture, and nation. But this approach presupposes a distinctive domain called "sexuality" that can be used in comparative analysis. Often, this sexuality is implicitly and sometimes explicitly rooted in a more deep-seated set of assumptions about reproductive sex as itself a biological given or in assumptions about a universal, biologically based pleasure. Thus sexuality becomes the pivot around which cultural differences are identified.

In her groundbreaking work on race and sexuality, Ann Stoler (1997b: 14) offers a partial corrective to this approach, noting that sexuality is constituted in and through colonial relations of governance, medicine, and education: "The very categories of 'colonizer' and 'colonized' were secured through forms of sexual control that defined domestic arrangements of Europeans and the cultural investments through which they identified themselves."[6] Herein, the possibility of organizing and devising a "science" of sexuality that is rooted in biological norms is shown to be contingent on the particular sociocultural engagements between colonizers and colonized. And yet, even here the presumption of sexuality as a nameable domain hovers as an implicit ground for comparative analysis.

Despite this long history of colonial engagement, presumptions of difference persist in the discussion of culture and sexuality, and these are still too often undergirded by assumptions about a sexuality that stands outside the contingencies of history, biology, and psychology. An ethnocartography of sexual practices has, as Kath Weston (1993) notes, predominated, leading to the reproduction of culture-bound comparative approaches. Our aim in this book is to move beyond this tendency to let "cultural difference" formulate theory; rather, we focus on how sexualities are constituted in and through projects that blur the boundaries between cultures, norms, and moralities.[7] In this effort, we build on the work of a number of authors who have begun to map out this territory.[8]

A useful corrective to the sociological work that uses sexual others as foils for a Western sexual constructionism looks at the "creation" of an object called "sexuality" as a historically emergent, often transnational, endeavor (e.g., Dikötter 1995; Donham 1999; Farquhar 2002; Kelsky 1996, 1999). Such accounts help to disrupt sociological readings of sexual others while returning us to fundamental questions about the meanings, forms, and practices of those phenomena that throughout the world fall into the domain of the sexual. In this sense, at least, ethnographic work that explores the elaborations of erotic desire, gender, and social relations in diverse locales continues to provide valuable insights into the interplay of meaning, structure, identity, and power.

Ethnographic studies also caution us against the practice of misinterpreting sexual practices by viewing them through the lens of inappropriate assumptions (Weston 1993). Just as historians have engaged in a rich debate on the stability of "homosexuality" across time (Halperin 1998; McIntosh 1981; Rosario 1997), so evidence from diverse contexts around the world continues to unsettle many categories used in the analysis of sexuality. Disjunctures between sexual identity, sexual behavior, and sexual ascription call into question "the (Western) correspondence model of gender/sexuality that assigns anatomical sex a constant gender and a prescribed object of sexual desire" (Weston 1993: 348; see also Jackson 1997a; Morris 1994; Patton 1996: 373).[9]

The assumption that sexuality can be bracketed off from reproduction is equally problematic (Manderson, Bennett, and Sheldrake 1999). The efforts in feminist and queer theory to question the disjunctures between sexed

bodies, gender, sexual identity, and erotic desire have disturbed the naturalisms of contemporary Western folk and scientific thought. However, insofar
as they have begun to establish new social scientific theories of sexuality, they
also risk misrepresenting societies where fertility is sexualized or where
procreation is central to gendered identities.

As with any other designated "domain" of social life, sexuality begins to
lose its coherence when subjected to careful cultural interpretation (Yanagisako and Delaney 1995; Herdt 1980, 1984, 1999: 17–27). Deborah Elliston
(1996) pushes the point further, noting that before placing these acts within
a set of questions about "sexual practices" we must first ask whether these
practices actually have an erotic significance. She cautions against the glib
assumption that simply by pointing to the presence of genital activity we are
able to recognize the sexual and the erotic across vastly discontinuous symbolic forms.

Ethnographers have faced the challenge of theorizing sexuality while leaving open the question of its symbolic configuration within social practice
(e.g., Clark 1997). Laura Rival, Don Slater, and Daniel Miller (1998: 296)
find that Western theories of sex and gender contain a pervasive "notion of
sexuality that . . . is not ethnographically grounded in any particular social
world." Their discussion of Huaorani people in Amazonian Ecuador presents a compelling case for situating sexual pleasures within mundane acts
of sociality:

> Sensuality in this culture is not centered on genitalia, nor is it the exclu-
> sive domain of adult heterosexuality; it should not, therefore, be assimi-
> lated to "sexual pleasure." . . . No distinction is made between the pleasure
> and contentment felt during sexual intercourse, the pleasure and content-
> ment of a 3-year-old caressing the breast of the woman from whom she or
> he is feeding, the merry feeling of someone stroking gently the body of a
> caressing companion, the gratification caused by the action of delousing
> someone's head, or the pleasure of being deloused by someone's expert
> hands. . . . Sexuality as an objectified domain referring to the physical
> relations between the sexes does not exist as such. (306, 309)

Rather than falling within the domains that Euro-American scholars have
mapped out as distinct categories of sexual identity, sexual pleasure, sexual
behavior, and sexual reproduction, reproduction among the Huaorani falls
within "the physical pleasure of harmonious living" (309). We soon find that
to map the domain of the erotic—and all its possibilities, sensualities, and

power entanglements—is to recognize how it is embedded in social institutions that far exceed those pertaining to the conjugal family, biological and social reproduction, and the pursuit of pleasure.

Thus, a theme running through the most sophisticated interpretations of nonmodern sexualities concerns whether the categories used to frame the analysis can capture a sensibility sustained within a very different social order (Manderson and Jolly 1997). This is an epistemological question concerning the limits of all projects of representation, especially those pertaining to cross-cultural interpretation or translation (Sperber 1985; Herdt 1999). To what extent does the effort to translate between symbolic worlds inappropriately distort—or entirely misread—social significance? That this tension inheres in acts of representation and analysis is not a reason to give up trying to produce subtle and sensitive interpretations across disparate regimes of common sense. With regard to the cross-cultural analysis of sexuality, Carole Vance (1991), among others, has wisely cautioned against inadvertently imposing one set of folk and scientific theories on others. Yet, from decades of debate, we know that where notions of body, self, and emotion are at issue, the task of thinking outside of one's own cultural common sense can be extraordinarily challenging.[10]

The language of social analysis leads us to imagine ourselves applying theory to culture with the intention of describing and explaining. Some think that to address the culturally and historically specific underpinnings of Western social theory is to commit a paralyzingly deconstructive move—one that undermines our ability to speak forcefully about the structures and processes that organize our world. Others think that critically reflecting on the historical specificity of contemporary theories of sexuality is essential to both analysis and activism.[11] It is not always easy to recognize where Western folk and scientific beliefs inhabit our explanatory certainties about sexuality. Perhaps the effort to definitively separate social "beliefs" from scientific "truths" is not as helpful as we once thought in considerations of global difference. Far from undermining the social analysis of sexuality, a recognition of the positionality of all social theory—including theories of sexuality—can foster a clearer perception of the multiple arenas in which specific claims about sexuality operate.

One way to look at sex within an international frame, then, is to look at it as a node in the negotiation of class-stratified transnational relationships. Under colonialism, gendered sexuality has functioned as a symbolic site for the elaboration of group boundaries and differences (Stoler 1992b, 1997) and it continues to function as such under postcolonial nationalisms (Findlay 1999; Jolly and Ram 2001; Kelsky 1996; Parker et al. 1992). Work in this area draws our attention to the social divides that make the sexual actions of particular types of people an issue within specific frames of stratification and identity. Given that actual sexual relations among individuals are transactional points within social networks organized through hierarchies of race and class, it follows that a social concern with the domain of the sexual functions to mark out differences. Thus, we argue that when science, medicine, and public health are the idioms through which sexual matters are articulated, the relational dynamics of power and difference are often forged around contested meanings of "the sexual."

Clearly, intensified global movements of people and information mean that territoriality and identity are no longer (if they ever were) simply arranged within localities encompassed within distinct nation-states. As Elizabeth Povinelli and George Chauncey (1994: 441) argue, to think "sexuality transnationally" means recognizing that "the dissemination of variously mediated forms of culture, embodiment, and desire happens at ever higher speeds and across long, striated distances in the context of reconfigurations and reconsolidations of economic, state, and national power."

Within studies of globalization, there is an active and important debate about the nature of the phenomena that the concept of globalization is meant to designate; we do not attempt to resolve these issues here. The complicated relations between the economic, political, and cultural axes of the systems now being identified as global remain to be fully researched. Anthropologists in particular have been critical of monolithic views of a singular globalization that pursues "the same outcomes everywhere in the world" (Rofal 1999b: 473) and of an a priori assumption that any global force must and will result in homogenization. To simply reverse the emphasis by describing the local in its specificity and diversity does not resolve the problem of understanding the processes we refer to as global (Massey 1994; Tsing 2000). As Lisa Rofel (1999b: 473) notes, globalization "is often treated in contrast to the local as if it were a deterritorialized force, without reference to the specific and uneven spatial groundings of the elements and processes involved." It is necessary to replace vague, monolithic, and often hyperbolic references to the global with a more measured and empirical curiosity about myriad "global projects" as specific, traceable networks of connection and exchange (Tsing 2000). This would enable us to understand the effects of these networks on the people caught up in them (or bypassed by them). It would also direct us to look at various discourses of globalization as forms of cultural production.

When we use the term "local" to signal the distinctiveness of a context, it is crucial to remember that locality is socially and historically produced in and through a dynamic of interaction. The local is not a space where indigenous sensibilities reside in any simple sense (Gupta 1998; Pigg 1992); global processes undo and remake the very particularism of the local as it stands in contrast to the seeming transcendence of the global.[12] Intimacy itself comes into question when globalization is brought into studies of sexuality because, as Povinelli and Chauncey (1994: 443) note, globalization "queries our commonsense referent of the proximate and the intimate, the subject and her space and time of being, and thus her forms and practices of desire." How are forms of subjectivity—and the identities and desires that manifest these forms—produced within contexts?[13] We believe that the answer to this is rendered partly visible through an analytic that recognizes the powerful moral underpinnings attached to things sexual and the powerful moral claims embedded within globalized discourses of development. A useful entry point for discussions of these contested meanings and experiences involves the ways in which moralities are themselves dislodged and attached, eliminated and reclaimed, in domains and practices that become configured as sexual. The transnational circulation of images of sexuality forges junctures among the erotic, reproductive, and sexual practices of various locations (Povinelli and Chauncey 1999: 445; see also Kelsky 1999). Modern notions of sexuality—formed in the melding of cultural processes and the scientization of sex—circulate in this manner and, more often than not, refer back to a notion of universality.

Development-oriented health, social reform, and population-control projects are surprisingly underrepresented in discussions of global exchanges and sexuality. International humanitarian and political institutions—articulated through nongovernmental organizations (NGOS), multilateral aid agencies, or activist networks—together create one of the most pervasive, influential, and mundane arenas in which sexuality is at issue. Whether their agendas are led by activism around sexual rights or management of sexual health, these projects, in their stated aim of social and behavioral change, become spaces of exchange within which sexuality is negotiated. Sexual practices are discouraged, promoted, named, and reframed (as the contributions to this volume vividly demonstrate). Target populations (men who have sex with men; sex workers; unwed mothers; multiparous women, etc.) are generated in these efforts and open up new lines along which "sex" becomes socially relevant.

Historical studies of sexuality, whether focused on Western nations or on their colonies, have consistently noted the role of science and medicine in forging and framing sexuality.[14] These studies also clearly show how science and medicine have been intertwined with projects of social reform, moral cleansing, colonial governance, and missionary work.[15] Yet when researchers, activists, and thinkers concerned with sexuality turn to the contemporary scene, the perspective changes. Health and human rights are conceptualized solely as arenas within which we apply our theories of sexuality rather than as contexts within which sexualities are actively made and remade. In this book, we make a case for incorporating into sex research and activism a reflexive understanding of how such efforts form new, often unanticipated, contexts—particularly in the field of health development.

Development

Worldwide, sexual practices have often been the focus of efforts to reform and modernize the nation. In the past, concerns with population vitality, racial purity, fertility, order and discipline, and economic productivity were merged in a focus on sexual reform for the sake of national progress (Connelly 2003; Hartmann 1995 [1987]; Sharpless 1997).[16] Malthusian concerns tied to eugenics formed an intellectual foundation for the development of the contraceptive sciences, which enabled planners to manage sexual relations that were presumed to lead to unwanted population growth and undesired racial mixing (Donzelot 1979). In the Americas, and later worldwide, the Rockefeller Foundation immersed itself in supporting what it saw as economic stability through population control while simultaneously investing in the development of reproductive sciences (Clarke 1998: 182–84). These sciences were internationalized by way of colonial and early postcolonial state-building projects that appealed to economic and cultural "progress" as well as to "national security" to justify and amplify reproductive interventions (Anderson 2003; Connelly 2003; Das 1993; Hunt 1997; Ram 2001). Consequently, a road map for the study of contemporary development projects can be found in accounts of colonial efforts to intervene in health by way of sexual relations (Hunt 1997; Manderson 1997a; Vaughan 1991), medicolegal mechanisms to control venereal disease (Levine 1993, 1997; Vaughan 1992), missionary projects focusing on the moral reform of the "native" through sexual and reproductive practices (Comaroff 1993; Reed 1997), and nationalist efforts to ensure a robust population (Anderson 2003).[17]

Today, the thematic links between nation, progress, and sexual conduct persist in altered form. Although appeals to "civilization" are less commonly heard now than at the beginning of the twentieth century, concerns with progress and modernization continue to be tied to dilemmas of sovereignty, economic strength, and international rhetorics of cultural worth and legitimacy. Questions of human rights, social justice, and survival, even when articulated in a self-consciously anticolonial manner, are usually tethered to the visions of progress inherent in secular liberalism, capitalism, and science. In our current era of postcolonial globalization, what kinds of regulation and control are being instituted and how are these regimes shaping everyday life? Who sees emancipatory pathways opening up through these configurations and who is investing what hopes in them?

In contemporary development efforts, one might read medical rhetoric about reproductive control, the control of sexually transmitted diseases (STDS), and so on as implicitly concerned with advancing ideas about what it means to be "modern" in one's sexual habits and choices. These continuities are what lend force to our question about the role of the rhetoric of modernization in shaping social relations by way of sexuality. Colonial histories of exploitation, justified through racial ideologies of exclusion and entitlement, make quite clear the stakes behind these questions (Ahlberg 1994; Levine 1993, 1997; Mani 1990; Alloula 1986). Further, the complicated effects of social change and the new forms of governance arising from these changes demand scrutiny of such processes (Asdar Ali 2002). The actual behaviors that result from these processes were and are often far from the intended outcomes of colonial leaders and/or health planners.

In much of the world, today's efforts at sexual reform and intervention are linked to larger national projects of development. In most developing countries, maternal and child health (a focus of colonial and nationalist attention for over a century) is now combined with population control schemes under the rubric of "reproductive health" (Dixon-Mueller 1993; Hartmann 1995 [1987]; McKinley 2003). The crisis wrought by the AIDS pandemic has expanded this arena to include what is termed "sexual health." In the wake of the Decade for Women (1975–1985) declared by the United Nations, issues of gender inequality and, to a lesser extent, sexual rights have now achieved normative status in development-type programs (at least at the level of rhetoric) (Petchesky 2000). In development programs, sexuality is medicalized—

and some practices and views pathologized—in ways that speak perfunctorily to local values while advancing donor and state concerns about population growth and disease control.

Worldwide, what we have termed "sexual reform efforts" occur in and through contraceptive promotion, sterilization camps, STD treatment centers, safe sex campaigns, sex education programs, gender awareness training, and so forth. These activities are set within legal structures and other forms of institutionalized social consensus that regulate family forms, organize public and private domains, and sanction deviance. Public health benevolence is cross-cut by other issues around which pointedly political organizing and activism occur: defense of the rights of sexual minorities or rights to sexual pleasure; community organizing based on sexual identity; curtailing of the trafficking of women; promotion of sex workers' rights; elimination of female circumcision; and control of the misuse of new reproductive technologies. The relations between mainstream health development and social activism are complex, working themselves out at regional, national, and international levels (see Fisher 1997; in relation to sexuality, see Barroso and Côrrea 1995; Cohen, this volume; Hoad, 1999; Larvie 1999; McKinley 2003; Morsy 1995). Matters of life and death—as they are made visible in sexuality—are also problems of modernity, especially insofar as they make use of the moral framings of modern science, technology, and objectivism to package their legitimacy and to invite social reform.

Developmentalism and the institutions it spawns can be placed within the larger context of projects of modernity and the kinds of institutional arrangements and cultural sensibilities this implies (Arce and Long 2000; Escobar 1995).[18] One way to define these arrangements is to describe the particular cultural forms that emerged out of the colonial, neocolonial, and postcolonial eras in relation to Western conceptions of science. This includes the possibility of shared assumptions about objectivity, scientific methods, technological solutions to social problems, and a host of associated political beliefs (Giddens 1991).[19] To place health development within the context of the modernities of particular regions entails expanding the temporal frame used to understand the goals, stakes, and effects of present-day development, which are embedded in relations of technology and sociality that exceed the nation and the stated goals of any given program. Transnational exchanges stemming from participation in international markets, media, social movements, immigration, telecommunications, and so forth surround and surpass development plans per se. At the same time, it is useful to focus on the particular ways in which received wisdom about one particular kind of exchange—that having to do with "science"—become a ubiquitous presence within "modernization," particularly when it comes to concerns over sexual behaviors targeted by health development.

This link between science and modernization is perhaps most clear in the epidemiological sciences. In epidemiologically driven international health development programs, the technologies used for data collection and the frameworks used to legitimize risk reduction offer new ways for states and international interests (such as bilateral and multilateral donors) to be vested both in the health of populations and in the project of modernity.[20]

The biological terrain here is articulated as a set of concerns about "populations," "fertility," and "health needs." It is also articulated as "sexual practices" and "sexual relations" and how they relate to fears about the "risk of death." Thus governments and policymakers are able to identify humanitarian projects aimed at "preventing death." And while such plans do actually prevent death in a number of instances, they also make possible a new kind of governance that, due to its reliance on science, some have termed distinctly modern. A technical language of health, while seeming to be solely about the well-being of bodies, emerges as a substitute for politics and in some cases for economics as well.[21] "Health" and "life" become nodes of control, dominion, and erasure; they are never straightforward road maps to humanitarian practice.

Once deployed in this way, the stakes of identifying what counts as success and what counts as failure become ever higher, in part because they are articulated as matters of "life and death" and thus become intensely morally charged.[22] Because of the moral position occupied by health development programs, it is difficult to talk about the unintended consequences of development projects targeting health and, especially, sexuality. Only recently have scholars applied the same sorts of critiques to sexual health development programs as they have to other kinds of development programs.[23] This may be due to the fact that health and sexuality are granted a quasi sacred character (Agamben 1998), making development efforts to safeguard them seem moral and unassailable.[24] That these are areas of political and moral struggle is clear: witness the difficult discussions around sex trafficking and female circumcision, around sexual rights, around human rights and AIDS, or even around the early efforts to develop a reproductive science in the United States (Clarke 1998). We believe that these debates are so vociferous because sexual intervention programs necessarily question the moral stability of all those phenomena that are identified under the rubrics of "sex" and "sexuality."

Sexuality has become a focus for interventions that reproduce this sense of life-and-death urgency, from post–World War II concerns with population planning (and the later emergence of developmental aid programs that focused on reproductive health) (see Connelly 2003; Greenhalgh 1996; Sharpless 1997) to the contemporary globalization of identity politics (supported, in part, by public health efforts to stem the spread of HIV and STDS) (see Cohen, this volume; Larvie 1999; Nguyen, this volume; Parker, Barbosa, and Aggleton 2000; Terto 2000). Yet we sense omissions in the health development literature on "sexual" topics that are very similar to those we saw in the early sociological literature on sexuality.

As programs to prevent sexually transmitted diseases rapidly acquire the prominence that has long accrued to family planning and contraception programs, there has emerged a more pointed attention to sexuality. Sexual health is increasingly linked to reproductive health, and as a result both sex and reproduction are framed, first and foremost, as medical matters. Yet the ensuing discussions about policies and programs occur as though "sex" were the same thing in all the locations where it is targeted (Pigg 2001a; Farquhar 2002)[25] and, further, as though interventions addressing it had consequences only for health. This discourse on sex creates a set of imaginings about what people do sexually, which in turn implies a vision of how they should respond to health programs.[26] From this arises an interpretive framework that places responses that run contrary to expectations within narratives about obstacles to progress and rationality.

How might the insights from social and historical studies of sexuality be brought into conversation with sexual and reproductive health policy and, beyond that, into a wider reflection on the contemporary politics of sexuality and governance?[27] Constructionist views stressing the cultural and historical specificity of the meanings of sexuality have been applied to curriculum design in sex education (Irvine 1995), as well as, in the case of male-male sex, to HIV/STD prevention. The crucial point has been made many times: attention to the local meanings of sexual relationships and acts is necessary not only to enable an understanding of people's behavior (including how it may put them at risk) but also to enable effective and appropriate modes of service delivery, intervention, and support. This profound recognition of the contextual specificity of all sexuality is, Peter Aggleton (2001) argues, the most important insight to come out of the past two decades in the social analysis of sexuality. It is also said to be the most relevant to projects of disease prevention and social improvement (see also Parker, Barbosa, and Aggleton 2000).

But is attention to local cultural meanings and to microcontexts in itself sufficient to enable an understanding of the forces forming the sexualities that are being targeted by these health-related policies and programs? Can this approach, on its own, shed light on what is at stake for various actors when, in the name of health, equality, and improved life, sexuality is fore-grounded as a target of intervention? What is the context within which the meanings of sexuality found in policies and programs are generated?[28] We see in social and historical studies of sexuality a blueprint for an approach that moves beyond describing the relation between sexual meaning and action in a given place and time. Rather than reading the record of the changing understandings of sexuality in the modern West solely as a lesson in cultural relativism, we question the picture of a world fostered by a syn-chronic view of local cultural differences—a world composed of myriad mi-crocontexts and localities whose contingency and specificity is transcended by a master view.

A historical perspective raises questions not just about change but also about influences and interconnections. Sexology, medicine, and the repro-ductive sciences were taken up and developed by elites, intellectuals, scien-tists, and authorities in a variety of places (Dikötter 1995; Farquhar 2002; Früstück 2000; Jackson 1997b; Srivastava 2001). The history of these varied scientific sexologies makes it implausible to approach as entirely new today's development interest in sexual and reproductive health. To contrast local cultural frameworks to a contemporary scientific understanding of sex and gender is to gloss over a more complicated and uneven history. In many parts of the world, rhetorics of sexuality and the medicalization of sex are already well developed and thoroughly imbricated in long-standing class-based in-vestments in the future of the nation.[29]

Caught up in varied regional projects of nation building and moderniza-tion, for some people medical, scientific, and development-oriented interven-tions have consolidated a certain shared, cosmopolitan common sense about sexuality, while for others these interventions have had little effect. This is why it is not at all uncommon to find that many of the people targeted by sexual health interventions frame sexuality in ways that share few (if any) of the underlying presuppositions of the medical and sexological frame. In some circumstances, development efforts address sex with a vocabulary that as-sumes a self-evident object capable of being described through the use of a common linguistic currency, despite the fact that linguistic referents for this concept do not exist in the targeted region. In other cases, what a Western observer might regard as the basic truths of reproductive science and sexology were altered when articulated as medical ideas in other locales.[30] Cases such as this lead us to ask: What are the past and present forms of the transnational migration of sciences of sexuality? How does an understanding of these histories alter how we interpret the form, aims, implications, and effects of today's interest in sexual and reproductive health? How and when is it possible to talk about the arrival or construction of sexuality? And to what extent is securing this sexuality part and parcel of health development?

Contemporary transfers of knowledge and technology occurring in and through health development reconfigure notions of sex and forms of sexual action—notions and forms that, as we've argued, should be understood to have a history. These transfers inevitably produce practical contradictions. They are based on taken-for-granted assumptions about bodies being biologically sexual; individuals having sexual natures; and certain actions being classified as sexual relations. It is not surprising, therefore, that one of the observations made again and again in the sociocultural research literature pertaining to HIV/AIDS is that the categories around which epidemiological and public health reasoning are organized do not map neatly onto existing realities. For example, it is not always possible to correlate how, in a given context, a variety of sexual contacts can be tied to specific identities through the use of development models of heterosexual sex and homosexual sex. Prostitution and marriage are similarly problematic terms. Because of the variety and fluidity of relationships that weave economic expectations into sexual transactions, the category of prostitution continues to pose definitional problems in public health efforts to target "commercial sex work" (de Zalduondo 1990). Destigmatizing prostitution by calling it sex work does not solve this problem, for the notion of sex work itself contains assumptions about economic compulsion, choice, and market demand that do not adequately describe certain economies of gender and sexuality (Wardlow 2001). There is a mismatch between specific contexts and the basic terminology of health development discourse. This mismatch certainly underscores the need for close-up and complex understandings of particular sites.

It also points to a need to look beyond particular contexts toward the ways that those contexts are themselves shaped by current events, including the recent wave of interest in sex in the name of health and development. If (as anthropological and historical research overwhelmingly shows) sexual identities, behaviors, and meanings articulate moral concerns within the family, the clinic, the community, and the nation, then how do medicine and science themselves become part of these social arenas as well as part of the milieu of moral reasoning in which people live?

Finally, we point to how internationalized rhetorics of sexuality have changed since being formalized into health development discourse. An earlier era of development did not discuss sex itself as a target for intervention; rather, sex was subordinated to concerns about fertility. A gendered objectification of sexuality was one effect of the development-related interest in reproduction. As women became the target of family planning programs—the node through which real "development" would occur for the family, the village, the nation—so too were they identified as having a sexuality that could be rendered both nonreproductive and an object for self-improvement. Policies directed at reproductive outcomes have more often than not contained messages about women being responsible either for carrying the burden of modernization (Anagnost 1995; Greenhalgh 1992) or for suppressing it (Kligman 1998). In both of these cases, without directly objectifying sexual practices, sexuality becomes the subtext of a far-reaching set of concerns about morality and the health of the nation (Ram 2001). Thus, for both health planners and contraceptive users, investments in reproductive behavior have forced a new kind of imagining about sexual relations. Indeed, although seldom explicitly stated or illustrated, the mediation of sexuality through contraceptive technology has been an important precursor of current efforts to directly confront sexuality as a health development concern.

With the HIV/AIDS epidemic, sexual relations have suddenly come to the forefront. No longer imagined indirectly through the proxy of fertility, sexuality has become scripted through the imperative of disease prevention and, in some cases, remains attached to concerns about family planning. Discussions of who is having what sorts of sex with whom are routed through an ultimate concern with disease vectors, echoing an earlier era when venereal diseases were central to moral debates that linked health to national strength (Brandt 1987 [1985]; Fordham 2001; Levine 1997). Yet compared to the social hygiene campaigns of the late nineteenth and early twentieth centuries, today's focus on disease and sexuality is more intensely explicit about sexual acts, pairings, and identities; more precise in its scientific elaboration of the physiological, even molecular, mechanisms of risk; more exacting and elaborate in its mathematical modeling of disease trends; and more deeply embedded in the political economy of medical research and pharmaceutical marketing. It is, in short, more tightly interwoven with science—not only through molecular biology and epidemiology but also through the sexual sciences.

The AIDS era has thus ushered in a critical shift in how sex is framed. What was once indirectly targeted as a matter of civility, population control, family planning, and public health is now targeted directly as a set of sexual practices, sexual identities, and sexual risks. Judgments about what kinds of

sex can be seen as prudent and "safe" are framed in a medical idiom, sometimes with a strong grounding in empirical research. But these judgments,
bolstered by pronouncements of science, can mask covert political and moral
ethnocentrisms implicit within the use of unexamined definitions of health
and sexuality (Patton 1990: 77–97; Fordham 2001). It is actually difficult to
disentangle assumptions and value judgments from scientific findings about
bodies, contacts, and risks because these findings are themselves predicated
on both universal objective indicators of health and on the modern, reified
concept of sexuality as an autonomous domain (see Pigg, this volume).

Epidemiological research and intervention strategies are two sides of the
same coin. At the epidemiological research end, there is an assumption that
there exists an objective, socially neutral standpoint from which behaviors
can be identified, named, and classified; at the intervention end, there is an
assumption that those addressed by programs will recognize certain desires
and actions as sexual behaviors that can be the object of reflexive fashioning.
Both of these assumptions have been subjected to criticism,[31] and both have
value as a means of discerning broad population-based patterns (in the case
of epidemiology) and in promoting at least one possible means of disease
prevention (in the case of intervention). Most of the discussion on these
issues revolves around optimizing health through disease prevention—certainly not an unworthy goal. As a consequence, however, little notice is given
to the extraordinary degree to which these efforts not only assume but also
create and attempt to enforce a certain definition of the sexual dimension of
body and experience.[32]

When sex is foregrounded in health-related research and development
objectives, what are the material implications for local sexual meanings and
practices? To ask this question is not only to call for paying better attention to
the particularities of sexual meanings and practices in various cultures (although this remains important) but also to recognize the contingency of the
pursuit of sexual health as an objective. It has been a struggle to introduce
the concepts of sexual health and sexual rights into policy discussions of
reproductive health (Cornwall and Wellbourn 2002; Petchesky 2000), and it
has been a struggle to introduce approaches to sexuality that are sensitive to
collective sociopolitical issues in the behavior-change dominated world of
AIDS intervention (Farmer, Connors, and Simmons 1996; Parker 1996). Yet,
as battles are being fought to introduce more robust and nuanced social
paradigms into these arenas of health development, efforts to look at sexuality in context have tended to overlook the much wider contexts of which
they themselves are a part.[33]

These questions do not imply that the use of the modern notion of sex and/or information from the sexual sciences are "bad" simply because they are identifiable as modern or as scientific; rather, the questions we ask point toward a more robustly historical and reflexive mode of thinking about the kinds of transformations and cultural negotiations under way in various parts of the world. Interventions contain hopes of change and visions of achieving a goal. These hopes and visions enter into complex social fields, in which the stakes for different actors may be divergent, fragmented, or contradictory.[34]

The hopes placed in sex education and awareness training as tools of empowerment have similarly ambivalent implications. Making sexuality into a matter of the body, to be addressed through an idiom of normality and health and described in terms of physiology and function, can partly defuse a morally explosive topic (Pigg 2002; Ram 1998a). It can also, however, introduce new grounds for discerning sexual deviance (Jackson 1997b; Rivkin-Fish 1999; Somerville 1997). The taken-for-granted biological universalism imputed to a medical and hygienic language of sexuality can offer people certain freedoms because it provides a way to discuss sex without discussing one's own sexuality. At the same time, it can be abstract and alienating. It can even be irrelevant to the conditions that structure one's lived sexuality (Setel 1999; Waldby, Kippax, and Crawford 1993; Ward 1991).

This book presents ethnographic cases that explore the intersections of the domain constituted as sex—in all its varied categories, practices, and meanings—at the transcultural junctures created by science, modernization, and development programs. These points of intersection raise numerous concerns about the conceptualizations of modernity and tradition. In many of the cases presented here, sex as a discursive and sensual possibility becomes woven into the possibility of thinking about being modern. It would be wrong to assume that the problematization of sexual intercourse is in itself a modern invention, as the scholarly explorations of things in India, China, and Tibet, for instance, clearly indicate (Adams, this volume; Dell, this volume; Farquhar 2002; Srivastava 2001). At the same time, exploring exactly how these historic formations meet up with and are transformed by a medicalized sexuality is one of the goals of this book. To this end, it is worth looking at what science studies has to offer.

Nature, Biology, and Technology: Science Studies

The moral object of sex can be viewed through the globalizing claims, practices, and power relations with which science endows development programs. Developmentalism holds out the hope that greater health and well-being can be attained through rational planning, and development regimes enlist people in efforts to carry out these plans by promoting technologies and educating them to modern consciousness. Science, of course, claims to have achieved an objective and hence universalizable knowledge of the organic world. To the modern consciousness, the "facts" of nature and the efficacious interventions that an understanding of them can generate seem to exist independently of context and to be applicable to all cultural values. The physicality of suffering is reduced to biological mechanisms that operate independently of human consciousness or cultural and social processes. Thus there comes a point in discussions of culture, politics, modernization, and development where one invokes the "bottom line"—where the problems of bodily suffering would seem to push to the back burner relativist concerns with historical contingency, contextual diversity, and cultural difference.

It is crucial that our argument not be misread as a relativist plea with limited real-world consequences or as a kind of culturalist fine-tuning of the larger project of improving health and well-being. The ethnographic case studies presented in the chapters that follow clearly dispute that type of polarizing account, with its foundational distinctions between the natural/fixed/universal and the social/variable/local. They show that, however accurately some of the component aspects of sex and reproduction might be known through science and effectively controlled through medical technologies, sexual and reproductive bodies never cease to be moral objects. This is because the ahistorical, decontextualized body posited by science does not exist in the real world—except perhaps in the discursive practices of science and development planning. Thus, even when scientific practices and knowledge claims are not directly examined, the situations descibed in these chapters point to fundamental conceptual questions about nature and society. We argue that the constructivism versus biological essentialism debate that has structured theoretical thinking about gender and sexuality is of limited use in understanding the real-world situations in which idioms of biology and techniques of biological manipulation mediate new framings of sexuality. We seek to sidestep the relativism versus universalism debate by drawing inspiration from science studies, which proposes a materialist view of the mutual construction of science and society.

Science, medicine, and technology are at the heart of questions of sex and development interventions, and efforts to scrutinize them quickly lead to a philosophical debate between realism and constructionism: either science records and manipulates the world as it is or its explanations are invented in context-dependent cultural schemes. Much of the writing in science studies has been at pains to stake out a third position (articulated, for instance, in Haraway 1997; Latour 1999) and to distinguish it from both prior constructionist theories and the project of "deconstructing" scientific knowledge in order to expose it as a contingent cultural production infused with ideological biases.[35] The alternative analytic offered by science studies acknowledges the role of empirical data collection and the processes of experimentation, evaluation of evidence, and so on; however, it also holds that the processes of scientific knowledge production are social from start to finish, as are their technological applications. To see science as a social practice is not to render its products any less "scientific" (Keller 1995); rather, it is to fully appreciate the grounded, real-world complexities and contingencies located within the actual practices of science. The posing of research questions, the designing of experimental procedures, and the interpretation of evidence all involve myriad decisions and choices that are made in a messy middle ground where scientists' interactions with the natural world are shaped by cultural schema and sociopolitical constraints.[36]

This perspective has also helped to recontextualize science within its so-called places of origin. Postcolonial science studies have made it clear that the work of science is always a result of transnational processes, historically drawing knowledge and practical insight not simply from the laboratories of Europe or North America but also from the experiences of colonial, missionary, and anthropological encounters that gave rise to certain scientific possibilities (Chakrabarty 2000; Prakash 1999; Harding 1993, 1998). If science is by its Western definitions a location of instability (Kuhn 1962), then it is important to explore the social processes that enable it to present itself within frameworks of universality. This view holds that "knowledge claims acquire the status of universal facts by virtue of the extent to which they become interwoven with the institutional settings and practices of scientists and their audiences" (Oudshoorn 1994: 10). Similarly, scientific applications cannot act in the world solely as objective forms of knowledge; rather, they are modified into a variety of "facts" within clinical, legal, educational and other contexts—all of which take on the personal, cultural, and political priorities of their users (Butt 1999; Martin 1994; Rapp 1988).

Development interventions that address sex and reproduction make a certain kind of use of scientific and medical research. In some cases—as in the current efforts to develop microbicides that would combine contraceptive efficacy with protection against sexually transmitted infections (including HIV)—the laboratory work is closely tied to the urgency of its anticipated application. Similarly, in an earlier era, from the beginning of their endeavor the scientific developers and financial backers of the oral contraceptive pill imagined that it would provide a technological solution to the perceived problem of overpopulation in the Third World (Clarke 1998; Marks 1997; Oudshoorn 1994). In other cases, health development interventions seek to extend the application of long-established scientific breakthroughs (such as bacteriological understandings of infectious disease) and related technologies (such as antibiotics).

The relationship between science and development is not an entirely straightforward one that moves simply from science to its applications. Development programs are dynamic institutional forms that create and sustain complex arenas of engagement.[37] Under the rubric of development, technologies are also prioritized and sorted, as when in certain countries fertility control—not treatment of infertility—is deemed appropriate to health care.[38] Development projects establish concrete sites where new sets of people are brought, sometimes suddenly, into relation with new knowledge and technologies. This is quite evident in programs offering sex education, with their introductions to topics as diverse as sex hormones, fertilization, and sexual identity. These encounters do not always follow the predicted route; what the new beneficiaries seek is not always what the planners have determined they should have—a contradiction vividly illustrated by a *hijra* in Hyderbad who, when told of a new sexual health clinic to be opened up (focused principally on STD and HIV treatment and prevention support), assumed that it would offer the breast implant surgery s/he hoped for (Reddy 2001). Development also ties class-based and state-backed investments in modernity to science, and it does so at both the level of implementation (as in population control programs) and the level of ideology (as in rhetorics that contrast knowledge and superstition).[39] There is thus much to be explored concerning the intersection of science, development, and sexuality, and this book can only begin this task.

The recognition of development as a kind of social presence, a loose assemblage of practices, institutional linkages, and discourses, can therefore be tied to an understanding of the social production of scientific facts. When insights into politics and practice are connected to questions about the social basis for the stabilization of facts, what emerges is a way of thinking about the politics of universalisms. Analytical questions about the diffusion, distribution, and uses of science, medicine, and technology can then shift registers, from free-floating philosophical arguments about "reality" or "rights" or "relativism" to grounded investigations of actual interactions and linkages. This is a starting point for investigating the postcolonial implications of how, worldwide, science and technology are producing new framings of sexuality.

At first glance, this global presence of science, with its concomitant biologization of sexuality, might not seem remarkable. Modernist thinking fosters the expectation that over time scientific views (simply because they are assumed to be true) will naturally replace "traditional" views. This way of thinking assumes that if people who were previously ignorant of, say, the chromosomal determination of embryonic sex, or the role of a sexually transmitted infection in causing genital sores, are presented with the scientific explanation of these events then they will recognize these as "better" accountings of their bodily experience than the ones they had before. From this perspective, the international role of science, medicine, and technology in framing sexuality would seem to be inevitable because it is easy to think that scientific views of sex have held sway in so many new contexts simply because they are "right." This is a teleology that assumes a singular unfolding from nature to society: the truths of nature are there, waiting to be revealed by scientists; once these revelations occur, their technological applications follow; these applications, taken up because they are so useful, become widespread and so have an impact on the societies that receive them.

However, if, as science studies hold, scientific truths are produced within concrete contexts of social practice, then the diffusion of science and technology needs to be explained in terms of institutions, practices, and relationships rather than in terms of natural determinisms. Through what institutions, in what forms, and through what practices do specific scientific views of sex and reproduction move from laboratory to application? Science studies proposes that we study the networks of actors that enter into new heterogeneous relations with each other through technoscientific endeavors. This brings into the open the multitude of mediations on which the acceptance and widespread use of scientific knowledge depends. Here, the key point is that facts acquire their facticity (i.e., their quality as context-independent truths) by being inserted into networks (Latour 1987). A fact stabilizes as indisputable and self-evident to the degree that it becomes "blackboxed" (i.e., becomes the accepted basis for a wide range of other actions and purposes). Much research in science studies has been concerned with tracing the transi-

tions from experimental uncertainty to knowledge claim, and from knowledge claim to universal fact (Latour 1986; Shapin and Shafer 1985).[40] Far
from being immanent within nature itself, the universalizable, decontextualized character of scientific knowledge is something that has to be achieved.[41]

These insights can help us to visualize what is going on in development
arenas, rescuing us from Luddite and/or romanticist critiques of the domination of Western science, for instance, and ensuring that we do not allow
a blanket suspicion of universals to serve as a critique. The planning rationalities of development are based on decontextualized knowledge, and
development programs require universal facts and work to extend their universalizability into further frontiers. The biologization and medicalization of
sex documented in the case studies presented in this book enroll people in
new networks of science. Within these networks universalizability is tied not
just to health interventions but also to political movements, identity formation, human rights, and new forms of sociality. And these practices raise
a final set of questions about the links between objectification and moral
erasure—about the creation of a discursive space within which morality is
presumed to be neutral.

Science-based networks of social activity are mediated by and constitutive
of moral claims and arguments, despite the overt suggestion that science, by
definition, operates in a domain devoid of moral judgment (Gould 1998).
"Factual" knowledge claims put forth by scientific studies—whether in the
form of biology, epidemiology, or medicine—tend to be treated as morally
neutral, even when behaviors set in motion by "the facts" arouse enormous
moral debate (Clarke 1998: 233–76; Ginsburg 1989; Paxson, this volume;
Rivkin-Fish, this volume). The biological sciences have played an important
role in shaping moral assumptions in the industrialized nations (e.g., notions of morally appropriate kinds of sexuality in relation to the sexual nature
of an inner "self" emerged hand in hand with advances in reproductive and
sexual research, from Freud to sexology to biochemistry). The idea of sex
hormones gendered the body at the molecular level; the concept of normality
in the research of Kinsey and of Masters and Johnson introduced new moral
ways of thinking about gender and sexuality. This kind of research concerning the biological bases of sexuality was carried out in a moral field that
authorized such research (and certain scientific questions) in the first place.

Scientific facts about reproduction and sexuality are constitutive of moral
positions; they are not neutral fields on which existing moral contestations
are perpetuated. The possibility of reading moral debate as itself an indica-
tion of the neutrality of "factual" biological claims (i.e., the idea that it is

possible to separate moral debate from the "facts") is brought into question in the chapters in this book that problematize the way that "scientific facts" are or are not recognized as neutral by the various social groups who are asked to believe them. Factual claims about sexuality, reproduction, and health are authorized under the auspices of new reproductive technologies, sex education, AIDS prevention, and so on, but the extent to which these claims are seen or understood as morally neutral certainly varies from place to place—in part because these programs (from medicine to health development) are always already invested with particular moralities. We see the domain of the moral as a form of politics in which identities, rights, and social and economic opportunities are deliberated in and through scientific claims that authorize one kind of moral justification over another. What the following chapters offer is a set of grounded examples of how efforts to make science "work"—by getting people to change their sexual behavior, to engage in "modern sex," and to become educated about "safe sex," "healthy reproduction," "family planning," and the biology of STDs—also function to unveil invisible moral positions. And this is not surprising, for the processes that make believable scientific claims about sex inevitably make evident the moral fields that have invested these claims with credibility. Our point, and it is a crucial one, is that moralities do not stand outside the processes of scientific object making and sociality; rather, they are constituted by them.

The chapters in this book articulate the lines of inquiry identified above as much by their overlaps and convergences as by their ethnographic contrasts. Numerous related goals demonstrate the linkages between chapters. Three of these are as follows: first, to provide concrete ethnographic illustrations of the mechanisms at work in negotiating and producing sexuality and the morally debated possibilities for subjectivity that follow; second, to illustrate the construction of sexual normativities as instruments of biopolitics, nationalism, and the creation of modernity; and third, to provide ethnographic descriptions of negotiations surrounding a morally based liberal humanism that is focused on creating sexual subjects and whose identity politics is in some sense inspired by new technologies and development efforts devoted to the management of things sexual.

Following from and elaborating on this introduction, the essay by Stacy Leigh Pigg delineates one of this book's central theoretical points by discussing the rise of a medicalized and biologized sex as a historical accomplishment. Pigg reminds us that the meanings of biological sex that are taken for granted in discourses on "the facts of life" must be continually re-created in locations where such ideas do not already exist. By arguing against the development view that a shift can occur from one understanding (myths and misconceptions) to another (a scientific view of sexuality), Pigg suggests that the scientific view of sexuality also involves shifts in investments in much wider networks and collective projects. There is a politics involved in this: What is the transformation that occurs (or can occur) through an acceptance of the idea that there are "facts" about sexuality? What sorts of erasures are made possible when one has "the facts" about sexuality? Unlike much of the development literature, which sees a conflict between facts that will liberate and cultural beliefs and attitudes that are harmful, Pigg's goal is to recognize how the biologization of sex draws more and more people into a set of globalizing projects that may restructure lives in ways that go well beyond replacing one set of ideas about sex with another.

The rest of the chapters are grouped according to three themes: the production of new subjectivities; the creation of normativities as a biopolitical project; and the negotiation of a morally based liberal humanism forged in a sexual identity politics tied to health development. Together, the chapters in this book show that although the effort to claim the moral high ground via appealing to universal facts is made over and over again, a cross-cultural comparative framework reveals the nonuniversalizable nature of such efforts (and, indeed, of such facts). The goal here is not to reconstitute a set of claims about social constructionism but, rather, to identify how such claims are able to produce moral certainties in the lives of people across cultures. These people are becoming increasingly "known" by way of their sexualized identities and, consequently, variously engage, resist, or reinvent moral certainties as they reimagine themselves as modern subjects.

Notes

We would like to thank the anonymous reviewers of this piece for their constructive suggestions on the shape of this chapter. In addition, Joanne Richardson provided her magic editorial touch at just the right moment.

1 This is perhaps what prompted the birth control campaigner and sex educator Marie Stopes to promote her book *Married Love* as an honest discussion of sexuality that would not require readers to wade through pages of turgid prose on lower organisms and faraway savages in order to find the information they wanted (Porter and Hall 1995: 209).

2 This separation of the social and biological dimensions of sexuality set the stage for the interest in "interactionist" theories that would explain the nature/nurture dynamic (see Abramson and Pinkerton 1995). Sociologist of science Bruno Latour (1993) argues that the essence of being modern lies in the investment in "acts of

purification" that separate biology from society within an analytic that fosters particularly intense (but denied) hybrids of the natural and the social. Sexuality research can be read through Latour's discussion of modernity as a set of ontological practices separating society from nature.

3 Connell and Dowsett (1992) go so far as to claim that "nativism" is obsolete as a theory of sexuality. We find it alive and well in many quarters, however, including development projects that draw on a scientific conception of sexuality as part of their legitimating rhetoric.

4 This paradox has most often been discussed among historians. The historical accounts by Foucault (1978) and Weeks (1989 [1981]) have mapped the consolidation, by the end of the nineteenth century, of a notion of sexuality. We now have a clear picture of the historical distinctiveness of modern Western ideas about sexuality: that it is natural and is the essence of an individual's identity, and that sexual acts are forms of self-expression. We are self-consciously aware of the peculiarity of sexology's attempt to classify sexual types and desires. These are the concepts of sexuality that have shaped sexual experience in the twentieth century in the West. Any study of current local sexualities can take this Western history of sexuality as a point of departure. This is because any theoretical frame for the analysis of sexuality shares at least a partial history with the "sexuality" the people studied understand themselves to "have." Weeks (2000: 130) comments that "sensitivity to context is one thing; doing away with the unifying concept of a sexuality is quite another. One of the problems with the new sexual history is that it is in danger of becoming a history without a proper subject. The history of sexuality is at the same time a history of a category of thought, which, if we follow Foucault, has a delimited history; and a history of changing erotic practices, subjective meanings, social definitions and patterns of regulation whose only unity lies in their common descriptor" (see also Padgug 1979). This issue is less often raised in terms of the problems of cultural difference. Review articles by Manderson, Bennett, and Sheldrake (1999) and by Weston (1993) discuss how any reading of the ethnographic literature related to sexuality is complicated by definitions, categories, and assumptions about domains that do not transfer across cultural frames.

5 Examples of this rhetorical formulation include Connell and Dowsett 1992: 68–69 and Weeks 1989 [1981]: 11. The concept of "sexual cultures" or "subcultures" (as, for instance, in Parker 1991), although heuristically useful, tends to reproduce this ahistorical sense of separateness.

6 Whereas the history of modern European sexuality tends to presume, by default, a stable West divided internally by class, gender, and regionalism but unfolding within the stable frame of the nation, the history of colonial sexuality shows the extent to which activities in the colonies shaped life in the metropole. (Indeed, Stoler forcefully argues that the metropole was a permeable and unstable formation whose boundaries continually had to be redrawn and rejustified in order to maintain rule.) There is nonetheless an embedded assumption in social and historical studies of Anglo-European sexuality that the spatial distance between metropole and colony dictated that these remain separate but parallel worlds, with a one-way traffic through which the social norms and values of the colonizers were transplanted on

new soil. The idea, from postcolonial theory, that what we call the West was created by its colonies has had little impact in the mainstream of sexuality studies.

7 Well-entrenched conceptual tools for the holistic analysis of culture consistently present "others" as types or forms existing outside of or parallel to "our" historicity (Fabian 1983). A vocabulary that stresses the differences "between" cultures offers few tools for analyzing complex historical processes of creolization and change. It is now widely recognized that a concept of culture that does not fully accommodate heterogeneity, contestation, and the fluidity of practice will not be up to the task of accounting in any way for the social complexities of border zones, hybrid spaces, global circuits, and translocal forms of consciousness that organize so many people's lives. Moreover, as feminist and Marxist anthropologists have pointed out, the emphasis on cultural difference elevates one line of cleavage to supreme importance for analysis, rendering differences (such as gender or class) within "cultures" to a lesser role as parts in the service of a social whole (Moore 1987; Wolf 1982).

8 For instance, Clark 1997; Hunt 1997; Reed 1997; Stoler 1997b, 1992.

9 The AIDS epidemic has brought the problem of assumptions, categories, and definitions into the realm of public health policy. Early efforts to address AIDS risk for "homosexuals" came up against issues of self-identification (Alonso and Koreck 1989; Cáceres 2000; Oetomo 2000; Parker 1987; Tan 1995). Patton (1996: 373) argues that the emphasis on condom use in projects that self-consciously try to work with local sexual categories has "produced a tendency, even in the most savvy projects, to accidentally produce western, urbanized sexual subjects among men who have sex with other men in other cultures."

10 See, for instance, Duden 1990; MacCormack and Strathern 1979; and Strathern 1988 for provocative feminist struggles with respect to conceptualizations of gender and the body.

11 See, for example, Bristow 1997.

12 Seen in this way, "the global" does not hover somewhere above localities, immanently transcending the parochial, embodied, particularistic—and by definition, limited and small—"local" worlds. Rather, the global, as a position that is achieved through locatable practices, is every bit as rooted, specific, and spatialized as the local (Massey 1994). Older models of preexisting "cultures," arrayed in well-defined territories and eventually penetrated by "outside forces" lead inevitably to an attempt to winnow an artificially reified authentic tradition from inauthentic borrowings. These models tend to reproduce versions of modernization theory that narrate a unilinear movement from tradition to modernity. Within anthropology, these models have been largely discarded in favor of a more dynamic emphasis on practice and cultural production. Yet in much of the sexuality literature these previous frameworks for imagining the confluence of local culture, Westernization, and globalization persist, to the detriment of our ability to understand both the process and the stakes of transnationalism (Manalansan 1997; Rofel 1999b). Rofel 1999b, for instance, unpacks the limitations of the modernization theory implicit in Denis Altman's discussion of the globalization of "gay" identity. See Appadurai 1996 for an attempt to theorize the "production of locality"; see Wolf 1982 for a view that explicitly addresses capitalist expansion.

13 Both psychoanalytical and Foucaldian theories of sexuality have developed a notion that the subject is "the nontransparent effect of a temporal unfolding of external social forms that constitute and are mediated by psychic and corporeal economies" (Povinelli and Chauncey 1999: 444).

14 See, for instance, Clarke 1989; Jordanova 1989; Mort 2000 [1987]; Weeks 1989 [1981].

15 See, for instance, Brandt 1987 [1985]; Hunt 1997; Levine 1997; Vaughan 1992.

16 In the 1920s and 1930s, for instance, intellectuals attributed Brazilian "backwardness" to Brazil's colonial history of miscegenation and to the sexual depravities stimulated by the tropical environment; in this context, progress was sought through rational engineering that would control (among many things) sexual deviance (Larvie 1999). Around the same time, in republican-era China educated groups became convinced that "control of sexual desire was the key to restoring the strength of the nation and achieving modernity" (Dikötter 1995: 2); hence, there was a proliferation of popular scientific and medical treatises on reproductive and sexual matters, and these formed a basis for later socialist state programs aimed at improving the "health" of the "nation" through intervening in the sexual life of citizens (Anagnost 1995). Somewhat later, postpartition Indian state efforts to recover the nation were articulated in part through the forced rehabilitation of "abducted" women whose sexual relationships cross-cut the divides between Hindu, Sikh, and/or Muslim groups. Interethnic relations were seen as a threat to the purity of the reformed and modernizing postcolonial nation states of India and Pakistan (Das 1993).

17 An especially vivid example of the lasting influence of colonial public health frameworks is the link between early-twentieth-century racialized understandings of venereal disease and contemporary efforts to explain the social dimensions of the AIDS epidemic. In the first part of the twentieth century, in much of eastern and southern Africa colonial public health interventions were focused on civilizing Africans by pressuring them to undertake new ways of being sexual (e.g., by eschewing polygamy). Venereal disease was framed within the larger problem of the flawed modernization of black male migrant laborers who, as "dressed natives," had abandoned their allegiance to traditional social values but had imperfectly adjusted to modern, urban conditions (Packard and Epstein 1991; Vaughan 1991: 129–54; Vaughan 1992). Decades later, in the 1980s, epidemiologists and social scientists found this same, deeply racialized, idea of flawed modernization to be a self-evident commonsense explanation for the burgeoning AIDS epidemic in parts of Africa (Ahlberg 1994).

18 The critical anthropology of development conceptualizes development as a historically situated moment emerging out of colonialism. It has attempted to look beyond economic determinism to understand the myriad dimensions of social practice occurring in and through contexts that come to be defined in terms of development. Early critical approaches framed development as a discourse that ordered and regularized forms of control through "the systematic creation of objects, concepts, and strategies" (Escobar 1995: 40). While this approach to development knowledge helps account for a certain degree of global uniformity in the power relations organized through applications of expertise and the rationalization of social im-

provement, it falls short of accounting for the heterogeneity and multilayered complexities of actual social practice in diverse contexts framed as development. It is necessary to take into account the ways that prior, locally specific histories of governance, planning, and visions of progress have already inscribed the social landscape in which present-day development activities take place (Moore 1999; Rutherford and Nyamuda 2000) as well as the regionally distinct histories of development itself (Sivaramakrishnan 2000). Further, looking at any given moment of development activity, the notion of a singular, coherent "development discourse" dissolves in the face of the different understandings that multiple agents have of their work (Gardner 1997). Moreover, the people targeted by development activities engage with them from positions shaped by processes other than development. As Rutherford and Nyamuda (2000: 841) state: "Those frozen in the 'development gaze' have also been motivated by other practices and concerns in their interactions with development . . . the actions and thoughts of these people are not subsumed or simply explained by development."

19 Arguments about the particular forms that emerge under the auspices of "development" work—and the micropolitics of their generation—have been made with respect to forest management (Sivaramakrishnan 2000), agriculture (Gupta 1998), income generation (Ferguson 1991), and resettlement (Moore 1999). These are a useful guide for understanding health development in relation to sexuality.

20 In this, they offer exemplary instances of Foucault's biopower. In most countries, the use of reproductive and sexual epidemiology is linked both to the management of the self and to the forms of citizenship that enable the state to manage population-level diseases, fertility, and so forth. Agamben (1998) and Haraway (1998) note that there is a pervasive effort to construe "bare," or biological, life as the foundation for all politics and, hence, as a qualifying feature of modernity. Politics here is played out not just in and through policy debates, voting, and structural governmental forms but also in all sorts of development programs that focus on death as the exception that always defines, and redefines, the rules for social behavior. Herein, decisions about issues such as how and whether to use contraception, with whom one can or cannot have sex, how one can or cannot have it, and so on are made into matters of state and national interest by being made into questions of life and death.

21 The concept of "the health of populations" is related to economy and governance. By tracing forms of power and legitimacy under modernity, Foucault (1978: 102) noted the importance of the notion of population "as a datum, as a field of intervention, and as an objective of governmental techniques." Colonial concerns with the vitality of the labor force gave way to neo-Malthusian preoccupations with overpopulation, while in affluent, industrialized societies health became a discourse on "risk" (Petersen and Lupton 1996). We find in these historic cultural practices the embryonic cultural forms that directly or indirectly would later become the foundations of the sciences of sexuality. Insofar as population levels are equated with risks of economic instability and national sovereignty, in contemporary programs we witness a merger of these concerns. Although deployed in a post-Malthusian era, national modernization programs in many parts of the so-called developing world still see population

control as a key to "making progress." In many developing postcolonial nations, science, medicine, and technology arrive as a unit that is articulated through, for example, "integrated development" (e.g., uniting fertility control, education, and agricultural loans). What has persisted are the assumptions, first, that interventions in the sexual life of "target populations" are invariably tied to modernization and, second, that sexuality can be seen as a primarily biological phenomenon, amenable to rationalized control through the sciences of reproduction, contraception, and population. Hindsight allows us to see more clearly how apparently "medical" questions about sexual and reproductive behaviors have been woven into a fabric of social relations that go far beyond the contours of the body and its health. These relations extend beyond the nation-state into transnational forms of corporate power. New corporate investments in life and nature are made increasingly possible by way of the sciences of sexuality (from contraception industries to vaccine testing to medicines for STDs), which weds pharmaceutical research programs to those for epidemiology and blurs distinctions between humanitarian and corporate politics, thus suggesting a kind of postgovernmentality. The fact that such marriages are carried out for the sake of "preserving life" often conceals the fact that entire categories of people must be "written off" in the process of achieving the aims of research and profit.

22 Within the development policy and planning literature the documentation of efforts to deliver important medical services, infrastructural opportunities, and health resources is often accompanied by an accounting of project failures and successes. Usually, the blame for failed development efforts is placed on target populations while credit for successes is attributed to the skillful work of program planners (Harding 1993). In contrast, critical ethnographic studies of development focus on the modes of engagement within development programs themselves, treating the problems of contestation over terms, forms, and practices as part of a larger inquiry into the unintended consequences of participation in "development" itself (Ferguson 1991; Gupta 1998; Li 1999; Moore 1999; Pigg 1992, 1996, 1997; Sivaramakrishnan 2000; Woost 1993). Despite years of self-identified failures in most programs, development discourse has usually been successful in depoliticizing and bureaucratizing regimes of control (Ferguson 1991).

It is necessary to look beyond the ostensible objectives of particular initiatives to appreciate what else may be accomplished by development activities. For instance, "participatory" and "community-based" approaches often bolster the position of local elites (Sivaramakrishnan 2000). Policies favor certain kinds of consciousness (Asdar Ali 2002; Ram 2001), and programs may actively form subjects accordingly (McKinley 2003; Ram 1998a). Ethnographic studies of population control and pronatalism provide ample evidence that development and public health interventions can indirectly reproduce local gender inequalities (Hartmann 1995 [1987]; Kligman 1998; Ward 1995; Morsy 1993; 1995). These studies also show that lack of attention to local understandings of gender relations and control over fertility often leads both to program failure and to the reproduction of political inequalities (Dureau 2001; Greenhalgh 1992; Kaufert and O'Neil 1993; McKinley 2003; O'Neil and Kaufert 1995).

23 Following earlier anthropological criticism of the cultural insensitivity of development programs, an enormous literature is devoted to studies of program failures to identify the mismatching of programs to actual sexual practices of a target population—whether for reproductive and family planning programs (e.g., Dixon-Meuller 1993) or for the control of STDs (e.g., Parker 1987, 1992).

24 This is in contrast to early efforts in the development of the reproductive sciences, which were treated as morally suspect.

25 Ruth Dixon-Mueller (1993: 270) has observed that between 1980 and 1992, "out of 2,100 articles on family planning only 76 incorporate some mention of sexual behavior or gender relations as they relate to reproductive health."

26 Vaughan (1991) makes this point with regard to syphilis.

27 We are not the first to propose these links; in fact, since the beginning of the social scientific interest in sexuality, there has been a constant intermingling of theories about sex and their application in policy-driven interventions. And because the last hundred years or so of social science interest in sexuality has generated numerous theories ranging from evolutionary psychology to radical constructionism, there are many assumptions about sexuality to be found within sexual and reproductive health policy. It is not a unitary field, and perspectives from feminism, social constructionism, and queer theory struggle to change how things are done at the same time as they propose different theorizations. For instance, the sex/gender distinction, which posits a heuristic contrast between biological sex and culturally formed ideas about gender roles, is now used in sex education and gender empowerment training throughout the world. Simultaneously, feminist literatures propose a deeper interrogation of assumptions about the distinctions between sex/gender and biological framings of sex.

28 For instance, Larvie (1999) discusses how constructionist arguments about local sexual meanings pertaining to male same-sex relations (which were used to stress Brazil's "difference") were debated in Brazil. Within the context of international neoliberalism, the notion that there was no coherent and singular "gay identity" on which community mobilization against AIDS could be based posed a problem for the Brazilian state's claim to have achieved modernity via committing to the public health notion of "best practices." As Larvie states: "How was the Brazilian government to develop a modern approach to AIDS prevention if its citizens did not have sexual identities organized around the modern discourses of sexual science? How could the administration of prevention programs be delegated to specific at-risk communities if no such communities existed? Perhaps most important, if communities of sexual others did not exist, the logic of delegating responsibility for prevention programs to nongovernmental organizations—imagined to be representative of specific communities—would fail. In short, the World Bank's strategy for modernizing public health initiatives in Brazil was threatened by a perceived lack of homosexual communities" (538). Larvie's discussion shows how an exegesis of sexual meanings can be reinserted into politics at multiple levels, thereby generating further sexual meanings.

29 We thank Kalpana Ram and Sanjay Srivastava for emphasizing this point.

30 For instance, in republican China, Dikötter (1995: 25) tells us that the anatomical, physiological, and endocrinological discoveries that supported Western views of the absolute difference between males and females and that were used as biological justifications for gender inequality (as described by Laqueur [1989], for instance) produced descriptions of homologous male and female bodies "different in degree, not in kind." This idea also used biology to ground gender inequality, though in a different way than it did in the West. And although in China in the 1920s and 1930s the emerging, medically justified focus on the regulation of the sexual body followed many of the patterns historians described for Euro-American countries (Foucault 1978; Weeks 1989 [1981]; Mort 2000 [1987]; Birken 1988), "no term for or conception of 'sexuality' appeared in twentieth-century China" (Dikötter 1995: 69). Sexological and medical texts in China spoke instead in terms of desires and pleasures, and they did so in ways that did not separate sexuality from procreation. Clearly, culture and science are not easily separated, nor can they be traced as distinct strands of influence on social attitudes.

31 On epidemiological categorization, see Bowker and Star 1999.

32 One example is the use of "Knowledge, Attitudes, and Practices" (KAP) surveys as a means of gathering baseline information for AIDS intervention efforts (Cleland and Ferry 1994). These surveys are directed toward uncovering beliefs and practices that may be relevant to prevention, and in some iterations they ask explicit questions about sexual behaviors. It takes an industry to mount this kind of survey; an industry to manage the information garnered from it; and an industry to teach people how to answer these sorts of questions "appropriately." As Farquhar (2002: 221) notes: "The sex survey . . . relied on neutral questions (i.e., suggesting no prior evaluation) that will elicit true statements from informants about their previous sexual experience and their preferences. These experiences and preferences are believed to have existed before the survey was administered and to persist unchanged after the survey has been completed; the multiple choice format dictates as much. Thus the survey instrument must presume that "sexual behavior" . . . enjoys an existence independent of the instrument's written questions and the carefully crafted sociological categories from which they are constructed." The taken-for-granted suitability of large-scale statistical survey methods in places like the United States or China is brought into question by evidence that shows how unsuitable they seem in places like Zaire or Nepal. But what is significant is that they are deployed anyway, in both places, and that they produce effects that are worth exploring.

33 For instance, in her lucid and influential essay "The Sexuality Connection in Reproductive Health," Ruth Dixon-Mueller (1993: 276) takes to task family planners who, "like their counterparts in demographic research, appear to have adopted a sanitized version of sexuality that treats intercourse as an emotionally neutral act." She argues (as do we) for a much more complicated picture of sexual acts—one that recognizes them as occurring within domestic, gender, political, and economic relations. Moreover, she notes how target populations reflect and deflect planned projects because of how these relations affect sexual encounters. As a development planner, however, she shifts from addressing family planning experts to making

recommendations about how to modify the understandings held by target groups. She is convinced that sex education and awareness of sexual values is a necessary part of the promotion of reproductive health, as is better and more thorough research on sexual practices. Her remedies assume the possibility of a socially neutral account of sex—an account that specifically overlooks her own critique. She advocates holding mock tribunals in educational sessions in which participants would put myths, misconceptions, and taboos about sexuality "on trial" in the form of debates. This pedagogical technique is now in use throughout the world. These are mock tribunals, of course, because we already know which point of view is supposed to withstand rigorous questionings. The scientific view of sexuality makes every other view, by definition, a myth, a misconception, or a taboo. If the health worker is to engineer the correct outcome of such mock tribunals, then what space is there within which to consider the possibility that the very notion of sex, which is the object of such trials, might be a foreign concept? Supposing that people are able to clearly separate overlapping and competing discourses about sex, then what aspects of the context—what domestic, gender, political, and economic relations—make one case about sexuality more convincing than another? What are the effects of an authoritative discourse that juxtaposes sexual acts within contexts against a purportedly context-neutral truth about sexuality?

34 For instance, some activists see the very notion of the sexual subject itself as the self-evident basis for an emancipatory politics and international solidarity around human rights. In the international gay movement, Manalansan (1997) observes, this conviction creates a narrative of progress that contrasts premodern "closeted" homosexualities to a modern sexual and political subject who is in the avant garde (see also Rofel 1999b). These distinctions offer both possibilities and limitations for those outside the Euro-American context who might be seen, and might see themselves, as gay (Cohen, this volume; Donham 1999; Manalansan 1997; Rofel 1999b). Foundational notions of the sexual subject and sexual identity provide a seemingly neutralized space from which to launch efforts toward achieving recognition and fair treatment. But the ethnographically grounded work of anthropologists suggests that such neutralized spaces can also inhibit the inclusion of existing meanings and forms of participation in certain cultural domains (including those we might call sexual) because they limit the conceptual space within which to participate—sexually, socially, and politically—in a modernity that is identified in contrast to prior social arrangements.

35 Hess (1997: 37) speaks of a "moderate constructionism" that would treat "the sociocultural and referential aspects of scientific theories as two dimensions of the same phenomenon rather than two alternative approaches to it."

36 Close descriptive research on scientific practice has demonstrated this effect many times over, making evident that other—equally scientific—procedures, pathways, and metaphors might have been used (Latour and Woolgar 1986 [1979]; Shapin and Shaffer 1985; Martin 1994. In relation to the gendered, sexual, and reproductive body, see Clarke 1998; Fausto-Sterling 1985; Martin 1986, 1990; Oudshoorn 1994). The image of science as an unmediated mirror of nature dissolves in the face of historical, sociological, and anthropological documentation of how scientific stan-

dards vary across time and areas of inquiry and of how controversies among scientists produce differing accounts of the objects they seek to explain. Within a science studies perspective, the view that scientific facts "suddenly leap into existence as the result of observations by clever scientists, who simply read the reality of nature" (Oudshoorn 1994: 10) is replaced by a view of knowledge production that takes into account not only the interactions of scientists with laboratories, bodies, molecules, and viruses but also their interactions with fellow scientists, the backers of their research, the institutions and agents who put their research to use, and the real or imagined users or beneficiaries of their labors (see also Latour 1987; Clarke and Montini 1993).

37 For instance, the controversial use of amniocentesis in India for sex selection is embroiled in cross-cutting development issues, including feminist efforts to strengthen women's social position, users' efforts to manage household economies by controlling the gender of their offspring, demographic views of a normal sex ratio, and the state's interests in all of these (Ratcliffe 1989).

38 On high-tech infertility treatment in India, see Bharadwaj 2000, 2002; Gupta 2000. Hunt 1997 records the case of the Belgian Congo, where colonial and neocolonial health development framed infertility and the resulting effect on the vitality of the labor force as the major development issue.

39 See Ram 2001; Pigg 1996; Adams 1998; and Adams 2003.

40 Latour (1999: 307) puts it this way: "The general drift of science studies is to make matters of fact not, as in common parlance, what is already present in the world, but a rather late outcome of a long process of negotiation and institutionalization. This does not limit their certainty but, on the contrary, provides all that is necessary for matters of fact to become indisputable and obvious. To be indisputable is the end point, not the beginning as in the empiricist tradition."

41 This point is important because it also gives us a way to think about changing scientific understandings. Again, research in the social studies of science has examined the procedures and practices that make "data" detachable from its context while preserving the stability of referential ties to the "real thing" about which claims are being made (Latour 1999: 24–79). These procedures actually can produce detachable knowledge that can be put to use in many contexts. But the accomplishment of this decontextualization is not without its vagaries. Oudshoorn (1994: 142) points this out with regard to the application of endocrinological research to the oral contraceptive pill:

> The decontextualization strategy suggests that technologies can be made to work everywhere, but this is not always so. Scientific artifacts require a specific context in which they can work, one similar to the context in which they arise. If this context is not available, scientists have to create it . . . Most contraceptive technologies are made in industrialized countries and therefore bear the fingerprints of western producers, including locally and culturally specific ideas of what ideal contraceptives should look like. Every technology contains, so to say, a configured user . . . Although pill researchers claimed that the pill was a universal, context-independent contraceptive, it nevertheless contained a specific user: a woman, disciplined enough to take medication regularly, who is used to gyneco-

logical examinations and regular visits to the physician, and who does not have to hide contraception from her partner . . . From this perspective it can be understood that the pill has not found a universal acceptance.

Interestingly, the dosages for the oral contraceptive pill were also developed on the assumption of a universal, standard female body with the same levels of estrogen and progesterone regardless of diet, living conditions, genetic background, parity, or age.

STACY LEIGH PIGG

Globalizing the Facts of Life

• • •

Sexuality has been the last domain (trailing even gender) to have its natural, biologized status called into question.—CAROLE VANCE

It is April 1997 and a week-long refresher course for youth "peer educators," run by a Nepali nongovernmental organization (NGO) with funds aimed at HIV/AIDS prevention activities for young people, is being held in a rooftop meeting room in a modest hotel for local travelers in the city of Pokhara in Nepal. Six months earlier this group of Nepali college students, ranging in age from eighteen to twenty-one, had spent two weeks learning about sexual health, sexually transmitted diseases (STDS), AIDS, and condoms. Now they had been brought together for an additional week of discussions, role-playing exercises, and education. A mild breeze flutters papers on tabletops as twenty students shift restlessly in their seats, hoping to cover up the fact that they cannot remember the set of vocabulary terms that they had been assigned to master in their first round of training. Each student examines a photocopied worksheet with three simple line drawings labeled "male genitalia," "female genitalia (external)," and "female genitalia (internal)." Arrows extend from the drawings to blank lines, where these peer educators in training are expected to fill in the correct term. Some of these body parts, like the penis, are easy enough to identify on the drawing, and young men and women alike know the appropriate technical term to write on their sheet of paper. Other parts are harder to identify; indeed, some are organs that these students have never had occasion to consider, much less name, either because it has never been considered important to do so or because these organs are not externally visible—or both. The black squiggles on white paper are drawn from an anatomist's or gynecologist's angle of inspection, and these peculiar renderings of the most intimate regions of the body do not necessarily match the landscape known to the embodied self.

When this worksheet was passed to me, I had a sudden flashback to the sex education courses I had sat through in church basements and in school classrooms as a teenager in suburban Milwaukee. The worksheets whose arcane information was confounding the Nepali students might have been taken from the same sex education textbook from which I had been taught. For that teenaged me, living some twenty-five years earlier in an American midde-class enclave coming to grips with the so-called sexual revolution, information about the reproductive organs, hormonal changes in puberty, the menstrual cycle, ovulation, and fertilization was fundamentally integrated into my concepts of "sex," along with "facts" about masturbation (normal), homosexuality (possibly okay but not normal), and gendered differences in desire (girls have to be careful not to lead boys on because the latter can't control themselves). I was awash in medico-moral discourses on sex, buffeted on one side by the sex education classes taught by the gym teacher and on the other by my reading of *Our Bodies, Ourselves*, the bible of the women's health movement (with furtive peeks at *The Joy of Sex* sandwiched in-between).

That April in 1997, watching the Nepali students struggle with their worksheets, it struck me that outside of this training session there were few (if any) other ways that they would encounter this particular configuration of information about the body. I realized then just how deeply my own body sense was informed by the sexual sciences. The facts of life that seemed obvious and basic to me and that shaped the way I handled my sexual relationships and my reproductive possibilities were not the same as those shared by the rest of the people in the room that day. The formats within which I have encountered this information, the myriad subtle ways it has always been echoed and reinforced in my world, and the uses to which I have put it have made it—and the phrase itself is telling—"second nature" for me. Would it become so for these Nepali students?

Stepping Back: Sex Education and Persuasion

Worldwide, health programs dealing with fertility regulation, reproductive health, and HIV/STD prevention are based on and actively promulgate a particular set of ideas about the sexual and reproductive body. Planned by experts in public health and development, set up within the context of national governments and donor-government-NGO relations, and tied to visions of social reform, these programs eventually take concrete form in the often mundane activities of education and service delivery. Some of these activities involve concrete alterations to the body (getting Norplant into arms, condoms onto penises, penicillin into bloodstreams, iron supplements into gestating women, etc.), but many others intervene in the social sphere (e.g., increasing the age of marriage for women, encouraging spacing of childbirths, urging husbands and wives to communicate about sexual and reproductive decisions) and involve complicated mixtures of education and persuasion. As a collection of activities, motivated by a variety of agendas and carried out in diverse locales, these endeavors form part of a larger historical phenomenon in which a particular set of institutional networks is internationalizing biomedically based knowledge and technology.

The internationalization of sexology and the sexual sciences is not new.[1] The well-known sexologists of the late-nineteenth and early-twentieth-century Anglo-European tradition were widely translated, and contemporaneous medical/sexological treatises were written by intellectuals in countries outside the West (Dikötter 1995; Früstück 2000). The elaboration of these imported and parallel sexual sciences was linked to state projects of modernization and, in some cases, decolonization. And, for the most part, it was a bourgeois elite who engaged with the new sciences of sex. Clearly, the sexual sciences have a history of being entangled with visions of social reform.

Although lower socioeconomic classes and marginalized groups have long been targeted by technological interventions (sterilization, contraceptives, medical treatments of venereal disease), the more recent wave of programs attempts to target such groups through sex education. Targeted groups are portrayed by experts and elites as either ignorant or, more benignly, as objects of pity when they are presented as voicing reasoning about their sexual and reproductive bodies that is nonscience based. Whether scoffed at, ridiculed, or gently corrected, difference as both inferiority and deviance is set in relation to the normative baseline of scientific fact. In such programs the idiom of rationality and the project of education often become vehicles through which class or racial distinctions are marked.[2] That the invocation of scientific facts can so readily function as a tool for carving out social superiority raises questions about the scope for diversity within sexual and reproductive health programs.

The sex education components of sexual and reproductive health programs aim to improve health and autonomy by improving the knowledge base from which people make their decisions, but there are persistent, troubling gaps between biomedical messages and local knowledge. Indeed, there is a pressing need to find a way to strike "a balance between respecting and building on what women know and giving them essential biomedical information" (Cornwall 2002: 229). For instance, women are often urged to use invasive contraception (such as the contraceptive pill, subdermal or injectable contraceptives, or the intrauterine device) with "no information at all on how the medicines or devices they are using work, or on what they do to their bodies" (219). When health workers do attempt to provide some explanation, they find that they are left to their own devices to search for metaphors that might bridge the gap between the biomedical "facts" and local knowledge. However, because women's concerns about the effects of these contraceptives on their bodies stem from indigenous understandings of reproductive health, even these explanations often do not address their worries.

Bringing biomedical knowledge into a nondominating relation with local knowledges is no easy feat. The educational arm of sexual and reproductive health programs restricts itself mainly to providing basic scientific literacy. Yet an instrumental faith in biomedical information fails to ask what people take on along with a biomedical view of sexuality and reproduction; what people in different locales actually do with this information and what they might seek from it and unintentionally derive from it.[3] These are questions about the processes through which people in diverse and often severely disadvantaged circumstances come to have (or not to have) stakes in a biomedical view of their bodies—questions that, in turn, demand that we take into account the various institutional stakes involved in this situation. The dominant frame for thinking about these issues persistently juxtaposes "facts" with "beliefs," "science" with "values," and "biology" with "culture." The optimistic hopes for achieving health via sex education sustain a view that, on the one hand, tends to overestimate the inherent, self-evident power of "the facts" to change the world and, on the other, to underestimate the degree to which the sexual and reproductive sciences are inextricably tangled in social issues.

In this essay I extract from my small ethnographic epiphany in Nepal a series of questions about the international presence of this particular conglomerate of ideas concerning the sexual and reproductive body. The vignette that opens this essay is more than a rhetorical gambit: that moment prompted me to ask a series of questions about the relation between theories of sexuality and the history of the sexual sciences. In this study I trace some of those connections by working outward from ethnographic specificity to abstract issues concerning the conceptualization of sexuality, biological facts, and globalization. Note, however, that although I begin with observations from Nepal my aim is neither to analyze processes taking place in Nepal nor to provide a cultural interpretation of Nepalese sexuality. Rather, my goal is for this study to function as a prolegomenon to the kind of inquiry called for by certain transformations around sexuality. We live in a time when sexuality is being increasingly biologized through international public health projects, while, simultaneously, social theory is prying it away from its association with the physical body. Thus there is a need to reexamine the theoretical tools used for thinking about biology and culture in relation to sexuality.

Biological facts elaborated through the sexual and reproductive sciences have been at the heart of the development of the concept of sex. A historical understanding of the codevelopment of, first, scientific objectivity with respect to the sexual body and, second, changing socio-moral debates concerning that body further confounds the self-evidence of the separation between facts and values, and points to how, on a global scale, a biologized notion of sex operates as a standardizing device. Lest we become mired in a negative critique of science as a Western particularism masquerading as a universal, these observations demand a robustly materialist way of envisioning the social production of facts.

A Scientific View of Sexuality

What is a scientific view of the sexual and procreative body, and why is it significant? Consider the following news article, whose headline screams: "African AIDS Epidemic Fueled by Sexual Ignorance." It sums up the case for sex education as a strategy for AIDS prevention:

> Westport, Ct (Reuters Health) May 16 [2001]—Sex and sexuality is at the core of the AIDS pandemic in sub-Saharan Africa and, according to a leading South African health official, researchers and politicians must involve the African public in a much more frank and open discussion of human behavior if they hope to successfully combat the disease.
>
> "Sex is regarded as a taboo in Africa—you don't speak openly about it," said Dr. Malegapuru William Makgoba, president of the Medical Research Council of South Africa [in an address to the National Institute of Allergy and Infectious Diseases in Bethesda, Maryland]. "We all know that this is a sexually transmitted disease and that's the bottom line," he said. "We're doing everything except focusing on the real major factor that determines whether or not you get the disease." . . .

African scientific and government leaders need to recognize that the AIDS crisis in this region is not just about statistics and treatments, Dr. Makgoba said, but involves a complex interaction between science, politics and culture. "The challenges facing science and its development today are no longer predominantly technical but largely social."

Research into the particular cultural backgrounds and sexual practices of Africans is almost nonexistent, he continued, with no focus being placed on combating the sexual mythologies, taboos, and ignorance that inform the sexual behavior of many African men and women . . . "The whole subject of human sexuality in Africa is . . . based on hearsay," Dr. Makgoba told Reuters Health. Addressing sexuality scientifically, "will make a lot of difference to people, both in the developed and the developing countries."[4]

The position articulated here by Dr. Makgoba (himself a prominent virologist) is a complex one. It is a plea to confront the HIV/AIDS crisis as a social issue. It is also a declaration that science must override the "politics" of the (merely) social disputes over the AIDS problem. The basis for an adequate public response to AIDS would involve the "frank and open" approach to sexuality made possible by the clarity provided by medico-scientific knowledge—a clarity that could trump narrow political interests. With his call for more research on "particular cultural backgrounds and sexual practices," Dr. Makgoba recognizes that interventions require reliable contextual understandings of behavior. Here the door appears to be open for conducting research into the contingent, complicated, and changing interactions between personhood, gender, kinship, domestic arrangements, economic strategies, and other factors that form patterns of sexual expression and sexual contacts within particular contexts.

Yet, in the next breath, Dr. Makgoba introduces a universal bottom line: these "mythologies," stemming from "ignorance," must be combated with facts. The sexual practices that increase the risk of HIV transmission can be shown to arise from "taboos," which in the hard light of epidemiological risk can be revealed to be shadowy collective delusions. A penis in a vagina or anus is an opportunity for the movement of microbes from body to body—period. As for ideas about masculinity and erotic longings; or about moral duties, coercion, and complicated goals and tradeoffs; or about hard life circumstances—well, these messy factors can be evaluated in terms of physiological harm (disease) and the "pure truth" of what we know about the sexual function of the human body. In a single sentence, the news article summarizing Dr. Makgoba's lecture leaps from a view of sexuality that could foreground the social (and the local) to a view of sexuality that emphasizes the biological (and the universal). Dr. Makgoba anchors the call for a scientific approach to sexual behavior in biological processes. For him, a "frank and open" public consideration of sexuality is one that makes it an object of medico-scientific knowledge, and this knowledge is assumed to be objective and neutral.

"Frank and Open" in Nepal: Putting into Practice the Scientific View of Sexuality

"Frankness" means speaking about sex in a scientific and sexological way. That this is a tautological imperative in public health became clear to me in Nepal during the course of my 1997 research on recently established AIDS prevention efforts.[5] The main issue preoccupying the Nepali NGO leaders, health educators, and AIDS workers was how to talk about sex in the Nepali context. International donors, program planners, and technical advisors took it as a given that discussions about AIDS required "frank" discussions of sex; "cultural" barriers were to be expected but could be overcome via some sort of compromise between frankness and the socially acceptable middle ground. Indeed, I noticed that AIDS workers were not simply engaging in this "frank and open" discussion but actually were doing a great deal of work to create the very discursive ground that would make this possible. It was as though they had been funded to run a railway, and to do so by planners who somehow believed that the job merely involved managing arrivals and departures when, in fact, it first involved the laying of the tracks.

Through HIV/AIDS prevention programs, with their attached emphasis on STD prevention, sex was put on the public health agenda in Nepal in new ways (cf. Parikh, this volume). The early 1990s saw a major infusion of donor funding to launch these programs. Under the rubric of disease prevention, new forms of institutional attention to the sexual activities and consciousness of Nepalis have emerged within a development framework, showing public concern (at least on the part of the urban middle class) over love marriages, trafficking in women, prostitution, and the moral dissolution caused by modernization (which has bled into a wider net of development-related problems).[6]

This institutional attention took several forms. First, because AIDS prevention programs revolve around changing the "risky" practices of individuals, some information about sexual practices is needed, especially information that is seen to be quantifiable (e.g., the average number of clients entertained per week by a sex worker; the age of first experience of sexual intercourse; the percentage of young adults who have had premarital sexual relations, etc.). Surveys of this type had never been conducted in Nepal: demographic research in support of population control restricted its focus to married couples and asked about fertility issues rather than sexual practices. With the new interest in AIDS and STD prevention, acts of sexual intercourse —frequencies, practices, and partners—came to be of importance in forming development objectives.

Second, STDS acquired a place on the public health agenda. Previously invisible to national health concerns, STDS had been regarded as an individual problem, treated surreptitiously by venereal disease specialists or (more often) on the advice of pharmacy owners. Public health programs had concentrated their attention on diarrheal diseases, malaria, tuberculosis and other respiratory diseases, and other major problems. The issue of STDS was introduced as a national health problem because certain STD infections can increase the risk of HIV infection. The public health discourse on STDS was new to Nepal, and in this respect Nepal's experience differs from that of India, Malaysia, and many eastern and southern African countries where colonial authorities, who were concerned with the vitality of the male labor force and the army (and, in some places, low fertility rates), had long viewed STDS as a national problem. In these countries discussions about AIDS have tended to echo earlier campaigns against venereal diseases, thus building on already established public frameworks. In Nepal, however, calls for sexual restraint for the purpose of disease prevention took hold with AIDS awareness.[7]

Third, sex education and "sexual awareness training" became core program activities. For programs aimed at youth, AIDS prevention was mainly interpreted as sex education (usually carried out in schools). Awareness seminars for adults also typically included sex education modules that offered information on the reproductive system, the sexual maturation of the human body, STDS, and exercises for exploring sexual values and attitudes. Efforts were made to train health workers, including those employed in family planning programs, to be more direct and sensitive when discussing sexuality. Planners saw these activities as providing the necessary scaffolding for achieving the concrete goals of reducing the transmission of STDS and HIV and increasing rates of treatment for the former. The guiding view was that more open discussions of sexual issues, together with more fact-based sexual and reproductive knowledge, were essential steps in accomplishing public health.

Manuals, curricula, and guidelines in use elsewhere in the world prov models for questions on "Knowledge, Attitudes, Behavior, and Prac (KABP) surveys; outlines for AIDS and sex education lessons; message___ AIDS awareness posters and pamphlets; and group exercises to "desensitize" participants and to enable them to discuss "myths and misconceptions" about sex. The curricular materials included role-playing exercises to "develop assertiveness skills," step-by-step directions (verbal and graphic) on "how to use a condom," and pithy handouts on "steps to behavior change." These materials intersperse medical information about reproduction and disease with exercises that encourage reflexive discussions on attitudes and values.

The international templates always include a statement about adapting materials to local cultural circumstances. This injunction, however, conveys the neutrality—and hence natural universality—of the frameworks and the information they contain by relegating cultural difference to a problem of fine-tuning information delivery. Understandings, explanations, objectives, values, and attitudes that deviate from the established norm of "facts" and "nonjudgmental" attitudes toward sexuality cannot find a place in the curriculum because these are precisely the misconceptions that sex education is meant to correct. "Facts" are parsed from "misconceptions" in subtle ways. This can best be seen in the lessons found in a highly professional manual titled "Talking Together: Integrating STD/AIDS in a Reproductive Health Context—a Facilitator Guide for the Training of Community Health Workers" (CEDPA and SCF 1997).[8] This manual was developed to help a wide range of health and family planning personnel take on the job of handling sexual issues when providing clients with HIV/AIDS, STD, and family planning information. Addressed to multiple audiences, it is meant both to educate health care personnel and to provide them with lesson plans appropriate to community education. It is thus part curriculum package and part textbook.

The first lesson in the manual addresses "gender and cultural issues in Nepal," the objective of which is to ensure that participants will be able to "name two of the strongest influences on behaviour in Nepalese society— (cultural and gender roles)" (CEDPA and SCF 1997: 2). The first exercise asks the group to consider the nature of men and of women, and then name similarities ("examples like both need water, food, love, warmth") and differences ("examples like childbearing, needing to shave, organs"). The facilitator is then supposed to lead a reflective discussion on why characteristics were attributed to either men or women. The exercise also requires a coda from the facilitator to drive home the point: "Conclude by saying that the only characteristics which cannot be changed are the PHYSICAL ones. Other characteristics like attitudes (men should not be sentimental) and behaviours (only women do household work and only men can talk with leaders and officials) are created by society. These things can be changed by individuals in the society" (2). The lesson here involves teaching participants to use the contrasting concepts of the natural/social to frame their conscious thinking about sex and gender. Indeed, the concept of a socially determined "gender" built atop sexual dimorphism is the lesson. In this exercise, local meanings are dealt with by eliciting stereotypes and then by objectifying them as "cultural" ideas that may readily be changed through conscious effort.

The fifth lesson, which concerns basic STD information, suggests beginning lessons by asking participants "to share local names and stories they have heard about STDS" (37). An earlier warm-up game had participants whisper a sentence in the ear of the next person in line until the last person repeats aloud what she or he heard (thus revealing how information can become distorted) in order to show "how easy it [is] to confuse facts." Then, in a small-group discussion, participants are to be asked to "come up with local names and myths and rumours related to local beliefs." In juxtaposition to the correct biomedical information about STDS, the handbook offers a shaded sidebar listing "some local terms for STDS" and "local beliefs" about transmission, symptoms, and cures. These lists pull together a diversity of terms and beliefs culled from the recollections of the health educators who provided input into the development of the manual. Few if any of these terms are known uniformly across Nepal, and none correspond in any simple way to the biomedical category of STD. Health educators who have attempted to teach about STDS remain aware of these local terms precisely because they are not easily converted into the biomedical category of STD. Attempts to discuss them in training sessions as "local terms for STDS" can create more confusion than clarification. The structure of this particular exercise appears to replace inaccurate "cultural" beliefs with correct biomedical information; however, health educators first inculcate the concept of the STD and then instruct participants to translate local terms so that they fit into this category. Only then can the lesson, as framed, do its intended pedagogical work.

The merger of "Nepali" content into the medical frame is accomplished in yet another way through the manual's sidebar stories. For example, trainers are told to tell the following story to the group:

I am a community health worker, and . . . a friend, Ram Maya, came to visit me the other day. She looked worried. We had some tea and talked a while and then she told me that she was having a lot of pain when she had sexual intercourse. She also said she had a thick and bad smelling discharge from her vagina. She felt embarrassed and shy to go to the health post about this and it was very difficult for her to even tell me.

Ram Maya got this infection from her husband, Jeet Bahadur, who works as a driver and travels out of the district almost every month. Ram Maya loves her husband and he brings money for her and their 2 year old daughter so they can live. She and her husband are hoping to have another child after a year or so—they want to try for a son. (41)

Recognizably Nepali names, places, and situations help to make connections between the abstract information being taught and its potential real-life relevance. Discussion of these hypothetical cases helps trainees learn to reason about ways of presenting information, and, certain contrived elements have to be introduced here to make the story work. The characters are always presented as seeking help in ways that are unlikely or implausible: a little too willing to confide in a health worker; a little too precise in their description of symptoms; a little too predisposed to make their sexual contacts into a medical issue. They are, in short, people who are already inclined to read their sexuality through a biological lens. These stories model the types of scenarios that health workers are supposed to bring about by educating people— but they are not the scenarios with which they actually deal.

International template materials, formulated by health education experts, provide well-thought-out and easy-to-use guides that save local health educators from having to reinvent the wheel. Useful as they are, however, these templates inevitably standardize information, priorities, and pedagogical techniques. For Nepali health workers, these models of what to do and how to do it came not only as a preset package but also as an orthodoxy. They were backed by the institutional authority of donors, whose goals and standards for handling the sexual component of reproductive health had already been developed in distant centers. More subtly, the materials carried the imprimatur of science and, with it, of modernity. These stamps of authority were important for the health workers thrust into the uncomfortable role of leading training and educational exercises about sex. The institutional and scientific legitimacy of the material buffered them from negative imputations about their personal moral character. Indeed, AIDS workers in Nepal found themselves in an awkward role: donor expectations concerning the "best" approaches toward AIDS education thrust them into activities that required them to be "frank," informative, nonjudgmental, and culturally appropriate, without providing them with much useful guidance about how to reconcile what, in practice, were frequently contradictory edicts. They therefore often felt the difference between what they were supposed to say, according to the materials in English from which they drew their own information, and what seemed to make sense in Nepal.

I was told by AIDS workers that they found something odd about the materials, something that didn't fit into the slot left open in the curriculum for listing their culture's values and beliefs about sexuality. What felt strange and foreign to them was the relentless attention AIDS work paid to the act, the behavior, the practice, the precise naming of body parts and desires—an excision of sexuality, as "sex," from its imbrication in morally saturated interpersonal connections. This excision was also variously seen as necessary, emancipatory, useful, vulgar, pointlessly impersonal, morally dangerous, erotic, and so on. But always it was seen as ever-so-subtly not entirely "Nepali."

Indeed, AIDS workers felt that many of the words in the templates had no equivalent in Nepali. Although there are many ways of speaking in Nepali about coitus, genitals, erotic desire, and the different kinds of relationships deriving therefrom, there is no Nepali term that groups all of these under the single category of sex. In mainstream international AIDS discourse, however, it is assumed that, although different societies might imbue different aspects of sexuality with various values concerning what is moral, erotic, embarrassing, desirable, normal, and so forth, these values are superimposed on what is in fact the same thing. People can be asked to "talk about" *it* or, in training sessions, "reflect" on their "values toward" *it*, or set up a program to provide "education" about *it*, or gather "baseline data" on *it*. The "it" referred to is the domain that in late-twentieth and early-twenty-first-century English we refer to as "sex." And "it" is assumed to be self-evident. However, for Nepali AIDS workers, their first task was to establish the self-evidence of this particular domain.

"Sex": A Modern Western Idea

Social historians looking at sexuality in Europe and North America have precisely traced the emergence of the modern concept of sex. They argue that "the separation, with industrial capitalism, of family life from work, of consumption from production, of leisure from labor, of personal life from political life, has completely reorganized the context in which we experience sexuality . . . Modern consciousness permits, as earlier systems of thought did not, the positing of 'sex' for perhaps the first time as having an 'independent' existence" (Ross and Rapp 1997: 164). It has been possible, since the late nineteenth century, to imagine sex as a discrete and demarcated dimension of human life—as an essence of the person, as an arena of social relations, and as an object of knowledge and investigation.[9] Urbanization altered the traditional forms through which communities regulated sexual behavior and alliances; migration separated persons from their communities of origin; and growing towns and cities widened the arenas of anonymous public space into which people entered as individuals.[10]

Concomitantly, the domestic sphere became understood as a "home"—a sphere of personal relations organized around emotional attachment and distinct from the realm of "work"—through an oppositional logic that sustains the notion of the "family" at the core of an ideology of intimate relationships (Collier, Rosaldo, and Yanagisako 1997: 71). Although these changes occurred in variable, complex, and nuanced ways in different places and for different categories of people, over the course of the nineteenth century there was a major shift in how sexuality was regulated as well as in how sexual alliances were understood. These shifts contributed to "the development of the concept of personal life, a sphere of individuality and self-development, based on material prosperity, but focused on the cultivation of individuality, which in its turn was to have important consequences on the specification of sexuality" (Weeks 1989 [1981]: 29).

These social changes fed public concern over a range of problems associated with what were seen as disruptions to "natural" family forms and gender roles. Intense debates over divorce legislation, women's rights, prostitution, venereal disease, legal sanctions against homosexuality, falling birth rates, contraception, eugenics, and miscegenation increasingly articulated matters of public policy and legislation in terms of the problems of sex. The vocabularies and frameworks used to address these issues transformed over time (documentation of this is especially rich for the period between 1850 and 1950). Cumulatively, the different ways that sex, as personal behavior, was seen to be at issue in a range of public social "problems" and reformist causes helped to consolidate a distinctive mode of attention to the "sexual" dimension of people's lives.[11]

This objectification was furthered by an increasingly refined scientific scrutiny of reproduction, sexual desire, and varieties of sexual behavior—a scientific project that was itself driven by the pressing social issues of the day.

Sexual "pathologies" became the object of description and explanation, and, through the use of scientific typology, sexual "deviance" became criminalized. The sexual body came under medical supervision through the treatment of venereal disease, management of childbirth, treatments of perceived aberrations of desire, and, later, through supervision of fertility and sex change operations. Both individuals and populations were increasingly imagined in relation to the "norm."

What we can see quite clearly is that the historical and cultural factors that intertwined in the social formation of modernity gave rise to a particular view of sex and sexuality. "In our society," summarizes Jeffery Weeks (1989 [1981]: 12), "sex has become the supreme secret ('the mystery of sex') and the general substratum of our existence. Since the nineteenth century it has been seen as the cause and 'truth' of our being. It defines us socially and morally; its release or proper functioning can be a factor in health, energy, activity; its frustration is a cause of ill health, social unorthodoxy, even madness." For sex to be conceptualized in this way, it must, as Weeks points out, be treated as a unified domain: "not just a series of acts, not a collection of bodies which can be eroticized, but a thing in itself, with its general causations and specified effects" (12). This notion of sex is also integrated into ideas about the self. Sex is seen as an act of self-expression that is deeply private and personal, and sexuality is seen as something that is "the essence of our individual being which asserts itself against the demands of culture" (12).

Questioning Cultural Specificity

If the ideas about sexuality used to plan and carry out most programs related to sexual health are culturally and historically specific ideas masquerading as universals, then do other cultures have other concepts of sexuality? Jeffrey Clark (1997: 195) has pondered this question in relation to the Huli, a society in highland New Guinea: "Clearly 'sexuality' as an area of study imposes a Western framework of beliefs and analysis, which assumes that a category exists 'out there' but does not ask whether this is also a category for non-Western peoples like the Huli. Granted that sexuality is an undifferentiated experience for the Huli, it seems undeniable that there is a Huli discourse about sexual practices and the body. If 'sexuality' is not (just) a private affair but a set of public beliefs about the practice and consequences of sexual behavior—and for the Huli these beliefs are based in and not separate from a cosmology which equates sociomoral relations with states of health—then the Huli could be said to have a concept of sexuality." How sexuality (in this looser sense) is tied up with reproduction, the aesthetics of pleasure, moralities, and the regulation of behavior then becomes a question for ethnographic investigation. The meaning of sexuality itself would have to be investigated; what is "sexual" cannot be assumed (Elliston 1995; see also Strathern 1988).

There are ethnographic techniques for asking and listening that allow us to closely follow local concepts and concerns and to arrive at some understanding of cultural differences regarding what we call sexuality.[12] Yet it is worth noting that such a study, done well, would likely be unrecognizable as a study of sexual behaviors and attitudes—at least in the eyes of the agencies concerned with planning sexual health programs. We might say that although sexuality is everywhere mediated by cultural meanings and structures of social organization it is not everywhere perceived as "sex."

My discussion would end here but for the fact that sex (in the modern sense, which allows it to be reified) is culturally present nearly everywhere (and where it isn't there are powerful institutions that act assuming that it is)—witness the dilemmas of Nepali AIDS educators and the lessons in the manual "Talking Together." Cultures are not hermetically sealed units. Their symbolic systems are not like the interior of a mirror-lined sphere that infinitely reflects back on itself (Fabian 1983); nor, in historical time, do cultures bounce off each other like billiard balls (Wolf 1982). Sexuality is experienced in social matrices, through organizing sets of public meanings, and within a history. Just as we would not want to project Western folk theories of the body, gender, sexuality, and the family onto this reality (see Ross and Rapp 1997), neither should we pretend that this reality is an unchanging site of cultural difference unaffected by wider processes of historical change. Further, the historicity of sexuality outside Europe does not begin, suddenly, with colonialism, urbanization, and other changes associated with modernity (Ahlberg 1994; Setel 1999). So-called traditional sexual norms were never as stable and unchanging as current AIDS-related discourse portrays.

There exists in many places a wide and porous zone where multiple meanings and cross-cutting social processes construct sexuality. In contrast to this porosity, public health interest in sexuality presents itself as a hard cusp where a particular kind of modern, reified, and biologized concept of sex pushes against other sexualities. In practice, however, what international health interventions produce are frayed and flexible edges where knowledge and practice is transformed.[13] Essentializing categories, which polarize "Western" and "non-Western" frameworks, are too crude to account for these transformations. The Nepali AIDS workers I discussed earlier found the reified, decontextualized, and ostensibly amoral discourse on sex distinctly odd—but they did not find it completely incomprehensible. Images of a monolithic process of Westernization inexorably rolling toward global cultural homogenization obscure too much complexity; images of "difference" as multiple sites of resistance to universalism obscure too many connections.

Rather than trying to rescue an image of a purely indigenous sexuality, distinct and untainted by "outside" Western influence, it is more useful to ask what kinds of interactions, connections, and conflicts emerge in the aforementioned porous zones. What sorts of claims to universality become plausible, and what kinds of stakes do various actors develop? What structures support and impel the wider circulation of the modern concept of sex, and what projects does this concept enable? Who takes it up, in what contexts, and why? How are other ways of knowing and engaging sexuality altered, refocused, or reinforced in the process? These sorts of questions begin to challenge the tendency to interpret events in terms of blanket concepts such as Westernization, modernization, and globalization.

A reified concept of sexuality can be said to have emerged within the context of an unfolding European modernity. In present-day Nepal, however, it arrives from elsewhere as a fully formed truth tacitly embedded in the programmatic assumptions of international health. Here the authority of science merges with a compelling techno-rational potential to control biological processes for desired ends (e.g., fertility regulation, disease prevention, the elimination of social discrimination).

Scientific Detachment as Social Engagement: The Question of Values

While many people working internationally in development, activist movements, and progressive causes recognize the "Westerness" of certain values attached to sexuality, this is not necessarily the case with regard to the "scientific" and "biological" aspects of these assumptions. Indeed, these "truths" are usually the ground for action and, as such, claim universality. Unpacking the socially specific dimension of these truths can seem dangerous because much is at stake and much is invested in the certainty of their universality. This claim to universality serves a political function by (ostensibly, at least) taking some aspects of sexuality out of the realm of moral debate. This move also has a history.

The sexual sciences that developed in the late nineteenth century "endeavored to escape or avoid association with pathology, individual or social"

(Porter and Hall 1995: 154) and "at least in intention, however compromised, set . . . out to apply the rigors of scientific rationality to a highly emotive area" in a way that Porter and Hall say "provided a radically new way to make, unmake, and remake sexual knowledge" (177). A language of clinical detachment came to be applied to sexuality, and in this way objectivity in relation to sexual matters acquired a cultural plausibility. Yet this stance has been (and continues to be) equivocal, for it has been (and is) used not just to observe nature but also to justify actions and policies on the basis of claims about nature. For instance, at the turn of the twentieth century prominent sexologists campaigned for the repeal of laws against sodomy, arguing that male homosexuals were natural sexual variants.[14]

Scientific research opens up new ways to manipulate nature, and these too are quickly linked to debates about the social good. The eugenics and birth control movements in the first half of the twentieth century are prominent examples (see Clarke 1998; Mort 2000 [1987]; Porter and Hall 1995; Weeks 1989 [1981]). With respect to venereal disease in the United States during World War I, for instance, newly discovered therapeutics (the Wasserman reaction, arsephenamine, and chemical prophylaxis) made it possible— to the dismay of morally oriented social reformers—for the army to control venereal disease among the troops through prevention and treatment protocols. Disease, rather than the immorality of extramarital sexual relations per se, became the problem, and "the demands of science outstripped the last vestiges of the rigid moral argument" through technocratic management in the name of efficiency (Brandt 1987 [1985]: 121). By the 1930s doctors and public health officials actively sought to "reduce the moral stigma attached to these infections in order to make it possible for physicians to deal with them more dispassionately" (137).

The social uses of detachment were not solely controlled by professionals. In the first and second decades of the twentieth century birth control activists Margaret Sanger (in the United States) and Marie Stopes (in England) sought to make fertility regulation directly available to ordinary women so that they would not have to rely on doctors. (Sanger, who was also a supporter of eugenics, later changed her strategy, making alliances with research scientists that eventually led to the development of hormonal contraceptives, an innovation that increased the medical control of fertility [Clarke 1998].) In England, at a time when booksellers required letters certifying legitimate scientific or professional qualifications from customers seeking to purchase medico-sexological books on sexuality and reproduction, Marie Stopes's marriage manual, *Married Love*, challenged this "conspiracy of silence, in order to enlighten the public" (Porter and Hall 1995: 218). This widely circulated book brought medical and scientific information about sexual function and fertility into bedrooms through idealizing marital sexuality as a form of self-expression leading to greater intimacy. Stopes promoted informed, frank talk between couples; the avalanche of letters she received from grateful readers seeking further enlightenment demonstrates that people were embracing the "facts" in order to rescue relationships. (Stopes's view of informed marital sexuality appears to be a model for the current wave of international sex education.) As all of these examples show, clinical detachment and scientific objectivity toward sexuality did not really lead away from social concerns but, rather, opened up new ways of dealing with sexuality as a social concern. Medical and scientific knowledge enables new forms of sociality (Foucault 1978; Haraway 1997; Rabinow 1996).

Biologization and Globalization

The scientific research that we now apply to sexuality pursued many separate but overlapping paths, including investigations into reproductive physiology, hormones, genetic inheritance, sexual functioning, orientation of desire, and the range and variety of sexual behaviors (Hall 2000). In an era of increasing professional specialization, the problems of sexuality fell under the purview of many emergent domains of knowledge, including social sciences (psychology, sociology, and anthropology), medicine (venereology, gynecology, psychiatry, public health), and biological sciences (reproductive physiology, endocrinology, genetics). Although not a unified field, cumulatively this work has solidified into a conglomerate of ideas about the nature of the sexual and reproductive body. As with all science, influential theories and important discoveries became the foundations on which further research and innovation was based. An undisputed fact is assimilated into other projects, and the more other projects there are whose stability depends on this fact, the harder it is for a dissenter to question it (Latour 1987).

International sexual health programs are not cutting-edge science; they are, rather, at the mundane end of furthering the application of that which is already well established. Explanations of the mechanics of reproductive physiology, of contraceptive technologies, of "normal" sexual functioning, of gender role and sexual orientation, and so on can be wrapped into a bundle— a bundle that passes as "a scientific approach to sex."[15]

In the sexual sciences, claims "just" to consider nature became firmly entrenched within strategies of disciplinary expansion.[16] By the 1920s and

1930s reproductive scientists in the United States were striving to separate their work from that of the more psychologically oriented sexologists in order to stake out an even "cleaner" and more "objective" legitimacy for their basic research, "providing [themselves] with the proverbial ten-foot pole with which they could touch reproductive organs with propriety" (Clarke 1998: 92). In the United States, funding designated for the holistic study of problems of human sexuality was channeled toward "basic science" research on reproductive biology carried out on animal models, thus pushing off center stage the direct investigation of human sexuality. Leading scientists resisted direct involvement in applied research on contraception so as to maintain a distance between their work and the mucky moral problems of human sexuality.[17] The influence of the decades of research conducted under this approach—not only the discoveries that resulted but also the modes of justification that developed—remains.

On the other hand, social constructivist approaches to the study of sexuality offer a trenchant critique of biological essentialism and introduce cautions against making inappropriate assumptions about the transcultural and transhistorical character of categories used in comparative analysis. This stance fosters an awareness that international sexual health programs contain many assumptions based on Euro-American folk beliefs.[18] Less evident to thinkers influenced by constructionism is that most constructionist arguments still implicitly assume that there could be a better, culturally neutral, version of these programs that would strip away the "beliefs" and work only through "the facts." Yet if the history and sociology of science has shown anything, it is that the dividing line between what counts as belief and what counts as knowledge moves over time and changes in relation to the perspectives from which it is viewed. And these changes are not easily explained as the automatic result of scientific progress. A social constructionist approach to sexuality tends, ultimately, merely to push to a further horizon the question of what is social and what is biological.

If social constructionist arguments are oriented toward uncovering the sociohistorical processes through which a current sense of obviousness about some object or idea has come about (Hacking 1999), then we should remember that such explorations are always focused on an audience that is itself historically located. And this is the crux of the problem with a constructionist argument. How could a Nepali AIDS worker distinguish between the facts and the folk beliefs that are melded within international approaches to sexual health? Encounters with different conceptions of the body, its possibilities and its functions, jar us into recognizing how many of our convictions are grounded in a knowledge of the sexual sciences. Folk physiological theories surrounding conception and fetal development do not simply look quaint to us moderns: they look patently untrue.[19] Relativist principles vanish when scientifically established truths seem so critically important to health and well-being that it would appear to be morally wrong not to educate people about them. Although such educational efforts may have numerous positive effects, they nonetheless relegate one set of action-generating knowledges about the body to the status of "mere belief." Thus certain actions come to be seen as "illogical," "superstitious," or, at best, in need of being brought into line with biomedical reasoning.

A distinction between facts about biology and beliefs about the body is used persistently—and perniciously—in international health, and although it may occasionally have strategic rhetorical value its main effect is to consistently position "culture" as a barrier to the solutions proposed by an expert knowledge (Yoder 1997). There is a colonial politics of knowledge at work here—one that plays itself out not only between "Westerners" and their "others" but also across divides of class—and this politics of knowledge determines whose views and voices will register. It has practical implications with regard to how officials, planners, educators, researchers, and activists imagine the purposes of their work.

What is going on in international sex education involves more than "facts" replacing "misconceptions" and more than cultures filtering knowledge about the body. A biologized notion of sex makes other ways of knowing and having a sexual body merely local, only cultural. The sexual sciences define the baseline of normality. The several meanings of "normal" are pertinent here: "conforming, adhering to, or constituting a usual or typical pattern," "functioning or occurring in a natural way," "the usual or expected state."[20] These ideas about normality are at work in international arenas in powerful and underexamined ways. Implicit in the sexual sciences is a call to enter into a specific international modality of engagement. The question then becomes: How are these normative and normalizing possibilities taken up, put to use, modified, or contested by various actors? What kinds of action become possible as a result?

Conclusion: Reenvisioning the Materiality of the Fact

Discussions of sexual and reproductive health seem always to come to rest, ultimately, on a distinction between facts and beliefs, a distinction that codes social positions within a hierarchy of knowledge and power. To work against this coupling we need a robust sense of the social processes through which facts are constituted so as to appear as transcendent truths lying outside any particular social arena. Here, some basic premises from science studies provide better leverage than culturalist explanations for thinking about the globalization of biologized notions of sex. First, by recognizing that the means of finding and describing nature is itself highly mediated, we can conceptualize facts without assuming that scientific research merely reveals an underlying nature that was simply waiting to be found and correctly described. "Facticity" is a quality that gradually emerges: "To be indisputable is the endpoint" of matters of fact, not, as the empiricist tradition holds, the beginning (Latour 1999: 307).

Second, we need to conceptualize—rather than assume—how the diffusion of ideas and technologies occurs. Numerous detailed empirical case studies of scientific innovations shows that scientific claims stick when they are taken up by others—not just fellow scientists who judge the findings to be sound but people for whom the insight solves a problem, bolsters a case, or furthers an aim. The finding becomes indispensable to the extent that it is melded with a wide range of interests and actions. (Indeed, anthropologists have long made a similar argument for the cultural and pragmatic embeddedness of beliefs.)

Third, we need to be able to imagine the spatiality of truth claims in order to address distributed diversity and inequality. If "facts" acquire their "sticking power" through their ongoing institutional and technological use, then not all facts acquire the same reach of facticity. Some networks become longer, more extensive, more stable, and even irreversible (Callon 1991).[21] To the extent that certain premises and standards already hold sway (i.e., they define the very starting points of engagement), facticity, as an effect of the binding capacity of wide networks, is within a closer reach of some people's projects than that of others. Proof, an event in one part of the world, can be a nonevent in another.[22] As feminist scholars have noted, the processes of stabilization move across a landscape made uneven by the power relations that organize difference (Star 1991; Haraway 1997).

This is why it is not very convincing to claim that the modern biologized frame for sexuality, on the one hand, and different cultural frames for sexuality, on the other, simply constitute parallel belief systems.[23] Belief, as Latour (1999: 304) has quipped, is "always an accusation leveled at others."[24] The ability to claim privileged, rational access to "reality" accrues to those most firmly connected within the longest and most stable network. These claims hold in the world because the networks hold; and the networks hold not just because a politically dominant group says they should but because of the particular and dense ways in which nonhuman actors (e.g., synthetic estrogen, HIV, latex condoms) are tied into them. Facts are indeed about processes, entities, and relations that exist outside the human mind. But they "exist" within collectivities; they correlate with the workings of a "real world" that has been brought into its current state through the entanglements made possible by the articulation of the "fact" itself.[25] If we think of science as a means by which nonhumans are actively socialized into new collectivities, then we can see arenas of applied science activity in international health as invitations to new sets of humans to become entangled in these new collectivities. Here, questions of science and society turn into questions about globalization.

Tsing (2000: 330) suggests that "we can investigate globalist projects and dreams without assuming that they remake the world just as they want."[26] The sexual sciences have been enlisted in an assemblage of globalist projects, including population control, struggles against gender discrimination, AIDS prevention, and activism for the rights of sexual minorities. These projects bind the biologization of sex to overarching claims to unity and universality. The notion of sex has to acquire its transcendence over what then comes to be positioned as "local belief and practice." Its global circulation requires what Tsing calls a "material and institutional infrastructure of movement" (338). When as intellectuals, researchers, planners, or activists we theorize sexuality, describe sexualities, or agitate for certain projects of social reform, we are part of this infrastructure, as are all of the people who are called into forms of collectivity around the notion of sex.

It is well known in both family planning and AIDS prevention circles that the acquisition of information alone does not change a person's sexual behavior (or even ideas about sexuality). In public health discussions about the promotion of sexual and reproductive health, there is a strong argument that both HIV prevention and fertility control should be envisioned as a collective endeavor. A transformation of social relations and of shared meanings would, in this view, precede modifications in individual behavior. Sex education efforts are often envisioned within public health and health activism as part of an effort to shift collective understandings (see, in this volume, Parikh; Paxson; Rivkin-Fish). The facts of sex are sometimes linked to projects of empowerment and social change that are meant to serve as levers for prying open existing assumptions.

In both individually oriented and collectively oriented programs science is drawn on as a supreme authority, removed from the social realm, trumping all issues of values and politics. In this kind of recourse to "the facts" and to a "scientific view of sexuality," the facts are endowed with a magical ability to change people's consciousness. Calling on them is construed as a socially neutral act, a way of stepping outside moral debate and even cultural particularism itself. Yet this escape from social investments is never really accomplished; the social investments are displaced because, as the social analysis of science reminds us, science and society are mutually produced.

Rethinking the notion of "the fact" and the role of science in social change provokes a set of questions about sex education that looks quite different from the more commonly heard set of questions about the accommodation of cultural differences and the harmfulness of misconceptions. What are the transformations that occur when "the facts" about sex are taken up? What kinds of investments in which social relations shift, and for whom? What kind of person in what kinds of social relations are people invited to become? To what institutions, technologies, discourses, and economies are people asked to join themselves by accepting these facts, and on what scale do these networks operate? "Insisting on relativism does not weaken the connections between entities," Latour has observed, "but multiplies the paths that allow one to move from standpoint to standpoint" (1999: 310).

We seem to be in an era, uncannily resembling the early twentieth century, in which the domain of the sexual is in the foreground of social struggle and international engagement. The internationally salient notions of sexual health and sexual rights can be a vehicle for certain struggles, and the sexual sciences might indeed be useful allies. However, if in retrospect the precursors to today's movements can be seen to have forwarded perspectives associated with both class privilege and racism, then this invites a humbler view of these activities. It is within this context that the consistent invocation of science against cultural beliefs concerns me, for it seems to work to demean a range of complicated reactions to a call to join in the extensive networks built around biologized notions of sex. If we pay attention to the myriad ways in which located people utilize how science reconfigures nature, then a critical understanding of the politics of the biologization of sex might emerge.

Notes

This essay benefited from many constructive discussions with Leslie Butt and Vincanne Adams, as well as helpful exchanges with Sanjay Srivastava and Kalpana Ram. Russ Westhaver and Kate Gilbert kindly read earlier versions, and their comments, together with those of the anonymous reviewers and Joanne Richardson, pushed me when I needed a push. I am grateful to the Joint Committee on South

Asia of the Social Science Research Council and the American Council of Learned Societies (with funds provided from the National Endowment for the Humanities and the Ford Foundation) for making it possible for me to conduct research in Nepal in 1997. The Social Sciences and Humanities Research Council small grants program at Simon Fraser University supported background research on public representations of AIDS.

1　I thank Kalpana Ram and Sanjay Srivastava for insisting on this point.

2　For instance, see Pigg and Pike 2001; Ram 1998a, 1998b.

3　In the field of sexual and reproductive health, there is much practical reflection on both the gap between knowledge and actual behavioral change and the community and social contexts that foster individual change. Although these discussions are extremely important, my questions here differ from them in that they attempt to address the conceptual framework itself—a framework grounded in biology, medicine, and science.

4　From www.reutershealth.com, accessed 19 July 2001.

5　More detailed discussions of AIDS prevention efforts in Nepal can be found in Pigg 2001, 2001b, and 2002.

6　The role of disease in bringing sexuality to public consciousness in late-twentieth-century Nepal is similar to the effect of the venereal disease campaigns in the United States during World War I (Brandt 1987 [1985]).

7　Public health information about STDs is nearly always encapsulated within information about HIV/AIDS, creating the impression among many Nepalis that STD is the first stage of AIDS.

8　Produced in Nepali as "Aapasi Kuraakaani." Expatriate and Nepali health education experts worked for a year to produce the English-language original, while only a month was allocated to translate it into Nepali (Deepak Koirala, personal communication, 1997). Although my discussion of this manual is largely textual, I chose these three examples because the topics/frameworks were persistent rough spots in the training sessions I observed. My discussion of these examples is informed by my participant-observation research with NGOs, including attendance at the workshop at which the manual was launched as well as a conversation with Deepak Koirala, whose job it was to convert the expatriate technical advisor's drafts into a "Nepali" form. All quotations here are from the English-language original.

9　Social historians have shown that this is a distinctively modern concept that arose gradually out of a series of shifts in social organization associated with industrialization and urbanization. My account here draws from D'Emilio 1997; Ross and Rapp 1997; and Weeks 1989 [1981].

10　Under industrial capitalism the family was displaced from its role as the main productive unit, changing the structures of interdependence between men and women and parents and children, with implications for patterns of courtship, marriage, fertility, and inheritance. The meaning of "family" (as well as the structures of actual families) changed over the course of the nineteenth century. The nature of these changes varied by class, region, and race, and their impact was experienced differently by men and by women. For some, wage labor opened new avenues for economic independence and, with it, possibilities for early sexual autonomy.

11 Changes in the usage in English of the word "sex" mark the consolidation of a reified domain of "sex" in modern thought. The predominant colloquial usage of the word "sex" has gradually drifted from a focus on qualities and differences of maleness and femaleness toward increasingly precise specifications of the "sexual" as "relative to the physical intercourse between the sexes of the gratification of sexual appetites" (*Oxford English Dictionary* [*OED*], Second Edition, 1989). It was only in 1975 that the *OED* defined the word in terms of "pertaining to sexual instincts, desires, or their manifestations" (as quoted in Caplan 1987: 1). To speak of coitus as "having sex" or just "sex" is a recent usage. A scan of the *OED*'s usage examples shows phrases such as "sex drive," "sex offence," "sex fiend," "sex education," "sex partner," and the like as dating no earlier than the late nineteenth century. Phrases like "sex feeling," "sex consciousness," and "sex experience," in use in the 1920s, sound slightly stilted to the early-twenty-first-century ear but reflect the newly distinctive concept of "sex," which by then had become cultural common sense. Even though the notion of sex has remained tied to gender and to procreation, over the course of the twentieth century it has increasingly come to be thought of as at least partly detachable from these concepts.

12 The term "sexuality" would have to be understood as a kind of shorthand for a more complex task of exegesis and representation, at the outer limits of which even the possibility for a universal language of social theory dissolves (see Sperber 1985).

13 The internationalization of gay identity is another instance, outside public health, of a homologous process (see Rofel 1999b; Altman 1997).

14 These arguments were tied to emerging scientific understandings of hormones, at least in the case of Magnus Hirschfield in Germany (Sengoopta, cited in Fausto-Sterling 2000: 151). Havelock Ellis in England was making a different kind of argument for the natural basis of homosexual orientation.

15 It might be argued that with respect to a socially charged subject like sex not all of these "facts" merit the label "scientific." In reflecting on the claims to universal truth that are contained within this bundle of ideas, it is tempting to try to separate the hard science from the soft, the good science from the bad, and in doing so to claim to be able to separate "real" facts grounded in nature from ideas tainted with cultural assumptions, thus arriving at a real universality rather than at a mere claim to universality. A critique of ideological claims embedded in science-based assertions has important uses. But some sociologists of science argue that it also has limits; namely, that the ideal of separating "nature" from "society" is itself a cultural value that obscures connections between nature and culture (Latour 1993). It is possible, as an alternative, to see "the scientific and the social as part of an inextricable system of ideas and practices—simultaneously social and scientific" (Fausto-Sterling 2000: 148).

16 The reproductive sciences and sexology are treated as separate arenas in the historical studies of science, a compartmentalization that itself reflects the cultural work involved in formulating the modern concept of sex.

17 In institutional contests over funding, the "biological side" and the "human side" of problems of sexuality were portrayed as separate, and research on the former came to predominate under a rationale that held that basic biological research (mostly on

nonhuman organisms) would illuminate the most fundamental aspects of sexuality and that it would do so through a more rigorous experimental design. These justifications also helped to bolster the legitimacy of research on sexuality and reproduction in the face of the continued stigmatization of researchers in these fields (Clarke 1998).

18 Vance (1991: 880), for instance, has insisted that "a social constructionist approach to sexuality must also problematize and question Euro-American folk and scientific beliefs about sexuality, rather than project them onto other groups . . . Thus, statements about the universally compelling force of the sexual impulse, the importance of sexuality in human life, the universally private status of sexual behavior, or its quintessentially reproductive nature need to be presented as hypotheses, not *a priori* assumptions."

19 These questions have a long and venerable tradition in modern anthropology. Consider, for example, Malinowski's discussion of Trobriand concepts of conception and paternity (see Franklin 1997: 17–72). It is not coincidental that Malinowski asked this question at a time when the reproductive sciences were consolidating their most important breakthroughs and when this kind of information was being popularized through marriage manuals. Margaret Mead's research in Samoa was also carried out within this context.

20 From the *American Heritage Dictionary*, New College Edition.

21 Although actor network theory holds that networks can dissolve as well as be built, it has been criticized for its tendency to idealize the expansion of networks. Further, it overlooks the problematic aspects of the standardization that a long, stable network accomplishes for those who live outside it (Haraway 1997; Star 1991). Feminist geographer Doreen Massey (1994) addresses the concept of "time-space compression" as an aspect of postmodernity in her critique of David Harvay's (1989) thinking about globalization.

22 Latour (1987: 100) says that we should be relativists when controversies erupt and disputes are in full swing, but that we should shift to realism when no one else is denying the evidence: "We do not try to undermine the solidity of the accepted parts of science." My example of the internationalization of knowledge through sexual health programs reveals that Latour is too quick to assume a homogeneous world.

23 Unfortunately, the alternative to this cognitive relativism pits "knowledge" against "belief" in a way that leaves no doubt as to who has the superior mind (see Good 1994).

24 Berg and Timmermans (2000: 45) discuss this relationship between universalization and what lies outside it in a connected but slightly different way. Forms engaged in ordering, they argue, "produce the very forms of disorders they attempt to eradicate." This way of understanding the standardization that occurs with the lengthening of networks challenges the notion that an encompassing network expands *over* an already existing but disordered, heterogeneous field, such that "there is nothing *outside* this unique yet all-encompassing space except that which has been erased or subsumed" (33).

25 Science is one means through which entities that are "in the beginning foreign to social life . . . are slowly socialized into our midst" (Latour 1999: 259; see also

Haraway 1997); there is a constant folding of the nonhuman into the human, crossovers between human purposes and potentialities in the material world. What science and technology produces are ever more intimate "imbroglios" between humans and nonhumans. These entanglements are mutually transforming: just as human social life is changed by new ways of knowing, tracing, and using events in the material world, so are nonhuman elements brought into new relations. If we feel that we know "more" now than we did a hundred years ago, it is because of the increasing scale and complexity of the entanglements that bind social institutions to nonhumans. Bruno Latour (1999: 304), for instance, invites us to imagine ourselves living not in "societies" that have a relation to "nature" that we observe or use but rather in ever-changing collectivities of humans and nonhumans formed though the process "by which the cosmos is collected into one livable whole."

26 Here Tsing is challenging anthropology to move beyond the sweeping claims about globalization as a historical trajectory, unitary process, and totalizing epoch.

PART 1

The Production of New Subjectivities

• • •

The first group of essays in this volume identify and illustrate the concrete technological, political, and medical instruments that are used in creating new sexual behaviors and sexual identities associated with sex education, family planning, fertility control, and AIDS prevention efforts. They show how reproductive identity and gender proficiency are tied to sexual practices, throwing into relief questions about what constitutes a modern moral subject. Similarities are seen here in the ways that scientific efforts create a self-conscious, autonomous subject who identifies his or her subjectivity in and through a medicalized sexuality—a sexuality that is seen as divorced from other domains of social life. At the same time, specificity of the politics and the cultural terrain that mediate these medicalizations render the lived outcomes quite different, specifically because the "sexual" refuses the isolating tendencies that its scientific rhetorics would give it. In some instances, "scientific" discourses underwrite the moral position against a "liberated" sexuality, and in other instances ethical debates spawned by the introduction of fertility control, abortion, and sex education provide the very groundwork for perceived liberation from traditional gender norms.

Michele Rivkin-Fish describes how sex education campaigns, that, in the wake of Soviet socialism, triumph science as the ultimate arbiter of truth, also produce naturalized discourses of traditional morally appropriate gender roles. The culture of "candid sexuality" heralded by the arrival to post-socialist Russia of pornographic films, sex magazines, and Western cinema is met by the medico-scientific writings and clinical practices of Russia's sexologists whose efforts are deployed to undo the "sexophobic" attitudes of the Soviet regime. At the same time, such practices reinscribe traditional gender hierarchies that differentially privilege males and females, both in terms of the practices of intercourse that are advocated by health officials and in terms of what those practices are meant to say about an individual's innate "constitution." Managing the genders by way of the sexuality of a young generation of postsocialist citizens entails managing inherent or "natural" sexual compatibilities—warning against marriage between sexually incompatible types and reiterating the possibility of biological differences between the genders. Postsocialist anxieties about "freedom" translate into efforts to reproduce maternal females and to control "oversexed" young men who, according to one Russian sexology lecturer, believing they are in love are simply being "deceived" by "sexual impulses." As biology is used to ground "truth," so sexuality is used to legitimize postsocialist moral concerns of the state. Herein, "scientific" discourse underwrites the moral position against a "liberated" sexuality.

Heather Paxson identifies similar processes in contemporary Greece where, she notes, an ethic of service that positions women in various fields of family, conjugality, and social responsibility is challenged by the introduction of medicalized sexuality. An ethic of well-being in which self-health, the body, and its hygiene become the focus of a virtuous life is posed as an alternative to traditional service-oriented gender performativity by way of a medical focus on sexual norms. But in contemporary Greece, efforts to manage fertility and sexuality tie virtue to nonprocreative sexual discipline at the same time that they reinscribe traditional moral codes on Greek women. Once again, emphasis on "scientific" discourse underwrites a Greek moral position against a "liberated" sexuality. Abortion in Greece signifies both lack of moral restraint (a position backed by scientific claims about the risks of multiple abortions) and the exercise of moral responsibility insofar as it can conceal acts of sexuality that are considered morally questionable. Sex education advocates and health planners deploy images of a responsible Greek sexual subject who adopts a "family planning mentality" and, as in Russia, the creation of a "new ethical subject" becomes "the moral object of sex."

Shanti Parikh traces the shift among Ugandan youth seeking sexual advice from traditional forms and venues such as "aunties" to newer forms such as "discos" and AIDS specialists. This shift is accompanied by an elusive shift in moral sensibilities. New rhetorics of "safe sex" claim a moral purity in messages about how to practice sexuality in ways that conform to "modern" standards of hygiene and beauty. But traditional "aunties" guided young women into the pleasures of sex in the context of lineage, village, religious, and ritual concerns by exploring and expanding the possibilities of physical manipulation and enjoyment. These traditional practices were carried out in the context of moral rigidity about sexual behavior and sexual prowess. In contemporary sex education and popular cultural media, questions of "morality" are foregrounded because of a public health concern with "risk" tied to modern Ugandan health campaigns. Notions of risk and pleasure that were intermingled in elders' memories about kin-based sexual learning have become unintentionally separated as sexuality has entered into more public (medico-moral and popular culture) domains. For many Ugandans, this new terrain of sexuality is morally bereft, despite its indirect self-claims to the moral high ground. Pleasure becomes a site for self-censure in ways that, in fact, directly undermine traditional ideas about the moralities of pleasure tied to appropriate conjugal roles, ritual practices, the potency of female sexuality, and more.

MICHELE RIVKIN-FISH

Moral Science and the Management of

"Sexual Revolution" in Russia

• • •

In the conference hall of a St. Petersburg hospital in March 1995, a group of thirty-six Russian obstetricians, midwives, and nurses gathered for an internationally sponsored workshop on improving women's reproductive health. Among the problems to be addressed was the long-standing reliance on abortion for fertility control, the ironic result of a pronatalist Soviet state disinterested in developing or importing contraceptives. Among the foreign public health experts leading the workshop was a representative of a North American pharmaceutical company that produces oral contraceptives. During the Soviet era the pill had been largely absent from national distribution networks, while the scant information made available about it derisively denounced the safety of "ingesting hormones."[1] With the end of the Soviet era and the incorporation of Russia into the global market, Western pharmaceutical firms viewed Russia as a promising "new market" for low-dose versions of oral contraceptives. The North America pharmaceutical representative, a marketing specialist with graduate studies in education, considered the training of local health providers in contraceptive counseling to be a necessary step toward changing attitudes and behaviors so as to legitimize contraceptive use after years of national anxiety. Ensuring "contraceptive acceptance and compliance," he told the audience of his family planning workshop, required providers to learn the appropriate skills to communicate with women. The challenge was to adopt a nonjudgmental, value-free attitude so a woman's individual needs could be fulfilled. He further explained: "When a woman or couple decides to use contraception, there are a lot of questions. Women bring their own understandings, fears, what they heard from their mother, their level of education, culture. And we also, as medical personnel, have biases. As providers of information, we need to be aware of our biases and give good information. Even if I think oral contraceptives are the best, and my colleague likes IUDs, we must give information to the women so that they'll have choices . . . It's very important to be supportive of her choice."[2]

Expressing support for women entailed an apparently simple set of steps: giving them alternatives regarding possible contraceptive methods and facilitating the fulfillment of the choices they make. Yet communicating in a value-free way required training and practice. So the representative divided the Russian participants into small groups and instructed them in a series of role-playing exercises to practice advising patients. Each exercise involved a hypothetical case describing a woman's reproductive goals and medical history; participants were to explain the contraceptive methods they would recommend, along with the pros, cons, and any counterindications they would consider in making their decisions. One scenario elicited particularly revealing insights into the Russian participants' view of this value-free model of provider communication. When the representative stated: "A 15-year-old girl with no previous births, abortions, or pregnancies comes to you because she wants contraceptives. What do you do?" a loud hum overtook the room and one Russian doctor burst out only half in jest: "First we're going to investigate the kindergarten that gave her such a bad upbringing!" A round of laughter followed, with many participants nodding in agreement. After the translator explained the comment in English, the Russian respondent continued by offering the kind of answer expected in the role-playing exercise: "Then we'll do a standard exam, try to talk to her and to her partner if there is one. We'll suggest barrier methods until her period, and then we'd suggest monophase [oral contraceptive] pills from the beginning of her period."

Pleased with this response, the pharmaceutical representative smiled appreciatively and stated, "Great! I think it's good to use oral contraceptives." While he commended the participant, other members of the group expressed diverging opinions in asides not intended for translation. A second doctor exclaimed, "Lock her up in her house!" And a third physician, a highly positioned public health planner in St. Petersburg, concurred, "Well, taking into account that she's changing partners and can get gonorrhea, I think I'm wasting my time here!"

This encounter offers a starting point for exploring the ways sexuality has become a key site for moral struggles over the future of the nation in post-

Soviet Russia. As the pharmaceutical representative guessed, physicians in Russia are positioned to create meanings about sexual practices that, at least partially, have the power to change such practices. But, while the representative and his fellow consultants promoted a model of professional neutrality as an explicitly political act of wresting power from experts and transferring it to ordinary women (an approach that linked new provider communication strategies with ideas of democracy and individual choice in post-Soviet Russia [Rivkin-Fish 2000]), the Russian physicians' discourses on sexuality reflect very different assumptions regarding their rights as experts to intervene in patients' lives. My goal in this essay is to explore why a paradigm of value-free expertise and individual choice about sexual and reproductive matters was not acceptable to the Russian physicians. More broadly, I wish to demonstrate how promoting notions of "choice" and "democracy" through a consumer development paradigm failed to gain legitimacy and even wrought unintended damage by ignoring local knowledge of moral selfhood. Instead, a view of sex tied to both "science" and morality prevailed in medical and clinical contexts.

I begin this essay by analyzing the historical narrative of Soviet sexuality developed by advocates of sexology—the scientific paradigm of sexuality—in the context of Soviet history. By contextualizing sexology and sex education work within the cultural and political contests raging in Russia over sexuality, I highlight the reasons that the principles of expert neutrality, objectivity, and free choice would be considered ethically untenable to the majority of Russian physicians, including those most supportive of open discussion and public expression of a differently construed "scientific" sexuality.

Some Histories of Sexuality in Soviet Russia

The dominant Russian narrative of the history of sexuality in the Soviet Union tells a story of severe repression by a "sexophobic" communist state whose policies of censorship and deceit distorted the population's understanding of human nature. Igor Kon (1995), the country's eminent historian of sexuality and a leader in efforts to develop public acceptance of scientific approaches to sex, has authored one narrative of sexual repression. An unflagging advocate of human rights and gay rights in a context where neither concept enjoys great support, his discussion of sexuality aims to highlight the role of state power in usurping individual authority and energy for collective purposes. Kon describes Stalin's campaign to eradicate sexuality from society beginning in the early 1930s as part of a wider process of purging any material that challenged the primacy of the state and diverted the population from an all-consuming devotion to communism.

In envisioning a nation of traditional, patriarchal families, Stalin criminalized sexual relations between men in 1934 (Kon 1995: 63–64) and abortion in 1936, reversing the 1920 decision of the revolutionary regime to legalize the procedure. Stalin's aim in the latter decision was to raise the declining birthrate, for if men needed to control their sexuality and concentrate on work, then women were expected to contribute their energies as workers and mothers. Thus with no contraceptives available, for the next twenty years women resorted to illegal abortions to terminate unwanted pregnancies. Overall, Kon explains the Soviet view of sexual energy and desire as dangerous because these dimensions of life raised the specter of diversity, nonconformity, and individualism, which the regime found especially threatening. In a study that partly challenges this view, the Russian scholar Oleg Kharkhodin (1999) has suggested that Stalin's obsession with harnessing people's commitments and engineering their behavior to fulfill state objectives revealed a systematic, purposeful cultivation of the individual as a most important unit of discipline. Drawing on this Foucauldian vision, continuities between the tactics of Soviet and scientific approaches to sexuality become visible; for if the two paradigms differently valued particular practices and pleasures, they each made sex a moral object of their own knowledge and power.

As the Soviet era progressed, physicians became even more implicated in either realizing or subtly revising official sexual ideology. Khrushchev loosened the tight control characterizing the Stalin era when he legalized abortion in 1955, yet he did not adjust the "sexophobia" of the regime. To help expunge "sexual immorality," he allowed the publication of popular literature intended to provide "sexual moral education" (*polovoe vospitanie*). Doctors became important resources for this campaign, instructing patients in ideologically appropriate attitudes and behaviors. Their clinic-based lectures, like published texts, offered select scientific information on anatomical and physiological processes such as menstruation and conception, yet their major purpose was to provide the proper ideological basis deemed necessary to maintain the boundaries of sexual purity. Conception, for example, was almost always described without any mention of sexual intercourse. Another theme was the harmful effects of masturbation. A typical text from this period described how "Children-onanists (*deti-onanisty*) are distinguished by secretiveness, obstinacy, and absentmindedness" and "easily fall into despondency and pessimism" (Ivanov and Pisareva, respectively; quoted in Field 1996: 130). Arguments against abortion also gained prominence. Official Soviet ideology blamed women who aborted for being selfish and betraying their maternal nature (Field 1996: 139). Physicians' advice to bear children was portrayed as beneficent, while women who failed to comply with the professionals' recommendations were told they would be punished with infertility (Field 1996: 141).

The responsibilities of the experts involved portraying sex as dirty and dangerous, imagining women through an image of chaste motherhood and as part of a family with strong patriarchal authority. Communist ideology condemned any sexual practice other than that between a husband and wife undertaken for procreative purposes. Premarital and extramarital sex, casual sexual relations, sex with more than one partner, and romantic relations with foreigners represented transgressions that needed to be actively uprooted (Field 1996: 116–20; Kon 1995).

Two notable and competing forms of knowledge about sexuality worked to challenge the official Soviet approach that viewed sex as an element that reduced people to their most base instincts. The first form comprises an extensive informal cultural repertoire of sexually explicit language, jokes, and limericks (chastushki) that proliferated in intimate circles of friends, most often among men (Cushman 1995; Yurchak 1997). If a Foucauldian perspective would encourage us to view these verbal forms as inciting productive efforts to regain control over the meanings of bodily practices, for sexologists the bulk of the informal sexual vernacular represented not a site of creative resistance to state repression but rather the vulgar and violent underside of a censorship policy that denied the value of erotic expression of any sort.

It was science itself that these scholars considered to be the most meaningful source of resistance to Soviet repression policies. From the 1970s onward, Kon along with Georgi Vasil'chenko struggled against Soviet authorities in order to develop the analysis of sex as an object of expert knowledge and power. Until glasnost relaxed restrictions on public discourses on sexuality, their work remained unpublished in Russia (or self-censored). Vasil'chenko, for example, in developing the scientific study of sexuality (then called "sexopathology"), focused largely on the biological dimensions of sexual problems that inhibited successful "family life," but virtually no mention of the psychological dimensions of sexuality was possible, including issues of desire and fantasy (Kon 1995: 92–96). With the end of censorship in the late 1980s, however, sexologists were able to publish works on "normal" sexuality in Russia, and in undertaking what they viewed as the undoing of Soviet thinking on sex they created the idea of a "normal" sex in relation to the scientific production of its truths. They expressed devoted commitments to ensuring that objective, scientific information about sex would be available to the public in order to debunk Soviet-era myths and taboos about the "harms" of masturbation, homosexuality, and nonprocreative sex.

Despite the presence of these counterdiscourses surrounding sexuality, many Russians accepted the view of sex as debasing and out of place in the public sphere. With the end of Soviet censorship, the conservatives organized widely publicized nationalist and church-sponsored campaigns attacking projects that appeared to support a freedom of sexual expression. They were spurred by the rapid increase in sexually explicit material in the media where, seemingly overnight, pornographic films entered living rooms during prime-time viewing hours, streetside kiosks sold instruction manuals depicting the variety of possible sexual positions, and imported Western films with nudity and violence flooded the cinemas, displacing the chaste products of Soviet censors. Indeed, in the eyes of many Russians today, Western-produced films, with their sexually explicit material, represent a frontal assault on family life that interferes with parental control and robs children of their innocence and purity. They blame Western and American influences for the rapid increases in teen pregnancy and out-of-wedlock births and the rise in sexually transmitted diseases that have occurred since the end of the Soviet era, and they look nostalgically to Soviet-style control or the Russian Orthodox Church for a renewal of moral purity and spiritual order. The sexologists' goals of renewing public knowledge of sexuality thus directly collided with conservatives and nationalists, who lumped together any form of sexual discourse as spiritually polluting and physically threatening to the vitality of the Russian nation.

The conservatives also relate a perceived Western-induced depravity to Russia's declining birthrate.[3] This argument is faulty on several grounds: falling fertility rates have been a source of anxiety in Russia since the 1920s (Solomon 1992; Vishnevskii 1999a), while numerous Western states, including Italy, Germany, France, and Greece express similar concerns over low fertility rather than—as Russians often assert—promoting it. Still, church activists and other nationalists associate Westernization with losses of sexual purity, romantic love, and the denigration of family values and childbearing. They define these losses as the erosion of traditional Russian culture, pernicious influences leading young women and men to promiscuity and a rejection of family life. Some have charged Western organizations that promote family planning and sex education—including USAID, WHO, and the World Bank—with conspiring to reduce Russia's population through propaganda and technology against childbearing (Medvedova and Shishova 2000).[4] These campaigns have had substantial success. In spring 1997 Russia's antiabortion organizations—along with a public committee called For the Moral Regeneration of the Fatherland, sponsored by the Russian Orthodox Church and nationalist activists—submitted petitions asking the government to rescind funding for family planning. The Duma (parliament) made the topic the subject of a roundtable discussion on family planning in the context of Russia's national security and consequently voted to end funding of its presidential family planning program that had been established in the early 1990s (Babasyan 1999: 5). On the legislative front, church organizers were instrumental in promoting a 1997 draft law that would have made abortion illegal in all but medically indicated cases. While this draft law failed to pass, the strength of the coalition between church-based abortion opponents and nationalist activists continues to grow. In 2003, strict restrictions were placed on abortion in the second trimester for the first time since the Stalin era.

Even many professionals who do not agree with theories of a Western conspiracy nonetheless concur that the declining birthrate is a sign that family values in Russia need urgent strengthening. A common argument of pronatalist politicians and demographers is that socialist approaches to women's full employment distort natural gender roles, pervert women's maternal nature, and emasculate Russian men. Low fertility is therefore considered a symptom of far-reaching moral decline in interpersonal relations stemming from socialist notions of gender equality. To reverse these trends pronatalists argue for policies including education on "sex-role socialization" and family life, to revive "natural" gender roles and thus instill the value of creating "mid-size families" of two or three children (Antonov and Medkov 1986; Antonov and Sorokin 2002; cf. Attwood 1990; cf. Rivkin-Fish 2003).

Needless to say, opposition to the kind of sex education being developed by the small group of maverick sexologists discussed here is far reaching and enjoys the support of numerous constituencies. This opposition is not limited to discursive criticism: bands of right-wing activists who see sex education as a threat to the nation's vitality have physically attacked sex educators during lectures, and at various times gay rights activists have been arrested. For sexologists such as Kon, Vasil'chenko, and those throughout Russia who follow their lead, battling such political trends is an important but unfortunate need, usurping time and energy from the task of developing sexual education and erotic culture.[5]

To defend the legitimacy of their mission, these sexologists feel obliged to oppose claims that teaching youth about sex entails the perversion of minors. They frame their task as "raising the level of culture" of the population around sexual and family matters, and they insist that sexuality and sex education—for professionals, parents, and youth—is a quintessential aspect of personal moral development. Kon, Vasil'chenko, and others position their science-based, "cultured" approach to eroticism and sexual subjectivity, in contrast to both the "pathological" sexophobia of the Soviet era and the current proliferation of "low-level" pornography. They strive to counter descriptions of sexuality education as promoting the rejection of childbearing. Claims to a moral science of sex enable Russian professionals to defend their work against accusations that they are betraying their nation, by insisting that their goals are beneficial, health restoring, uplifting, and in moral support of the well-being of Russian families. They cannot, consequently, remain silent in the face of a fifteen-year-old girl who admits she is having sex. Failing to express moral outrage would be interpreted as condoning the loss of sexual purity, shame, and decency that such behavior is widely thought to represent and thereby becoming complicit with it. Providing the girl with contraception based on a seemingly value-free consumer-service model would be perceived not only as expressing indifference to this individual's destiny, but also working in concert with hostile Western forces to endanger the continuity of the Russian people.

Educating the Educators: Russia's Sexology Training for Health Providers

Given such virulent public opposition, the struggle to advance a moral, scientific approach to sexuality is largely waged in classrooms for expert retraining and in selective public outreach programs. During my fieldwork in 1994–95 I participated in two month-long programs attended by physicians and psychologists from around the Russian Federation who had come to St. Petersburg specifically to study sexology. The programs were held in conjunction with a department of psychotherapy and sexology at one of the city's medical institutes, with lectures and training held daily for over four hours. The topics covered ranged from ancient sexual cultures and modern sexology to sexuality over the life cycle and a practicum in psychotherapy. I discuss below two central themes of these programs—the use of statistics and a Russian version of anthropometry applied to sexual traits and experiences—and I describe how these themes shaped physicians' clinical work and educational projects to selectively normalize sexual practice and construct them as moral.

In the St. Petersburg programs a key way that science offered lecturers an authoritative means of constructing sexual normalcy was through the presentation of statistics on the widespread character of specific sexual behavior. Lecturers used statistics compiled by Alfred Kinsey and William Masters and Virginia Johnson, to establish the commonality of behaviors like masturbation, as well as the proliferation of what is called in Russia "alternative forms of sex"—that is, noncoital activities that Masters and Johnson call "petting" and "necking." Due to the impoverished state of Russian libraries and the extraordinarily low salaries provided to lecturers, the most recent editions of these classics in sex research were not available to the educators. Instead they relied on earlier editions, such as the second volume of Masters and Johnson's *Women's Sexuality*, published in 1953.

Sexuality throughout the life cycle formed a central component of the program and was an important arena for distinguishing the current scientific truths from Soviet-era propaganda, which disparaged the existence of sexual urges and desires for all but married adults devoted to procreative purposes. Age was presented as an important component of the definition of "normal" sexual activity inasmuch as different behaviors are considered "normal" or "pathological" at different points in the life cycle. Lecturers in the course on sexology emphasized that infants and young children are "naturally" sexual beings, and that one's sex life may extend into old age as well. The idea that "gerontological sexuality" or sexual activity after childbearing years following menopause is "normal" was described as a radical and progressive change in Russian approaches to sex.[6] Among young children, the lecturers emphasized, sexual games between siblings are common and "absolutely normal," which was an issue of particular interest to many participants who were parents.

Uncovering the "normal" in human sexual nature became especially crucial in the case of teenage sexuality, for if Soviet and post-Soviet opponents never recognized chidren's or postmenopausal women's interest in sex they anxiously pathologized teenage sexual interest as evidence of a degenerate upbringing or the perverse product of Western influences. The lecturers explained that youth sexuality is characterized by two main tendencies: first, its experimental character, including homosexual experiences; and second, the discrepancy between sexual impulses and emotional abilities. Homosexual experimentation and even sexual play with animals were described as "normal" and no cause for concern in teenage years. While enumerating the range of possible behaviors that could be considered "normal," a main topic of discussion involved masturbation.

Statistics on masturbation were provided from Masters and Johnson, Kinsey, and others detailing the commonality of the practice, especially among male teenagers. One lecturer went into extensive detail about masturbation but also sought to demonstrate that recognizing its "normal" character was actually nothing new to sexologists. Alluding to the potential ignorance of his students, he stated that "although sexology long ago recognized that masturbation is normal, the level of sexual-erotic culture of our population requires us to discuss it." Another topic reviewed at length in connection with teenagers was "alternative forms of sex," or noncoital forms of sexual activity. Lecturers constructed these acts not only as "normal" but as positive ways of avoiding sexually transmitted diseases such as AIDS.[7] Finally, the lecturers roundly emphasized the importance of ensuring open communication with teenagers and actively working to avoid the creation of sexual taboos: educating parents in the scientific truths of sexual life and then promoting these understandings with their children (that is, the moral deployment of science) was the key to developing normal and healthy sexuality in the teenage and adult years.

The language of statistics drawn from international sexuality research offered program participants authoritative conceptual weapons against those in Russia who continued to portray sexuality as spiritually polluting and morally debasing. By offering a scientific language and conceptual framework for managing sex, sexologists are able to domesticate its meaning: no longer the sphere of wild, chaotic danger, sex becomes a "natural" part of life and an arena knowable by experts. At the same time, by speaking in a language of statistics and universal science, the Russian lecturers modeled their identities as sex professionals—thereby establishing themselves as educated, cultured, erudite experts who repudiate the folly of those who would repress sex in the name of utopian spiritual purity; who would make it the object of political manipulations aiming to reorient human energy to "socially valuable" aims; or who would distort its emotional complexity by trivializing it through commodification. Sexologists contrast themselves and their universalizing project to those of communists, nationalists, and pornographers by insisting that sex understood as "natural" could also enter the province of the moral (Foucault 1978, 1990).

As a consequence, the need to harness sexuality for societal needs is not absent in this post-Soviet moral economy of sexual value. Culturally significant questions concerning male-female differences and their successful complementarity for marriage and reproduction formed the base for a second theme that the educators used to define human sexual nature and to detail its firm boundaries between normalcy and pathology. They found a key resource for this task in the anthropometric work of Vasil'chenko, which was most extensively elaborated in his 1990 volume *Sexopathology* (*Spravochnik Seksopatologiia*). Most specifically, classes drew on Vasil'chenko's notion of human sexual constitution to establish quantifiable measures for the natural (and implicitly moral) bases of male and female sexuality. The notion of the "human sexual constitution" draws on theories of anthropometry applied to sexual anatomy, physiology, and production. It is used to conceptualize an individual's sexual disposition and the kind of sexual activity said to be "normal" for him or her. In essence, the notion of sexual constitution offers a typology of sexual subjectivities based on the idea that each individual is endowed genetically, biologically, and to a lesser degree socially with a certain degree of sexual strength. Further, the effort of ascertaining whether someone's behavior is "normal" or "pathological" must take into account the individual's sexual constitution—that is, their physical predisposition toward sexual expression. Yet the broader parameters of normalcy with which any individual's sexual constitution is compared and assessed stem from the normative measures of his or her gender: there is a range of normal indicators within masculine sexuality and within feminine sexuality, and any given individual should fit somewhere within these borders.

These parameters defining the ranges of sexual constitution were offered in the lectures as a means for physicians to assess the character of a patient's sexuality (as normal or abnormal) through quantifiable measures in their clinical work. While physicians might briefly discuss the concept in sex education efforts, it was primarily presented as a diagnostic tool for sex therapists. Thus, even though sexual constitution did not comprise a central theme in educators' lectures with teenagers (mentioned only in passing by a few lecturers I observed), the implicit and explicit assumptions about sexual activity and men and women's sexual natures informing this theory shaped the idea presented in many lectures.

Portrayed as an "objective" evaluation of the relative strength of an individual's sexual disposition, the notion of sexual constitution is a descriptive and numerical representation of the arithmetic average of seven indicators that are taken as signs of sexual potential. The indicators for male sexual constitution are as follows: age at which the libido is first aroused; age at first ejaculation; an anthropometric measure of the relationship between leg length and overall height (called the *trokhanternyi* index or TA index); the amount and shape of pubic hair; the greatest number of acts of sexual intercourse with ejaculations in a twenty-four hour period (or what Vasil'chenko calls "maximal excess"); the number of years after marriage when a stable sexual rhythm averaging two to three acts of intercourse per week is established (which Vasil'chenko [1990: 61] labeled the theoretical physiological rhythm or TPR [*uslovnno-fiziologicheskii ritm*]); and, finally, the age at which this stable sexual rhythm is developed.

Based on these indicators, sexual constitution is understood to be firmly predetermined by genetic and biological factors (many of which occur during puberty), and only to a lesser extent shaped by social factors, such as when one's sex life becomes "stable." Indicators such as the relationship between leg length and overall height or the amount and shape of pubic hair draw on the anthropometry of sexual features—an area of research developed by Vasil'chenko on the basis of earlier Soviet studies of anthropometry and morphology. Vasil'chenko explains the significance of the relationship between the leg length and overall height as a sign of the parameters of the growth gradient during puberty, which themselves indicate either hormonal normality or malfunctioning of the endocrine system during the phase of sexual development (1990: 149–50).[8]

In examining an adult to determine his or her sexual constitution, a physical would assess the TA index in order to ascertain whether puberty had been delayed due to a pathology of the gonads (Vasil'chenko 1990: 152). Pubic hair is described as forming in a "feminine fashion" (*po zhenskomu tipu*) or "masculine fashion" (*po muzhskomu tipu*) and is also used as a sign that puberty may have been delayed due to pathological processes in the endocrine system. By drawing on Soviet research from the 1930s conducted by examining the sexual characteristics of soldiers, Vasil'chenko notes that although pubic hair develops over time and a "feminine type" of sparse hair may eventually become more "masculine," the presence of a "feminine type" may also signal preexisting pathologies that affect an individual's current sexual constitution (1990: 157–58).

In contrast to these indicators, female sexual constitution is seen as directly connected to a woman's reproductive capacity and experiences in giving birth. The seven indicators evaluated for assessing a woman's sexual constitution are as follows: menstrual function, including age at first menstruation and the regularity of menstruation; childbearing function, including the length of time taken to conceive after beginning sexual activity as well as the character of the pregnancy; the anthropometric measure of the relationship between overall height and leg length; character of the pubic hair; age at which the libido was first aroused; age at first orgasm and length of time after becoming sexually active until achieving orgasm 50 to 100 percent of the time (1990: 78–79).

While the goal of these sexology courses involves training physicians to "raise the level of culture" of the population by unraveling the complex emotional and moral components of normal sexuality, the use of the notion of sexual constitution suggests that biological determinism remains central to the post-Soviet definition of sexuality. What is evident in this paradigm of sexual constitution is how extensively the vision of "normal" sexuality—in its putatively scientific dimensions—is shaped by rigidly normative assumptions about what it means to be a man or a woman. Men's sexuality is an inherent, biological drive that undergoes a linear progression from a period of "hypersexuality" in the teenage years and early adulthood until sometime after marriage, when a stable sexual routine is established. "Normal" adult sexual activity is thus by definition not only heterosexual, but based in marriage. Women, in contrast to men, are defined as sexual inasmuch as they are reproductive, with the course of their pregnancy and menstrual patterns integral to how their sexuality is evaluated. There is a built-in expectation that women will not seek to prevent pregnancy after becoming sexually active, for one measure of the childbearing function involves the length of time taken to conceive after beginning sexual activity. The idea that a woman may not want children or may want to postpone childbearing while enjoying sex is virtually absent in the formulas for sexual constitution, except in one indicator alone: a "strong" sexual constitution is signified when a woman gets pregnant despite using contraception.

The use of anthropometric models by Russian physicians to delineate human sexual nature and free post-Soviet subjects from the taboos and repressions of the socialist era carries more than a small amount of irony. Soviet-era ideology and practices, repeatedly portrayed as the wellspring of ignorance and the vector of disease for an entire population robbed of the knowledge of their own sexual nature, slips unnoticed into current discourses intended to free Russians with the truth of human nature. It can do so because, for one, anthropometry is not marked as "Soviet" and thus retains the authority of being "scientific," a tool for discerning "nature." No less important, it remains legitimate, even welcomed, for its perceived ability to offer clear measurements of sexual dimorphism and differentiation. Anthropometry is viewed as a useful tool for reestablishing and quantifying the differences between maleness and femaleness and thereby helping to "return [society] to nature."

In B. M. Vornik's encyclopedic reference on sexology (which was used by several physicians participating in the program) the theory of sexual constitution is presented as an objective tool for determining the truth of one's body and sexual subjectivity. Male and female subjectivities are inherently polarized, and while there is said to be a reciprocal influence between genotype and "external" or psycho-social characteristics for men, the psychosocial factors thought to shape male sexual practices are defined vaguely and thus narrowly:

> Although maximal excess, and the time when a stable routine of sexual activity is established consisting of 2–3 acts of intercourse per week, are linked to genotype, they substantially depend on external, situational factors. Therefore to a significant extent they, in and of themselves, reflect the level of mature sexuality or the index of constitutionally conditioned sexual activity. The genotype and degree of sexual activity are interrelated. On the one hand, the frequency and form of sexual relations are determined by a man in relation to his temperament, that is, his sexual constitution; on the other hand, the level of sexual activity influences the functional condition of the sexual system. (1994: 213, 215)

While this work acknowledges in a vague way that social influences, or "external, situational factors," affect the routinization and regularization of sexuality, it is ultimately a man's own inherent personality and temperament that determines the frequency and form of sexual relations undertaken (his partner's needs, societal expectations, material conditions, etc. are not seen as having a role here). For women, the situation differs most noticeably with the case of indicators concerning orgasm, which "although are partly also determined by hormonal status, strongly depend on upbringing or moral education [*vospitanie*], psychological and behavioral particularities of the woman, individual experiences, the partner, etc." (216). Women's sexual subjectivity, it becomes clear, is a consequence not only of genetic predispositions but also of moral imperatives lodged in her psyche during childhood, of men's demands, and of other "external" factors.

This text also provides a handy formula for conceptualizing the ways that sexual constitution may be used to determine a patient's sexual "normality" or the presence of pathology: "If the genotypic indicators and level of sexuality are close, then the development of sexuality is harmonious, in accordance with the sexual constitution. If some indicator is off the scale or there is a large difference between several indicators, the character of difference may determine the presumed defective syndrome" (216). In other words, a person lives harmoniously and healthfully only to the extent that the needs established by his or her genetic sexual constitution are fulfilled physically and socially. This, of course, is only possible by the appropriate frequency of sexual activity.

Comprised of a series of prescriptive assumptions, the concept of sexual constitution establishes normative meanings of adulthood, masculinity, and femininity; and it affirms the notion that physiological and genetic factors have a deterministic influence on sexual interests, proclivities, and behavior. Moreover, because sexual constitution is based on the idea that sexual interest and activity stems from inherently biological potentials, it is conceptualized as a largely individualized characteristic, as if larger social contexts and relationships with an individual's partner, social milieu, and family background have minimal influence on his or her sexual interest and activity (except in the case of women's orgasms). The possibility that adults who live together may undergo periods of experimentation, abstinence, and/or non-coital forms of sex is not acknowledged as part of "normal" adult sexuality.

The participants in the sexology courses I attended seized on Vasil'chenko's formula for determining sexual constitution as a means of helping their patients understand sexuality and create realistic expectations for their married lives. The physicians eagerly accepted the notion of sexual constitution as a diagnostic tool they could use for both assessing and treating physiological processes as well as conducting therapeutic interventions. For example, one participant asserted that sexual constitution would be a very useful tool for conducting sex therapy and marriage counseling; by determining the sexual constitutions of fiancées, a physician could advise against a marriage in cases where sexual constitutions are deemed incompatible. The deterministic character of this theory did not seem to present a cause for concern or doubt among participants. During an interview, I conveyed to participants my disbelief that sexuality, sexual expression, and interest were biologically determined and constitutionally stable. Speaking with one participating physician and her husband, also a doctor, I skeptically protested, "What does a woman's ability to get pregnant sooner or later have to do with her ability to enjoy sex?" My acquaintance responded with certainty: "But a woman's sexuality is entirely related to her ability to get pregnant. Whichever force it was, nature or God, [it] gave us orgasms as a reward for childbearing. If sex weren't pleasant, the human race would die out. Women's main function is to bear children. It's perhaps not a rigid relationship [between sex and reproduction], but it's there." I have frequently found such views expressed by health providers, laypersons, and the media.

Statistical and anthropometrical discourses lend legitimacy to discussions of sexual processes and pleasures in part because they are viewed as reflecting human nature, not political ideology; placed in contrast with the discredited policy of Soviet egalitarianism, associated with "turning women into men," current claims that sexology is scientific carry important cultural authority here. Framed in this way, the embrace of sexology becomes characterized as the decidedly moral revival of previously concealed truths.[9] The nature it discovers is not a value-free grounding of human life but rather a realm of moral imperatives that beckons people's return in the wake of Soviet ideology's perceived disastrous manipulation of sex and gender through politics. Proponents insist that scientific approaches to sex will further humanitarian causes: unearthing the truths of sex will restore access to pleasure and health for individuals and the nation without sanctioning a reckless indulgence in vulgar sexual enjoyment. Moreover, discourses on the biological basis of sexuality articulated within the paradigm of science can be seen as offering a means of legitimating sexuality as "natural," domesticated, and ultimately a force that serves the nation's future. With motherhood at the core of women's "human nature," sexuality becomes a channel for harnessing reproductive biopower in tandem with national needs for population (Foucault 1978). With this logic, as educators weigh in on the meanings of sex as normal and natural, and simultaneously define the borders of pathology, they articulate concern for the welfare of the nation and the health of youth, mothers, and future generations. Their concern establishes their authority and responsibility to pronounce, adjudicate, and determine the value of specific behaviors of their patients. No less important, it provides a morally valid response to nationalist discourses equating sex with decay, decline, and the dying out of the Russian people, for the sexual pleasures and practices it legitimates are fertile and maternal.

Bringing Sexological Principles to Teenagers: Sex Education Courses

As stated above, efforts to establish sex education classes throughout Russia have encountered virulent and not infrequently violent nationalist opposition. Elsewhere I have discussed some of the main themes of these programs in St. Petersburg, which include the "natural" character of sexuality and the "normalcy" of masturbation, as well as the dangers of STDs and abortion (Rivkin-Fish 1999). While many of the physicians conducting sex education classes are gynecologists who devise lectures based on their personal sense of what needs to be addressed with young people, I concentrate here on lectures by participants in the sexology course described above. In particular, I explore the ways in which the lecturers drew on biological and moral precepts to construct male and female sexuality and to distinguish them from each other, as well as to warn of the dangers involved in starting sex "too early." These topics reveal the deep ambivalence on the part of health providers regarding the desire to normalize sex as a natural part of life. They strive to oppose Soviet modes of characterizing sex as "antisocial" and deviant, while still dissuading teenagers from believing that sexual activity is appropriate at this stage of life. The resulting discourses combine capsules of sexological knowledge about "normal" and "cultured" sex, sexual pleasure, and appropriate female and male behaviors, with ample warnings about the physical and moral reasons that teenagers should not be having sex.

As in the sexology courses for experts, the lectures for teenagers emphasized the idea that sexuality is a normal and important part of daily life. Sometimes explicitly and often implicitly, this issue was framed in contrast to the negative views of sexuality that led to shame, silence, and disease under the Soviet era: "No matter what they have or haven't told you, sexuality is just as much a part of human existence as drinking, breathing, etc. And therefore to speak of sexuality as something sinful is fairly unjust, and, I would say, even pathological" (quoted in Rivkin-Fish 1999: 807).

The establishment of sex as "normal" rested largely on its basis in human biology. Biology, however, was frequently described not in acultural or objective terms, but as a deterministic force containing the inner truths of the self for both the present and future. Much is at stake, therefore, in biological processes, where the "abnormal" lurks dangerously close. This is evident in the lecture of one physician, who described the puberty years of ages twelve to eighteen as "a period where the body undergoes a colossal restructuring. So, what's going on with you now, maybe you don't especially notice it, but it is playing a role, it is the foundation on which your entire future life will be based. Normal or abnormal, happy or unhappy, both with relation to health, as well as, naturally, psycho-sexual development."

The lecturers portrayed male sexuality as activated and propelled by physiological functions. The brain, hormones, and nervous system figure prominently in conditioning teenage boys' and men's sexual motivations, behaviors, and needs. Emotions, by contrast, are virtually absent. Even if an adolescent boy believes he is "in love," one lecturer stated, he must realize that he is being deceived by his sexual impulses:

At 16 to 17 years of age there is another fairly unpleasant moment in psycho-sexual development of the [male] teenager. This period is called hypersexuality. What is this? The body develops, produces sperm. A certain kind of defect appears when an overflow of sperm in the excretory path, mediated by the brain, leads to the need for sexual activity, sexual contact. Why am I telling you this? The thing is that it is considered an entirely normal phenomenon when a teenager understands this normal physiological process as love . . . This is the work of your sperm glands. Therefore I ask you to remember, please, that not all love at 16 to 17 years old is true love. Remember that a purely physical process is playing a great role here.

The primacy of biology as men's inner sexual essence is further developed in another description of the "normal" adult male sexual nature:

For men, the sex act . . . is fairly primitive in its structure. The neuro-humoral system plays the main role for men in the sex act. What is this? It means that in men during the sex act the most important role is played by nerve impulses, which go along the nerve paths, along the spine. A man looks at a woman, he likes her as a sexual object, nerve impulses are sent out, and an erection occurs, that is, pressure in the sexual organ. Next comes the sex act and orgasm. A man does not perform the sex act without orgasm, remember that please. Every ejaculation ends with orgasm. It is a deep pathology when ejaculation does not end with orgasm.

This lecturer continued by contrasting the biological determinism of men's sexuality with the determinants of women's sexual pleasure. Teenage girls are portrayed as future mothers who do not undergo the notorious phase of "hypersexuality," while adult women are in need of emotional warmth and physical affection, not sexual intercourse per se. Teenage boys are told that becoming a cultured person and having a successful marriage requires that they learn about women's sexuality in general and their partners' needs in particular:

There is a colossal difference in women. In women the psychological situation plays the most important role in the sex act. If overall the vast majority of men are fairly indifferent where the sex act takes place—there is pressure of the sexual organ, having sex is necessary, and with enough arousal it can take place anywhere—the woman is far from indifferent. Women have an absolutely precise take on a certain partner, specific situation, and her partner's acts. Therefore, the concept of foreplay was introduced, which includes caressing the erogenous zones and not immediate penetration when the man suddenly wants it.

The differences between men and women are clearly not limited to the physical mechanics of sex but extend also to their social priorities and values. The lecturers instructing boys outlined these multiple differences specifically to instill a sense of moral obligation that understanding the general female biological and social makeup, as well as their partner's individual constitution, was necessary to become a decent husband in the future:

> It is necessary to know your partner; when there is no knowledge of your partner's body, when the man's goal is to undertake the sex act in order to satisfy himself, the end result is that the partner will either put up with him her whole life quietly hating [him], or will simply leave him. Knowledge of your partner's body is absolutely necessary for not only a normal sex life but as a consequence, a normal family life. . . . While for the man there's a precise organization of life—career, work, periodic sex acts generally for self-satisfaction—for women the main thing is the family.

This same idea was articulated in several lectures. One typical comment asserted: "Please remember that if a girl has sex with you then therefore somewhere in the depths of her soul she sees you as a potential future husband. Think about your responsibility—this person who you supposedly love at the moment, you are basically cruelly deceiving."

The lecturers all stated that the decision to begin having sex was a personal one, and that "no one else has the right" to tell someone what to do. Nonetheless, they concentrated on enumerating the physical and moral calamities that could befall those who began sex too early, ranging from contracting disease and even becoming infertile to losing the "sexual function" to ruining one's future marital happiness (one gynecologist who did not take the sexology courses spoke of girls who would "wilt" like a prematurely and forcefully destroyed rosebud [Rivkin-Fish 1999: 811]). In these discourses, the biological and moral dimensions of sexuality are deeply intertwined. They construct a set of moral imperatives lodged in biology, which exacts retribution in the form of physical pathologies against those who contravene the moral principles of sexual restraint:

In addition to anatomy [and] physiology, sex includes aesthetics and other such dimensions. Sexuality achieves its full value only when it is not a purely mechanical act . . . Empty knowledge of the technical leads, first, to complete ignorance, and second, it ends with great misfortunes . . . The soulless [*bezdushnoe*] use of technique leads to unpleasant consequences in life around twenty years later. Nature is a pretty evil thing [*Priroda—ona veshch' dostatochno zlaia*]. If a person is supposed to go through specific stages in his sexual development and if he tries to deceive this nature then nature will punish [him]. Girls who began having sex at fifteen as a sport or for some other reasons sometimes develop what is called frigidity—sexual coldness or the entire absence of interest in sex. Men develop this more rarely, of course; men may develop impotence or sexual weakness, which is much more common in couples who had sex early without sufficient psycho-sexual development; that is, the body's development and spiritual growth. They develop disharmony in marriage and also always in sex. It ends in that both the man, to a lesser degree, and the girl to a greater degree become, well, not repulsed, that would be an exaggeration, but in any case [there is] absolutely no understanding, [they are] having sex with very little satisfaction.

Propelled by an urgent hope to assist young men and women in navigating the spiritual and physical morass of sexual life and death, the messages conveyed in these lectures attempt to combine two rather competing ideas: they strive to acknowledge the centrality of sex to human life, while struggling nonetheless to ensure that sex remains contained within the safe boundaries of maternity, marriage, and "cultured" masculine power. Sex becomes "normal" and "moral" for Russian health experts when it is located within a broader logic of postsocialist change that is imagined to involve a "return to nature": masculine men and feminine women. Nature, this educator asserts, is "evil," but only when betrayed because it exacts revenge from moral transgressors. As the excerpts given above make visible, sex education lectures ultimately aim to revive traditional relations in the family that are comprised of responsible, solicitous masculine authority and a femininity that is maternal and vulnerable.

In these ways, the Russian science of sexuality has provided a legitimate idiom for discussing sexual processes and pleasure while also reaffirming the medical aspects thereof. Program lecturers rely on the authority of science to characterize their claims as objective truths, while their discourses present culturally specific images of men and women's unique relationships to sex and their distinct physical, social, and psychological needs in order to make moral arguments about appropriate gender differences and relations. The sexual taboos of the Soviet era may have been overturned, but sex continues to be channeled into domesticated, reproductive ends in the name of "cultured" social change and moral renewal.

Conclusion

When the North American representative of a pharmaceutical company producing oral contraceptives directed Russian health care workers to role-play a scenario in which they were to assist a fifteen-year-old girl requesting contraceptives, the representative assumed that the only relevant information they needed was the patient's medical history. Questions concerning why she was having sex, who was responsible for her behavior, and what could be done to stop it were by implication irrelevant. In the representative's view, such questions were beside the point, inasmuch as the teenager was clearly demonstrating her maturity and responsibility by seeking to prevent an untimely pregnancy (yet as one Russian participant noted, the representative seemed far less concerned about preventing STDS). In portraying health care workers as "providers of information," the representative's moral stance required them to keep their opinions to themselves and to present the teenaged girl with safe and suitable contraceptives, just as they would any other consumer.

It is notable that in some spheres of Russian health care, a model of provider behavior based on the sanctity of consumer demand has taken root, and it has resulted in profound experiences of empowerment for those who until recently had encountered only the Soviet system of shortages and a complete lack of individual choice. Since perestroika, for example, private and semiprivate dentistry has flourished in Russia, and patients with the ability to pay for care are presented with a series of options and individual choices for determining their course of treatment. During my research, the improvements in technology and new forms of provider communication in dentistry were repeatedly celebrated as a positive outcome of market reforms in health care.

My argument here is thus not that Russian health care providers simply cannot for cultural reasons offer women choices about their health care and in this way facilitate their individual empowerment; rather, it is that doing so is limited by debates about the moral implications of sex and the ways that a science of sexuality has configured "normal" sex. When the pharmaceutical company representative raised the scenario of a teenager asking for contraceptives, he failed to appreciate the fact that Russian society has been in the throes of painful, anxiety-filled discussions about the role of sex, and the meaning of teenage sexuality in particular, as the nation struggles to come to grips with the implications of democratic openness for its health, welfare, and future. For many Russians, the notion that a fifteen-year-old girl would not only be sexually active but would approach sex in a purposeful and nonprocreative way by planning ahead for it with rational, calculating decisions, confirmed the worst assumptions of those who bemoan a breakdown of moral standards by Westernization and democratization: the idea that Russia is enduring a rapid and fatal process of moral decay and degeneration of human relations; that Russians today are governed by a ruptured system of values and have no spiritual navigational system; and that they are beset by a loss of romance and a denial of love, purity, and chastity in favor of a pragmatic, cynical approach to the body and intimate relations. The final outcome, it is supposed, of this rational, utilitarian approach to interpersonal relations—such as that demonstrated by the pharmaceutical representative— would be nothing less than the rejection of childbearing as witnessed in the request for contraceptives.

Working with these views, the Russian participants disputed the idea that remaining scientifically "neutral" about teenage sexuality was ethical. While the representative presumed that his refusal to intervene in a patient's decisions was a sign of respect and a recognition of her maturity, it appeared to the Russians as a sign of utter indifference regarding the questions that mattered most: why she was having sex, who was responsible for her behavior, and what could be done to stop it. This indifference, moreover, seemed to them to confirm wider societal critiques that what the West was ultimately conveying to Russia was a package of unrestrained sexuality and disorder in human interactions; the rejection of marriage, children, and family life; and a rational approach to human behavior that represented the antithesis of Russian spirituality, romance, and soul. Unwittingly, this would-be advocate of democracy and individual choice threw himself into a cauldron of discourses brewing over the topics of teenage sexuality and the influence of the West on Russia, Russian youth, and the nation's future. With this culturally inadmissible hypothetical scenario, the pharmaceutical representative discredited not only his communicative paradigm of providers' neutrality but also the larger goal of working to facilitate women's self-defined needs. We can only imagine what kinds of possibilities might have been inspired had he raised the question of provider-patient communication about sexual health as a topic for discussion and debate, with the problems of rights and responsibilities, coercion, compliance, and culture as matters for contemplation; or, at a minimum, what outcome would have occurred had he himself prepared by reading Vasil'chenko's provocative texts.

Notes

1 Soviet central planners endorsed a pronatalist stance and took minimal efforts to produce or import contraceptives throughout the seventy-year duration of the Soviet regime. Planners briefly introduced high-dose pills in the late 1960s, but they soon removed them from pharmaceutical distribution networks due to the negative side effects. In the 1980s, surveys found that approximately 12 percent of women used IUDs to control their fertility. Condoms were considered uncomfortable and of poor quality. The vast majority of people relied on withdrawal, the rhythm method, and douching to prevent unwanted pregnancy, and resorted to abortions as a backup (Remmenick 1991): twice as many pregnancies ended in abortion than were carried to term (Field 1995: 1472; Remmenick 1991).

2 All quotes by lecturers in this essay are taken from the recordings I made in 1995. In total during my fieldwork on women's health and postsocialist change I conducted sixteen months of participant-observation research in St. Petersburg and Moscow between 1993 and 2000. I observed and taperecorded thirteen sex education lectures and conducted twenty-six interviews with sex educators. While the sexology courses and sex education lectures on which this chapter is based took place in 1995, I have remained in contact with some of the lecturers and have followed the intellectual and social development of their projects. In 2000, sex education for school children in St. Petersburg was canceled due to the sustained public outcry by nationalists and other conservatives against the lectures, which were characterized as the "perversion of minors." However, efforts continue there and in other cities to reinstate and develop the programs. I would like to thank the Andrew C. Mellon Foundation; the Council on Regional Studies, Princeton University; and the Peter B. Lewis Fund of the Center of International Studies, Princeton University, for support of this research. All translations are mine unless otherwise indicated.

3 Fertility fell from 2.016 in 1989 to 1.386 in 1994 (Vishnevskii 1996: 14), while life expectancy for Russian men plunged from 64.87 years in 1987 to 57.49 years in 1994 (103). The rates of STDs and other infectious diseases have increased exponentially. Syphilis, at present one of the most serious threats to public health, reached a rate of 277.6 per 100,000 population in 1997 (which represents a 64.5 increase since 1989) (85–86).

4 See also "Planirovanie Nebytiia" in *Novaia Gazeta*, vol. 32, 1999, 1, 13.

5 It is important to highlight that while both Kon and Vasil'chenko advocate the scientific study of sexuality, their approaches differ in important ways. Most notable is that Kon is a sociologist who veers away from biological determinism in his discussions; Vasil'chenko is a medical doctor who makes it the premise of his work.

6 This concept is considered new to many Americans as well, as discussed in a May 2000 *Newsweek* magazine article promoting elderly women's sexuality (Brown 2000).

7 The use of condoms as a means of preventing HIV transmission was not discussed.

8 "Due to the law in which only one part of the body grows at a time, which is most evident in puberty, the result of the vector-interaction between the intensiveness of growth of the length of the tubular bones of the extremities and the axial skeleton at the moment when all growth zones close (at the end of puberty) always fixes the parameters of the characteristics of the growth gradient" (Vasil'chenko 1990: 150).

9 This vision of nature as inherently moral articulates a rejection of the Soviet socialist experiment in which obsessive compulsions to plan and fantasies to engineer all of human life and society formed a core component of Soviet public policy. In celebrating its use of science, technology, and the instruments of modernization to gain control over nature, the environment, and human life, the Soviet regime announced its utopian promises in the idiom of transcending nature. Yet its failures to improve human life and the damage it wrought on the environment led opponents to see the Soviet system as "opposed to nature" and as a hostile, perverting, and debilitating attack on nature as ecology and on human nature, which it tried to distort through changing the place of sexuality and the form of gender relations in society. Current visions of postsocialist change often work from this commonsense understanding that with the end of the Soviet Union and its planned economy, Russia may return to the "natural" course of societal development; this "return to nature" is especially discussed with regard to gender roles and relations. Nature in this vision stands in contrast to Soviet images of human life and becomes an inherently moral grounding of human imperatives that no societal or political entity has the right to engineer or manipulate.

HEATHER PAXSON

Family Planning, Human Nature, and the

Ethical Subject of Sex in Urban Greece

• • •

In urban Greece since the 1970s, family planning—the calculated use of contraceptives to achieve desired family size—has been forwarded as a new, liberating practice, a clear alternative to so-called traditional strategies for birth control that rely on sexual restrictions, frequently backed by abortion. Family planning advocacy in Greece considers it a human right that people be able to have the number of children they want and when they want—without women having to resort to abortion (Margaritidou and Mestheneou 1991; Apostolopoulou 1994). What is more, advocates see family planning as introducing a moral dimension to the efforts made by Greeks in fertility control; promoting women's physical, social, and emotional well-being by stressing the responsibility to care for one's self. In so doing, they hope to "modernize" these practices in line with Western liberalism. Here, however, family planning advocates neglect how morality has already been central to women's sexual and reproductive agency in Greece. In this essay I examine how efforts to establish scientific discourses of sexual health in Athens have produced a partial, uneven shift in the ethical terms through which many urban Greeks consider sexual and reproductive issues. This not only impedes contraceptive uptake and safe sex practices, but leads to a moral conflict for women, who are at once asked to inhabit two ethical bodies and to realize competing moral objects of sex.

I detail here how modern family planning rhetoric and Greek reproductive discourses that have come to be labeled "traditional" turn on conflicting notions of agency, responsibility, and nature. The moral object of sex is figured differently within the two ethical frames. For family planning advocates, the moral objects of sexual responsibility is the personal achievement of physiological and psychological health, something considered equally available to women and men—that is, gender neutral. Family planning advocates intend for an individuated *ethic of well-being* consistent with the philosophical commitments embedded in biomedicine (what Robert Crawford [1980] has termed "healthism"), to replace a set of virtues castigated by family planners for being "backward" and for compromising women's autonomy. Under the extant ethic—what Athenians might recognize as Greek cultural tradition and what I term an *ethic of service*—the moral object of sex has been directed at realizing social expectations within patriarchal models of family and nation. In both cases, I argue, the moral object of sex in Greece encompasses the creation of ethical, and gendered, subjects. Thus, it is through a rescripting of this moral object from social to physical well-being that ethical (and gendered) subjectification has begun to shift. This shift—and the ambivalence it produces for women—is made particularly audible in the ways that people talk about the appropriate uses of abortion and the means of protecting against HIV and sexually transmitted diseases. Through tracing such narratives, and by situating family planning rhetoric in the national context of Greece's declining birthrate, I hope here to suggest reasons why middle-class Athenians have partially adopted modern evaluations of fertility control without necessarily adopting the modern methods themselves.

My arguments are based on wider ethnographic research into meanings of motherhood and practices of fertility control carried out in Athens between 1993 and 1995, during which I was interested to learn where professional and lay theories converged and diverged on what counts as appropriate sexual and reproductive behavior for both women and men. I draw on a range of sources, including public discussions of the social and demographic impact of family planning; professional conference lectures where gynecologists evaluated medical approaches to family planning; media analysis; interviews with family planning volunteers, physicians, psychologists, demographers; and discussions with middle-class women ranging from retired grandmothers to doctoral students, most of whom were living and/or working in the residential neighborhood of Pangrati. Niki, a thirty-five-year-old homemaker who was looking for employment when I met her, reflected tellingly on the changes in gender roles that have occurred since she moved to Athens from a nearby village nearly two decades ago: "Of course it's changed a lot because they're trying to change us. From the television and in the schools they speak to us, all the politicians, they're trying to change us, to make us European because we are Third World. So the foreigners say."[1] The most recent aspects of Greek modernity are embraced as progress by its participants in one moment but distrusted in the next as foreign condescension and imposition (see Sutton 1994). Changing gender roles and sexual mores are no exception.

In this essay, after contextualizing the 1970s introduction of family planning ideology and methods to Greece, I trace the promulgation and reception of the ethic of well-being—and its negotiation with an ethic of service—through two family planning initiatives in the 1990s: first, the warnings of the damage that abortion can do to a woman's body; and second, the fight against AIDS and HIV transmission. In both cases, an individual's right to good health is translated into a personal, moral responsibility to control what happens to the body, as the social sphere of sexuality is reframed as a medicalized site of personal, physical health. In light of these two cases, I consider one reason why even the most "Western" of urban Greeks are not fully embracing the biomedical understandings of "nature." Indeed, I argue that customary Greek notions of nature are entangled not only in ideologies of sexuality but in national narratives. I then move on to discuss how the Westernizing rhetoric of the safe sex campaign has prompted a backlash upholding a romantic, deeply gendered sexual discourse of Greek national character. In this context, I consider how the moral object of sex articulates what it means to be a properly Greek woman or man in the midst of morally ambiguous economic, social, and political change. Both Greek and biomedical ethical models of sexuality are amenable to the interests of larger political communities, in part because gender and sexuality have long provided a framework for the discussion of Greek national identity (Dubisch 1995; Herzfeld 1997: 96–97). What this national identity comprises has been subject to recent debate in Greece amid the ongoing issues of European Union integration, contested claims to "Macedonian" history, and territorial disputes with neighboring Turkey. More particularly, the process of maintaining a strong body politic through appeals to men's and women's gendered embodiment, especially through heterosexual behavior, has been brought into sharp focus amid anxiety over the declining (below replacement level) birthrate commonly rendered as a "crisis" of national demographic weakening (Emke-Poulopoulou 1994; Paxson 1997; Halkias 1998). But before I begin my analysis, I wish to situate the ethical claims made on sexual practice within the contrasting metaphysics of Greek notions of "nature" and those of biomedicine.

The Metaphysics of Greek and of Biomedical Notions of "Nature"

Arthur Kleinman has argued that one feature of biomedicine unique among all medical forms is "its peculiarly powerful commitment to an idea of *nature* that excludes the teleological" (1995: 29). Biomedical nature simply *is*: it is imbued with neither design nor purpose. Under the biomedical gaze, filtered as it is through the logic of Cartesian dualisms separating mind and body and reason and emotion, the "nature" of the body is reduced to inert material. As Kleinman states: "The psychological, social, and moral are only so many superficial layers of epiphenomenal cover that disguise the bedrock of truth, the ultimately natural substance in pathology and therapy, the real stuff: biology as an architectural structure and its chemical associates" (1995: 30). But in Greece, *anthrópini físi*, the "nature" of the human, of *ánthropos*, is not fixed but rather is realized through social practice. Nature here is as much characteriological as biological, and it has a kind of teleology: the formation of ethical gendered subjects.

Humans, *ánthropi*, are expected to realize gendered natures through activity appropriate to either women or men, conforming to normative behavior learned through example. Juliet du Boulay, writing of a Greek village where she conducted fieldwork in the 1960s, keenly recognized and described this issue through the idiom of divine destiny:

> The people of Ambeli do not argue that gender characteristics are inherent in the biology of both sexes; they argue from the gender characteristics themselves, with both men and women being understood to possess a "nature" and a "destiny" as a direct inheritance from their society. What I [call] "destiny" is an ideal pattern that is prescribed a priori, while what I [call] "nature" consists of the observed deviations from this destiny that answer to the pattern of temptation in daily life. The villagers themselves, however, do not use the terms "nature" or "destiny" but embody these concepts in images—on the one hand, of Adam and Eve, and on the other, of Christ and the Mother of God. (1986: 157)

According to du Boulay, both Eve and the Madonna are inevitable and therefore (to villagers) justifiable components of the condition of womanhood. The moral woman "transforms" Eve into the Mother of God; she recognizes and accepts her fallen "nature" but overcomes it by fulfilling her maternal "destiny." In du Boulay's formulation, the moral woman, the maternal woman, is also the true complete woman. While the religious dictates described by du Boulay were not so audible in Athens in the 1990s, it remains clear that Greeks must be seen to live up to gendered expectations. As one young woman said to me while we were discussing reproductive decision making: "All one's actions and everything that one does, one does in the interest of what others will confirm about one's self." And a professor of midwifery explained to me why as many as 95 percent of abortions continue to be performed in the private sector when national health insurance would cover them in state hospitals: "I think it's the Greek ethics. It's what other people will say about you."

A connection between virtuous and customary behavior was made explicit by Aristotle, for whom ethics concerned the socially orchestrated actualization of potentialities provided by nature. In "Nicomachean Ethics," he writes: "Neither by nature . . . nor contrary to nature do the virtues arise in us; rather we are adapted by nature to receive them, and are made perfect by habit" (II.I). I cite Aristotle not as evidence of any cultural survivalism, but because I view contemporary Greek culture, supported by Orthodox Christian theology, as organized by a virtue-based ethics which moral theorists attribute to Aristotelian thought and term "naturalism." Such a notion "views the moral project as teleological, its *raison d'être* being to bring to fulfillment those features of our humanness which are present as potentialities within us and which constitute our uniqueness as human" (Parsons 1987: 390). I view gender in contemporary Greece as working in just this way: as du Boulay and others have recognized, here gender operates as a system of virtues. Women and men feel the burden of ethical responsibility differently, not because they live under different moral systems (pace Gilligan 1982; Noddings 1984), but because ethics and gender are mutually constitutive means of organizing social identity and inequality. Lela, a thirty-four-year-old mother of a toddler son, offered this telling comment in an interview: "Boys and girls I think are just the same. Society is the one that makes the difference between them." While manliness is largely established through demonstrating the virtue of *eghoismós*—what Michael Herzfeld has glossed as "aggressive self-regard" (1985: 49)—women are seen as naturally, and properly, self-controlling, and are supposed to cultivate this disposition through habit (Campbell 1964; Hirschon 1978; Herzfeld 1985, 1991; du Boulay 1974; Friedl 1967; Iossifides 1991). Put another way, women demonstrate virtue through the habituated control of their own nature.

I focus here on what women must do to realize proper femininity through morally responsible action because Greek family planners, operating under a common assumption that reproductive issues are essentially women's issues, pitch their efforts primarily at women. To get Athenian women to think differently about abortion and contraception, family planning advocacy has worked to encourage them to think differently about sex, about themselves as subjects, and about their own agency. If Athenian women have not whole-heartedly taken up medical contraceptive practice—taking the pill, having IUDS inserted—I found that scientific discourses of the body are working to transform the substance of the "nature" that a woman is to control to demonstrate womanly virtue. In the past, women have been asked to exercise a social control over their natural sex drive—a legacy from Adam and Eve—in the service of lineage and family and with the aid of ever-watchful fathers and husbands (Hirschon 1978; Iossifides 1991: 135). But these days, family planning ideology holds that "modern" women should engage in reasoned manipulations of their bodies' biological nature, their fertility, by using medical contraceptives and thus obviating the need for social control of sensuality. As the ethic of service is being pushed aside to make way for the ethic of well-being, the "nature" that women are ethically to control is pressed inward into the realm of the biological. As I demonstrate below, this personalizes both reproductive responsibility and gender proficiency.

In order to understand Athenians' fertility control practices within local meanings of gender, sexuality, embodiment, and ethical subjectivity, it is necessary to comprehend the world of (Greek) humans as simultaneously natural and fabricated, biological and social. The biomedicalization (cf. Zola 1976) of fertility limitation in Greece engages metaphysical and moral issues in which, as I examine later, the well-being of the body politic, or nation, is ultimately at stake. This formulation resonates too with Nancy Scheper-Hughes and Margaret Lock's call to "reconnect the social and biological worlds" that biomedical practice often works to separate, a call that seeks to trace the particular interrelationships between "three bodies": the physical body that houses the self; the cultural body that authorizes processes of signification in and through the body; and the regulated political body, part of an aggregate body politic (1991: 412). To do this, and following the lead of Athenians, I introduce a fourth body: an ethical body that coordinates the other three and that helps us to comprehend reproductive agency from the level of the individual, to institutions of family and medicine, to the nation. I am proposing, then, that the ethical questions asked of sexual and reproductive practices in particular settings can allow us to scale—to measure and analytically ascend—the body politic (see also Ginsburg and Rapp 1995; Gal and Kligman 2000).

Introducing Family Planning Ideology: Toward an Ethic
of Well-Being

In the mid-1970s British-trained gynecologist George Kakoyanis (a pseudonym) worked with a group of concerned housewives and politicians to establish the nongovernmentally affiliated Family Planning Association of Greece (FPAG). They believed that if women were better informed about the pill and the IUD then the nation's soaring abortion rate would decline. Middle-aged women in the 1990s explained to me that in the 1940s and 1950s their mothers "discovered" abortion as a crucial means of limiting family size amid war-time famine, urban relocation, and economic struggle (see Blum and Blum 1965; Comninos 1988). Abortion offered women a backup to the contraceptive methods they knew, which included natural sponges doused in lemon juice but primarily consisted of withdrawal, abstinence during fertile days of the menstrual cycle, and condoms (Arnold 1985; Emke-Poulopoulou 1994; Georges 1996a).

While abortion was becoming medicalized as a routine (albeit underground and illegal) gynecological practice, it was brought to national attention only after a birth control survey in the late 1960s suggested a link between abortion and the nation's dramatically declining fertility rate.[2] According to this study (Valoras and Trichopoulos 1970), women having abortions were "to blame" for as much as 40 percent of the declining birthrate not only, or even primarily, through an accounting of "Greek lives lost" to terminated pregnancies (although see Dorkofiki 1985), but because repeat abortions reportedly resulted in women's secondary sterility (see Paxson 1997). By the 1980s, as many as three hundred thousand abortions were being performed each year in Greece, at nearly three times the live birthrate (Comninos 1988; Margaritidou and Mesteneos 1992: 30). During this same decade, the nationwide fertility rate dropped to 1.4 children per woman of reproductive age (Emke-Poulopoulou 1994). The FPAG (which in 1985 became an affiliate of the International Planned Parenthood Federation [IPPF]) acts primarily in an outreach educational capacity, although their efforts have been somewhat hampered by a suspicion that "family planning" has exclusively to do with strategies by the industrialized nations to suppress population growth in the developing world (e.g., Apostolopoulou 1994: 14). In fighting legislative limitations, family planning advocates have learned that it is expedient to speak to Greece's "demographic problem." An FPAG publication, for example, clarifies that family planning in Greece "secures the human rights of the population and of the individual, promotes general health, and in addition . . . is the tool for materializing the policy of birth increase within the frame of the country's potentials and needs" (1993: 7).

In this context, FPAG members work to educate people about biomedical contraception, the damage that abortion can do to a woman's reproductive organs, and the need to prevent the spread of sexually transmitted diseases. They do this by hoping to "introduce" a moral dimension to women's attitudes toward abortion because in the view of many, as reported by state-employed social scientists in 1990, "abortion is not a moral issue of any dimension in Greece, and . . . there is a general lack of guilt about the subject" (Agrafiotis et al. 1990: 38). In categorizing abortion as Greek women's "main method of birth control" (cf. Apostolopoulou 1994: 14), professionals imply if not assume a sexual perverseness among women who have repeat abortions.

The offices of FPAG are located in a dingy building on Solonos Street, near the University of Athens. On my first visit to the association I found Evangelia, an experienced volunteer counselor, leading an informational seminar to a coed group of about forty university students. These seminars, along with publications addressing AIDS, contraception, infertility, and abortion, represent the bulk of the association's activities. Standing in the back of the room, I was impressed with Evangelia's frank discussion of such "traditional" methods as withdrawal and abstinence during fertile days, acknowledging these to be valid "methods of family planning," if not as reliably effective as such "technical" methods as the pill or IUD. As Evangelia said to me in a later interview, "Today we try to enlighten people to see that the effects of whatever method of contraceptive she uses will be less than that of having an abortion." At the same time, however, family planning advocacy works to update "traditional" methods through scientific knowledge. A booklet titled "Conception and Contraception," published by the state office of the General Secretary for [Gender] Equality (which I picked up at the FPAG office), includes a two-page schematic diagram of how ovulation and menstruation proceed, day by day, over a twenty-eight-day cycle. The idea is to offer women a way of testing their understanding of when contraceptively "safe" days happen against scientific knowledge of female reproductive biology.

Biomedical "knowledge" of human nature thus becomes a key tool that family planners offer women. A booklet published by FPAG, "What Do You Know about Contraception?," explains the premise of the work done by the association: "This booklet aims to give information about how the reproductive systems of the man and the woman work, how conception happens, and how you can control your fertility. Thus you will be able not only to prevent an abortion but to plan your family responsibly and consciously, without stress and without danger to the health of mother and children." Here, biomedical knowledge signifies the autonomy promised women once they learn, as an FPAG board member said to me in an interview, "how their bodies work [and] what they're doing to them—in a sense, to feel in control." The commitment to education as a key element in changing behavior is one that Greek family planners share with U.S. public health programs (Oaks 2001: 81) and with the feminist consciousness-raising movement (Evans 1979) that reached Greece in the 1980s.

However, FPAG members further recognize that the popular uptake of medical contraceptives requires more than mere "knowledge" of biology and methods. Spermicide and female condoms are openly displayed in middle-class neighborhood pharmacies in Athens. In the mid-1990s a woman could purchase triphasal contraceptive pills over the counter at pharmacies for between US$4.50 to US$9.00 per cycle. And yet Greek women report the lowest rate of oral contraceptive use in the European Union; IUD use is only slightly higher; diaphragms are used largely by women who first used them abroad; and the abortion rate continues to exceed the live birthrate (Margaritidou and Mestheneou 1991; Creatsas 1994). Even middle-class urban Greeks, those who set "modern" cultural and social standards, continue to rely heavily on nonmedical contraceptive means. Condoms, for generations associated with disease prevention and prostitution (and customarily purchased at outdoor kiosks), have not been thought of as contraceptives—and have not been used in marital relations—until quite recently (they are now stocked on supermarket shelves).[3] The low rate of use of medical contraceptives, at least in urban areas, cannot be attributed to a lack of awareness or availability (see also Georges 1996a).

Greek demographic and sociological studies, taking Western European and U.S. cases as standards for comparison, tend to make sense of Greek women's reliance on abortion by referring to the tenacity of a culture that impedes medical contraceptive uptake (see Paxson 2002). Members of the FPAG stressed to me in interviews (and discuss in their publications) that contraceptive use requires the willing acceptance and adoption of the idea of prevention. Some professionals reason that abortion has been popular among Greek women precisely because it operates as a post hoc therapeutic measure, which also was the conclusion of a 1990 study conducted by FPAG board members to assess the effectiveness of their decade-old hospital-based state counterparts.[4] State-run family planning centers, they found, operate primarily as women's health clinics, with the majority of clients using the services for Pap tests and breast examinations (Margaritidou and Mestheneou 1991; Margaritidou and Mesteneos 1992). The authors interpret this as part of a wider cultural tendency among Greeks to approach medical services for curative and therapeutic benefits, with little regard for health promotion and disease prevention (Margaritidou and Mesteneos 1992: 31).

Elaborating on this idea, Dr. Kakoyanis told me in an interview that in his opinion the greatest obstacle to family planning in Greece concerns "cultural" notions about proper sexual practice, notions that were more diffuse than could be explained by religious proscription. "The Orthodox Church is not so demanding a tradition as the Catholics. Abortion is traditional birth control. Despite all this education, people still resist the pill. They don't like to interfere with the spontaneity of intercourse—I think it's more cultural, the attitudes of people. Because everybody knows that contraceptives exist, especially young people. And the stranger thing is that the doctors—they know there is contraception—but they don't push it." After dismissing any suggestion that the church impedes family planning messages (as many Athenians schooled me, "We have no pope!"), Kakoyanis astutely acknowledges that physicians operate within the same cultural system as their patients and thus can be disposed against contraceptives like anyone else. Yet here he reduces "culture" to "tradition," to something that people "have" and can overcome.

As with other modernization programs, family planning advocacy presupposes that to be modern, people must think themselves away from cultural biases, and further, that if people give up collective mentalities based on folk belief for "modern" subjectivities, personal liberation will follow. As is evident in Kakoyanis's words, family planners often conflate a lack of preventative action with cultural assumptions of feminine passivity in heterosexual relations, viewing "traditional" birth control methods as reinforcing prevailing patriarchal norms that posit men as active participants in sexual relations and women as passive recipients of it (Campbell 1964: 227; du Boulay 1986: 150). Consequently, whereas "old fashioned" methods such as withdrawal, condoms, and abstinence via the rhythm method require the (implicitly unreliable) cooperation of male partners, in their literature and presentations the FPAG (along with state-sponsored family planning publications) define "modern" contraceptives as being for women to use in their own interests. Backed by biomedical authority and committed to Enlightenment notions of individual subjectivity and prescriptive morality, family planners frequently translate women's "traditional" sense of reproductive agency, reliant on post hoc abortion, as a moral flaw marked by the "failure" to take preventative action.

Members of the FPAG believe they can succeed in encouraging women to think differently about abortion precisely because they see themselves introducing morality, in the form of rational self-interest, to reproductive decison making. Editorializing in *Planned Parenthood in Europe*, IPPF consultant Evert Ketting explains that their "broader mission indicates that 'family planning' . . . is a philosophy of life. It is based in the conviction that human beings will act responsibly if they possess the knowledge, skills, and means to do so" (1995: 1). This "philosophical" dimension links thinking and ethics. From a family planning perspective, moral virtue is realized through control of the physical body via preventative health care. Being well requires doing good (cf. Comaroff 1982). Greek women have approached abortion "amorally," they declare, not because women undervalue motherhood or act out of selfishness—as U.S. women have become accustomed to hearing—but because they "lack" a sense of preventative action and have been "ignorant" of the physical damage and threat of sterility that repeat abortions pose (see, for example, "The Triviality of Abortion in Greece" [Naziri 1991]).

Family planning ideology shares modernity's commitment to rationalism, to a sense that our primary moral responsibility should be to our self-interests. Even sex, often regarded as appropriately emotional, is drawn in to a realm of calculated logic. Thus family planners assume that given proper knowledge about biological nature, women will choose contraception over abortion because as rational beings they will accept scientifically backed promises of safety and surety (see Thompson 2000; Paxson 2002). What is more, the ethic of well-being moves what it takes to be proficient at being a woman toward being a properly autonomous individual, thereby flattening gender difference.

In discouraging abortion practice, then, most Greek physicians and politicians do not appeal to some "sanctity of life" at conception or to the "rights" of an "unborn child." Instead, as I detail below, the family planning strategy has been to apply the ethic of well-being, first, to exhort women to protect their own bodies from the potential damage done by repeat abortions and sexually transmitted disease, holding over them in particular the threat of subsequent sterility; and, second, to encourage women and men to think of "sex" as separate from procreation, and therefore as something that can be properly prophylactic. Because, as we will see, the ethics of abortion have "traditionally" aimed at hiding the evidence of inappropriate sexual relations, discussions of abortion in Greece are always indirectly about sexuality and gender and thus also plug into the safe sex campaign to prevent HIV/AIDS.

*Case 1: Negotiating an Ethic of Well-Being and an Ethic of
Service in Abortion Narratives*

In a variety of pamphlets with titles such as "Do You Know? It Could Happen to You: Abortion," the FPAG warns of abortion's biomedical dangers, listing allergic reaction to anaesthetic drugs, hemorrhage, perforation of the uterus, damage to the neck or interior of the uterus, inflammation, fever, and endometriosis and salpingitus which increase the danger of ectopic pregnancy or sterility. Such family planning rhetoric actively challenges the popular belief that abortions in Greece are safe, even "the safest in the world," as an older woman once assured me. The FPAG publication "Conclusions of the Seminar on Women and Family Planning" warns: "Abortion is a violent dilation of the cervix, and scraping of the fetus from the uterine cavity by mechanical means. It is not a natural medical practice, but a violent intervention that . . . [leads] to devastating consequences for the woman's mental and physical and psychological health" (1993: 10). Women who regard Greek abortions as the world's safest are thinking of the low risk of maternal mortality when abortion is practiced by physicians versed in the technique. Family planners seek to recalibrate the "safety" of abortion in line with an ethic of well-being by emphasizing the risks of abortion to one's well-being. When state pronatalism picks up the family planning message, abortion's "safety" also becomes an index for demographic health: the body becomes emblematic for the culture as a whole (Scheper-Hughes and Lock 1991: 412) as the empty womb, scraped out and destroyed, transposes barrenness onto the national body politic. At the same time, family planners voice concern over the effects of abortion for women's emotional health. Not only will a properly modern, "enlightened" woman "know better" than to find herself with an inopportune pregnancy she must rid herself of through abortion, one demographer writes, she will also learn how to "maintain her psychic, bodily and social well-being," having been released "from the anxiety of an unwanted pregnancy and childbirth" (Emke-Poulopoulou 1994: 79). Thus the ethical body created by the ethic of well-being promises health for the three bodies: physical, cultural, and political.

But what do women think? Several of my interviewees mentioned to me having seen American-style television talk shows featuring medical experts discussing the new reproductive technologies, contraceptives, and the medical dangers of abortion. Doctors in Greece are highly respected and their word is rarely questioned (Arnold 1985; Lefkarites 1992; Tsalicoglou 1995). Nadia, whom I met when she appeared at my door selling English-language cassettes, had seen such programs. During a later interview she volunteered that while repeat abortions can lead to female infertility, she believed that new techniques are making them more safe: "Does abortion clearly damage the organism? I believe this is not a matter of opinion because it's a medical issue. Of course the doctors maintain that some methods [are better], for example not to scrape a piece of the uterus [dilation and curettage] but to use suction, like with a cupping-glass, you understand. Today I think it's done with suction [aspiration]. Now, how successful is it? I believe that after some two or three abortions you always do harm to the organism for the next time you want to keep a child. I have heard of cases where [a woman has] had around two abortions with the result that [she] can't have a child."

When I asked twenty-five-year-old Vasso about how having an abortion affects a woman, she stated that there "must be" some "psychological effect" but went on to clarify that the "worst" thing that can happen is "maybe in the end, when [women] finally decide to have a child after they already had abortions, then many women can't because something has been damaged." Other women I interviewed spoke from direct experience. Litsa, who at age thirty had a child after using in vitro fertilization, confided she was rendered unable to conceive "naturally" after having an abortion in her youth.

Middle-class Athenian women know the medical dangers of abortion. But they speak of abortion in relative terms, in the register of an ethic of service keyed to responsible motherhood. Lela, whose parents look after her child while she is at her civil service job, reveals how Greeks qualitatively assess fetal life in terms of the potential social life of a future child: "It's bad for you to have an abortion. But then who will bring up the child for you [if you're at work all the time]? And if your relationship is not working, is it better to bring up your child in a disintegrating family? It is better to have an abortion than not be able to give it a good life." Pressed into ethical service of family and community, abortion has been presented as a solution—albeit fraught and imperfect—to a pregnancy that occurs when a women is not in a position to fulfill the social requisites of being a good mother.

If abortion can symbolize either a woman's patriarchal obligation and dependency or her free exercise of personal choice (Wilt 1990; Pitch 1992), I was struck by how many middle-class Athenian women of various ages expressed the former view as opposed to the latter. As a means of family limitation, abortion has enabled women to better care for the children they already have, but it has also provided women with a means of coping with a careless or uncaring husband, with a too-forceful lover, or with an incestuous male relation. Women have frequently been compelled to have abortions, especially "in the past," I was told, when men did not shoulder their responsibility in sexual relations so as to avoid conception. Eleni, the mother of three grown children, forcefully conveyed how abortion practice in the Peloponnesian village where she was raised and married related largely to a lack of male responsibility in sex: "I know a woman who had forty-one [abortions] and five children. I know that particular woman felt sex as a rape, not at all as sex—because her husband would get drunk, come home, make love to her and the next month she would have an abortion." This woman's husband apparently conceived of marriage as a property agreement whereby a husband owned access to his wife's body for sating his sexual desire and for producing heirs. Prior to 1982 there were legal grounds for this type of behavior, although morally speaking it was understood that men as well as women were expected to at least attempt to exercise sexual moderation (Campbell 1964; du Boulay 1974). Middle-aged and older women like Eleni frequently distinguished between "good" and "not nice" husbands in terms of whether their wives had to resort to abortion to cover over men's lack of sexual control.

If frequently abortion is ethically motivated by proper motherhood, under an ethic of service it becomes a moral issue in that it is a woman's moral responsibility to hide sex: hiding an abortion hides from others evidence of sexual impropriety. Of sexual transgressions, a friend of mine explained: "If you don't talk about it, it doesn't exist." Robinette Kennedy reports of Cretan women speaking similarly of extramarital affairs, and she quotes one as saying, "When I don't say anything to my husband, the evil stops right there. Nothing happens. But if I tell anyone about it, the bad thing goes on" (1986: 125). As demonstrated in the honor and shame literature (cf. Campbell 1964; du Boulay 1974; Herzfeld 1983, 1991; Gilmore 1987), silences surrounding abortion in Greece uphold repute because this depends less on what one does as on what others believe one does; as the midwife said, this is the "Greek ethics." Meanwhile, discreet actions can achieve useful ends. A woman who finds herself with a husband who "isn't nice" can, and indeed should, attempt to correct for his moral weakness (unfettered sexuality) with her moral strength (terminating pregnancy). However, it is not the case (as modernizers hold) that Greeks view hidden behavior such as inappropriate sex or abortion as exempt from moral evaluation; rather, morally questionable behavior that goes undiscovered is allowed to continue.[5] With this history in mind, a gynecologist and feminist activist I interviewed pronounced abortion—and patriarchal complicity with it through institutions of family, church, and medicine—as "part of the violence against women" in Greek society.

And yet, such cases demonstrate a disjuncture between the "appearance" of male authority and the "reality" of women acting behind the scenes to safeguard the family's ethical/social well-being (Friedl 1967; Dubisch 1986). In other words, and contrary to the assumptions of both "honor and shame" and of family planning ideology, Greek women have not been merely the passive victims of male sexual dominance. Or, they have at least framed recourse to abortion as in keeping with womanly dispositional virtues of self-control and maternal sacrifice. Maro, a thirty-eight-year old unmarried dentist who lives two blocks from her parents, who followed her to Athens from their village, stated to me: "The mother, for me, plays the most significant role in the house. However, because society is androcentric [*androkratikí*], the world appears male and the father thinks he has the upper hand. For although anymore they both generally work, say, in the shop, and in the majority also both participate in the home, the woman is the one who is responsible for the house, for the kid—the father participates less in the common responsibilities because he's tired, he's going to go to see his friends, he'll read his newspaper and sit around—this is the classic Greek family. It's generally thought that the role of the father is more important, when in essence it's the mother's." Women have had abortions not only to terminate inopportune pregnancies but also to conceal immoral sexualities (see Schneider and Schneider 1995: 178)—ranging from incest to having "too much" marital sex—and they have done so in service of family, community, and even perhaps nation. In so doing, they demonstrate virtue. This is the ethical service that family planners miss as they hope to instill a different kind of ethic that pushes for women's individual acquiescence to state interests in modernity and larger families by protecting personal health and future fertility. These challenges may compromise women's reproductive agency.

Whereas "in the past" the immoral sexuality that abortion kept from public scrutiny included extramarital affairs, incest (an issue raised in several interviews), and sex between spouses after "a certain age," at present this list has expanded to include "irresponsible" (nonprophylactic) sexual relations. And while abortion and sex are discussed more openly today, Athenians wanting to espouse "modern" views may be more quick to label abortion as a shameful last resort. The moral questions deliberated are significant—and the moral doubt understandable—because what is at stake in questions of intent and agency is not only the moral character but the gender proficiency of women. According to the traditional ethic, matters of sexual propriety are decided on the basis of established character, meaning that a woman must attend continually to her public appearance and to others' opinions: having a moral reputation results in morally appropriate behavior. In contrast, under the biomedical ethic of family planning ideology, repute is after the act: abortion is damaging to a woman's body, and because it is avoidable it is morally unsound, and thus a woman who has an abortion is lacking in forethought and moral judgment. Well aware of this distinction, the middle-class Athenian women I interviewed commented on the high incidence of repeat abortions in Greece; most offered stories of friends and relatives who had had abortions and only a few offered their own abortion stories.

At twenty, Nia was the youngest woman I interviewed. A university student, she lived down the street from me in a neoclassical house with her elderly widower father. Nia, who is close to many surrogate mothers, her aunts, and the wives of her fathers' friends, filtered her analysis of the Greek habitus (Bourdieu 1977 [1972]) of abortion through the lens of both ethics: "I've heard of women who have had an abortion, married with older children already—they feel ashamed that, having a child of twenty, they go and get pregnant again. And they and their husbands know only this way. It is for them the solution. They have had children, it can't harm their system." Here Nia is making a secondhand evaluation of "traditional" practices—even as she makes excuses for them—in light of scientific knowledge about the harm abortion can do to one's reproductive system. Nia believes that women who might regard abortion as birth control must be older; they are mothers. She makes rational excuses for their "ignorance," even suggesting that abortion in their case is not such a bad option because at their age it can't harm them anyway. Realizing that the ethic she might apply to her generation is not fairly applicable to older women, she excuses herself from having to judge them: "Since women are today more informed, they believe it is better to be preventative, so they consider abortion as a last resort. If you can't do anything else and a child comes to you suddenly—and at an age when you can't have a baby—then I think you resort to an abortion." (Nia's report is outdated: in fact, the Greek abortion rate is rising most rapidly among teenagers.) Women are able to draw on a legitimate ethic of service in talking sympathetically about others, while reserving for themselves a more contemporary, scientifically underwritten, moral position.[6]

This ethical brokerage indicates that family planners, in order to foster the modern mentality they believe will produce modern contraceptive use, must do more than frighten women into wanting to avoid an abortion: family planning advocacy must change the way women and men approach sexual relations and think about their own agency. The new sexual ethic that family planners hope to instill is well illustrated in a column in the May 1993 issue of *Yinéka* (Woman) magazine. There Anthi Doxiadi-Trip observes that "the problem with prophylactics is not that no one has told [adolescents] about them, or that they've never heard of them. The problem is that, because they do not have the proper 'psychological training,' it goes in one ear and out the other."[7] She advocates training children to adopt preventative practices early in life: if kids grow up using sunblock to prevent skin cancer and brushing teeth to prevent tooth decay, they will be more inclined in later years to use condoms to prevent inopportune pregnancy and sexually transmitted disease. Doxiadi-Trip champions a decidedly modern type of agency: "To give them the sense, the pragmatics [to realize] that many of the things that seem to happen to them are in their hands to make happen, not let happen to them" (321). The ethic of well-being asks women to realize morally appropriate behavior through enacting responsible decisions that are explicitly self-interested, rather than finding self-worth through service to others.

To help facilitate a shift in people's understanding of control as it relates to fertility, the family planning pamphlets and newspaper articles described and quoted in this essay frequently replace the Greek word *érotas* (passionate love) with the English word "sex," represented in either Greek or Latin characters. While socializing with Athenian teenagers as an American exchange student in 1988, anthropologist Joanna Skilogianis told me she never heard the word "sex"; "back then," she said, "people 'made love' [*kánoun érota*]." Another friend recalled to me: "My grandmother wouldn't talk about 'the act'—that's what she would call it, *I Práksi*, with a capital I and a capital P." Today, the public use of the foreign word "sex" (which is strewn throughout magazines and newspapers, heard on television, and voiced by doctors) expands the allowable parameters of acceptable and valid sexual practice beyond (unprotected) vaginal intercourse. Being "Western," the word "sex" simultaneously connotes pleasure and rationality. Family planners, committed to the liberating promise of rational action, also need sex to be pleasurable as a way of disentangling morally appropriate sexual practice from its "traditional" mooring in the possibility of procreation and generating proper families. A "modern" mentality amenable to contraception would take pleasure, not social repute, as the object of sex. In the family planning rhetoric (including FPAG and state Ministry of Health literature, as well as in such popular media as pregnancy test advertisements), the modern pleasure ethic of "sex" is set apart from a traditional "procreative ethic" (Katz 1990), which can still be referred to through *kánoun érota*, or "making love." The word "sex" signals the advent of nontraditional sexual practice: primarily guilt-free sex outside marriage without intent to marry, but also including anything that is not monogamous marital sex, men having sex with prostitutes, or incest (all of which might be considered more "traditional")—the kinds of sex that abortion has covered over.[8] But "sex" on the model of Western modernity, as Carole Vance (1984) has noted, is if pleasurable then simultaneously dangerous. And this brings us to the second element of the 1990s family planning campaign: the promotion of safe sex practices.

Case 2: AIDS and HIV Transmission and the Marketing of "Safe Sex"

The phenomenon of AIDS not only participates in the opening up of public and private discussions about sex, but the AIDS awareness campaign provides a window onto how Greek family planning and its attendant ethic of well-being must reconcile the promises and perils of being modern. The first cases of AIDS in Greece were reported in 1983.[9] "The last few years," thirty-eight-year-old Maro said to me a decade later, "now since AIDS appeared and the campaign about AIDS began, the prophylactic has begun to enter into people's lives." An article published in a leading daily newspaper, *Ta Nea*, reported: "The male prophylactic is almost the only method of contraception that young men know and the majority of them use it—not for contraception, but for their own protection from the diseases which are transmitted by the sex act [*me ti seksoualikí práksi*]."[10] Consensus among the family planning community suggests that the abortion rate has been falling since 1992 as a welcome by-product of the increased use of condoms to prevent HIV infection.[11] "Fear of AIDS and the increased use of condoms has apparently led to a 50 percent drop in the number of abortions in Greece," *Ta Nea* reported on 19 April 1995.

In Greece, people's fear of AIDS has been focused on the virus itself, which seems to be looming in "today's world." According to popular opinion, AIDS "appeared" in Greece via tourist "carriers." AIDS, always otherized through its English acronym (in line with the use of the English word "sex"), is depicted as a symptom of modern times and not as, say, a disease put on the earth to punish individuals for engaging in certain practices. It was striking to me how infrequently AIDS was mentioned in conjunction with homosexuality or gay men; more often, it is attributed to IV drug use, another modern import.[12] Amid the collective memory of centuries-long struggle against occupation and foreign rule, this view is in keeping not only with Greece's historically rooted "underdog imagination" vis-à-vis the "West" (Diamandouros 1993) but also with an understanding that homosexuality reflects a weakness of sexual will rather than concretizes a sexual identity. Homosexuality, like overenthusiastic heterosexuality, is a natural (if morally problematic) phenomenon that can be blamed on the characteriological human condition of original sin. The HIV virus, in contrast, is seen to come from "outside" Greece. When HIV is not ghettoized among a "sexual minority," the health message is that anyone can contract the virus.[13] According to FPAG: "All sexual acts are dangerous without prophylactics"; "Any kind of sexual activity without proper use of a prophylactic is very dangerous"; "AIDS attacks anyone regardless of sexual orientation."[14]

In the informational literature put out by the FPAG and by the Ministry of Health Center for the Control of Infectious Disease, it is *seksoualikí epafí*, or sexual contact, that transmits disease as well as causes inopportune pregnancy. The FPAG literature on HIV prevention can be quite sexually explicit. One leaflet cautions readers to remember that "oral sex" [*to somatikó sex*] is very dangerous during menstruation or if the active partner has a cut in his mouth, swollen gums, ulcers, bleeding wounds, etc." In saying that any sexual practice or "contact" is potentially "risky," the literature acknowledges that any sexual practice, regardless of procreative potential, is indeed, sex. An article titled "Save Safe Sex" that appeared in a 1995 issue of *Flash* magazine (which is geared toward young men) voices the newly sanctioned permissiveness with the voice of traditional authority (parental figures): "We would never tell you (like your mother) to find a good girl so [you] can have a family and put your mind at ease. We tell you, 'great, go out and screw this summer,' because the winter is miserable, because all the country's babes are now unwinding and you can't miss the party!"[15] Young people are being told that sex is not shameful—so don't be ashamed to carry a condom. Sex in this view—safe sex—can be enjoyable, but still it is not something to be engaged in "freely" with "abandon." As this article's title reveals, sex "for pleasure" will not be much fun if it leads to disease or inopportune pregnancy.

By playing to a collective fear that every instance of "sexual contact" can transmit HIV, the AIDS information campaign presents its message as the light at the end of the tunnel, as a glimmer of hope in a fallen world. If *kánoun érota* (making love) refers to an almost quaint ideal of "traditional" relations between romantic and/or conjugal partners, *seksoualikí epafí*, by its ability to transmit disease, is a tarnished, contemporary form of the old ideal. However, there is redemption after the Fall: seksoualikí epafí has been brought out of the silenced sphere of the family and into the public domain of scientific medicine. True, every instance of sexual contact runs the potential risk of disease, but family planning fights modernity with modernity by retooling and reapplying (for instance, within marital relations) that ancient technology, the prophylactic. As noted by FPAG: "The surest method of *protection* is to *insistently demand* that your sexual partner wear a *prophylactic.*" Here, prophylactic sex and the "traditional" sex acts that spread disease are distinguished as having sex versus "making love": "Don't make love in any way with a man who refuses to wear one. Your own life and your partner's comes first."[16] In these lines of officialized discourse, people are told they can do good and have sex—any kind of sex, as much sex as they want—so long as it is safe from disease and other "undesirable consequences,"— namely, inopportune pregnancy that would likely lead to abortion, which, like a disease, is potentially damaging to biological fertility and health. Family planning advocacy, then, works to frame "sex" as a medicalized space of rational, autonomous control separate from constricting patriarchal relations and symbolic links between procreation and motherhood. The latter, recalling Kakoyanis's words, are relegated to the more "cultural" category of "making love."

As shown in the example above, promotional campaigns for condoms frequently act on traditional stereotypes of gender and sexuality and pitch their message toward women and not men. The August 1992 issue of DIVA, a glossy fashion magazine targeting middle-class young adult women, was during my fieldwork prominently sold at kiosks covered in plastic that also encased a silver-wrapped condom. Moreover, I once bought a skirt of Greek manufacture from a centrally located shop that had affixed to it a paper packet labeled "AIDS" that contained a male condom. Here, family planning efforts neglect to realize that in feminizing a traditionally "male" contraceptive, the burden of contraceptive accountability is increasingly placed on women. While it is unequivocally good that condoms are becoming commonplace (indeed, as mentioned earlier, a side effect of increased condom use to prevent HIV has been the drop in the national abortion rate over the last few years), a feminist gynecologist once complained to me that condoms were never advertised extensively when their primary purpose was to prevent pregnancy: "You see how unfair it is. How many years have we tried as women to make men use the prophylactic, the condom! They will *try* it for women, but the partner, he will not accept it. But now with the AIDS problem it's really advertised everywhere. This was never done for pregnancy. Not to save the poor women's life [by reducing need for abortions], but it's only to save the man's life. I find it outrageous, actually." Just as it has "traditionally" been viewed as a woman's maternal duty to limit the size of her family, it is a "modern" woman's duty to protect the heterosexual family from disease.

Under the ethic of well-being, each person is held morally responsible for her or his own actions in terms of the possible resultant health consequences—that is, infection from disease or sterility from abortion. This is in contrast to how "traditional" moral codes of sexual relations are aimed at upholding God's will and family solidarity; the repercussions of premarital or adulterous sexual activity have to do with what others would say about the transgression: "How will what you've done reflect back on the rest of us?" It is not merely the moral codes—what people are or are not allowed to do (or admit to) sexually—that are changing, then. The bodily ethic of health also requires a change in "the way in which the individual establishes his relation to the rule and recognizes himself as obliged to put it into practice" (Foucault 1990: 27). An ethic of well-being is "new" in how it imagines the ethical subject. Put plainly, the new ethical subject is the moral object of sex.

The narcissism of this subject is made explicit in Doxiadi-Trip's magazine column: "The difficulty is the meaning of prevention, the meaning of 'I have control over things that concern me,' the meaning of communication, of discussion as a form of intimacy. And above all else the meaning of *erota* [passionate love] and devotion, profound respect for the body—our own and others" (1993: 320). As FPAG states in one of its pamphlets: "AIDS is combated if each one, individually, takes measures! Looking out for myself means looking out for the one I love!"[17] Here, in taking "love" as something that motivates behavior in sexual relationships, family planning advocacy hopes to encourage not only new understandings of sex but also of love. Motivated by an ethic of well-being, love can take one's very self as its object. And yet, paradoxically, the family planning notion of sex, divorced from reproduction, is also morally divorced from the specificity of particular relationships. Under an ethic of well-being, a properly moral attitude toward sex will approach it rationally, each instance of sex being morally equivalent to any other because the moral object of sex is one's own personal health and well-being. The family planning "philosophy of life" depends on this new object of sex which is encouraged by a new object of erotic love: love thyself. Passionate love—being swept away by pure emotion and physical urge—is irrelevant to the pleasure of rationalized sex.

What would it mean to take passionate love out of the ideal picture of sexual relations? In Greek cultural thought, sexual attraction (érotas) is defined as a matter of physical attraction and recognized as a "natural impulse," but it is largely valued (perhaps especially by women) because it may become a path to *aghápi*, the enduring love of the heart (Papataxiarchis 1991). As Phoebe, a forty-year-old divorced administrative assistant, explained to me: "Érotas, with the meaning of sex, or passion which you feel for an individual, is something that is passing. Aghápi is something that stays forever. That is, I believe, as you set out in your relationship with an individual you start out first with érota, this attraction between two persons, and then either it will fade—it will never become anything else—or it will be followed by aghápi and this lasts, certainly, for all the years of your life." Eva, a 25-year-old administrative assistant, concurred, noting that "after érota comes aghápi. When I'm *erotevméni* [in *érota*] I have a passion for this man. I like him, I want him [sexually], then after awhile I believe that the passion and my érotas will continue to exist, but aghápi will prevail." Physical attraction and sexual relations come before and potentially lead to enduring love, a point that Athenians explained to me as being in contrast with the more puritanical American or British way of doing things. Family planning and safe sex rhetoric, cast in this foreign mold, asks Greeks to bring aghápi to their érota, so to speak. The repercussions for conceiving agency and subjectivity are significant. In this context, it is not surprising to find a backlash against safe sex mandates: a proliferation of romantic visions in Greek public culture.

Nature and Nation: Siting Sexuality within the Moral Politics of National Identity

In Greece, the backlash against safe sex mandates is unleashed in the context of a cultural imperialism where the safe sex campaign is often viewed as a sanitizing threat to a wild, unruly, and virile sexuality that many Greeks claim as an apect of national character—the kind of male sexuality that women's use of abortion has often been directed at correcting or, perhaps, enabling. To demonstrate this briefly, I draw further on magazine images; because Greek media often mimic Western formats, media representations of gender and sexuality offer an incisive view of the ambivalence that characterizes a young urban Greek gaze toward the West, emblematically represented by the United States. *Flash* magazine's "Save Safe Sex" article appealed to "the person who wants to live and not to survive. Who isn't closed up in his room, traumatized by hysteria, paroxysms and prohibitions, who has no taste for either 'abstinence and temperance' or self-service. *Greek folk wisdom* said it years ago: 'masturbation [*malakía*] is fine, but with sex you know the world.' Save sex! And do it safe! [emphasis added]" (72). Here Greeks are recognized to be "customarily" incurable romantics and insatiable lovers. The tourist T-shirts with their slogans such as "Greek men are the world's greatest lovers" remind us, though, that this "tradition" has revolved around gender asymmetry in sexual relations.

Such popular images reveal how Athenians' receptions to family planning rhetoric are tuned to the wider political culture of a nation-state where gender and sexuality provide a framework for debate over national identity (Dubisch 1993: 281). Gendered, sexualized imagery figures widely in national stereotyping because "like gender . . . nationality is a relational term whose identity derives from its inherence in a system of differences. In the same way that 'man' and 'woman' define themselves reciprocally (though never symmetrically), national identity is determined not on the basis of its own intrinsic properties but as a function of what it (presumably) is not" (Parker et al. 1992: 5). In the early 1990s, the virile component of a Greek national character may have been most potently portrayed by the country's late septuagenarian prime minister, whom the mainstream press could not help but admire for his bold move to court and marry a "tall—taller than 80% of the men in [his] PASOK party—blonde and sexy" woman, a contemporary of his children.[18] Far from being raked over the coals of media morality for leaving his (American) wife of several decades and the mother of his children for a significantly younger (Greek) woman (and an Olympic airline hostess at that), Andreas Papandreou was credited with rekindling the national flame of érota "in the years of a spiritually crippled Greece." Another heterosexual men's magazine waxed poetic: "Oh men of Athens, anatomists of History. Come let us avenge the prime-ministerial member for the adolescent pursuits of dawning érota. . . . It's true. Andreas Papandreou, this fearsome generator of aghápi and myths, did it for you. He, whilst having a rendezvous with death, collided with érota. He dressed his feathers and set off on a solo journey, an odyssey to the depths of the soul . . . Érotas swept like a conflagration over the hypocritical 'don't' and 'must' of constipated neohellenic society. He came like a spring rain to sweep away the dust of aged ideas."[19]

Papandreou's much-publicized exploits were seen to breathe new life into the "Greek spirit" that had been flattened, presumably, by institutionalizing forces whose parameters for sanctioned behavior today include safe sex mandates. If Papandreou could let loose and find happiness at his age and in his position then hope is not lost for the Greek masculine/national ideal according to which "Greeks" are mortal (male) adventurers in a land of female sirens. As the probable sarcasm of the authorial tone itself suggests, this article belies an ambivalent view of "the West": in a magazine explicitly modeled after Western prototypes lurks implied "condescension toward the effeteness of the West" (Herzfeld 1986: 222). Just as women's supposed sexual weakness ultimately reveals their strength, the Greek (male) lack of sexual control in practice (a normatively feminine characteristic) ultimately testifies to the nation's virility. This contradiction (or better, inequality) is not particular to Greece but rather appears in the nationalist rhetoric of many modern nation-states. David Horn, for example, writes of early-twentieth-century Italian fascism that "the virility of the social body, like that of the individual male, was seen to depend crucially upon women" (1994: 65). The moral object of sex under construction through family planning turns out to threaten the "natural" fixity of that masculine sexual energy (responsibly channeled by women's post hoc birth control) that helps to distinguish and reproduce Greeks as a unique and special people. The ethical body is a gendered body.

What is perhaps most striking about this sexual idealism in the Greek case is that it revolves around men's romantic, emotional inclinations. A decade or two ago, men's magazines were more apt to celebrate the "calculated, unemotional skillfulness" that a certain subculture of men, *kamákia*— literally, "harpooners"—applied to "the hunt" of foreign women for recreational sex (Zinovieff 1991). When the promise of sex (along with sea, sand, and sun) is seen to draw tourists to Greece from wealthy nations (Zinovieff 1991), the irresistible, charming, and sexually prolific "Greek" (male) carries national value as a marketable commodity. The practice and social status of kamákia has declined since a fear of H I V infection has induced more men to use condoms in casual sex, to abstain from its practice, or even to settle down and marry. In the wake of rational safe sex campaigns, and perhaps inspired by Andreas Papandreou's amorous adventures, in the early 1990s the Greek media added a romantic, marital "happily ever after" to the lure of Greek male heterosexuality. The virile/fertile Greek lover is, after all, not only a marketable tourist commodity but a potentially crucial national resource, a sexual service worker in the production of new Greeks—if, like Papandreou, he stays home and marries the Greek girl. While the stereotype of virile masculinity may help placate government anxiety over a declining birthrate, as with the gendered assignation of "blame" for infertility problems Greek men (including politicians) can still hold Greek women primarily accountable for this decline, thereby translating the nation's underfertility, its "demographic problem," into its "woman problem."[20]

What all this means for Greek women is that now more than ever many may feel pressure to be alluring to men, to make themselves sexually available to men, and to flatter men's sexual egos by letting men sweep them off their feet. Greek men, in Athens and in other tourist areas around the country, complained repeatedly to me, a young *Amerikanídha*, that "local" women were not nearly as exciting or accommodating as foreign women (see also Zinovieff 1991). While discussing her former marriage over dinner one night, my friend Moira advised me: "A woman must be interested in what the man is interested in." Indeed, as soon as forty-year-old Moira began expressing interest in her own projects and goals rather than devoting her time to cheering on her husband's career in television production, the marriage fell apart. How are women to reconcile the pressure to play the supporting conjugal role at the same time that media articles and advertisements and even their doctors exhort them to "take control" of their sexual and reproductive lives? Needless to say, debate ensues: How are "modern" Greeks supposed to talk about sex and go about romantic relations? To phrase this in the Aristotelian frame I introduced at the outset of this chapter, how are people to act morally and realize their gendered "natures" when they are pressured to adopt practices that directly challenge customary relations?

When gender remains crucial to the construction of the Greek nation-state and is symbolically enacted by male-dominant heterosexual relations, it becomes easier to understand why Greek women can eagerly consume a biomedical model of pregnancy (Georges 1996b; Mitchell and Georges 1997) and birth (Arnold 1985; Lefkarites 1992) while remaining wary of medicalized female contraceptive practices that challenge the moral symbolics of heterosexuality. We can also see how those among the Greek medical establishment who advocate family planning construct their own orientalizing stereotypes of "Greek women" in explicating an irrational "preference" for abortion. Michael Herzfeld elucidates this Greek dilemma as follows: "As self-styled Westerners discursively seek to distance themselves from the 'atavistic' Balkan and Muslim worlds, usually by decrying a supposed lack of rationality in those populations, they find themselves imitating precisely the same paradoxical strategy of simultaneously exoticizing their own past and pointing to it as the source of their national character" (1997: 110; see also Sutton 1994). Greeks frequently view proudly their sexual proclivities as more "Eastern" or "Mediterranean" (*mesoghiakés*)—that is, more in line with the Turks who are similarly "hot blooded" and "passionate" as opposed to, say, the "cold" Brits who, in being stereotyped as overly rational and unemotional, are seen as emasculated and "effete." But while Greeks are berated for having far fewer children (and hence producing a far smaller army) than do Turks, Greek politicians nevertheless praise their constituency for being "modern" enough to validate Greece's membership in the European Union, the privilege of which Greece officially finds Turkey undeserving. Nationalism colludes with patriarchy in demanding that family planning, responsibly employed by modern citizens, rationalize the "nature" not only of sex and fertility but of population growth.

Conclusion

In this essay I have taken an ethical view of gender and sex so as to demonstrate how the desires of family planners to introduce a moral dimension to fertility control overlook an existing set of ethical precepts that are densely woven into women's sense of abortion and that inform Athenians' ambivalent reception of safe sex imperatives. In describing how Athenians struggle to update their ethical evaluations of sexual and reproductive practice, I have demonstrated that family planning advocacy underestimates the powerful role that gender plays in shaping ethically appropriate sexual and fertility control practice under both biomedical and customarily Greek models. The ethical body required by the ethic of well-being—like that summoned forth by the ethic of service—is a gendered body. In recognition of this, and counter to modernization theory, I have argued that if knowledge of biomedical fertility control facilitates a "modern" shift in the ideal site of reproductive agency—from the social realm of sexual relations and the post hoc arena of abortion toward the biologized space of conception and contraception—this does not signal an automatic gain in women's autonomy. The ideological commitments of family planning advocacy produce an ethical indeterminacy that is played out in assessments of women's virtue as self-controlling and that multiply the kinds of sexual impropriety women are charged with concealing. Athenian women's gender proficiency is judged in a context in which patriarchy and liberal individualism are in uneasy—sometimes consistent, sometimes contradictory—coexistence. Conflicting social/ethical expectations become especially burdensome in an era when the very same irrepressible—even immoral—sexuality that family planners want women to overcome continues to inform the "nature" of Greek national identity, thereby helping to distinguish "Greece" from the encroaching and dominant

"West." By superimposing an ethic of well-being onto an ethic of service, family planning rhetoric, far from facilitating modern women's liberation, has furthered women's lived contradictions as Greek women.

Ethics is what makes the physical, cultural, and political bodies stick together, and ethics is an important place to look to understand how people respond to social change, including the transcultural transfer of medical technology. In Greece, an ethical view of gender tunes us into the way a characteriological "nature" to be socially realized in the frame of Aristotelian naturalism and Orthodox theories of sin (Campbell 1964) conflicts and combines with the material "nature" of biomedicine: recall Aristotle's notion that "neither by nature . . . nor contrary to nature do the virtues arise in us; rather we are adapted by nature to receive them, and are made perfect by habit." Today, Athenian women are asked to realize through habit a new kind of nature, one presented by family planners as asocial and biological, even as it is to be adjusted to through ethical modification of habit. Even biomedical nature is socially realized through ethical action. The recognition of this notion reveals how sexual and reproductive agency is neither a matter of free will nor of resistance to the imperatives of a fixed nature or a constraining culture. Agency emerges in ways that reconfigure and reproduce identities and social relations, including relations of gender and global inequality. To conclude, I would like to suggest here that this lesson about nature and agency might helpfully be extended beyond the Greek case—that it might be bent back to reflect critically on the definitively "modern West," the post-Enlightenment source of healthism, which embodies moral reasoning consistent with biomedicine. What is "real" about human nature here, too, is not its fixity or inevitability but its realization through social practice. The physical, cultural, and political body is a creature of habit, of ethical habitus realized at a variety of scales at once.

Notes

This essay draws on field research sponsored by Stanford University and the National Science Foundation (grant SBR–93–12633). I would like to thank the following people for their thoughtful comments and helpful suggestions regarding various pieces of the argumentation presented here: Vincanne Adams, Jane Collier, Stefan Helmreich, Michael Herzfeld, Thomas Paxson, Stacy Pigg, Michele Rivkin-Fish, and Sylvia Yanagisako.

1 All undocumented quotas in this essay are taken from interviews I conducted during the course of my fieldwork in 1993 to 1995. The thirty-eight women I interviewed about their personal stories range in age from twenty to seventy; around half

are mothers and several are divorced. Their occupations include student, civil servant, salesperson, professional, and homemaker. Most recognize themselves—in explicit contrast to their mothers and grandmothers—as "modern" or "contemporary" women.

2 The earliest research into contraceptive use and abortion in Greece was conducted in the mid-1960s by the (now defunct) University of Athens Centre of Demographic Research. This survey of 6,513 married women throughout the country found that since World War II abortion had served Greek women as the best known and most available and effective method to avert inopportune births. Among those who "admitted" to having had an abortion (35 percent of the women surveyed), women averaged two abortions each in rural areas and nearly four abortions each in the greater Athens area (Valaoras and Trichopoulos 1970; Comninos 1988). The following figures (Valaoras and Trichopoulos, 1970: 290) reflect responses to a question posed by researchers regarding "methods of family limitation" (see also Symeonidou 1990): coitus interruptus, 49.2%; condom, 22.0%; induced abortion, 20.6%; other [pill, IUD], 8.2%; total: 89.5%.

3 A 1994 article published in the progressive youth magazine o1 (Lykouropoulos 1994) reported that many Greek companies that package foreign-manufactured condoms do so without sterilizing the imported product, which has never been tested for tears or other damage. Indeed, in March 1998 seven brands of imported condoms were removed from the Greek market after they were found to be defective. Included among these were models of the top-selling brand DUO, which is manufactured in Malaysia and packaged in Greece under the German-based multinational Beiersdorf corporation (reported in "Faulty Condoms," *Athens News*, 12 March 1998, A3).

4 In 1980 (not coincidentally, the year before Greece became a full member of the European Union) the Greek Parliament legalized female methods of contraception and legislated the establishment of family planning (*ikoyeniakós programmatismós*) clinics in a select number of state hospitals. By 1990, thirty-eight state-sponsored clinics were in operation throughout Greece (thirteen others had by then shut down), eight of which were in the Athens area. These state-run centers operate apart from FPAG, but because the number of qualified instructors is limited, private and public initiatives and memberships overlap. Evangelia, for instance, volunteers her time to FPAG but is paid by a state insurance agency to give similar kinds of presentations.

5 In a social world where the operational notion of "self" is "rooted neither in individual impulses nor in institutional roles, but in changing, situated pressures" (Derné 1992: 260), morality becomes a matter of character development, of conformity to normative standards of propriety. Discrete actions are left to achieve pragmatic ends. This is somewhat different than in, say, Catholic Ireland where women may keep a history of having an abortion from others "to protect themselves from the criticism of others" who condemn abortion as "wrong" in and of itself (Fletcher 1995).

6 For a similar observation of U.S. women's moral evaluations of smoking during pregnancy, see Oaks 2001: 112–13.

7 Anthi Doxiadi-Trip, "Pro-Profilaktiká" [Pro-prophylactics], *Yinéka*, May 1993, 320–21.

8 The difference between "having sex" and "making love," or between modern and traditional sexual practices, may be one of semantics. People may now simply be talking about a variety of sexual practices that others have quietly been doing, happily or in resignation, for generations. One friend told me that she heard the older women in her "husband's village" giggling one day in the fields, telling dirty jokes, and the women started saying things like, "Oh, you know sex, it's really good" (not the attitude they were supposed to convey); "and you know if you don't want children you do it from behind!" My friend, a Greek American, was aghast. "No really," a woman of her grandmother's generation assured her, "how else are you going to do it and have a good time—you just do it from behind!" The correlation between anal sex and contraceptively safe sex has been noted for additional areas of the Mediterranean (Delaney 1991: 50–51).

9 In 1989 an estimated 8,000 persons in Greece had tested HIV positive (Agrafiotis et al. 1990). In 1993, 721 cases of AIDS had been reported. These numbers are low in comparison with other European countries, where in 1993 22,939 cases were reported in France, 17,029 in Spain, 15,780 in Italy, and 6,929 in the United Kingdom (Hellenic Archives of AIDS 1993: 141, cited in Tsalicoglou 1995: 95). But as noted in Tsalicoglou 1995: 85, the relatively small numbers in Greece should be considered in light of an increasing rate of occurrence: in 1992 there were thirty times more new cases than in 1984. By early 1994, 871 persons were reportedly living with AIDS in Greece, of these 779 were men and 92 were women (35.2 percent of the women were infected by their husbands) (Lazanas 1994).

10 Based on surveys done in 424 general military hospitals of male patients from urban areas, aged eighteen to twenty-seven (presented at the Ninth Northern Greek Medical Conference in Thessaloniki, 6–10 April, as reported in "They Know Only the Prophylactic," *Ta Nea*, 1 April 1994).

11 I heard this in numerous interviews with physicians and social science researchers; see also Emke-Poulopoulou 1994.

12 Official statistics on means of infection do not quite match up with popular understanding: 58 percent of AIDS cases were linked to homosexual contact, and only 4 percent to IV drug use; 10 percent were reportedly due to blood transfusion (despite a state center for the Control of Infectious Diseases pamphlet's assurance that you can get a blood transfusion without fear of contracting HIV); 15 percent were infected from heterosexual contact; and 11 percent were linked to "unknown source" ("World AIDS Day," *Athens News*, 28 November 1993).

13 Indeed, traumatic images of AIDS victims from around the world had in the 1990s instilled a fear among Greeks that bordered on paranoia. A German man working at a small inn in Mytilene, Lesvos, complained to me in 1992 that over the past few years Greek tourists had begun to grumble noisily about having to share a bathroom with "other" (meaning foreign) guests; they feared they would "catch AIDS" from the toilet seat. In early 1994 a health clinic/social center opened in a working-class neighborhood near Piraeus, a place where people living with AIDS or with HIV could

come for support, care, and counseling. According to newspapers, children at a nearby elementary school staged a strike claiming that the "air was bad," while a neighboring restaurant owner complained that his business had suffered since the clinic's opening. So widespread are the misperceptions of how one can contract HIV that a KEEL pamphlet goes through a list of thirteen items that one can do and not be in danger, including embrace someone, shake hands, give a simple kiss, be near someone who sneezes, use someone else's books or pencils, use a "foreign" toilet, shower, or used towel, swim in a pool, eat in a restaurant, handle foreign plates or glasses, be stung by mosquitoes, fall with an open wound, give blood, get a blood transfusion.

14 The quotes here are from the FPAG leaflets "AIDS: *O gnostós 'ágnostos': gnósi horís prokatalípsis*"; "AIDS *ke alliós . . . Profilaktikó!*"

15 "Save Safe Sex," *Flash*, August 1995, 72.

16 From the FPAG leaflet "AIDS: *O gnostós 'ágnostos': gnósi horís prokatalípsis.*"

17 From the FPAG leaflet "AIDS *ke alliós . . . Profilaktikó!*"

18 "Love in the Time of Cholera," *Colt*, February 1996.

19 See "Dhimografikó: I yinékes ke páli énoches" (Demographics: women are again to blame), a piece written by the Greek Chapter of the European Forum of Leftist Feminists that appeared in the newspaper *Mesimvrini* on 12 December 1993. See also Paxson 1997; Halkias 1998.

20 Vasili Bonio, "O érotas sta chrónia tis choléras," *Colt*, February 1996, 59.

SHANTI A. PARIKH

From Auntie to Disco: The Bifurcation of Risk and Pleasure in Sex Education in Uganda

• • •

All those social controls . . . which screened the sexuality of couples, parents and children, dangerous and endangered adolescents—undertaking to protect, separate, and forewarn, signaling perils everywhere, awakening people's attention, calling for diagnoses, piling up reports, organizing therapies. These sites radiated discourses aimed at sex, intensifying people's awareness of it as a constant danger, and this in turn created a further incentive to talk about it.—MICHEL FOUCAULT

The proverbial question of who should teach children about sex was an issue being debated by national planners in Uganda in 1999 when I was there to conclude the first phase of my research on youth sexuality.[1] Although proud of their remarkable and widely cited success for reducing HIV prevalence rates from as high as 36 percent in some urban sites (with the national average at 21 percent) in 1991 to the low of 8.3 percent in 1999, planners grappled with a new dilemma—the reality that their 1986-initiated AIDS campaigns had aggressively thrust sex into the public domain by offering ways to reduce sexual risk without talking directly about the sexual acts themselves. Much of the medically constructed talk about safe sex assumed a certain level of knowledge about sexual activity and a shared moral code, thus circumventing discussions about the pleasures that attracted people to the potentially deadly act. For those young people without firsthand technical knowledge about sexual practices, the safe sex messages became catchy mantras repeated in public celebrations as part of a medico-moral toolkit removed from affective relations or political-economic context.

The silence about sexual pleasures in public health messages became a space readily filled by other kinds of images, messages, and rhetorics generated outside the HIV/AIDS and reproductive health industries. In Uganda's burgeoning commercial and mass media sectors images of pleasure proliferated in Western pornographic movies and romance novels, local music halls and bars, newspaper gossip and advice columns, radio talk shows, and "soft sex" and social life magazines. These venues were not, however, without their critics. Establishments that directly addressed the erotic and displayed sexualized bodies received constant reprimands from social critics in public and private forums. Letters to the daily newspapers, irate radio callers, public gatherings, and grumblings among elders passionately bemoaned the decline of traditional morality. Disgust became a powerful tool in the moral criticism of these ubiquitous visuals of sexual erotica. As the social critiques increased, more media sold and the venues prospered. In an interview with the managing editor of a monthly soft sex magazine (who was in his late twenties with a B.A. in religious studies from Uganda's prominent state university), he asserted that, "Before [the publication of a controversial cover and the resulting flood of public outcry] no one said much about our magazine, although there were definitely uneasy feelings about what we were doing. Now it is thought to be a dirty magazine. And sales have really soared."[2] For the critics, the scantily clad covergirls dressed in bikinis or miniskirts became the embodiment of impropriety, emblematic of a world recklessly defying the way things should be.

Since the first public HIV billboard was built outside the capital of Kampala in 1986 (see figure 1), Uganda's successful HIV/AIDS campaigns have inadvertently sharpened the bifurcation between discussions of sexual risks and sexual pleasures that, according to my interviews with elders in Bulubandi village and the reports in the ethnographic record (Fallers 1969; Mair 1969; Roscoe 1911), were previously intertwined at the local level.[3] The HIV campaigns did not cause the bifurcation; rather, this compartmentalization in public discourse had been in progress since the colonial campaigns against syphilis in the early twentieth century (Lyons 1999) and were further prompted by the medicalization of childbirth practices and reproduction (Hunt 1999; Thomas 2003), religious and legal discourses on sexual immorality (Comaroff and Comaroff 1991; McCulloch 2000), and the anxiety surrounding youth sexuality in coed schools (Stambach 2000; Summers 2002). Unlike the sexual health campaigns in the past, however, the HIV/AIDS

1. The risk of sex. Uganda's first AIDS billboard, built in 1986 outside the capital of Kampala. Photo by Shanti Parikh.

education campaigns have inserted the sexual into the public space in unprecedented ways (see Pigg, this volume). The aggressive state-backed and internationally funded HIV/AIDS programs, the "time-space compression" (Harvey 1989) of newer media technologies to reach more people in shorter time, and the inescapable local realities of AIDS burdens have interacted and legitimized the entrance of sexuality into the public realm (see Parikh 2001). In the process of medicalizing sexuality, new moral sensibilities have emerged and the categories surrounding the sexual have become codified in ways that distilled and sanitized risky behaviors from sexual pleasures. At the same time, capitalist forces have repackaged and commodified the historic role of sex educator—the paternal aunt, *sôngá*—by removing her from the local kinship system and transforming her into a genderless, faceless commercial "sexpert" that no longer speaks to pubescent girls but to a sexually knowing mature adult audience. She now offers advice on the art of erotic techniques to an adult audience seeking modern romance, love, and multiple orgasms.

In 1998 I conducted a formal survey with 260 primary and secondary school students in the Iganga town area in Uganda.[4] Of the total number of students 87 percent stated that their greatest fear about sex was contracting HIV or another STD, and 10 percent, mainly girls, stated pregnancy as the greatest fear.[5] When asked where they learn about sex, none of the 260 students stated the source as reproductive and sexual health campaigns. The students did not consider information from the public health campaigns or religious teachings to be a primary form of their sexual learning; instead, most young people ages nine to twenty said that they learn about sex from discussions with friends, by watching older people flirt at local social places such as discos and bars, and through representations of erotica in popular culture. The same students said that they would prefer to learn about sex, which older youth defined as sexual intercourse (including foreplay, sex techniques, and physical desires) from schools, parents, and health professionals.

Significantly, the authoritative adult voices that warned about managing risk remained silent about sexual pleasures and intercourse. This silence was motivated by the moral view that direct reference to pleasure and intercourse would stimulate otherwise dormant adolescent desires (for a similar discussion about the United States, see Irvine 2002; Patton 1995). Notions of morality based on parental consent that had in the past regulated sexual partnerships, particularly for young women, were seen as the strongest guarantee of premarital sexual abstinence.[6] While adults grappling with the erosion of historical authority retreated into a silence, young people sensed the uneasiness that floated on the sidelines of sexual health messages. For youth, the silences in health messages spoke louder than the warnings of sexual risk. Thus, while the AIDS industry helped define youth sexuality as a national problem, it remained inadequately equipped for, and uncomfortable with, educating youth about sexual acts and pleasure.[7]

The result of this reticence was a separation of public sex talk into that about risk and that about pleasure (Vance 1984). Influential public-interest players such as religious leaders, state policymakers, and traditionalist groups closely monitored the former; the latter was motivated by the burgeoning capitalist marketplace. Unlike the ABCs of risk reduction—Abstinence, Be faithful, and Condom use—there was no unified voice for discussing sexual pleasures; rather, a variety of local, national, and global commercial cultural brokers produced erotic messages that were diverse, inconsistent, and misleading. The commercial marketplace for sexual information operated alongside the public health campaigns bringing sex talk and underlying ideas about sexual morality into the public arena. This process rearranged vocabularies of sexual morality that include new standards of bodily hygiene and grooming, medico-moral notions of reproductive health and risk reduction, and religiously infused rhetorics that equate sexual purity with sexual unknowing. The gradual disruption of historical processes of sexual learning has led to what Philip Setel (1999: 59–78) has called "cultural dislocation," in which demographic, economic, and social changes have converged to create new ways of conceptualizing sexual morality (also see Schoepf 1997).

Locally, people in Uganda had already felt the weakening of the role of the family in educating young people about the morality surrounding risk and pleasure. This had less to do with the messages in the national HIV/AIDS campaigns than with the historical decline of kin-based sexual learning resulting from mobility and migration, along with the rapid emergence of privately owned recreational venues, popular culture, and the mass media. For adults in Bulubandi village and Iganga town (the ethnographic settings examined in this essay) the fading of kinship authority in the sexual learning of young people is unequivocally symbolized by the urban space of Iganga town and possibilities it offers for unsupervised interaction between boys and girls in schools, recreational venues, and the lively evening *kayola* (bazaar).[8] Listening to elders describe the ideal process through which young people become sexualized selves, one might think that they are talking of a different place altogether. Youth today have little connection to or knowledge of it. Thus, the larger aim of this essay is to address the question of how the recent processes of medicalizing sexual risk and commercializing sexual pleasure have interacted with local histories of practices, discourses, moralities, and conceptions of sexual selves to fashion new moral objects of sex.

Village and Town, 1950–1999: Social Change along the HIV Corridor

Iganga town lies in eastern Uganda along the trans-Africa highway that runs from the coast of Kenya into the Democratic Republic of Congo. Commonly known as the "HIV corridor" in the international media reports and academic writings of the first decade of the AIDS epidemic, the highway is portrayed as a series of sexual networks replete with truckstops and social venues for commercial sex work and entertainment (see Patton 1997). Areas along this highway, including Iganga and its outerlying village of Bulubandi, still record some of the highest HIV prevalence rates in Uganda (UNAIDS 2000; Obbo 1993; Pickering et al. 1996). Speakers of Lugosa are the predominate group in this agrarian region, where they live in highly dispersed patrilineal clan units, marry according to exogenous rules, and follow patrilineal lines for inheritance, political succession, and affiliation (see Fallers 1965).[9] Although kin groups remain the primary safety net for individuals, gradually over the last fifty years changes in the market economy and in education, along with sectarian political unrest and the rise in civic associations have enabled some people to forge identities and gain access to resources based on nonkin relations.

Today, changes in economic opportunities, prestige hierarchies, urban migration, and marital patterns ranging from polygyny to monogamy with "outside wives" or other various configurations of extramarital relations, have begun to dramatically shift the social landscape within which Ugandan youth configure their ideas about gendered morality, pleasure, and risk. Hence, just as today residents in Bulubandi draw both from kin networks and from wider civic networks for access to status and wealth and for making other sorts of claims, so too do Ugandan youth look to wider social and civic networks for making sense of their sexual selves. As stated earlier, among the most prominent historical transformations in this process is the changing role of the *sôngá*, a traditional female kin-based sexual advisor, usually an older paternal aunt whose role has recently been professionalized and incorporated into larger public infrastructures concerned with sexuality. In her commercial form, this advisor need not be related by kinship to those she advises, and any professional sexual counselor can be known in the neighboring language of Luganda as "*ssenga.*"[10] A crucial role of the kin-based sôngá involved individual instruction on preparing and sexualizing the young female body by instructing on how to lengthen the labia minora; yet in today's commercial form, this intimate role has disappeared.

Today, professional ssenga are recruited to help mediate and negotiate a growing popular culture milieu of sexual opportunities by changing youth expectations for what it means to be sexual.[11] The latter are provoked by a domain far beyond the reach of the sôngá or by her commercialized, contemporary equivalent, and discos, magazines, films, videos, and radio culture provide opportunities for sexual engagement that even traditional sex counselors cannot adequately encompass. I wish here to begin my account of this transformation with some stories of past ways that young people came to know about "sexuality," after which I move to a comparison with the contemporary ways that youths know and make sense of their sexual selves.

Traditions of Sexual Coming of Age, circa 1930–1950:
Sexualizing the Female Body and Satisfying Male Pleasures

Most elders in Bulubandi village have similar views regarding the ideal kin-based system of learning sexual roles and the proper presentation of gendered sexual selves.[12] When elders lament that past ways of learning how to manage and present the sexual self differ greatly from today, the idealized past serves as a moral lens through which they understand the emergence and magnitude of the AIDS epidemic. Through discussions of difference, expressions of disgust, and comments on cultural disarray, elders express a sense of loss over the waning of the role of kin in sexual learning and the moral development of young people. As elders tell it, the past may have been uncivilized but at least it was orderly.

The commentary of older people needs to be interpreted carefully. As scholars of Africa remind us, there have always been changes in traditions and variations within the ideal. In challenging the idea of depicting a static folk model of sexuality in Africa, Setel posits that "the idea that 'once upon a time' there were clear and rigidly obeyed cultural rules and social institutions governing sexuality is not truer for Africa than it is for Europe" (1992: 27). Yet Setel also emphasizes that elders' depictions of an idealized past frequently serve as ideological moral commentary about present social problems such as AIDS and out-of-wedlock pregnancies. Historical narratives, therefore, provide insight into how contemporary public culture has shaped local discourses and understandings about shifting sexual landscapes.

What is collapsed under the modern-day rubric of "sex education" by state and development discourses and by the media and residents of Bulubandi village exists in elders' narratives as a much longer, broader, and fragmented process. The process of becoming a sexualized adult in the past included not only actual practices leading up to sexual intercourse but also the presentation of the sexual self (e.g., comportment, dress, and hetero- and homosociality) and obligations to kinship and matrimonial groups. The transition from child to adult involved the gradual development of a sexual self that enhanced expected gendered roles in the family and society. These sexualized selves were to be fully actualized in marriage where they were appropriately intertwined with reproduction, family reputation, and marital obligation. Whereas sexual acts were considered a private matter as long as they did not breach a taboo (such as bestiality, prolonged same-sex sexual relations, and incest),[13] a person's presentation of sexual self including reputation and adherence to moral codes concerned the extended family (see Jeater 1993: 37). Locally, breaches of sexual taboos were perceived as corrupting the entire clan and as being brought by bad spirits or witchcraft; hence, even when enacted privately, elders depict taboo sexual acts as a cosmological concern for the clan, requiring cleansing ceremonies to protect the family from further harm.

Male (specifically fathers, uncles, and older brothers) and older female clan members had vested interests in younger women's reproductive capacities and sexual respectability, which resulted in the close monitoring and regulation of female sexuality. As anthropologist Lloyd Fallers observed in the 1950s, "the ideology of male dominance . . . centers about the sexual and child-bearing potentialities of women" (1965: 78). Several elder women spoke about being prohibited from leaving the family compound without permission because their families feared that the young female would be seduced away or "stolen" by a man.[14] Female sexuality, unlike male sexuality, was a great source of anxiety for families primarily because it was believed to hold significant reproductive power and hence power over men.

This difference between female and male sexual powers is reflected in the lack of ritualized sexual coming of age for males because Lusoga-speaking boys do not undergo formal rites of passage to manhood.[15] In stark contrast, female sexuality required direct shaping, controlling, and grooming. Interviews with elder women reveal that although the sexuality of girls was groomed primarily for the purpose of satisfying male sexual pleasures and desires, the satisfaction of a woman's own sexual desires was not ignored.[16] Molding a girl's sexuality was the joint responsibility of her mother and her designated sôngá— paternal aunt selected by the father, often an older sister whose bridewealth was used to assist his marriage. The mother oversaw the transition of a girl's body by stressing the importance of modesty, which centered around the hip and thigh area, the core of female sexuality, physical attractiveness, and reproductive powers. The mother's gaze and instruction began at a young age and intensified after a girl began menstruating, so as to prevent pregnancy in her father's house and the possible reduction in bridewealth or her marriageability.

Whereas the mother's persistent surveillance ensured proper embodiment of adult female modesty, the girl's designated sôngá directly guided her sexual development and later served as a sexual advisor. The father's lineage, from which the sôngá came, had great stake in the sexual actions of offspring because it was in the service to the clan that its members' sexual means of forging kin relations was to be directed (cf. Jeater 1993). Instruction from the sôngá began before menarche, continued during puberty, and became more focused and intense after a girl was betrothed. The official role of the sôngá ended after the girl's wedding night but, depending on the relationship between the two, the aunt remained a close advisor and confidant to her married niece.

A pattern of child lending, in which a girl resides with and assists her sôngá and the matrimonial family of the sôngá, created an opportunity for a girl's sexual instruction. Child lending at earlier ages might coincide with the sôngá's pregnancy or to ease the financial burden in the girl's natal family, a practice still common today. These immediate, practical needs also helped manage the growing tension between the girl's desire for more freedom and the strictness of her parents or of a stepmother.

A crucial role of the sôngá concerned instructing the girl to stretch or pull her labia minora (*okusika enfuli*) until they reached a few centimeters. Pulling involved numbing the area with a sticky substance, most likely sap from a tree, and rolling the inner vaginal lip around a twig. A girl received instruction and commenced this activity at around the age of eight or nine and continued until she began menstruating, for after menarche, it was believed, the lips became too tough to pull. Although males knew of the act, pulling was considered a female secret and was referred to as "going to collect firewood" (*okujaa okughelera enku*) or "visiting the bush." These terms are commonly known today because of the attention that pulling has recently received in Uganda's mass media, as discussed below.

Pulling formed a central part of sexually preparing the female body both for sexual activity with her husband and for childbirth. Norah, an elderly birth attendant in her late sixties, provided for me in an interview a common explanation: "Long ago they used to say that if you do not visit the bush to pull you would not give birth. In reality," she continued, "pulling is useful because if you never pulled, during the time of delivery a baby will fear to come seeing that she is coming in a very open place. And even the men did not like to have sex with women who never pulled. To men, a woman who never pulled looked to them like entering a house that has no door." Similar to Norah's explanation, elders commonly invoked the idea of a vagina needing a cover and the image of a door, associating both with a sense of modesty. Similarly, Lusoga-speaking men were not circumcised (unless they were Muslim) because it was believed that exposing their uncovered genitalia was, as one anthropological observer put it, "an act of indecent exposure" (Orely 1970: 13). As Norah suggested, pulling was closely associated with ideas of fertility as well, linking a female's external genital transformation with her reproductive capacities (see also Jeater 1993: 24). A girl received a stern warning that if she did not pull she would either be unable to give birth or would experience complications during delivery. On a more social level, "visiting the bush" provided girls a safe forum for sharing information and gossip with their peers, thereby helping to establish a heterosocial network of age-mates. One woman with whom I spoke laughed as she remembered visiting the bush with other girls. Although pulling was painful, she said, girls would take longer than necessary just so they could temporarily escape constant supervision and the drudgery of housework.

In addition to covering the opening of the vagina, pulling increased a man's sexual satisfaction by elongating the passage through which the penis passed, and was considered one of the most effective ways of "winning favor of a husband." This was especially important in polygamous unions in which existed sexual competition among cowives. For instance, Faridah, an affable and almost blind widow in her seventies, was the third of five cowives and, as the rumor went, she was jealously known by the other wives as the favored one. When I asked Faridah about the importance of pulling, she replied: "If a woman who never pulled was in a polygamous family, her husband would give her less [sexual] attention than her cowives who had pulled. She could be disliked." When I asked if that was why she was the favorite wife, she laughed, paused, and then thoughtfully answered that she had a *sôngá bulungi* (a good aunt). The sôngá received credit or blame for a young woman's sexual conduct and moral behavior. A sexually well-groomed young wife would be a source of pride for her sôngá, an extension of the aunt's own sexual-social self. Likewise, a sexually lackluster young bride reflected the sexual inadequacies of her sôngá. In latter cases, the flow of gifts from the young woman's disappointed husband to his in-laws, including the sôngá, would diminish over time.

The apex of a sôngá's sexual instruction occurred during the period between the formal engagement ceremony (*okwandhula*, or introduction) and the wedding ceremony. Again, child lending facilitated this process in that a secluded, betrothed girl might be sent to live with her sôngá where she was taken care of by female relatives.[17] A sôngá advised the betrothed girl about "bedroom tricks" (*okulamba obukodyo bwomubulili*; literally, "advice about techniques of the bed"). Further, mainly through observation rather than verbal instruction a betrothed girl would gather tips on how to perform her sexual duties. A few older women recounted rumors of sôngás who discreetly arranged for the betrothed girl to hide in the aunt's bedroom or directly outside the bedroom while she and her husband had sexual intercourse. The "bedroom tricks" included bedroom dancing, or moving the hips, both during foreplay and coitus. Important to bedroom dancing was the proper wearing and use of the waist beads (*obutiti*) given by the sôngá to the betrothed girl. Waist beads are ten strands of colorful plastic beads (before the introduction of plastic beads, dyed seeds were used) joined at the ends and tied loosely around the waist. Imbued with sexual significance, waist beads were guaranteed to cause great sexual arousal in men.

The sôngá also gave the girl a cotton *kitambaa* (cloth) to use for cleaning the man after sexual intercourse.[18] Along with instruction on proper use came the stern warning that if her husband ever found her carrying the *kitambaa* when she was not in the bedroom with him, he would have sufficient evidence to accuse her of adultery. Another important lesson involved proper hygiene of her body, including how to cleanse it and rid it of foul odors by using herbs and other vegetation (see also Burke 1996: 23–31). Although boys were also taught hygiene and washing techniques, these were cast for them as acts of cleanliness rather than means of enhancing sexual attractiveness.

While on the one hand a woman was encouraged to enjoy sexual acts herself and play the subtle seductress role with her bed dancing and waist beads, she also learned that the man should believe he is the sexual innovator and initiator. His pleasure, she learned, should be seen to supersede hers. To achieve this, betrothed girls received coaching in the disciplined management of expressions of sexuality, such as bedroom sounds. One older woman, aged sixty-four, described her experience as follows: "I was also told that during the real act of sex, sexual intercourse, I should not keep quiet but I must make some sounds showing the man that I am enjoying what he is doing to me and it will also encourage the man." Noises were thought to further arouse the man, making him more eager to please the woman. Mastery of sexual play also entailed social risks for women. If not managed carefully, a woman could be accused of adultery or having engaged in premarital sex, which were often collapsed into a single category of being a prostitute (or *malaya*).[19] Although it was fairly agreed on that sexual intercourse should satisfy both the man and the woman, social validation of sexual pleasure did not mean that all sexual encounters were consensual and pleasurable for both. I heard several stories from both older and younger women about being coerced or forced into having sexual intercourse, especially in their first sexual experiences (also see Fritz 1998: 153).

Consummation of marriage marked the official transfer from father to husband of the rights over a bride's sexuality. "On the wedding night," Fallers documented (1957: 112), "the bride is accompanied to the bridegroom's house by her brother and her father's sister, who remain for one night to assure themselves of the bridegroom's potency and who, on the following day, must be given a token gift 'to drive them away.'" According to elders I spoke with, the sôngá was also interested in assessing the effectiveness of the girl's education or whether or not "she was able to play sex as accepted." If the girl was a virgin, as indicated from blood on the bedding (often made of banana fibers), the sôngá was rewarded with a goat. If the girl was not a virgin, however, no action was taken against the girl or sôngá.

Some elders claimed that the sôngá and other relatives would witness the consummation of the marriage by standing outside the door or, in later days, by lying under the bed, although the latter seems improbable given that many rural residents slept on floor mats.

Village gatherings and ceremonies provided informal venues for learning about sexual morality and sexual means of relating. These gatherings included naming ceremonies for newly born twins, burials and funerals, housewarming functions, clan meetings, marriage and introduction ceremonies, and beer drinking parties. One elder recalled burial ceremonies in the 1950s: "Young people used to learn about sex through burial ceremonies. These ceremonies used to take more than one month. During this time older people used to do a lot of adultery and the young people used to watch this. That is how they came to know about sex." He later made specific reference to the songs performed during twin naming ceremonies. The songs, which contain unusually sexually explicit content and refer directly to genitalia, are performed in gender role reversal dramas as men and women exaggerate sexualized behaviors and comportment of the opposite sex. Colonial observers at the time incorrectly assumed that the songs represented the "licentious" practices of the people (see Roscoe 1911: 72); however, elders and later ethnographic accounts are clear that the sexually explicit nature of songs during ceremonies are indeed particular to these social spaces and in other contexts they would not be considered proper.

Intergenerational social functions not only offered youth a chance to watch adult flirtation but also, through dance, provided a publicly acceptable stage for gendered rituals of seduction. For males, the dances centered on competition; for girls and young women, the dances were a display of feminine sexual allure. A good dancer isolated her waist and, while keeping her shoulders and trunk still, propelled her hips in precise and rhythmic jerking motions. Mothers instructed girls in this dancing technique, and at certain events skilled dancers were the center of attention. To further emphasize the ideal feminine body—a small waist with pronounced hips and upper thighs—today, and perhaps in the past, a cloth is tied around the waist, which is then passed around as different women and men enter the spotlight. Similar to bedroom dancing, improvisation and personality constitute a successful performance.

Other elders recall the importance of childhood games in experimenting with gendered sexual selves. An elder in Balikabona village remembers a game called "house": "When we were young we used to play together with girls. And we used to divide ourselves into a father, a mother, and children.

Those who acted as the father and mother were always the eldest in the group and they used to be of opposite sex. In the process there would come a time when those acting as parents would tell the children to go and play and that they would call them if they wanted them, or they would say that it's time to go to sleep. The two people—the father and mother—would sleep together and sometimes we used to pretend to play sex at an early age." Young people today play similar games and also cite such games as being early sources of sexual learning and spaces for the articulation of adult gender roles.

Uganda has experienced profound social changes over the last half century, and these transformations have altered the ways in which young people learn about the pleasures and risks of sexual relationships. As sexual learning has gradually detached from the kinship system and village settings, the idiom of a regulated sexual morality has shifted from notions of family obligation and reproduction toward newer discourses by the modern nation-state regarding a healthy population. Historically, against the backdrop of high rates of syphilis and infertility in East Africa from 1910 through the 1950s, colonial missionaries, physicians, and government officials introduced new and often competing rhetorics of morality that focused on the need for tighter regulation of female sexuality through the means of religion, reproductive policies, physical exams, laws, and notions of domesticity (see Ahlberg 1991; Davis 2000; Hansen 1992; Musisi 2002; Vaughan 1991).

More recently, HIV/AIDS education campaigns and the commercial economy have been powerful forces in shaping how sexuality education and morality is conceived locally. These cross-cutting visions are at the heart of intergenerational tensions. For elders in Bulubandi village, for example, the loss of kin-based control over the molding and control of youth sexuality, particularly that of girls, is the cause of a decaying system and a major reason for the rise of many social problems—including AIDS, prostitution, and premarital pregnancies. Reconstructing what elders see as the cause of the changes to the idealized past that they recall is a way to provide insight into how local populations place AIDS in historical perspective.

The Emergence of the Commercial "Sexpert" in the 1990s and the Commodification of the Ssenga

Today, an emerging group of public culture producers has found that past sexual practices and ideas make ideal material for their profit-driven ventures (see figure 2). Many of the young producers are part of an educated elite group that has been exposed to global media forms and thus keen insights

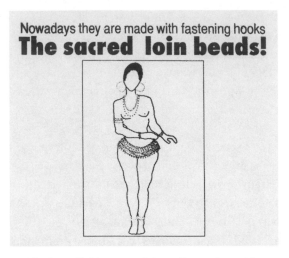

Nowadays they are made with fastening hooks
The sacred loin beads!

2. "The latest fashion craze." According to the article, waist (loin) beads "were part of a women's beauty and sexuality" (from *New Vision*, 6 May 1997).

into blending foreign media with indigenous popular cultural expressions to create new forms of cultural genres and consciousness (Barber 1997; Fabian 1978). These techno-savvy producers bring into radio, magazines, or TV a constant interplay between an imagined Ugandan past and a glimpse at possible future modernities. This construction of modern Uganda adds yet another moral lens through which sexually curious youth and adults understand sexuality. The public "sexperts" offer advice to young and old on radio shows and in newspaper columns and counseling centers, blurring the boundaries that once established differential access to information between young and old and male and female (see Birken 1988). Today, access to such information is limited by an individual's access to media. Within this new democratized public space, the commodified and commercialized ssenga has become an easily recognizable icon and sexpert.[20]

One day two excited girls ran into my office in Iganga town waving the 21–27 February 1997 issue of *Chic*, a soft sex/leisure magazine whose cover sports a different scantily dressed covergirl each month. In this issue the title of the feature article boldly occupied the glossy cover of the magazine: "Ladies: To Pull or Not to Pull Is the Question." Unlike the reasons for pulling given by elder women in Bulubandi, a version in the magazine linked the practice of pulling to increasing a woman's sexual pleasure. Using testimonial from an informant, the article explained: "The results [of pulling] are usually pleasurable, some women admitted. 'Every time I shower with warm water I feel great down there,' Joy confessed. By increasing the sensitive surface area, pulling is believed to enhance sexual desire and masturbatory pleasure. 'Ever since I carried out that function I have found jogging more enjoyable. I don't need a man to get an orgasm; all I do is jog!' Mary, an athlete, said."[21] The article concluded with a brief description of an expensive Western surgical procedure that cost twenty-three hundred British pounds and provided what the article described as the same "effect as the traditional African [practice]." The author challenged the reader to consider the irony: "What Europeans today pay top dollar for, we have been doing for years and for free." In the magazine's creatively refashioned version of the practice, pulling satisfied female sexual desires rather than being done for reproductive purposes and male satisfaction as depicted in Bulubandi elders' narratives. The refashioned version of pulling was implied possibly to lead to the obsolescence of men in women's sexual pleasure, thereby providing an even greater threat to historical patriarchy and reformulating moral sensibilities about female pleasure.

Yet another version of pulling appeared in a sex advice column in Kampala's daily newspaper. A perplexed, perhaps fictitious, reader asked: "At the tender age of 11, I was made to extend the outer [sic] labia of the genitals . . . What is the purpose of extending the outer labia?" The advisor responded: "You are one of the few lucky modern ladies who had the opportunity to perform this ritual at such a tender age, and didn't shun it . . . The purpose of extending the outer labia of the female genitalia . . . is plainly to increase your partner's satisfaction during sex . . . That is why women are advised to perform it, because it keeps their men satisfied and limits their wandering."[22] According to the author of the column, it is the outer labia—not the inner ones as described by elders—that are the parts of the genitalia that are pulled. Pulling, the girl and the public are informed, increases a man's sexual pleasure and discourages him from "wandering" to other women.

Whereas the testimonials in the first article serve as a device to inform the public about the (supposedly) rare practice of pulling, the question-answer format of the column quoted above couches pulling as a practice that an expert can explain. In both reports, pulling is spun into a tale of modern sensibilities and pleasures, a sign of Africa's sexual revolution that draws from traditions in its precolonial past. For many young men and women, such popularized versions of past sex practices that are generated by the unseen yet omniscient sexperts are the source of their knowledge about sex, the old days, and their own bodies. These frequently male advisors recast versions of tradition formerly based on clan reproduction through a modernist lens of the individual pursuit of pleasure.

As the sexpert trend was taking hold, Uganda's historical sex counselor, the ssenga, emerged as one of the most profitable mass-produced sexual icons. She became a cultural reference to the old days, a time without AIDS. Simultaneously, the Lusoga form of sôngá was overshadowed by the ssenga of the Luganda. The commodified ssenga plays on the roles, duties, and sexual wisdom often attributed to the kin-based sôngá and is conveniently packaged into a powerful symbol of cultural heritage and modern knowledge. Advice columns, radio shows, counseling centers, education seminars, and TV programs that comprise the flourishing sexpert industry bear the functionally recognizable name ssenga. People in Bulubandi can easily identify this new counselor, a familiar and trusted person. For example, every Wednesday the *Monitor* (Kampala) newspaper features an advice column called "Agony Column with Ssenga Nambwere." Another "Agony Column" appears in the competing newspaper in the women's section. In both columns the ssenga consoles broken hearts, advises on modern romance and love, and offers solutions to sex problems (such as impotence or genital warts) and anxieties (such as first sex experiences and intercourse during menstruation). The columns encourage the modern reader to seek help from the expert: "Want to share your problems or seek help? Write to Ssenga Nambwere, c/o the *Monitor*" (the troubled modern sex citizens could also fax or e-mail their questions). The columns were given titles such as: "He Loves His Ex," "Is It Okay to Use a Vibrator?" and "How Do I Tell if My Wife Reached an Orgasm?" The once private conversations with the sôngá are now shared with a wider audience blended along lines of gender, class, and age.

While many grassroots HIV/AIDS education campaigns are conducted in local languages, perhaps not surprisingly public culture discourses about sex and sexual pleasure are commonly done in English. Using English provides a certain license for discussions that would be considered too vulgar or inappropriate for public consumption if uttered in local languages. A radio talk show about sex broadcast in Luganda was cancelled after conservative traditional leaders complained about the program's indecent content, yet a similar radio program aired in English remained on the air.[23]

In the process of commercial packaging, the ssenga that emerged is removed from the private lessons taught to girls and is now targeting an audience of adults who are interested in improving their sex lives and getting answers to questions about their bodies that the AIDS campaigns do not address. Once associated with the instruction of prepubescent and betrothed girls, the ssenga has been transformed into a counselor for "mature" men and women, married couples, and sexually precocious young people, according to local perceptions. The ssenga as a modern-day cultural icon has been seamlessly woven into an invisible and expert voice in affairs of love, romance, and the banal business of relationships between adults. Partly because of the faceless nature of the media, ssenga are able to creatively push and merge the distinctions between tradition and the modern and can unapologetically defy the boundary between illicit and acceptable.

Whereas the public ssenga has risen to national prominence, in Bulubandi the role of the sôngá in teaching pubescent girls about sexuality has virtually disappeared. Today the sôngá who acts as the bride's representative is selected more for her social status in civic society than for her role in the girl's sexual development. For example, in 1998 I was invited to one of the year's most talked about ceremonies of introduction or engagement in which a well-known businesswoman in Kampala who was also a former member of parliament performed the role of the sôngá. She played her role appropriately, appearing insulted when the initial bridewealth offer was made and wincing at subsequent upgrades. At one point she leapt up and boasted about the physical, intellectual, and personal qualities of the prospective bride. The dramatic negotiations settled on a price of five cows, which was exceptionally high for the cattle-poor region. The master of ceremonies announced that the five cows represented "a church wedding, monogamy, faithfulness, honesty, and hard work," and the audience laughed at the clever modern symbolic twist. After the ceremony, the sôngá got into her Mercedes and rode off—there would be for her no lying under the bed waiting for a bloodstained sheet and no goat. The sôngá thus remains the representative of the prospective bride and the means of her public presentation, including her sexuality, yet at the same time may not have had any conversations with the bride about sex.

If the role of the sôngá has declined and the religious leaders do not feel comfortable talking with youth about sex, who should perform this function? The two common answers in Iganga are parents and schools. It is seen as culturally inappropriate for parents to talk directly to their children about sex, although indirect communication through riddles or strategically situated gossip exchanges has long been accepted and normal. An elder woman in Bulubandi expressed another perspective to the idea of parent as sex educator. She stated that it was the current adult generation and their promiscuity that had caused the rampant spread of AIDS, and since adults cannot seem to control themselves sexually how could they possibly teach young people about sex and sexual morality? In her opinion, adults should be embarrassed because their unregulated sexual behavior after Uganda's independence in 1962 and during its political instability thereafter (1966–1986) caused the rampant spread of HIV/AIDS. Although many parents do not discuss sexuality with their children, it is the parent who is blamed or criticized when their children's sexual behavior defies the boundaries of propriety.

Most young people believe that school is the ideal place to learn about sex, asserting that teachers are socially respectable and knowledgeable. Compared to magazines and videos, students feel that schools "would give correct information on sex." While young people enjoy the erotic images and public sex counseling programs, they are often confused about the accuracy of the information. However, in the schools around Iganga, sex education contains a unit on the biology of reproduction, another on anatomy, and, increasingly today, scientific lessons about HIV/AIDS. As one fifteen-year-old girl remembered: "When I was in primary five [equivalent to the fifth grade] a teacher talked about sex one day. She did not want to talk too much about it but the children kept on asking her so many questions, and we came to realize that sex has been there since our great grandfathers' time. But she wouldn't talk more." What is revealed in the girl's statement is that by the age of ten or eleven these students knew vaguely about what has recently become lumped under the term "sex" by virtue of information from AIDS campaigns, radio programs, local gossip, or observing older siblings. They respect their teacher's knowledge and feel that the classroom and not gossip is the best place to learn about sex and sexual morality. They are eager to know what no one would tell them.

Teachers, however, are reluctant to discuss sexuality and morality for fear of being accused of seducing students or of encouraging premarital sex among students—a concern that continues despite the reality that youth have access to unregulated mass media and popular culture messages about sex. When I asked Mr. Waibi, the headmaster of Iganga secondary school, if his school had instituted the sex education curriculum as presented in the Ministry of Education's moral education module, he responded: "At the moment, no. I remember having tried to introduce sex education here but when the parents had a general meeting, they stopped it. They thought that when you talk about sex you are telling people to do it or you are describing the real act of sex. Yet we wanted to reflect to what the sôngá used to teach. But the parents had a misconception about it . . . We first should educate the parents about the need to educate the children and have the sex education at hand. So, there is no sex education in the school, although we sent someone to train and she came back but we are reluctant to [have her] teach because of the parents' attitude toward it."

Mr. Waibi was open to introducing sex education in his school. Like parents, however, the school needed first to learn how to teach it. Although the sex education curriculum had not been implemented in the Iganga schools when I conducted my research there, it is revealing that the curriculum was included within the section on marriage and moral education. The curriculum module treats sexual intercourse solely as a marital obligation, not as one of desire or love. Therefore, because people only need to know about it when they are preparing to wed, schools as well as other adults are excused from teaching details about sexual activity and sexuality. The embedded moral message suggests that sexual pleasure leads to dangerous consequences such as unplanned pregnancy or HIV.

Sources identified as ideal sex educators, such as parents, religious institutions, and schools, do not feel comfortable or enabled to discuss sex with a group of people who moral doctrine dictates should not be sexually active. The sôngá, on the other hand, has been transformed from a sex educator for girls into a broader educator for both males and females, often neglecting the biological and sociological questions of youth. Furthermore, public health and HIV/AIDS campaign workers view their role as educating people about health risk reduction not sexual pleasure. People in both Bulubandi and Uganda in general acknowledge that sex education for young people is needed, but they remain uncertain how to institutionalize it in a way that accommodates the concerns of adults and the needs of youth.

Learning about Sex beyond the Ssenga, 1962–1999: Discos, Bars, and Video Halls

Young people in Bulubandi associate education with more than risk reduction, safe sex messages, and the biology of reproduction. For them it also includes the processes preceding sexual intercourse, such as gendered codes in meeting, flirting, persuading, negotiating, courting, and foreplay. Young people learn cultural scripts of sexuality and morality by observing older people and sharing information among peer networks about male and female interactions in sources such as discos, bars, marketplaces, the village, and in Western pornography.[24]

For older people the venues of discos, bars, and video halls symbolize a myriad of conflicting changes in society—changes such as the fading of tradition, assimilation into modernity, blending of local and foreign, youth gone wild, and new opportunities for youth (Parikh 2003b). Discos and bars epitomize the long-awaited freedom of movement, association, and economic opportunities now feasible after Uganda's twenty-five-year period of internal strife that followed independence from British rule. These recreational venues are not new—many have been in Uganda for decades—but they continue to serve as targets for accusations of social and moral decay.

Over the last fifty years, much entertainment has moved from private homes and local politicians' residences into commercial settings in town. Elders remember the emergence of discos after independence in 1962 when towns opened up to Africans and electronic equipment became increasingly available. According to one elder man, soon after news of independence reached Iganga "there was a sudden increase and excitement in the social life of Basoga. People began to learn the Western cultures—new styles of dancing, music, both Western and Zairean, dress, and bars. There was a big change in such a short time." Elders recount stories about the forced decline in traditional entertainment after a conflict that occurred between Uganda's first postcolonial president, Milton Obote, and the king of Baganda (Kabaka) resulted in the king's exile and increased restrictions on mobility and public gatherings. Under heightened postindependence national insecurity, village functions became strictly regulated and eventually village social events became the domain of local politicians who sought to increase their following locally and gain support by national officials. By Idi Amin's reign in the 1970s, the politically motivated parties that replaced kin-based functions began to give way to commercial social establishments; mainly disco halls with traveling bands, bars, and local-brew drinking places.

The recent rise of the Ugandan celebrity in the form of radio personalities, disc jockeys, and musicians has further increased the popularity of disco halls and bars. The symbol of the celebrity man together with the naughty, lipstick-wearing "detoother"[25] has helped create the urban-inspired, youthful disco culture found throughout Uganda today (also see Ferguson 1999). This culture is popularized by its print equivalents—the soft sex and social life magazines. The smuggling (*magendo*) economy that flourished in the 1970s under the regime of President Amin brought other forms of entertainment into Uganda, most notably pirated American, European, and Indian videos and the concomitant emergence of commercial video halls throughout the country. After President Yoweri Museveni took over in 1986, the resultant peace, liberalization of the economy, and social freedom facilitated a further multiplication of social forms and venues, and the rise of commercial leisure had a firm hold.

Today, school holidays offer young people an opportunity to explore town life through visits with schoolmates who live in neighboring villages (Kinsman, Nyanzi, and Pool 2000; Konde-Lule, Sewankambo, and Morris 1997). "Transnight" discos that run through the night stir excitement during school breaks. To announce transnight disco events, pickup trucks with large speakers blasting dance music and carrying groups of men in urban wear slowly cruise through busy market areas. Young and old stop their activities and come out from offices, homes, and informal selling shacks to watch the colorful truck and listen to the fast-talking disc jockey and the loud dance music. Some frown in disapproval and turn away but others wave and cheer at the sign that Iganga is part of a global urban network. For youth, the display announces another opportunity for them to see adults at play and maybe indulge in a little adult play themselves.

The dress code at discos is "modern casual"—jeans, baggy pants, T-shirts, colorful rayon shirts, brimmed hats or baseball caps, miniskirts, low necklines, satiny materials, and dress shoes—and individuals select from a variety of aesthetic styles, depending on financial abilities and how they desire to create a public identity. The atmosphere of discos and bars is created by modern stereo systems, disco lights, a mixture of Western and African (mostly Ugandan and Zairean, but more recently South African) dance music, bottled beer, and energetic disc jockeys. Early in the night, men dance in groups with other men and women with other women. As the night wears on and libations flow, social mixing of the sexes increases; the songs, dancing, mingling of sexes, and flowing beer are common images that guide sexual narratives of youth. As one secondary student offered: "Young children today easily learn about sex in discos. In slow songs men and women hold each other while the young ones watch. At times from such moments of close contact men and women end up playing sex in dark corners or in the bush while the young children see them." For this and other youth, the excitement is not with whom people go to the discos but with whom people leave. He continues: "After seeing, the young people go and practice what they have seen." By watching intently, youth learn the secrets of adult sexualized interactions only to share their disco narratives with their friends, until the narratives become well-known sexual scripts among youth (see figure 3). If young people lack the financial means to enter the disco, simply congregating outside itself presents a form of entertainment and a social scene that can be shared with classmates. One girl recounted a story of a man

3. "Where young people learn about sex." A composite
drawing of a disco by boys ages eleven to fourteen at
Nakigo primary school in Iganga, Uganda.

trying to convince a woman to leave with him. After the man bought the
woman drinks and danced closely with her, the couple wandered off to a dark
corridor behind the dance hall. Another boy expressed similar thoughts:
"The disco is the best place to learn sex. This is because you are able to see
how a boy begins to approach a girl, how the affair develops until you see
them playing sex." Other venues such as bush discos held in the village to
celebrate political victories or parties for a housewarming or a marital engagement offer youth other chances to observe adult play and flirting.

Western videos, particularly those shown at night, provide an up-close
look at sex acts. During the day and early evening video halls show U.S.
action movies, kung fu films, Indian melodrama-romance musicals, and
sports tapes. At night "blue movies" (pornographic and X-rated movies)
from the United States and Europe replace the daytime films, providing
youth with images of interpersonal sex scripts that emphasize sexual positions, noises, foreplay, and visual plots (although often far removed) within
which youth can imaginatively insert themselves (see Larkin 1997). Young
boys secretly flock to these video halls, either peeping through windows or
paying the admission to go inside and watch foreign men and women indulge in sexual intercourse. Girls, often too embarrassed to expressly watch,
catch glimpses as they pass by slowly with their friends on detour from an
evening market trip. One secondary school boy commented that from blue

movies one learns the "best styles of playing sex." Another student added: "Young people [most] like to attend video shows concerning sex. This is because they want to improve on their ability. So because of this they always want to attend sexual films. I think they are also most interested in watching films about fighting—for example, boxing. In this way they get skills on fighting their enemies. But they also like videos concerning sex, especially girls need to know what to do in bed. And also young people are interested in sex films so as to learn many skills and styles and to know which one is the best."

Even if young people do not view these films, the details eagerly retold and embellished by friends offer the visual imagery and sexual scripts through which they can imagine sexual possibilities void of local realities. Same-sex and mixed peer groups allow youth to further discuss and explore issues of sexuality with older youth acting as experts. Through these networks young people make sense of sexual behaviors and begin to understand their own sexuality. Although they are very critical about what their peers say about sex, many do not feel that they have a trusted adult with whom to speak openly without fear of reprimand (see also Dilger 2003).

The venues through which youth gather sexual scripts have specific gendered constructions of sexuality. Women who frequent bars and discos are often referred to as promiscuous and are perceived as defying sexual propriety. This often sends mixed messages to young girls. For them, discos and bars are a place where men and women perform gendered sexuality, but girls are not sure how to enact these roles without jeopardizing their own reputations. As one girl told me: "The women in the bars are beautiful, but they are not good women." Girls and some boys must grapple with this tension between the risk of scarring their reputations with pleasures of recreational leisure and developing their own sexual subjectivities.

Sex Education and Morality in a Changing World, 1950 to the Present: Migration and Foreign Religions

Egulansi, an elder woman in Bulubandi, offered the following commentary about generational tensions in sex education:

The relationship is very poor between the young and old. Today young people hardly listen to any advice from old people. Whatever they are told they will always say, "that's of the past and it can't work now." Youth believe that they have a generation with everything new . . . Today people who get educated see it as a shame to ask or be told by sôngá about the things to do with marriage or sex. At the same time young people today claim to know everything. Worse still, young people today do not give elders the chance to teach them, especially about sex. For instance, so many young people today, especially the girls, get into sex before they reach the age at which we used to teach about sex. So today they find out the bad and the good by themselves.

Many adults and elders share Egulansi's sentiments (also see Stewart 2000). For them, the idea of young people "finding out things by themselves" signals a shift away from sexual knowledge tied to the family and village setting toward newer "technologies of sex" (Foucault 1978) generated by national and global cultural brokers. This shift is accompanied by a shift in moral sensibilities. Newer sources of sexual information generate categories for analyzing, targeting, and discussing sexuality in ways that are not always compatible with those elders use to discuss the past. Hence, elders and adults feel marginalized in the sexual development of young people, yet are aware of the complexities of life that youth face, including HIV/AIDS, uncertain futures, limited jobs, and the desire for foreign things and ideas. Young people, on the other hand, desire to learn more than the risk of sex that is presented in the HIV/AIDS and reproductive health campaigns.

Rapid change over the past fifty years stimulated by new forms of state regulation under colonial and postcolonial regimes and increased mobility and flows of people, goods, and information has facilitated unprecedented transformations in social arrangements. Key external forces include moral discourses of Christianity and Islam, medical and scientific pedagogy about sex and reproduction, and the commercialization of sexual advice in the media and through counseling centers. Yet these forces are not merely acting on residents of Bulubandi. Rather, old and young residents actively appropriate, interpret, and deploy newer ideas of morality to understand and critique local concerns of HIV/AIDS, unplanned pregnancies, and sexual learning by young people. Attention to the wider political economy and an analysis of elders' perceptions of how these historical changes are linked to sexual learning reveals the more subtle shifts that have been in motion for a while.

To older women in Bulubandi, the diminished role of the sôngá and the practice of pulling epitomize the transition from the traditional to the modern era of sexual learning. Indeed, several elder women (who came of age between the 1930s and 1950s) and adult women (who came of age in the 1960s and 1970s) with whom I spoke did not reside near their sôngá. Some adult women were not assigned one until they were betrothed. Although many of the now middle-aged women lived with a sôngá for short periods during their youth, few said that their sôngá provided them with the extensive sexual training that they described, and only some said they were formally instructed on how to pull. When I asked these same women if they had discussed issues of sexuality with their nieces, very few said that they did. Others explained that strained relationships between their brother's wife because of jealousy over children or wealth or differences in ideologies or religious beliefs also contributed to the reluctance in performing as the sôngá.

At the demographic level, a long history of dispersion of kin groups has contributed to the declining role of the sôngá. The diffusing of kin groups was common in precolonial Basoga (Cohen 1986) and was further exacerbated by colonial programs to relocate populations near Lake Victoria in an attempt to eradicate sleeping sickness (Musere 1990). After colonial rule ended in 1963, the opportunities for mobility fluctuated during Uganda's unpredictable periods of civic strife and peace. Some people relocated for economic opportunities and education while others fled areas when local political situations shifted against them. This mobility increased during Idi Amin's regime, when new economic opportunities opened up for Africans in regional and international trade. Given that Iganga lies along the trans-Africa highway, smuggling and other long-distance trade provided a viable economic activity for men as well as for women, yet carried very different social implications. For example, "Dubai traders" became both a derogatory and a deferential term for women who traveled to the Middle Eastern trading hub and returned with suitcases of luxury goods and a new sense of economic independence and social freedom. During the mass killings of Milton Obote's second regime in the early 1980s, elders in Bulubandi remember opposition followers retreating into villages to flee from potential political violence in the capital. As the residential dispersion of kin groups increased, the ability of the sôngá to carry out her duties as described became increasingly difficult and unrealistic.

It is commonly agreed that most girls in Bulubandi today do not pull, and I did not meet any females under the age of thirty-five who told me that they had attempted the practice.[26] For elder women, the decline of pulling is closely linked to the presence of British missionaries because, they recall, the missionaries believed that pulling was masturbation or body mutilation and hence uncivilized and immoral. Furthermore, female missionaries stationed at schools and health wards asserted that pulling promoted promiscuity by introducing girls at an early age to their genitalia and sexual sensation.

Nabirye, a seventy-three-year-old woman who had an unusually high level of education for a female of her time, told me that in the 1940s the nuns in her Catholic boarding school forbade the practice of pulling. Fearing that the twin liabilities of education and not pulling would jeopardize her niece's chances of marrying and reproducing, her sôngá advised Nabirye's parents to transfer her to another school, which they did after some convincing. Nabirye thus never finished pulling, and as an adult she had a string of miscarriages, divorces, and episodes of barrenness. Indeed, Nabirye attributes her series of misfortunes to not pulling and to witchcraft sent by a jealous stepmother.

Nabirye's story represents how, since the late nineteenth century, foreign religions have interacted in complex and multiple ways with local ideas about sexual learning and morality through the colonial project aimed at "civilizing" African sexuality (see Hansen 1992). During the early part of the twentieth century, a long debate ensued among missionaries, colonial officials, and local (male) elders about how to achieve the goal of creating ideal African subjects who would serve the larger economic and political interests of the colonial government and companies. As the process progressed, Christian marriages emerged as the ideal model through which to domesticate and create a group of African elites (Morris 1967; Musisi 2002; Kalema Report 1965) and "churches and hospitals [were seen] as the proper places for sex education and care of reproductive health" (Giblin 1999: 313). As a result, church and health centers became important interventions for reformulating African bodies, sexuality, and moral codes (see Bastian 2000). The sexual development of young people became constituted with intertwined notions of premarital abstinence and sin, and such notions were easily appropriated into local rhetorics and ideologies of sexual activity—notably parental permission for daughters' sexual activity.

Today in Uganda the national governing bodies of colonial-established mainline religions—specifically, the Catholics, the Anglican Church Mission Society (CMS), and the Sunni Muslims—are frequently consulted on a variety of national policies surrounding sexuality, ranging from HIV/AIDS education to issues about polygyny and divorce. More recently, African independent churces, splinter groups, folk Catholicism, Pentecostal revivals of the "saved" (balokole) and other popular movements have attracted new followers with their emphasis on "prophecy and spiritual gifts that challenge the authority of the established churches" (Spear and Kimambo 1999: 240). These churches attract followers who want to distance themselves from the highly political nature of the mainline religions and who appreciate the lively and energetic services and the spirited music played on electronic keyboards that accompanies these gatherings. Led by charismatic speakers, decentralized and independent churches are strategically positioned to address the needs of local communities by weaving familiar idioms into religious rhetorics and appealing to local anxieties, including ideas about sexual immorality, HIV/AIDS, and urban youth culture.

The highly visible movement of Pentecostal *balokole* has had tremendous local influence. This movement began in Rwanda in the 1930s and thereafter spread throughout East Africa, fading and reappearing at various political, economic, and social moments. The *balokole* doctrine stringently advocates monogamous relationships and sexual abstinence before marriage. While I was in Uganda, the movement gained considerable strength in Iganga, especially among the young; among women who desire to escape from wayward husbands; and among single professionals who had migrated from the capital to work in nongovernmental organizations or other offices. Within Islam, the Tabligh movement (in Arabic, "to instruct or educate people about Islam") is the most pronounced splinter group in Iganga. Sallie Simba Kayunga (1994: 324) notes that in Uganda "a major concern of the Muslim fundamentalists is the reinstatement of women in their 'rightful' place under the control of men." According to Tabligh leaders in Uganda, part of the solution to reversing Uganda's moral decay is bringing women back into the modesty guidelines set in the Koran. These guidelines dictate that women must be fully covered except for their eyes and, I was told, also prohibits them from riding bicycles, thus further restricting their physical mobility and access to sexual enticements.

Churches and mosques in Iganga have remained virtually silent regarding the sexual learning of young people by maintaining that unmarried people should not engage in sex and learning about sex should correspond with pre-wedding arrangements.[27] Sexual learning most commonly finds its way in the marital counseling required by most religious institutions, and it focuses on gendered sexual obligations, the role of reproduction, and fidelity. More commonly, however, sex becomes an object for invoking moral projects. When I asked Reverend Kemba of the CMS in Iganga about the HIV/AIDS education campaigns in Uganda he applauded them but was highly critical of what he saw as the overemphasis on condoms. He argued that "encouraging the young people to use them [condoms] means that we are encouraging prostitution and adultery, which is against the Biblical teaching." For Reverend Kemba, as for others, teaching about condoms is equivalent to encouraging people to engage in unrestrained sexual activity. To illustrate his point, he recalled a dance at the adjacent teacher's college. The day of the dance, a nongovernmental organization held an HIV/AIDS education program during which they demonstrated and distributed condoms. The day after the dance, according to the reverend, used condoms and wrappers were scattered everywhere. He assumed that without access to condoms the young people would not have engaged in sexual intercourse.

Another church leader stressed that young people today are learning "incorrect ideas about sex" from videos, books, and discos. He stated that the role of the sôngá in sexual learning was the ideal, and he contended that it had disappeared. When I asked if his church had tried to replace the teachings of the sôngá or had encouraged the congregation to reinstitute the practice, he replied: "In fact the church has tried to incorporate that in its teachings. For example, that's why we have opened up counseling clinics and we send people especially from the Mother's Union groups to these clinics to go and teach the young people. So, these have taken up the role of the sôngá after realizing its importance." For this church leader, as for many, sex education centers around females and it is the responsibility of women to educate younger generations of females. According to the chair of the Mother's Union, however, the union does not offer sexual advice to unmarried or childless females. Instead, she explained, it assists poor rural women with pre- and postnatal health advice and shows them "proper" techniques for running a household and caring for new babies and toddlers—an effort akin to the domesticity projects of the same organizations during the colonial era (Allman and Tashjian 2000; Hunt 1999). The criteria for assistance established by the union resembles that of other reproductive health programs—in order for a young female to receive assistance she already has to have a baby or be married.

Religion is invoked to explain the decline of historical practices, yet simultaneously it is woven into commentaries about today's sexually misbehaving youth. Christianity led to the erosion of traditional morality, yet critiques of modern-day impropriety are infused with Christian and Islamic imagery and values. Whereas discourses of morality based on family obligation and reproductive choices shape older people's narratives of the past, their critiques of the present draw from Christian and Islamic rhetorics in ways that merge preexisting moralities into discourses of sin. While religion provides a rhetorical framework in discussions of sex as a moral object, I almost never heard anyone in Iganga say that religious institutions or leaders are the ideal sexual educator of young people. Nonetheless, foreign religions have played a major role in shaping how people in Bulubandi and Uganda perceive appropriate sexual learning for young people today.

*Conclusion: Reconciling Risk and Pleasure in the Age of
Public Sexuality*

I began this essay with a question that is continually debated by sexual health
professionals and other planners: "Who should teach our children about
sex?" Ironically, as sex becomes a moral object of public scrutiny rarely do
planners seek to understand the current ways that youth gather sexual information and the underlying moral codes that fall outside their clinical discourse and vision of ideal. Nor do most adult planners consider exactly what
it is about sex young people want to know. In an attempt to educate without
sensationalizing the HIV/AIDS epidemic the public health industry adopted
a clinical discourse that distills responsible sex into three compact tools:
abstinence, faithfulness to one partner, and condom use. Filling the void of
sensual content, the commercial media invoke sexually explicit codes that
claim to draw from a vernacular discourse about sex while simultaneously
creating a new space for audiences to imagine sexual possibilities. The competing moral codes tend to separate notions of risk and pleasure in the minds
of young people who are beginning to explore their sexual selves and the
possibilities.

Young people consider HIV/AIDS and reproductive health education to be
a negligible form of sex education; it informs them of the risks of sex in ways
that are detached from the emotive or political economic contexts in which
sexuality is enacted. Yet the rise of the commercial sexpert industry, from
which adults gather information about relationships and romance, does not
adequately address the very real hormonal as well as socially based sexual
changes that adolescents experience. With the transformation of the sôngá
from an intimate and personal educator of girls to a public icon speaking
about "healthy" relationships within national projects of modernity, young
people learn about sexual relationships before learning about their bodies
and the sexual acts themselves. The historically prescribed roles of the paternal aunt and uncle in educating youth about the morality of sexual risk and
pleasure have virtually faded, and has been replaced by public health messages on one side, and by peer networks, discos, pornographic movies, and
romance novels on the other. Young people today observe various sexual
interactions in easily identified spaces around the village and in town and
spread their newly acquired sexual scripts among their network of friends.

Wider social and economic transformations (such as schooling, newly
emerging local religions, and the emergence of commercial sexperts) have
caused in young people's orientations of sexuality a shift from kin-based

duties of reproduction to the individual pursuit of pleasure or management of risk. The public discourses circulated by health campaigns and the mass media offer young people ways to understand the sexual learning they acquire from local leisure spaces. Hence while authoritative adults debate from who, how, and what young people should learn about sexuality and morality, Uganda's emerging future adults forge their own ideas by combining messages about risk and pleasures in ways that are experimental; often contrary to the intended message; and sometimes detrimental. In the current moment in Uganda's thus far successful campaigns to reduce HIV transmission, the challenge will be to merge within health messages ideas about sensual pleasures in ways that offer young people the range of sexual possibilities within the reality of local landscapes while not alienating parents and other adults in the process.

Notes

I owe many thanks to Vincanne Adams and Stacy Leigh Pigg for their invaluable feedback and suggestions on this article. I would also like to acknowledge Harold Scheffler, Kamari Clark, Linda-Anne Rebhun, and Richard E. MacKay for comments on an earlier version, and thanks also to my insightful research assistants Janet Kagoda and Gerald Isabirye.

1 "Who Should Teach our Children about Sex?" was the title of one of many articles on sex education and young people that appeared in the daily newspapers in the late 1990s. The debate continues to receive considerable public attention and there is little consensus about how to educate young people about sex and what constitutes sex education.

2 On the controversial cover, the low camera angle revealed what some thought was the corner of the covergirl's underwear.

3 Although it appears that notions of risk and pleasure were bound in many historical contexts in sub-Saharan Africa (Ahlberg 1994; Jeater 1993), there are some exceptions. For example, Philp Setel (1999: 920) argues that the Chagga people in northern Tanzania "appear never to have had a positive cultural emphasis on sexual pleasure . . . None of the accounts of male initiation speak of teaching that husbands were entitled to sexual pleasure or that wives experienced desire." This is not the case among the elder men and women I interviewed, for their historical narratives reflect a culturally specific notion of sexual pleasure. Note that all undocumented quotes in this essay are taken from interviews and conversations held during the course of my field research in 1996 to 1999.

4 Of the 260 students, 150 were primary school students (ages nine to sixteen) and 110 were secondary school students (ages fourteen to twenty). The group is equally divided into boys and girls.

5 Other fears about sex included friends finding out (4.6 percent), "no fears" (2 percent), and parents finding out (1 percent); and, with less than one percent, addic-

tion to sex; God; too young; getting tired during sex; getting arrested; and the financial expense of sex. Some students listed more than one fear.

It is important to note that the significantly disproportionate mention of fear of HIV (87 percent) relative to fear of pregnancy (10 percent) draws attention to Uganda's recent history with national development priorities and flows of international funding. Unlike the neighboring countries of Kenya (see Ahlberg 1991; Thomas 2003) and Tanzania that have had continuous and internationally funded family planning campaigns throughout the 1980s and 1990s, Uganda's sexual health efforts since 1986 have focused primarily on HIV/AIDS education and reduction. The difference in priority is in large part because much of Uganda's development programs and international funding ceased during the nation's internal insecurity during the regimes of Milton Obote (1963–1971 and 1980–1986) and Idi Amin (1971–1979). When the country emerged from civil war in 1986, the politically astute President Yoweri Museveni welcomed aid from international agencies that were eager to situate themselves at the "epicenter" of the AIDS epidemic. This act brought in a flood of foreign donors, development workers, and public health specialists (Bond and Vincent 1997; Lyons 1997).

6　These kinds of contradictions between the stated ideals and what actually takes place in managing the sexual risk experienced by young people are regular aspects of life and are stimulated by the heightened anxiety surrounding youth sexuality. For a detailed discussion of one possible way this contradiction can be articulated locally, see Parikh 2003a.

7　There are notable exceptions including *Straight Talk*, a monthly newspaper feature insert for youth. Like other public attempts to address sexuality, the organization receives continual monitoring from many sides: one prominent Catholic clergymen called the program "condom pushers" while other concerned groups say the publication does not go far enough.

8　There is a growing literature on youth sexuality and modernity in East Africa. See, for example, Durham 2000; Fugelsang 1994; Mutongi 2000; Parikh 2001; Smith 2000; Stewart 2000.

9　Lusoga is the language; Musoga refers to a single person and Basoga is the plural form; Busoga is the region; and Kisoga is a noun that is used to indicate things of the Basoga people, such as Kisoga dancing.

10　The Luganda spelling *ssenga* is more commonly recognized in public culture in Uganda than is the Lusoga *sôngá*, and the former is used in print materials such as newspaper advice columns and articles and in the terminology of counseling centers. The predominance of the ssenga spelling is because many media outlets are located in the Luganda-speaking capital and because of the historical and contemporary dominance of the Baganda (the ethnic group that speaks Luganda, who live to the south of the Basoga).

11　In an article in the *Boston Globe* on 28 October 2003, correspondent Rachel Scheier chronicles daily activities of a modern-day professional *senga* (*sic*) in Kampala as she hosts a two-hour radio talk show, runs a monthly seminar, and offers private consultation to an audience composed mainly of married couples and young adults seeking love. She notes that AIDS education methods featuring the ssenga are now being tested, but the idea has received some criticism from university students for being too old-fashioned.

12 It is difficult to know exactly when this ideal system existed in practice, but it is likely that it started around the beginning of the twentieth century. This estimate is based on the general history of British colonial presence, elders' accounts, and works on similar sexual education systems in southern Africa (e.g., Jeater 1993). Previous ethnographic work was undertaken in the same subcounty by anthropologist Lloyd Fallers (1957, 1965, 1969) in the 1950s and early descriptive accounts by missionary John Roscoe (1911, 1915) were based in Uganda from 1893 to 1911. This substantive part of the historical account presented in this essay has been constructed from my interviews with elders.

13 While no one with whom I spoke mentioned same-sex sexual activity, this does not mean that same-sex desire or activity does not exist. Historically what is important is that individuals marry and reproduce, which is seen as the proper role for adults. Engaging in same-sex sexual activities at one point in life (for example, at boarding school) can be overlooked if the person actualizes his or her adult duty of marrying and reproducing. In much of East Africa, the practice of female-female marriage locally is not seen as a same-sex sexual activity because of the nature of the union. Specifically, another woman is brought into a marriage between a male and female with the purpose of bearing chidren for a barren wife or a wife whose profession or occupation financially and socially enables her to fulfill her reproductive obligations through another woman. Such a union is labeled a female-female marriage because the wife is responsible for identifying a surrogate mother and paying bridewealth and her upkeep.

While I was in Uganda from 1996 to 1999 and again in 2002, there was a heated public debate about "homosexuality" (the term used in the media and public speeches). The dominant thought expressed was that homosexuality is a sin imported from the West and did not exist in "traditional" Africa. In much of the debate, there is a conflation of same-sex sexual activities and "gay" identity that may not have existed before. Similarly, Murray and Roscoe (1998: xv) write: "Today, especially where Western influences (notably Christianity and Marxism) have been strong, the belief that homosexuality is a decadent, bourgeois, Western import has become common."

14 Fallers (1969: 96) recorded that 30 percent of the cases brought to the local African courts involved disputes by males over female sexuality. These offenses included alleged violations against the owner of a female's sexuality (e.g., adultery), disputes about the proper owner of a female's sexuality, or a father "harboring" a daughter for whom another man had given bridewealth.

15 Elsewhere in Uganda, such as among the Bagisu speakers, male circumcision ceremonies are performed (La Fontaine 1977; Heald 1999). For Lusoga speakers, however, there is no set age at which a boy socially or symbolically transforms into man.

16 A common ethnic stereotype that I heard among Basaga as well as non-Basaga is that Basaga women are "sexy," meaning that they are sexually less inhibited and care about their own sexual satisfaction. In addition to the practice of pulling and the role of the sôngá, this ethnic stereotype is partly fueled by the long-standing idea that

Basaga women are ideal wives because they work hard yet their families demand little bridewealth.

17 I found little historical description in Faller's work regarding the period between a couple's introduction and wedding ceremonies. Faller (1957: 112) writes: "The bride is secluded until the wedding under the care of an elderly woman, who bathes and anoints her and teaches her wifely duties." During this period of seclusion the girl is to have only limited interaction with people and certainly not with her future husband. In reality, however, this period could extend for an indefinite duration because of difficulties faced by the groom in securing the agreed-on bridewealth and other prerequisites, such as completing his home or paying off debts.

18 In his study of the history of the commodification of cleanliness in Zimbabwe, Timothy Burke (1996: 29) writes that the historical accuracy of the practice of a wife washing her husband after sex is "a subject of considerable debate and ambiguity among women and men today." He found that while men "enthusiastically supported the practice," women held a variety of opinions about it. I did not encounter any outright debate about the practice of washing, however, and it seemed to be a fairly accepted and noncontroversial idea.

19 As Hodgson and McCurdy (2001: 1) observe in sub-Saharan Africa: " 'Vagabond,' 'prostitute,' 'wayward,' 'unruly,' and 'immoral' are just a few terms used to label and stigmatize women whose behavior in some way threatens other people's expectations of 'the way things ought to be.' " As the essays in their edited volume illustrate, women who challenge the "boundaries of 'acceptable' behavior" by surviving without the assistance of kin or husbands, often get cast as sexually immoral. For a historical perspective in Uganda, see Davis 2000.

   Similarly, for residents of Iganga the term "prostitute" (or the Kiswahili word *malaya*) serves as a method of controlling the actions of women by stigmatizing certain behaviors (such as dress, physical mobility, and comportment) and normalizing others. It is a powerful category that is often invoked when people discuss the moral decline of young people, females in particular. Even if a female does not engage in direct acts of commercial sex work, she may be labeled as a "prostitute" by merely appearing to have unrestricted physical mobility and by acting in ways that defy normative notions of female propriety.

20 I will use the Lusoga sôngá to refer to the paternal aunt in Bulubandi, and the Luganda ssenga to refer to the commercial sex counselor who bears the name in the mass media.

21 "Ladies: To Pull or Not to Pull Is the Question," *Chic* 1 (2) (21–27 February 1997): 32.

22 "Dear Ssenga," *Monitor* (Kampala), 11 October 1997, 11.

23 For a similar debate in Nepal, see Pigg 2002.

24 I use the term "cultural scripts" to refer to patterned behavior invoked by young people when describing various sexualized interactions between men and women (see also Gagnon 1990). Scripts are significant in that they become a gendered and cultural toolkit of acceptable or possible behaviors that young people might draw on when they encounter a new sexual situation.

25 A "detoother" is a woman who cleverly manipulates men into buying her drinks or other items, but she does not necessarily have sexual relations with them. This

femme fatale extracts money from the mouths of mesmerized men, hence the notion of "detoothing." She is not seen as a prostitute nor does she lack individual agency. In fact, in local talk and the media the detoother is constructed as a powerful seductress while her male victims are considered powerless and sexually frustrated.

26 Several educated Luganda-speaking women residing in the capital proudly told me that pulling is still done in their areas. While I cannot access the extent of this claim, the statement itself is consistent with the cultural revivalism currently occurring among some elite Baganda.

27 When I was in Iganga no church or mosque had a sex education program for youth. Two visible programs did exist in Kampala: the Baptist program "True Love Waits" and the Catholic program "Youth Alive." Both programs focus on abstinence by offering young people activities (such as worship, skill training, or planning for the future) to divert their attention away from sexual activity.

PART 2

The Creation of Normativities as a

Biopolitical Project

• • •

The second analytic trajectory addressed in this volume—the construction of sexual normativities as a result of the new arrangements of biopolitics and the moral arbitration aroused in their wake—is made visible in the following essays by Leslie Butt, Heather Dell, and Vincanne Adams. The idea of sexual normativity, found under the rubric of some form of "normal sex," is herein identified as a project that in some sense instantiates modernity in most of the contexts where this terminology is used. "Normal" sex is identified by way of its counterpart "deviancies" as a means of pathologizing practices that are seen to be in violation of the moral standards of the modern and/or colonial as well as the postcolonial nation-state. The project of classification (as Cohen notes in this volume) is often seen as central to the possibility of objectifying sexuality as a biopolitical domain. It is also central to the idea that we can read this creation of "normative" sex as a modern project deeply tied to the fields of colonial and postcolonial health development, and nationalism, in and through science.

In diverse locales, ideas about normal sex are brought into existence in ways that simultaneously and alternately play into and contest existing debates over gender identity, the impact of modernization, and the impact of colonial relations. But the possibility of reading this process of "normalization" as distinctively modern is made somewhat questionable by a historical inquiry into the ways that sexual relations are studied, classified, and rendered problematic in not-yet-modernizing contexts and discursive formations found elsewhere in the world. In one instance, a notion of "common-sense sex" becomes formalized in and around state interests in regulating the sexuality of women simultaneously with elite interests in negotiating the push toward modernity. In another instance, the idea of "ordinary sex" is shown to be already highly contested prior to the arrival of modern notions of "sexual" identity and sexuality.

Leslie Butt examines the intersection of competing forces of modernity among the Dani people of Highland Papua (Irian Jaya). Javanese bureaucratic state efforts to govern marginalized Dani in highland Indonesia by way of the deployment of ideas about "commonsense sex" become enmeshed with local gender relations, notably young women who dare to become "runaway wives" resisting traditional marriage arrangements. Butt's point is not simply that government efforts to categorize Dani sexuality as marginal, backward, and most critically, out of control, are instruments for subjecting Dani to the demands of a modern state. She shows the pivotal role of local bureaucrats as they almost indiscriminately select certain highly visible features of everyday modern social life and render them as proof for simplified models of deviance. In imagining and rendering legible a normalized deviant sexuality, bureaucrats plumb the domain of cultural intimacy but rely on highly objectified visual practices to pass judgment and implement social policies. The Dani reclaim power to some extent by appropriating the superficiality of the bureaucratic ideas of "commonsense sex." By dressing the part or resisting it by "running away," Dani both reinforce state ideals of restrained sexuality and provide themselves with a partial means of moving beyond those ideals.

Heather Dell's exploration of sexual practices in postcolonial India examines the unexpected outcomes of an identity politics set in motion by colonial relations and the importation of Western pornography and videos as articulated around practices of contested sexuality today. The construction of an "ordinary sex" of "home" versus an imported "English sex" that includes practices deemed "foreign" by middle-class Indian housewives (oral and anal sex in particular) suggests a conservativism that wraps notions of Indianness into the practices of "acceptable" sexual engagement. But Indian middle-class housewives' certainty that "foreign sex" presents them with the burden of moral and nationalist insult is matched by the equal certainty among some prostitutes that it is precisely this sex, consumed by Indian middle-class men, that will bring them the comforts of financial security and social redemption once they have left their profession. Dell notes that that "the migration of so-called foreign sexual practices into the Indian homeland is a form of inverse deterritorialization" wherein the historic contrast between "respectable wives" and "colonized prostitutes" is rendered indistinct as the foreign is absorbed into home, contested, and yet found capable of "transforming home into the world" in the process.

Vincanne Adams explores the history of Tibetan concerns with things sexual by way of a review of liturgical and popular literatures devoted to the topic of appropriate sexual behavior in the Tibetan historical context. Tibetans historically made distinctions between "ordinary sex" and Buddhist "tantric sex" as a way of noting the moral weakness of the former in contrast to the moral purity of the latter. Political shifts in Tibet ushered in socialist modernization by way of an overt concern with female sexuality. This shift, Adams argues, did not change the fact that sexual intercourse was morally problematic or that it was recognized as a potential "matter of state" in historic Tibetan society. In this sense it would be wrong, she argues, to presume that "sex" as a problematic topic did not precede modernity in Tibet. However, she notes that socialist reforms offered a new set of ethical possibilities with which to think about and practice sexual intercourse. These new possibilities required the production of a biologized sex that was tied to concerns about population, political allegiance, and socialist ethics. Whereas moral concerns advanced by the theocratic state were articulated in rhetorics of celibacy and the virtuous bliss associated with tantric meditative practice, sexual relations and practices under Chinese socialism were ascribed primary importance as vehicles for revolutionary commitment, population-based family planning, and secular rational modernity. Debates over the virtues of this new kind of "sex"—the kind that Tibetans call "sex without love"—are today a foundation for moral debate on the streets and in the nightclubs of contemporary Lhasa. Contestations over this kind of "sex" are tied not only to tensions between government institutional forces and Tibetan traditional conservatives but also among differently "modern" contemporary urban Tibetans. Focusing on the moral object of sex is, for many Tibetans, both a means of rejecting tradition and a means of sustaining it.

LESLIE BUTT

Sexuality, the State, and the Runaway
Wives of Highlands Papua, Indonesia

. . .

In the highlands of Papua, Indonesia,[1] in a valley accessible only by foot or by plane, indigenous Dani men describe how an "epidemic" of runaway wives has shattered their notions of being in control of the political affairs of the valley. These runaway wives are women who abandon their husbands or intended husbands, often leaving at dawn to meet a preferred suitor or to return home to parents or kin. While women abandoning husbands or arranged suitors has long been a feature of highlands New Guinea marriages,[2] Dani men reason that these patterns have changed, especially since 1969 when the former Dutch colony was incorporated into Indonesia and restructured as part of an authoritarian state system.[2] Dani women can now challenge norms within marriage by using new technologies such as easily accessible contraceptives distributed through Indonesia's nationwide family planning program. They now have recourse to a village judicial system that promises to adjudicate runaway wife cases. Increased mobility offers women the opportunity to destabilize a sexuality once primarily constituted within regional exchanges and alliances. During my fieldwork in the Baliem Valley in 1994–1995 and in 2000, for example, I found that in one village almost half of the women had at some point run away from their intended or actual husbands.[3]

The runaway wife problem brings to the fore the effect of changes in the domains of sexuality and reproduction among the indigenous Dani. It also highlights the extent to which the many Indonesian in-migrants who dominate social life in the valley affect the understanding of and practice surrounding sexuality. To these migrants, runaway Dani wives do not confirm the success of Indonesia's efforts to promote family planning, enforce pacification, and instill values of modernization. On the contrary, runaway women validate the reverse: they confirm local migrants' constructions of deviance that are associated with inappropriate sexual desire and behavior. A good modern woman, according to Indonesian in-migrants, simply does not run away.

Since 1969, some seven thousand Indonesians have moved to the Baliem Valley in a steady trickle in order to assume dominant political and economic roles as bureaucrats, civil servants, and entrepreneurs. The Dani, who are of Melanesian descent, are lumped together by these newcomers with other highland indigenous groups under the term *asli* (indigenous, or original). In turn, the Dani call these migrants *pendatang* (newcomers). *Rambut lurus*, or "straight hairs," is also a common term because migrants are of Malay-Indonesian descent, arriving mostly from the islands of Java, Sulawesi, and Ambon, and have straight hair and lighter skin than the Dani. Pendatang now comprise roughly two-thirds of the inhabitants of Wamena, the Baliem Valley's only town, and make up about 10 percent of the total valley population.[4] Like most Indonesians, newcomers have internalized the ideologies propagated by Suharto's New Order regime (1966–1998), which promoted restraint and control in the domains of sex, domesticity, and family responsibilities. Indeed, the regulation of intimate domains was targeted as a necessary step in the successful control of population growth, itself the cornerstone of national development policy. Restraint in choosing with whom one has sex, and how one bears children, have become markers of individual acceptance of "development" and of claims to be "modern" in Indonesia (see, e.g., Suryakusama 1996; Bennett 1999; Blackburn and Bissell 1997; Robinson 1998; Murray 2001; Boellstorff 1999).

The role of the Indonesian newcomer in promoting a restrained sexuality is a crucial feature of local forms of state authority. Monolithic policies are not enacted in remote locations at the margins of the nation-state in the same way that they are conceived and rationalized in the seat of decision making, Jakarta, located some three thousand miles away. An analysis of the normalizing effects of strategies throughout Indonesia misses the key issue of *how* discourses of "normal sex" contained within state ideologies and institutions concerned with gender, domesticity, and development trickle down, and *who* is involved in the process. From this angle, one of the most important means to understand contemporary Dani experiences is to look not at the Dani but rather at how the region's newcomers understand the Dani.

In implementing state objectives, including the ideals of a restrained, family-based sexuality, the pendatang of the Baliem Valley have invented or refined a number of idiosyncratic policies that are specific to the region. I call this regional construction "commonsense sex." Commonsense sex derives its legitimacy primarily from three arenas: ideas of a constructed, racialized Other that places Dani women, and men, as potentially marginal; a discourse of reproductive control that places women's bodies at the service of the nation; and a discourse of sexuality that enmeshes sexual restraint within a host of other domestic accomplishments. Pendatang use their interpretation of the scientific claims undergirding state policies to justify their actions. These rationalizations transform into specific policies and practices at birth control facilities, family planning programs, and clinics for sexually transmitted diseases. In these locations, judgments about hygiene, manners, courtship, and education enable the construction of a commonsense sex that reaffirms the authority of the pendatang by aligning restraint with the modern.

The commonsense morality that is locally constructed and enacted pushes the politics of sexuality and reproduction far into the realm of embodied action. As Akhil Gupta (1995: 378) argues, "everyday interactions with state bureaucracies are . . . the most important ingredient in constructions of 'the state' forged by villagers and state officials." However far these bureaucrats seem to deviate from formal policy, through their practices they nonetheless implicate the state deeply into the "minute texture of everyday life" (375). In this essay, after first reviewing broad-based Dani and Indonesian moral claims about sexuality and reproduction, I explore newcomer ideas of commonsense sex in the Baliem Valley. Notably, newcomers claim to be able to read sexual deviance in appearance, clothing, and demeanor. Runaway women's behavior, for example, is rationalized and simplified as a form of sexual and emotional irregularity, whereas the review of Dani experience suggests that the choices made by young wives intersect with multiple other factors. Here I pay special attention to the health policies implemented in the name of the common good and to how these policies simplify, encode, rationalize, and reaffirm the difference between "subversive, unproductive sexuality and productive, patriotic sex" (Stoler 1997a: 35).

Is There a "Dani Sexuality"?

If the term sexuality is in itself hard to define, claiming norms that are representative of a group is an even bigger challenge. Jeffrey Clark has urged that caution be used in discussions of sexuality in Melanesian societies, where Orientalist assumptions have regularly skewed interpretations about the sexuality of others. He warily suggests, for another highlands Melanesian society, that sexuality is "not just a private affair but a set of public beliefs about the practices and consequences of sexual behavior . . . based in . . . a cosmology which equates sociomoral relations with states of health . . . . It is a reasonably systematic set of beliefs about relations among the body, coitus, and power/knowledge. . . . It controlled young men, children, and women, not through punishment or incarceration but through concepts of pollution and, to some extent, surveillance" (1997: 195–96). Such a definition suggests the extent to which sociality, the interdependence of collective lives, both defines and assimilates sexuality as an outcome of socially mediated relationships among the Dani. Politics notwithstanding, men's and women's behavior reflects back, and stands for, the well-being of the society.

For the Dani, multiple nodes also link sexuality and reproduction. The capacity of men and women to produce healthy offspring is central to the collective ritual and practice aimed at carrying on clan names and bringing honor to a patrilineage. The Dani exchange subsistence crops and pigs in primarily status-driven negotiations, which culminates every five years in a major celebration known as the marriage festival (*ebe akho*). In this polygynous society, young girls are often wed to men many years their senior, who may already have several wives. Ongoing brideprice payments between two families may keep exchange relations alive for several years afterward (Heider 1970, 1972; Peters 1975).

Tied within systems of exchange and marriage are symbolic constructions of female and male potency. Because of these, sex is a site of both desire and ambivalence. According to Dani men, menstrual blood can poison men's bodies, food, and pigs, and they consider vaginal sex largely toxic and potentially debilitating. Women possess an essence that is potentially destructive: drought, famine, and in particular, child death and the cessation of the future regeneration of Dani society, can occur if women merely look at the sacred ancestor bundles that men keep in secret ritual houses. On the other hand, women fear the toxicity of sperm, especially if it enters the body in the wrong place or at the wrong time. The Dani continue to adhere to a strict postpartum taboo, where parents of a newborn child appear to refrain from having sex with each other for up to six years while the mother is actively breastfeeding. If a couple has sex, sperm can enter women's breast milk by traveling up through the body, and the sperm mixing with breast milk can cause the infant to get sick or die. Many men try to initiate extramarital relationships during this putative period of abstinence even as they try to prevent their wives from doing the same. Overall, the dividing practices of gender and generation that are deployed by Dani men succeed in some measure in regulating women's behavior, although women are by no means subservient.

Changes brought about through modernizing practices, state interventions, new technologies, and the media all modulate Dani sexuality. Moral claims about polluting bodily substances, for example, have taken on new hues in the face of enticements such as cash, novel forms of prestige, and changing status values (see also Knauft 1997; Clark 1997; Wardlow 2002). In the Baliem Valley, Dani men and women regularly violate moiety strictures in sexual encounters, and some couples publicly admit to having sex during the postpartum taboo, although child-spacing patterns have been retained. Some women use state birth control. A few Dani women now marry outside the marriage festival, and more love-based marriages take place now than in the past. More households organize along nuclear family lines. Young women are increasingly drawn to the urban center of Wamena, with its commodities, food stalls, and reduced restrictions on behavior. With increasing ease, young women who are unhappy with arranged marriages can justify their choice to run away.

The following case illustrates the complex effects of modernization on young women's choices. At one wedding I attended in 1995, an alliance chief named Ukumhearik, who was rich with pigs, land, and influence, wed his fourteen-year-old daughter Neli to a prominent ally, an equally wealthy man who was older than his daughter by two decades. Neli cried incessantly throughout the entire proceedings, wailing that she was not willing to marry the man her father had chosen, and that she would not stay. Amid the whoops and hollers of women welcoming her into their clan, the chief bid his daughter an emotional farewell (see figure 1). She was then led away from her homestead (see figure 2) to that of her new husband, who was deeply embroiled in the politics of brideprice payments. Neli told me that she already had a boyfriend—a sixteen year old from across the valley—whom she had met during her year at the Catholic boarding school in Wamena, when she undertook, and failed, her first year of high school. Unlike her arranged husband, her boyfriend from school "loved" her for who she was not for whose daughter she was. Not surprisingly, two days after the marriage ceremony she ran away at dawn.

After it became clear that Neli had been welcomed into her boyfriend's family, her father took on the delicate task of mollifying the rejected suitor. Not only did Ukumhearik have to negotiate a return of the brideprice, he also had to begin talks with the family of Neli's boyfriend, who were equally eager

1. Giving away a daughter. Photo by Leslie Butt.

2. A gift of pork. Photo by Leslie Butt.

to establish good relations with him. The terms of agreement got bogged down in petty disputes over the proper allocation of resources and, on two separate occasions, this runaway wife case ended up before the local judiciary. Timoteus, a Dani man appointed village head within the government's village structure, sat with his local advisors in the dusty village office and, after much consultation, pronounced judgment on the case. Like most cases, he judged in the first husband's favor and forced Neli's return. A few days later, however, she ran away again at dawn.

Neli's case illustrates how much the freedom to move through territories once controlled by tribal enemies, and to develop new networks through time spent in town, destabilizes the embeddedness of sex in other cultural processes. Yet for these mobile women, the act of sexual intercourse, which they may or may not engage in with their husbands or boyfriends, is not the most important issue. They are also concerned with the politics of brideprice payments, with asserting their independence, with thwarting parental expectations, and with improving their overall well-being. For researchers viewing the Dani from afar, however, coitus becomes the imagined center from which Dani sexuality emanates.

In 1970, Karl Heider (1972) documented one of the earliest attempts by approximately twenty pendatang, including military and police officers, civil servants, and Dutch Catholic mission workers, to formally regulate the Dani marriage system. These outsiders observing the marriage festival felt that many of the girls were too young to marry. In order to discourage the girls, and ignoring the fact that a space of several years typically separates the event of marriage from the act of consummation, outsiders legislated the following: no girl should be forced to marry against her will; no polygynous marriages could take place; and anyone who married could no longer stay in government school. None of these policies were adhered to at the time, but they set a standard in which concern with sexual intercourse within marriage remained a key feature of interventions in domestic relations.

Informed anthropological research conducted in the 1960s did little to clarify perceptions about sex. In one paper, Heider (1976: 189) describes a culturally generated ethos of sexual restraint among the Dani. It was so encompassing, he argued, that the Dani should be classified as having low sexual energy: "The Dani level of sexuality is so clearly beyond the general range that we will have no trouble in saying that it is 'extraordinarily low.'" Heider based this conclusion primarily on the long postpartum taboo and on an absence of evidence—based on Dani men's equanimous attitude about sex—that this taboo was being violated.[5]

In dramatic contrast, just thirty years later Dani sex is alleged to have gone wild and out of control. According to a recent study conducted by members of Indonesia's Institute of Scientific Research (LIPI), the Dani regularly attend "free sex parties." These are "frequent traditional ceremonies, variously named *pesek*, *tem*, or *wisilum*, and [involve] dancing and feasting, [which] often also include pairing off to engage in sexual relations" (Hull, Sulisyaningsih, and Jones 1999: 32). Researchers deemed these parties a major public health problem by concluding that public events led to frequent events of unregulated premarital sex (Hartono, Rumdiarti, and Djohan 1999; Ingkokusumo 2000; Hull, Sulisyaningsih, and Jones, 1999).

From an extraordinary absence of sex to an extraordinary excess of it: Which is the case? The answer, of course, is neither. But it is critical to note that bureaucrats never took up Heider's ideas about a low sexual energy among the Dani. "Sex parties," "traditional" pairing off ceremonies, and "runaway wives," in contrast, are the constructions widely used to decry sexual norms. Newcomers view Dani sexuality as deviant, and more out of control, than expected or desired in contemporary Indonesian society, and government officials constitute Dani practices as a "serious problem" (Hartono et al. 1999: xvi). In light of this, I now turn to the roots of some of the commonsense rationalizations used to code current ascriptions of deviance.

The "Commonsense Sex" of Newcomers

When newcomers set up their lives in the Baliem Valley they arrive as citizens of the state but also as the local voice of authority. On one hand, they respond to what can be understood as totalizing state ideologies of sexuality from a mainly middle-class vantage point. On the other hand, they use those same values to render legible the domain of sex in others. They transform ideas about sex into specific, local policy based on how they judge what they see. The pendatang arguably do not identify themselves as national citizens or as aspiring middle class as much as they claim the role of local, neutral arbiter based on a rationalized set of "commonsense" ideas about sex. The observations and interviews I carried out suggest that local factors and individual predilections play a vital role. Commonsense sex includes idiosyncratic interpretations of a national ethos of sexual restraint, constructions of racial difference, and proof sought and found in the domain of the visible.

NATIONAL SEX • During the New Order regime (1966 to 1998, and to a significant degree since then), President Suharto harnessed the economic discourse of postwar development theory to serve the interests of his state policies. A highly authoritarian regime, New Order government controlled dissent, quashed efforts to develop a civil society, and gave the military significant political power (see figure 3). In Papua, the military wields considerable economic power as well. It guards its interests through violence and through symbolic displays of dominance which together regulate dissent and undermine local forms of political power. However, the creation of large governing bodies formed only one part of the strategies of rule. Suharto also engineered a hierarchical system of state authority that extended down through regional and village offices through to the smallest level of the state, defined as the household. The claim to have selected the most appropriate "development" for Indonesians serves to render mundane the invasion of the state into everyday, domestic domains, wherein development becomes "an arena in which 'the state' can continuously repeat its raison d'etre and become legitimized in routine processes and events," while claiming to serve "a 'national interest' apparently above politics" (Li 1999: 297).

In the name of "national interest" men's and women's bodies and their sexual and reproductive practices have been opened up to scrutiny and regulation.[6] While the state harnessed the considerable powers of the bureaucracy and the army to implement programs, it also employed subtler means directed at securing the willing cooperation of its citizens, a process that

3. At the "War Festival." Photo by Leslie Butt.

Suzanne Brenner (1998: 227) has called the "refashioning of society from the inside out."

Population control serves to rationalize interventions in intimate realms.[7] Birth control in Indonesia is free and easily available. As the visible, scientific, and technocratic arm of population policy, birth control provides a seemingly neutral, sophisticated, and pragmatic solution to the perceived overpopulation of some Indonesian provinces. A successful way to co-opt the family into prescriptive state ideologies of development and reproductive control has been to enact the "family principle" (*azas kekeluargaan*). This is a key principle of state ideology, which places the family as the funamental unit of the nation. Within this model, the nuclear family—husband, wife, and only two children—embodies the ideals of the small, healthy family. While there is no formal policy requiring women to adopt the family principle, conformity to a domestic, two-child family is nonetheless valorized to such an extent that the model is disseminated widely in the media, in government-run women's activities such as PKK community outreach (Pembinaan Kesejahteran Keluarga, or Support for the Prosperous Family), and in the Civil Servants' Wives Association.[8]

Inextricably linked to these legislated moralities are middle-class values about sex, which Linda Bennett (1999: 54) sums as "silence, shame, and secrecy." In Indonesia, the middle-class draws from Javanese cultural ideals of hierarchy and power, and from Islamic prescriptions promoting deferential female behavior: "meek, passive, obedient . . . sexually shy and modest" (Wieringa 1998: 148). In Jakarta, for example, the categories of *perek* ("experimental girls") and *mimi-momo* (Indonesian girls who sell their virginity for large sums of money) have been excoriated in the press (Utomo 2002). Considerable evidence exists that suggests that while actual sexual practices deviate from ideal norms, sanctions against improper sex are strong enough that a culture of sexual secrecy has evolved in several regions of the country (Jennaway 2002; Bennett 2002). Thus bureaucrats in Baliem Valley, like their counterparts in the rest of the country, eschew unsanctioned sexual relations, decry an essentialized Western challenge to tradition, and privilege heterosexual, monogamous relations as against all others, often lumping all extramarital sex under the derogatory term "free sex" (*seks bebas*).

COMMONSENSE SEX • As the district director of the regional family planning office, Pak Ake trains outreach workers to promote family planning and other health objectives. He also oversees contraceptive distribution, known locally by the acronym KB (*keluarga berencana*, or family planning). In the highlands, clinic workers meeting with Dani women promote Norplant, an implant inserted into the upper arm, and DepoProvera, injections that prevent ovulation for several months. The birth control pill is not available to the Dani, although it is widely promoted elsewhere in the country. The family planning board does not promote condoms in the Baliem Valley because they are associated with prostitution and disease prevention, not family planning.[9] Unlike condoms, which are safe and simple to use, Norplant and DepoProvera are technologically complex, invasive short-term forms of sterilization that Pak Ake deems well-suited for Dani women who are "not yet ready" (*belum siap*) to assume responsibility for taking contraceptives on a daily or as-needed basis.

A number of outreach workers run family planning workshops in the villages across the valley. The pendatang family planning workers I interviewed echo state ideologies about family responsibility and the value of birth control in bringing about healthy families. In three separate interviews, three field workers I spoke with articulated a reductionist logic that they use to promote the use of contraceptives to Dani women. Even though each woman prefaced her summary to me by saying that she always told Dani women that this was her own opinion, the outreach workers all located the production of normal and healthy families in a rejection of Dani practices. Here I paraphrase their position: "Yes the Dani have KB *asli* (traditional family planning methods, notably the postpartum taboo), but this doesn't keep their children alive. If they use our KB, then the women will be able to concentrate more on keeping their children healthy because the women won't have to concentrate on not getting pregnant. This will make it easier to keep their children healthy." This is clearly a tautologous statement, true by virtue of its logical form alone. What is disturbing about a circular argument being used as a motivational argument is, first, that it recognizes no other possibilities. It also places contraceptive use firmly within the hegemonic narrative of the nation-state. Most striking, however, was how consistently the three separate women's commonsense rationalization denied alternative models of families and family planning.

Another commonsense opinion rooted in national policy is the need to restrict birth control only to married Dani women. In the highlands, health services directed toward reproductive control and healthy sexual behavior are geared only for the heterosexual married couple. In an interview I conducted with Pak Ake, he sketched out for me his most recent challenge. After fourteen years on the job, he was now implementing a new state policy called KISS (*kampanya ibu sehat sejahtera*), a campaign to promote healthy and prosperous wives. Of the twelve campaign items, he took special pride in promoting monogamy (versus polygyny); an increase in the age at marriage; breastfeeding; and the use of birth control.

When I asked Pak Ake how he dealt with cultural beliefs in the KISS campaign, he pointed to a pair of photographs on his desk that eroticized two beautiful, young, bare-breasted Dani brides sitting docilely at a marriage festival. Speaking to the photographs, he said, "I respect these people. I listen to them." He says he modifies KISS policies to deal with pragmatic realities, such as being less harsh on polygyny than what is called for in the campaign. But it goes against common sense for him to make full allowance for the range of cultural practices that constitute sexuality, ideas of the body, desire, gender relations, and more. Even after living in the region for more than twenty years, his cultural knowledge is limited enough that he cannot make appropriate exceptions but instead enforces his ideas of common sense.

Pak Ake's biggest frustration has always been convincing the Dani to follow proper protocol. They are the most "difficult" (*susa*) of all the people in the highlands district, he noted. To illustrate his point, he stated that half of all of the Dani women who come to the family planning clinic don't qualify for the services: they are turned away because they haven't obtained their husband's permission to use birth control. "These women want birth control, but they just ignore all the rest of the campaign," he complained. He also suggested that they were too lazy to get the documentation they needed: "These women can just get a letter of permission from the [male] village chief saying they are married. If we have that letter, then they can get KB. But they don't want to go to any trouble." Despite the complexity of Dani marriage patterns, and the antagonistic gender relations often preventing women from taking control of their reproductive lives, fully half of the women who wish to regulate birth patterns are denied the chance because a normative ideal of a spouse, and a supportive spouse at that, is the commonsense criteria by which newcomers such as Pak Ake judge suitability. For Pak Ake, this is merely common sense. Women who use birth control should be married; husbands should be informed; and women who don't have husbands or don't want to tell them about birth control are behaving in such a fashion that they should not qualify to receive the service.

The following case suggests that this commonsense conclusion also reso- nates with Dani ideologies. Deli was a particularly troublesome runaway who generated a flurry of gossip when she impetuously moved back and forth from her husband to her former husband several times over the course of a few months. Some Dani condemned her for setting a bad example; others rejected her actions because she abandoned one child and seemingly caused the death of her second infant. Many supposed she had begun a course of birth control as a means to more readily ensnare a new husband. This abuse of technology was seen "as the worst form of irresponsibility," said one courtroom observer during the judicial wrangling. Many Dani felt that women who use birth control irresponsibly should receive the most severe forms of sanctions. In this case, the discourse of villager and civil servant on the "appropriate" use of KB closely parallel each other: both rely on a commonsense assumption—imagined and enforced locally by civil ser- vants such as Pak Ake—that KB should be used only by married couples.

COMMONSENSE RACISM • In the Baliem Valley one of the most striking divisions runs along the lines of race. The migrant newcomers and the indigenous Dani often construe identity along racial lines. Racial categories have historically played a major role in Indonesian sexual politics, with colo- nial officials regulating sexual relationships on the basis of skin color and on attributes of breeding, character, and disposition (for example, see Stoler 2002). The internal malleability of ideas about a racial essence allows race to be deployed as a strategic category enabling authority. Throughout most of Indonesia in the postcolonial period, however, sexual regulation by race has been replaced with more generalized regulation of the home and family by the state. But in Papua, where Indonesians have arguably sustained the role of colonizer once held by the Dutch, race still matters as a category of difference and a semirigid taxonomy, despite adamant claims to the contrary. The differences in lifestyle, values, social class, and traditions between pendatang and Dani become conflated as racial difference. It is not an exaggeration to say that the Dani fairly represent the primitive other relative to mainstream Indonesia. Among the many isolated groups on the margins of the nation-state, few have as iconic and as visible a status as the Dani, the "penis-gourd wearing," "war-loving," "wife-stealing," "stone-age primitive" of the Baliem Valley (see figure 4). They are endlessly referred to as some of the "most primitive people on earth," not only in media reports and by tourists and missionaries but also by a large number of pendatang who live in the area. As Benedict Anderson (1987: 96) puts it, military personnel tend to see the indigenous peoples of Papua as "racial and cultural inferiors" to the Malay-Indonesian majority. Anderson also argues that these values pervade a government bureaucracy that cares more about Papua and its abundant natural resources than about the people who live there.

If the nation-state's policies have racist overtones then, locally, common-sense differences grounded in ideas of race and class are likely to gain ready support because they echo unstated expectations. The near total dichotomization between Indonesian/ruler and Papuan/ruled that I observed in 1994 to 1995 has been tempered somewhat with the recent increase in political power of Papuan politicians, yet racial values pervade social relations. Inter-ethnic marriage between Papuan and pendatang, while rare on the coast, remains nonexistent in the highlands. Pendatang soldiers may engage in short-term relationships with Papuan women, typically as a temporary live-in lover, or with the woman as an informal sex worker, but not in spousal relationships. Such unions are not prohibited by law; they simply do not happen.

Racism within health care relations often remains overt.[10] The following example demonstrates a recurring pattern of discrimination in the attitudes of pendatang health workers toward their indigenous patients. Pendatang health workers use the term *asli* (a double meaning of indigenous and original) to describe all their indigenous patients. Ibu Tina, the Javanese director of the family planning clinic in the town of Wamena, is an imposing, authoritative woman dressed in immaculate nursing whites. During her tenure, she has implemented a special segregated service in Wamena for family planning checkups: asli days and pendatang days. "All asli are dirty," she

4. Dani warriors. Photo by Leslie Butt.

said, "and newcomer women do not want to be examined on the same table for fear they might catch a disease." To avoid imagined ills, the director has organized the weekly schedule to privilege migrant clientele. The one day a week set aside for Dani women allows the director to clean the clinic for the migrant clientele who use the service on the remaining four days. In commonsense terms, all Dani women are asli and all asli women are dirty. The segregation policy goes unquestioned by the provincial health officer and is supported by the local head of the Department of Health, even though the policies result in reduced access to reproductive health services for indigenous women.

COMMONSENSE ABSTINENCE · Of all the moral claims about deviant sexuality, pendatang have taken the most dramatic affront to extramarital sex and premarital sex. Commonsense sex means monogamous sex within a monogamous union. Pendatang officials widely condemn parties, using putative rates of sexual relations occurring at those events to try to bring a stop to nighttime public gatherings. One advocate even suggested burning abandoned traditional dwellings to prevent young couples from making them a secret site for sexual rendezvous.

Newcomers have also attempted to stop extramarital relationships by imposing a fining system at government clinics for Dani patients who are diagnosed with a sexually transmitted disease (STD). Indeed, for the past twenty years, asli patients diagnosed with STDs must pay a fine before receiving treatment at a government clinic. In 1995, for example, therapeutic options for STDs could be obtained at the hospital and at several smaller government health centers where a diagnostic visit costs rph. 1,500 (about US $0.15). However, the fine ranged from rph. 15,000 to rph. 25,000 (US $1.50 to $2.50), or about ten times the cost of the clinic visit. According to Gunawan Ingkokusomo (2000), the fine system was started at a clinic run by missionaries outside of the Baliem Valley. The mission, opposed to adultery, established the fine in order to try to reduce rates of extramarital sex.

By 1985 the regional clinic directors, all Indonesian migrants, had agreed unilaterally to impose the fining system at all clinics in the highlands district. Even though this fining system was never approved by the provincial health ministry, it has been applied consistently through to the present. As Ingkokusomo (2000: 26) cryptically states, "the fine was effective," by which he means that a steady number of people came to the clinic and were fined. What is less clear about this practice is the logic through which it became common sense to assume that there was a necessary effect between Dani extramarital sex and STDs in the first place. It also presumes a positive association between fining and a renewed commitment to monogamy. Ironically, the fine came to be applied to all patients who needed treatment for an STD, not just married patients. The goal of promoting monogamy, which had given legitimacy to the policy in the first place, faded in importance as the fine came to apply to any indigenous person with an STD who requested treatment.[11]

Another direct regulatory mechanism aimed at pre-marital sexual practices occurred at the Wamena nursing school. For Dani girls who finish high school, one of the few ways for them to enter the civil service is to take a two-year nursing course. Competition to get into the nursing school is fierce, and once accepted, girls must submit to regular pregnancy tests carried out at random intervals. If the test is positive, they must leave the school. This test thus discriminates against anyone whose pregnancies do not follow planned patterns. According to Pak Topy, the nursing school director, the nursing school is limited to unmarried women because husbands often claim the right to interfere with their wives' school program. Also, married women are likely to get pregnant, he notes, and drop out of the program. He claims that antagonistic Dani gender relations force him to make up these policies, rather than recognizing the extent to which assumptions about a deviant Dani sexuality provide him with the categories by which to curtail access.[12]

Young Dani nursing students are mostly compliant regarding these requirements. Some young women drop out after a time, but most know that in order to get through nursing school they have to avoid sexual intercourse for a three-year period. Sexlessness in women is thus equated with seriousness and moral purpose, and many of the young women at the school take propriety to exceptional levels by emulating the actions of their pendatang supervisors in clothes, dress, and deportment. They revile those women who seem to take marriage as fluid and brittle, and they draw on burgeoning class aspirations and essentialist constructions to make every effort to paint themselves as different from women caught up in "traditional" ways. One young Dani nurse, a twenty-year-old named Robina, began work at the STD clinic at the Wamena hospital immediately after graduation. She took great delight in demanding that patients pay their STD fine. The monogamous wife of a man engaged in extramarital sex is as much to blame as the husband, she argued. If the wife had behaved well, she reasoned, the husband wouldn't go off looking for another woman. According to Robina, anyone who comes to the clinic with an STD is automatically at fault. As she says to the patients: "You went walking on the wrong side all on your own [kamu jalan salah sendiri]," then she adds, "now you have to pay up."

Common Sense at the Margins

As I fly over 150 miles of jungle and jagged mountains separating the valley from the capital on the coast I am reminded how far away development activities in the highlands district are from the state ideals. In an environment where mudslides wash out roads with alarming regularity and clouds control the volume of air traffic there is little hope of achieving the standard of orderly, organized health and reproductive services sought by the state. As Steve Ferzacca (2002) has noted for other parts of Indonesia, the technologically sophisticated treatments that would reinforce the state's modernist goals are neither always available nor always appropriate. In the Baliem Valley, timed birth control technologies or STD treatment regimens fail to achieve target goals, not just because the Dani are ambivalent about these services but because constantly challenging weather, outdated or missing medical supplies, and desultory distribution can confound even the most ardent efforts to establish a program. Under these difficult circumstances, many pendatang express their commitment to their work and believe that they are doing the best possible job.

Doing a good job requires local knowledge. In other regions subject to intense, if inconsistent, development efforts, interpretations of development and scientific discourse are also used to legitimate claims about local values. The province of Papua is no exception to this. But the way these local values are created and contested is more than a realistic local modification of authoritarian policies. In a critical reassessment of the discourse of Indonesian "development," Tania Li (1999: 295) clarifies the two-pronged nature of state efforts to constitute governable subjects. The first achieves its effect through multiple processes of normalization, including those in the domestic realm; encouraging monogamy by building houses designed for nuclear families is one such strategy. However, a second process is also at play, and it surfaces in the places where the actual accomplishment of rule plays itself out—that is, in the space of cultural intimacy.

The manipulation of assumptions about sex and how people engage in it also helps constitute subjects. This domain, unlike the architecture of houses, is particularly subject to commonsense rationalizations. Constructions of an improper sexuality are far more likely to occur in groups classified as marginal by the state because constructions of sexuality—which can be neither proved nor disproved—offer an optimal means to establish and legitimize classifications of order and disorder on the periphery. Those who use commonsense sex to reinforce state systems draw sometimes on certainties offered in scientific claims and at other times from authoritarian decrees. Common sense is reductionistic, and as Margaret Lock and Mark Nichter (2002: 11) argue: "Reductionist correlations of risk . . . provide those who are so inclined with a seemingly 'objective' and scientific substitute for other forms of prejudice." Available technocratic solutions such as "appropriate" birth control usage and idealized "normal" sexual relations help confirm imagined difference by linking together local practice with broader regulatory objectives.

One of the most intractable difficulties with refashioning society from the inside out is that many processes remain invisible according to standards of legibility. The entire exercise of state regulation of the minutiae of sexuality must necessarily depend on forms of objectification of visible practices and of inventing categories or units that are visible. This objectification, according to James Scott (1998: 183), needs to occur if the state is to succeed in refashioning its marginal populations, for "legibility is a condition of manipulation." Laura Stoler (2002) has suggested that the power of categories rests in their capacity to impose the realities they ostensibly only describe. Yet, to a certain extent, commonsense sex is less about the management of sex among Papuans than about the appearance of sexual subjugation and a compliant citizenry. If Dani women move into government "healthy houses" built for nuclear-style families, remain married to the father of their child, and attend family planning sessions, they may engage in the most deviant forms of sexual activity without raising as much ire as would a woman who conforms to state sexual ideals but does so in such a way that appears otherwise (see figure 5). The amount of effort expended in the Baliem Valley to imagine and render legible a deviant sexuality can hardly be justified through centrist objectives alone. Efforts such as the STD fine or the convoluted logic of KB outreach workers reinforce not only the objectives of the state but the necessary deployment of locally relevant categories to achieve the appearance of success.

Health messages become more authoritative in nature as they stray from the scientific claims rooting the policy. Pendatang obtain their information almost exclusively through highly ritualized three-to-four-day workshops, where attendance lists are scrutinized more closely than course content. Health seminars are crucial sites where disjointed, incomplete information propels local formulations of commonsense sex. The scientific language of health promotions provides the means to gloss racialized and sexualized categories of difference with a patina of rationalizations drawn from core scientific assumptions. These informative sessions about contagion, the goal of KISS campaigns, or the dangers of STDs offer just enough information to allow participants to claim familiarity with policy and to manipulate it to fit with local understandings. Social categories that are "easy to think" lessen the burden of administration by simplifying knowledge requirements (Stoler 2002: 207).

In many cases the simplification of scientific categories transforms into overtly racist practice on the ground. From the Dani point of view, racial difference has had a dividing effect as increasing numbers of pendatang have moved to the valley. Despite the different backgrounds and experiences of newcomers, real integration with the Dani remains rare. Even among the most dedicated outreach workers in development projects, I have yet to hear any discussion about health and sexuality that was not ultimately reducible to a discourse of "us" and "them." Most Dani are aware of this and distinguish on similarly oppositional lines between the very few pendatang in positions of power who would support the empowerment of Dani in political and economic circles and the vast majority who do not. The simplifications inscribed in categories of racial difference, unlike those more subtly encoded in visual categories of sexual deviance, arguably have a more devastating effect on overall well-being. Notably, the force and feeling encoded within

5. A "model" nuclear family. Photo by Leslie Butt. To all appearances, this family emulates codes of progress. Fredy has a job as
an assistant at a local clinic and Maria makes efforts to adopt the
clothing and childrearing habits expected of her by pendatang. But
Fredy's sexual behavior challenges ideals, and Maria is just fifteen,
having run away from an arranged marriage the year before this
photo was taken.

local constructions of racial difference have legitimated an increase in the use of violence as a strategy of containment, particularly since October 2000 when a racially motivated revenge attack left more than thirty pendatang and Dani dead in the streets of Wamena.[13]

Conclusion

Despite the tendency of many Dani to remain on the periphery of much development activity, they nonetheless are drawn into the work of nation making. Like other groups on the margins, the Dani intimate a possible failure of the state to reach all of its citizens. At the same time, they represent the challenge that state policies can best meet. How they are included makes little concession to the preexisting bases for regulation that are embedded in the structural institutions of Dani society—notably marriage, exchange, and male authority and leadership. The objectification of sex as a moral act reduces the range of possible unions, from polygynous, fluid brittle, and socially embedded forms of marriage, which privilege men, to the actions of runaway wives, which subvert male privilege by allowing a woman the possibility of having more than one long-term relationship over her lifetime. Instead, pendatang-run agencies offer only the monogamous, two-parent, two-child family model in which sexual risk is absent. Development discourse initiated in Euro-American societies propels a heteronormative imperative, buried deep in initiatives such as immunization, family planning, higher ages at marriage, and lessons in parenting.[14] Risk is associated with deviance from norms. Of necessity newcomers must imagine the Dani more simply, as lacking inherent restraint and as being out of control. The homogenizing discourse of development, filtered through the vernacular of commonplace sex, delegitimizes existing cultural structures of constraint even as it undermines the ways that Dani women have chosen to deal with the range of options now available to them.

The young Dani women at the epicenter of targeted policies struggle with the strictures they face. Many women's domestic situations or personal predilections prevent them from taking up the challenges of fuller participation in a "modern" lifestyle. In keeping to the margins they expose themselves to multiple labeling practices, of which "runaway woman" is only one. But in running away they try to create conditions that have the potential to challenge existing regimes of power. Many other women put their energies into conforming. For some, this means following the marriage festival tradition and seeking to gain power through having children and regulating the domestic domain. Others emulate newcomers and embrace their notions of common sense. Among the young women who are admitted into the nursing school, for example, one popular activity involves having a photograph taken of themselves in a photo booth, against a backdrop of an imagined exotic locale. To prepare for the photo the girls cake their faces in a white powder to create the illusion of lighter skin, and they grease their hair back into round, smooth buns similar to those worn by straight-haired beauties in state promotions. They apply bright red lipstick and pose awkwardly in conservative dress and high heels. Between this extreme image of demure conformity, and the eroticized images of Dani brides in Pak Ake's office, lie a host of power-laden confluences of desire and sexuality. It takes the docile, bowed-down bride-in-waiting on Pak Ake's desk, the white-face conformity of the schoolgirl, and the dashing, defiant runaway on court trial to validate commonsense judgments and to create the local conditions for moral constructions of difference so vital to the broader narratives of progress.

Notes

1 Papua is the most recent name given to this former Dutch colony. It was formerly known as Irian Jaya from 1971 to 2000, and this name is still widely used by Indonesian officials in the central provinces. From 1949 to 1971 the province was called West Irian (Irian Barat). To further confuse matters, the province is regularly called West Papua, a term used widely by political dissidents in the province and their supporters outside of it.

2 On the basis of accounts from highlands New Guinea there is evidence of a long history of women who run away from their husbands. Reasons have been variously attributed to notions such as a fluid form of marriage in which alliances are easily made and broken or to norms where men hold a privileged status in constituting relations of inequality favoring them. For example, see Brown and Buchbinder 1976; O'Brien 1969; and Butt 2001a.

3 My research in Indonesia in 1993, 1994–1995, and 2000 was funded by a Social Sciences and Humanities Research Council of Canada (SSHRCC) doctoral dissertation grant, a SSHRCC standard research grant, the Office of the Dean of Humanities at the University of Victoria, the Asia-Pacific Foundation, and a McGill University graduate studies fellowship. I am grateful to the Indonesian Institute of Sciences (LIPI), to Cenderawasih University, and to the WATCH Project and the Eastern Indonesia University Development Project for facilitating portions of this research. Editorial insights from Vincanne Adams and Stacy Leigh Pigg helped sharpen the arguments in this essay. An earlier version of this paper was presented at the American Ethnology Society annual meeting in February 1999. The names of all of the people in this paper have been changed, although the places and institutions have not. All undocumented quotes are from my interviews and notes taken during my field research in 1994, 1995, and 2000.

4 There are approximately sixty thousand Dani along with about five thousand indigenous people from other parts of the highlands living in the Baliem Valley.
5 Over a decade after Heider conducted his research, Van der Pavert (1986) recorded a
complex ritual that seemed to challenge Heider's claims that the Dani exhibited a
low sexual energy. The *ima wusan* ritual absolved Dani participants of blame for
engaging in sexual relations with members of their own moiety. Clark (1997) has
also critiqued Heider for basing observations on a Euro-American conceptualization of sexuality that posited a naturally strong sexuality controllable through cultural mechanisms.
6 Women take center stage in efforts to contain sexuality and reproduction. In Indonesia gender constructs serve as a means to emphasize progress and renewal of the
"masculine" state, often at the expense of idealized communitarian village values or
other "traditional" ways, which are often depicted as "feminine" (Sunindyo 1998).
7 A partial list of the social policies directed at regulating reproduction and sexuality
includes a regulated sex work industry; a marriage law establishing age at marriage; a nationwide family planning policy; policies promoting "small, happy, and
healthy families"; and the regulation of sexuality through informal and formal
means among civil servants and other state-sponsored groups such as the Civil
Servants' Wives Association.
8 Regarding the media, see Sunindyo 1998; Brenner 1999. For PKK see Newberry
and Ferzacca 1999. For a critique of the Civil Servants' Wives Association, see
Suryakusama 1996. For regulation of prostitution, see Hull, Sulisyaningsih, and
Jones 1999.
9 Contemporary AIDS prevention efforts have to date had limited success in modify-
ing this widespread association.
10 While many locals have articulated this point in informal conversation, it is only
very recently that Indonesia's research institute has formally acknowledged the
problem of racism within health care services (it was stated in a widely distributed
report in 1999). See Hartono, Rumdiarti, and Djohan 1999; Hull et al. 1999b; and
Butt 2001b; Butt, Numberg, and Morin 2002.
11 At present, two of the clinics have stopped charging for drugs for STDs and it is
expected that others will follow soon. Rates of STDs, treated or not, skyrocketed
during the time of the fines.
12 Rather than test girls for pregnancy, a more productive test would be to interview the
husbands of potential students. The director presumes that sexual activity indicates
an absence of commitment on the part of the girl.
13 In late 2000, political strategists in Jakarta, concerned with the strength of the local
Papuan separatist movement, particularly in the highlands, strategically incited
racial hatred among the Dani by taunting separatist youth at a flag-raising event.
Angry youth gathered and murdered some thirty pendatang soldiers and women
and children before dispersing. Mote and Rutherford 2001 provides a full analysis
of this event.
14 Bornemann 1996 argues this point more generally; Boellstorff 1999 describes its
effects on gay identities in Indonesia.

HEATHER S. DELL

"Ordinary" Sex, Prostitutes, and Middle-Class Wives: Liberalization and National Identity in India

· · ·

In their struggle for power, colonial nations and the people they have colonized have leveled the charge of women's sexual impropriety or even sexual depravity against each other. Among the colonial powers of Europe in the nineteenth century, normative sex "was put forward as the index of a society's strength, revealing both its political energy and its biological vigor" (Foucault 1978: 146). In European ideology, women's sexual propriety was one key index in measuring the moral superiority of nations, which could then be ranked in a hierarchy ranging from civilized to savage. In the British colonial encounter, England ranked itself at the apex of civilized development, with India imagined to rank far below it. This ideology of sex as a measure of political power was often compelling both for colonials in the British empire and for those peoples they colonized.

How have Indians used not only sexual discourse but also sexual practice to contest social territory in colonial and postcolonial India? Under colonialism, the Indian middle class constructed a nationalist/colonial difference between the ideal Indian middle-class wife and the proletarian prostitute. They used the wife ideal to locate a domain of nationalist, class-based respectability that supposedly stood quite apart from colonial influence. In contrast, they constituted the prostitute as the ideal wife's other: a sexualized, disreputable identity that symbolized the threat of colonization as well as a loss of class standing. The former became a woman sheltered and surviving inside the Indian nation in the face of an occupying foreign colonialism. The latter, the prostitute, became a boundary subject positioned on the divide between Indian nation and British Empire.

These icons of femininity embodied the imagined difference between the Indian home and the colonized world. Yet in postcolonial India the wife/ prostitute opposition is being challenged due to the influx of pornographic videos into middle-class homes, which in turn is creating "new" sexual demands in ways that change the division of sexual labor between wives and prostitutes. Because these videos and the practices depicted are sometimes called "English" sex, meaning oral and anal sex, they resurrect debates about what is Indian and what is foreign. Even more frequently, however, the debates are marked implicitly though an insistence on "ordinary" sex. The shift in the sexual division of labor between prostitute and wife has now made it possible for an interesting inversion to occur in the opposition between wife equals home and prostitute equals foreign world. Indeed, the prostitute is now capable of becoming a bearer of "home" by her ability to refuse "English" sex while the good wife may be asked to become the purveyor of the "foreign" in the intimate site of the home itself because she may not be able to refuse the sexual desires of her husband. This inversion is not, however, complete or tidy, as I will explain below.

Oral and anal sex are not new to India: such "newness" is an invented absence because these practices have been depicted in books, paintings, and temple sculpture in India for centuries. As one Indian doctor remarked to me with irony: "If you go through the history of the development of sexuality and practices, I think from this subcontinent you could say we have produced the best possible books, . . . if you can visit even all these temples, say the Surya Temple, Sun temple . . . the practice of oral sex and others was there . . . Anything new that appears to a person, it may not be new."[1] Hence what is now thought of as *saheb's* (European) way has played some part in Indian culture for a long time. The "foreignization" of such practices is a major way in which "a nation can consolidate its identity by projecting beyond its own borders the sexual practices . . . it deems abhorrent" (Parker et al. 1992: 10).

In considering this "new" shift in sexual demands on wives and prostitutes, I adapt Arjun Appadurai's (1996) term "deterritorialization" from the use he gives it in marking the migration of bodies. Instead of looking at how immigrants struggle to reconstruct their imagined communities in a foreign location, I offer a preliminary exploration of how the migration of so-called foreign sexual practices into the Indian homeland is a form of inverse deterritorialization, seemingly transforming home into the world, a foreign place where social reproduction becomes a similar source of struggle. This inverse deterritorialization is taking place in the globalizing market of world capitalism and, more locally, in an India that has recently implemented a liberalization model of economic development. Due to its liberalization policy, India has recently opened its borders more fully to a phenomenal flow of goods, including "English" sex videos. The permeability of India's borders in a transnational world has intensified a debate about how to maintain and reshape a national identity and its national sovereignty. In this essay I suggest that sexuality, not simply gender, is pivotal to this negotiation of the home versus the world, or national identity constructed against what is said to be foreign. The colonial Indian history of the wife versus the prostitute and the construction of the good woman of the nation shaped current Indian culture, and it is here that I begin this examination.

Respectable Wives, Colonized Prostitutes, and Nationalism in Colonial India

Sexual discourse had been a locus for constructing "indigenous" and colonial identities even before the British first arrived in India and sent runners to villages to recruit women to service the sexual demands of their troops (d'Cunha 1991).[2] Sexual discourse was further reshaped in the rise of industrialization in the eighteenth and nineteenth centuries that brought thousands of male villagers to factories in urban areas like Calcutta in Bengal and thousands of rural women to brothels to "provide" for them. The impetus for these changes in the economy has been explored extensively elsewhere (Dell 1999; R. Chatterjee 1993); what is important for this discussion is the notion that "common prostitution" became an icon for aspects of colonialism—or foreignization—in the eyes of the rising Bengali middle class, or *bhadralok*.

In the nineteenth century, India was a society under pressure from the British who often used selected depictions of "barbarically oppressed" Indian women as a means of legitimating their direct rule over India. At the same time, after the Great Rebellion of 1857 the British administration brought in far more troops to hold India—troops that were assisted in finding sexual gratification among Indian women. Members of the administration argued that this supply to *lal bazaars* (or regimental brothels) in no way was an imposition on Indian society because prostitution preexisted British occupation and was said to be less stigmatizing to women in India than it would be in Britain.[3] It was a society where the British often took female seclusion as an index of oppression and yet also instituted the Contagious Diseases Acts that allowed Indian women found outside of seclusion to be branded as prostitutes and subjected to arrest, gynecological examination, and extended treatment in a hospital (Ghosh 1994). In short, British rule left the identity of respectable Indian womanhood and therefore the bhadralok without much physical or ideological ground to stand on. It is little wonder therefore that for the bhadralok sexual discourse as well as sexual practice together became an intriguing yet frightening site for contesting the boundary between the "indigenous home" and "colonial world" as well as the divide between the newly emerging Indian middle class and those deemed below them.

Many scholars of South Asia have written on the construction of the idealized Hindu woman as a representation of a nascent Indian nation (P. Chatterjee 1989; Mani 1987; Nair 1993). Partha Chatterjee (623) argues that the formulation and survival of an Indian nation in the belly of a British Empire made it necessary "to cultivate the material techniques of modern Western civilization [in the outer sphere of work] while retaining and strengthening the distinctive spiritual essence of the national culture." Recent analyses of the formation of the idealized *bhadramahila* (or Bengali middle-class woman) place emphasis on the woman as guardian and preserver of broad notions of Indian morality. Centrally, these women were not to "become *essentially* Westernized" (627).

In bhadralok discourses on sexuality, the emphasis on respectable Indian reproductive femininity at home highlighted the dilemma of social reproduction in a disjunctive colonial world (Appadurai 1996). Modesty and chastity—sexual practices that create and maintain social distance—were crucial to Indian nationalist claims that Indian women were culturally superior to and separate from women from the West. In contrast to Partha Chatterjee's early emphasis of the binary between the uncolonized Indian private sphere and the colonized public sphere, Dipesh Chakrabarty (1994) offers evidence that the Indian home was never as purely "uncolonized" as we might think. Instead, Bengali middle-class domesticity contained contradictory impulses that made it unstable. It emphasized domestic improvements that accommodated colonialism as well as retained aspects that resisted assimilation into British habits.

Bengali elite domesticity drew on "the promise of 'improvement', of being allowed into the tiny coterie of the 'leading' nations of the world" that made the "Victorian fetishes of 'discipline', 'routine' and 'order' . . . the most privileged elements in Bengali writings on domestic and personal arrangements" (55). According to this construct, these attributes of the European home were extolled as the key to political empowerment and prosperity that the Bengali elite home required. The work of the elite Bengali housewife was to establish a highly rationalized routine that her family could count on, including providing direct care that would improve her children's physical and mental vigor and running the home economically as commensurate with household income.

At the same time, this rigorous improvement, however transmuted by Bengali culture, was problematic. It structured the household in terms of the demands on men of participating in the colonial civil political sphere with its long working hours and punctuality. An alternative elite domestic sphere was envisioned as a separate space that allowed the bhadralok householder to leave the self-in-the-world on his doorstep for a more spiritual, transcendental self within the home. The purification of bathing, a change of clothes, and a different sense of duty within the family were only some of the ways the bhadralok household was constituted as an alternative sphere, a location where Indian nationhood could survive and flourish until independence could be obtained. In these two constructs, Chakrabarty (1994) suggests, the ideal household and ideal bhadramahila as both improved and uncolonized were therefore contradictory and unstable in their multiplicity.

The indigenous/foreign instability in the identity of the Indian household no doubt fed the anxiety that Sumanta Banerjee explores regarding the bhadramahila's ability to leave the Indian home and therefore the nation for the apparently freer life of a prostitute. If colonialism was transforming the Bengali household then the movement into the fully colonized world might be enticing. Would women, the chaste guarantors to the Indian culture, forsake their household duties to follow their husbands into the colonized streets? The anxiety regarding the bhadramahila's chastity is clear in an 1846 edition of the newspaper *Tattvabadhini Patrika*: "When they, being imprisoned [in the women's quarters of their homes] see how free the prostitutes are, when many among them find their own husbands addicted to frolics with prostitutes, is it surprising that they also would be fired with the desire for such vices, mistaking them for delights? We learn that many such women have left their homes to join the ranks of prostitutes" (quoted in S. Banerjee 1990: 156).

The ability to transgress this divide made the differentiation between bhadramahila and prostitute even more crucial to the survival of an Indian nationalist imaginary. Due to the strong effect of purdah secluding respectable women in households, the rising numbers of Indian prostitutes in the streets of Calcutta made them one of the most visible representatives of Indian feminine identity in the mid-nineteenth through early twentieth century. These numbers were particularly damaging to the bhadralok because the British administration was able to specify that these women were bhadramahila, because reportedly they were "chiefly recruited from the ranks of Hindu widows . . . women of good caste" (Mackenzy, writing in 1872; quoted in R. Chatterjee 1993: 162).

Members of the bhadralok responded by differentiating the bhadramahila as wife/mother ideal from the *beshya* as the colonized prostitute (R. Chatterjee 1993; Nair 1993, 1996; Banerjee 1990; I. Chatterjee 1990). Hindu high-caste widows and prostitutes who usually had been identified with the same term, *rarh*, in the early 1800s, later became distinguished by the separate terms *bidhabha* for widow and *beshya* or *kulata* for prostitute (R. Chatterjee 1993: 163). Ratnabali Chatterjee examines the discursive centering of the bhadramahila's "virtue" through the construction of the prostitute as her other. Moral tracts that were in circulation emphasized an opposition between the chaste wife (*patibrata*) and the prostitute (*beshya*). The opposition was succinctly set out in the 1874 publication *Advice to Women (Stridiger Prati Upadesh)*: "The good wife, patribrata, is shy silent, does her duty and is totally undemanding, stays away from men, keeps her whole body covered and does not wear flashy clothes." In contrast: "The beshya is loud mouthed, always restless, bares special parts of her body, falls on men, demands jewelry and continuously wears revealing clothes" (anonymous, writing in 1874; quoted in R. Chatterjee 1993: 167). This formulation of the beshya in specific ways echoed Indian elite critiques of Western women as "fond of useless luxury, car[ing] little for [the] well-being of the family, . . . immodest, and somewhat coarse mannered" (I. Chatterjee 1990: 26). Westernization—symbolized by entering the public sphere—for the bhadramahila in the nineteenth century might invite accusations of being "brazen, avaricious, irreligious, [and] sexually promiscuous" (P. Chatterjee 1989: 630).

Sumanta Banerjee (1989, 1990) also emphasizes the process of bhadralok claims to reputation, and therefore leadership, through distancing. Indian newspapers from the 1840s through the 1870s argued for the exclusion of prostitutes from public gatherings. Banerjee notes that the increasing public criticism of prostitutes as corrupters of both the bhadramahila and the young bhadralok was part of the process of segregating "elite chastity" from so-called dangerously promiscuous common women. Bhadralok newspapers and books regularly criticized women performers who had visited high-status women in their homes to the point where the performers themselves were banished from elite domiciles. Still other women who had greater access to the public sphere of the marketplace, the street, or festivals were more often than not excluded from the bhadralok home. These "disreputable" women were literate and comparatively independent Vaisnavite women, women of the working classes, and prostitutes. Sumanta Banerjee concludes that idealized bhadramahila domestic roles and feminine cultural pursuits took on a new "private chamber character" that emphasized "a private and defensive world insulated from the mainstream of the streets" (1990: 167).

The hierarchy of femininities between reputable and disreputable women was inscribed in the more rigidly differentiated social spaces of elite home and street. The space of the bhadralok home was necessary for the creation of the feminine, elite identity of the bhadramahila. This home was built on exclusions of types of femininity damaging to Indian elite respectability—those deemed sexually promiscuous and corrupting. The bhadralok construction of this space of the elite Indian home was central to a claim to social territory within a British colony, a bhadralok space that co-opted British virtues and transformed them by combining them with elite Indian ideologies in order to establish themselves as an elite within the Indian community and fend off British racist accusations of cultural inferiority. Yet, the cultural production of "proper marital sexuality" for the bhadramahila was accompanied by the construction of an "excess" of sexual need for the Indian elite male that had to be directed to prostitutes. The honorable wife as mother and the disreputable, nonreproductive prostitute were two aspects of the imagined landscape of Indian elite masculine identity. Nonetheless, the wife/whore opposition took shape in an increasingly colonized society in which not only sexual discourse but sexual practice was being used to contest social territory.

Sexual Practice and National Identity in Postcolonial India

This bhadralok opposition of the respectable Indian wife and the Westernized whore has reemerged in India recently with the flow of vcRs and international pornographic videos into middle-class Indian homes. Today, some husbands are asking wives to accept "blue films"—sexually explicit or pornographic videos—from the world into the home. And, some are asking their "chaste wives" (patribratas) to view the videos, thereby making consumption into a marital practice. Videos from Japan, the United States, and other countries are thus seeping across the territorial boundaries of these imagined domains of Indian respectability.

This consumption of foreign videos fits Bruce Robbins's (1998: 261) idea of a new global cosmopolitanism, "a long-term process of translocal connecting" that has been supported by an increasingly complicated transnational flow of people and commodities. He argues that Appadurai's invitation to "fish for cosmopolitanisms in the raw" broadens the search beyond Euro-American flows or beyond First to Third World unidirectionalism (Appadurai 1991, quoted in Robbins 1998: 259). Robbins notes that such fishing for cosmopolitanisms "clinch[es] the point that the concept is neither a Western invention nor a Western privilege" (259). Such fishing is well illustrated by Karen Kelsky's (1996) work on vacationing Japanese women's sexual liaisons as a mode of consumption of American men in Western destinations. Although her analysis is complex, at the very least it reverses the Orientalist Madame Butterfly motif of Western consumption of a sexualized East, offering an instance of the exoticization of the West by the East.[4]

For India, in contrast to Japan, things British have not been thoroughly domesticated—and, for many, British commodities are still somewhat alien and colonizing. This may be because India's independence from the British Empire was won just over half a century ago, and until recently India has chosen to remain largely closed to foreign products. I offer this example to challenge models of cosmopolitanisms that suggest either the untroubled or naive acceptance of things Western in nations of the South or an assumption that West exoticizes East, particularly when the commodity is sexual.

Although cosmopolitanism has been marked by "the idiom of travel and the crossing and inhabiting of borders" or "culture as travel" (Kelsky 1996: 175), the most intense impact in Indian may be the consumption of "foreign" commodities that offer a cachet of global cosmopolitanism. The liberalization of the market in India, particularly in the 1990s and beyond, has opened its borders to an unprecedented influx of products, especially media products that bring a "knowledge of the outside world" (Kottak, quoted in Liechty 1998: 109). In turn, the consumption of such "foreign" and therefore "foreignizing" commodities has contributed to a refiguring of this foreign/indigenous instability in some Indian middle-class households. The challenge is to consume what is presumed to be the foreign yet remain normatively Indian. Such syncretism—reminiscent of the nineteenth-century Indian middle-class struggle to absorb and yet render indigenous British middle-class practices—in this current case means availing oneself of the perceived consumption patterns of "the Jones's" and yet steadfastly remaining "the Chatterjees."[5] It is reminiscent of the colonial nineteenth and early twentieth century, but not parallel.

The postcolonial dilemma of national identity is different. The adoption of a neoliberal development policy by India, rather than the older comparatively isolationist self-sufficiency model of development, has thrust the nation more forcefully into world capitalist relations. Rather than dealing with the colonial imperialism of the East India Company that was ultimately directed by Britian, India is now facing participation in a market filled with transnational corporations that are so large and mobile that few countries can easily contain or direct them. (Nonetheless, these transnational corporations are identified with the West and often benefit Western stockholders.) As Gupta (1998: 336) has argued, the entry of transnational corporations due to India's national neoliberal models of development "have made it difficult for policies to be resisted and reformulated by democratic means at the national level." This world capitalist system (and its increasingly speedy delivery of goods across ever more permeable boundaries) has destabilized national sovereignty as well as national identity. This, then, is why the conundrum of consuming "the foreign" and yet remaining Chatterjee becomes culturally significant. It serves as an individual citizen's micro experience of a nation's dilemma on the world market.

In South Asia, VCRs have functioned as markers of middle-class membership (Liechty 1998). The viewing of Western videos, however, is seen as more risqué. For many couples in South Asia, the explicit videos are used as a form of internationalized sex education.[6] They provide a welcome lifting of demanded silences and policed omissions. Two male consumers I interviewed in 2001 contrasted Indian or Hindi films with what they classify as English: "The videos we see are 'outsiders' or Western. But a little while ago I saw a Hindi film like that, but it had nothing compared to English video," stated one. The other continued: "No, it is as good as showing nothing. [Indian films] show the breasts, but it takes forever, ten hours, for her to remove the panties and even when she does, it isn't shown clearly . . . In English video, it's beautifully detailed."

While some welcome the explicitness of "English" video, for many others the videos are a source of marital discord. Tension in some homes may be escalating not simply because of embarrassment but rather because of the husbands' requests to wives for different kinds of sexual practices. Men's requests for oral and anal sex, as depicted by foreign women (and men) in the videos, are being met with objections by some wives. In an interview on 7 July 2001 with two-middle class wives, in Santoshpur, West Bengal, both agreed that they were not likely to accommodate change. As one said: "For people like me who have education and awareness, who know about [oral and anal sex], we know that this is not wrong, that there can be several ways to give pleasure. I think because of the way we are raised, we are [told] or have said that there are things that are wrong, wrong, wrong . . . Naturally, it is very difficult for a woman to change tomorrow. Even if I knew about it and I believe that it is not wrong, still I will not do it myself because that is how I have been brought up." Watching risqué films, never mind enacting the content, may make some women "fear being labeled as loose or vulgar" (Liechty 1998: 118). This has led to a redeployment of nationalist narratives in debates about what is Indian and what is foreign.

These foreign videos, regardless of country of origin, are coded as "English film," with all of the implications of cosmopolitanism and colonization that such a label brings with it. In a global landscape where more sexually focused media programs have been assumed to represent Western consumption patterns, it is important to see that what is identified as English in India has more to do with Indian assumptions about England than England itself. Sexuality, specifically, is often projected onto other nations (e.g., "French" kissing). An article in the *Hindu* invites us to "just look at the names of recently released films—'Red Meat', 'Jealous Love', 'Sexy Tommy.' "[7] While some blue films are of Indian origin, the use of "English" to name them points to a practice of locating them well outside of the imaginary community of the Indian nation. Representing one such perspective in Indian politics, the government of Maharastra in 1995 "vowed to usher in a new era of conservatism in India culture, which in recent years has been dramatically influenced by exposure to the West."[8] Minister of Culture Navalkar recommended a ban on pornography, while new rules against sexually explicit advertising on television led New Delhi cable television operators to stop their coverage of the 2000 Olympics.[9] Yet some censor boards have applied different standards to Indian and foreign films. In the south Indian city of Hyderabad, "English" films are left uncensored by the censor board.[10] But now "English" film, or rather "English" videos, are making their way into middle-class homes. After a century of the respectable bhadralok home being imagined as a "non-colonized space" (Nair 1993), the very intimate relations of some middle-class marriages are becoming subject to a territorial re-negotiation. What is the normative divide between the Indian home and the neocolonial world?

Foreignizing Deviance

Nationalist narratives may code "English" sex practices much like AIDS—as something deviant and therefore foreign. When I arrived in India I was told that many believed that AIDS was not a problem there because Indians were not promiscuous like people in the West. When I began conducting research in a red light district in Calcutta, I was asked if I was HIV positive because my eyes were blue. Social workers explained that sex workers tried to avoid getting infected by refusing to have sex with anyone with blue eyes—in other words, a foreigner.[11] These examples, of course, are clear evidence of how many Indians have foreignized the sexually charged topic of AIDS. The World Health Organization's massive campaign to slow the spread of AIDS in nations of the South has included the circulation of sexually explicit AIDS prevention discourse. This discourse has emerged from earlier development discourse that targeted fertility; in other words, the "high" birthrate that was seen as indigenous to Indian culture. Yet development discourse that focuses on AIDS is seen, at least among many in India, as a discussion of unsafe (read foreign) sexual practices like oral and anal sex.[12] In this case, it is a bitter irony that the problem, as well as the corrective, is understood to rely on a double foreign invasion: first AIDS, then AIDS discourse. Some may wonder if the "cure"—broadcasting sexually explicit information about safer sex—is a part of the solution or a cause of more problems.

According to such views of the foreign, Indian wives as reputed reservoirs of chastity and spirituality supposedly should be exempt from AIDS as well as "English" sex. Nonreproductive sex may be categorized as a perverse activity to the so-called true women and mothers of India. Oral sex, and certainly anal penetration, does nothing to beget sons or even daughters, wives may suggest. Because many women continue to gain some standing in families by bearing sons, the difference between practicing reproductive versus non-reproductive sex has a very real impact on their lives. But, as I was told by one interviewee in 1997, given the imbalance of power within marriage, the denial of husbands' demands sometimes may result in domestic abuse and divorce.

Some argue, however, that the pressure for change is coming from women. A recent column in *India Today* asked if Indian women were shedding the image of *Sati Savitri*, [or] *Bhartiya nari* (i.e., "Indian woman virtuous and pure as the venerable goddess Savitri"), because female bachelor parties, themselves unheard of several years ago, include the screening of blue films, if not a live performance by a male stripper.[13] Husbands and mothers-in-law, therefore, may be the ones objecting to this foreignization or loss of the Bhartiya nari image, not wives. The "foreignization" of oral and anal sex and the revalorization of "ordinary" sex are a renegotiation about the cultural norms of gender, race/nationality, and sexuality.

Yet oral and anal sex as entirely foreign to India is an invented tradition or, more precisely, an invented absence: "If you go to the villages, the rural areas, ancient paintings, people have always used women's bodies that way . . . If you see our *Kama Sutra*, the Western Countries cannot go above that" (Sinha 2001). Indeed, these sexual practices have been described in the *Kama Sutra* and depicted on some temple walls in India for years. While these instances of elite male culture and presumably tantric art cannot stand in for all of India, they do however suggest that these practices have not been entirely absent from South Asian sexual relations. Yet the *Kama Sutra* has been marginalized:: "How many people are educated about the *Kama Sutra*? Even I myself have not really read it . . . and I have been told it is a bad book" (Sinha 2001). The minimizing of Indian sexual diversity through marginalization leaves room, ultimately, for seeing it as foreign, from elsewhere.

Nationalism and Cosmopolitanism in Red Light Districts

Elspeth Probyn (1999: 48), in her research on the figuring of women's sexuality as a central and ordinary part of a national regime, invites us to share her preoccupation with "what different national regimes incorporate as ordinary." She identifies ordinary not only as what is expected but what is assumed to belong within a jurisdiction. I suspect that Probyn would find an excellent example of this notion in the inclusion of "ordinary" sex within the jurisdiction of India and the supposed exclusion of "English" sex. As Probyn states: "In turn, jurisdiction reminds us both of the space in which power is exerted and the modes through which it is carried" (48). A pivotal mode through which power is exerted is sexual, in both discourse and practice. After all, sex has been and continues to be imagined as a central signifier of a nation's political strength (Foucault 1978). What, then, is the space through which national power is exerted in a globalizing world—where world capitalism ships new products at great speed to more and more places, potentially erasing national boundaries as it does so? Does power still reside in the mobilizing of a national imaginary (e.g., being the good woman of India)? Or is power better exerted by being Indian yet cosmopolitan (being an Indian who practices "English" sex)?

Even among Indian sex workers, the division of sexual labor between

Bhartiya nari and prostitute is not so simple. In interviewing Calcutta sex workers in 1993 and 2000, I found that some see themselves as respectable enough to reject the growing demand for "English" sex. "Young educated men," said a sex worker, "they see English movies and they even bring books with them. They want oral and anal sex. But, we refuse." Echoing the discomfort of some middle-class wives, prostitutes in Kalighat officially disparage the practices as disgusting. Remarked one prostitute, "I refuse anal and oral sex . . . even kissing [on the mouth]. How is it possible to indulge in this [anal sex] when one uses it to pass stools? I pray every night, how can I put this thing in my mouth?" What bothers her is this mixing of incompatible territories of the body. Much like the separate sovereignty of India and Britain, these territories do and should have separate functions. "But, to please them," she explains. "I do kiss on his chest, hands, say nice things to him, to make him feel loved." These practices, she suggests by contrast, are normative.

Most sex workers insist that they provide only vaginal intercourse, which they code as "ordinary" sex. As one sex worker said, "I tell them to leave or I just have ordinary sex with them." Even in a tough market like selling sex, such a worker would rather lose a client than practice something other than ordinary sex. In her eyes, Indian men are more likely to ask for out-of-the-ordinary practices if they have lost their supposedly Indian inhibitions through drinking: "People who come drunk are the ones who want the out of the ordinary, and therefore I don't entertain them." Yet the very fact that there is the term "ordinary" sex suggests that there is pressure to provide the supposedly nonordinary.

Some Calcutta prostitutes count themselves less as border subjects and more as women of India—practicing what is collectively assumed to belong in the jurisdiction of India, which means ordinary sex. By this, they work to resist being othered or foreignized themselves. Such behavior, although perhaps not expected, is historically consistent with those sex workers who practiced nationalism in the mid-1800s by raising substantial funds to overthrow British rule during the Great Mutiny and the siege of Lucknow (Oldenburg 1990). Prostitutes then continued to be active in the nationalist movement in the twentieth century, gathering and donating money to the Tilak fund. During this same period, however, Gandhi dashed their hopes of full membership in the movement by refusing to speak to a meeting that prostitutes had organized. Bandyopadhyay (1989) reports that Gandhi also cynically commented that if prostitutes could form socially accepted organizations then why not burglars and ruffians? Nonetheless, sex workers have often taken the role of citizens doing community work. They have been active in maintaining the Indian nation by doing charitable work to help Indian refugees of social upheavals and natural disasters (Dell 1999). Many prostitutes, then, like the good Indian wife, have and continue to locate themselves as women of the nation. Their sexual conventionalism is consistent with this. As one woman said: "Just because I am bad, I don't have to be bad all the way." Among some prostitutes, therefore, there remains an insistence on membership that keeps ordinary sex in place as a normative practice in many prostitutes' everyday lives.

Bad versus good—as it was in the colonial period—is still being negotiated and tied to the notion of foreign versus national. Good or moral practices are inflected with the need to protect a woman's moral and bodily integrity, thus coinciding with protecting the body of the nation. The demands of a nationalist morality are different, however, depending on gender. As Uma Narayan (1997: 409–10) comments: "Men seem to be permitted a greater degree of latitude for such cultural changes, changes that are often not labeled 'Westernization,' where parallel changes on the part of women are. I have only fairly recently begun to see that one common thread that linked what was forbidden to me at various times under the rubric of 'Westernization' involved cultural norms relating to female sexuality." The practice of "foreign" sex by men does not call into question their membership as sons of India. Yet even for women, this good/bad as national/foreign is not holding entirely. As I have suggested, wives may or may not supply this "English" sex, thereby challenging their traditional identities as moral preserves of the nation, while prostitutes may or may not refuse "English" sex, thereby undermining the stigma they face as vectors of "foreign" sexual practices, pollution, and illness.

Sex workers in Calcutta's red light districts such as Kalighat Khidderpure and Sonagachi, however, say that demand for "English" sex is increasing as more young middle-class men arrive with videos, books, or magazines. "Just as days are changing," mused a sex worker I spoke with in 2001, "so are sexual practices. Yes, of course, we learn from foreign movies . . . If a twenty-one-year-old boy watches a blue film, can he stay sane? He has to try it out." And as another sex worker commented in 1993: "Men see a lot of movies and pictures and get stimulated by this. And they know if they will spend Rd. 20 to 25 [US $0.66–0.82] they can have what they've seen." In fact, older men with money should be acknowledged as part of the group creating this demand. Sex workers explain that oral sex provides the stimulation that this older clientele needs to maintain erections and climax.

Some prostitutes have begun to see middle-class "hegemonic masculinity" (Connell 1987) as more problematic than working-class masculinity because working-class men still want the same "ordinary" sex that they have requested for decades. Prostitutes describe those who want "English" sex as "men from Bombay, sailors, men with a little money—a shopkeeper, driver, someone exposed to the world. But not the poor—the rickshaw puller, cart puller, the ordinary coolie. They don't ask for anything else [but ordinary sex]." The working poor tend not to have such ready access to these specific types of global commodities, and hence they do not traffic in the type of cosmopolitanism that constructs middle-class status.

The othering of oral and anal sex is evident in the way prostitutes speak around it by naming it as something that is simply outside the boundary of ordinary sex. The practices also are othered by how clients ask for them by number. Without an illustration, customers can simply say that they want "number two" or "number three." A Calcutta sex worker in 2001 described to me a brothel system in Bombay where requests to view women who would perform "number one" (ordinary) or "number two" (oral) sex were signaled by the flashing of a green or a red light respectively. Number two girls, like the practice of oral sex itself, were seen as less "kosher": "If a girl did number two work, then we told her not to use our plates at mealtime as she has had oral sex. That's when we started writing our names on individual plates . . . We describe [oral sex] as saheb's way." The foreignization of such practices is explicitly accomplished by calling them saheb's way or the European way and by using English terms to refer to them. Oral sex is referred to using the English term "suction" or "sucking." As one sex worker described to me in 1993: "For some women, there are fixed customers. . . . The reason is that these women perform certain sex activities such as [she states in English] 'sucking,' 'from behind,' and so on, which are paid for at a high price by a certain group of customers." The use of foreign terms marks the cosmopolitanism of the product yet also serves to maintain the foreign/indigenous divide. Better to ask for such things in the sordid but exciting language of English slang than to use the Bengali and Hindi that have served as the languages of Indian culture and political sovereignty.

A 1992 study of Sonagachi, the major red light district of Calcutta, tracked "English" sex customers in the eyes of prostitutes. This clientele is seen as middle-class or wealthy men who go to moderately priced or more expensive prostitutes. Most Sonagachi prostitutes reported that they sometimes performed oral sex but rarely provided anal intercourse. Yet the study also suggests that there is a core of sex workers who now specialize in oral sex—

more than 18 percent of the practitioners in Sonagachi (All India Institute of Hygiene and Public Health 1992: 30). This specialization means that prostitutes obtain fixed customers, as they are called, who form a regular clientele. Such financial stability in Calcutta's red light districts, which are crowded with competition, is rare indeed. As one sex worker told me in 2001: "Our women in this line have increased, and so, they try to get money any way they can. This is my body, of example, and I have four chidren. I have not earned a single penny. If a man comes along and wants to do it, then even though it is against my will and desire, I remember the faces of my children and am obliged to do it." Another sex worker recalled a friend whose father, mother, and brother used to arrive to collect the money the woman had earned through oral sex. She did it "her whole life just to maintain her family" who, in turn, did not realize that they were living on something other than ordinary sex. This explains why some prostitutes, even those who count themselves as the daughters of an Indian nation, are willing to offer "English" sex.

Sex workers see the availability of "ordinary" and "nonordinary" sex varying by red light district. Locations like the red light district of Kalighat with its more working-class clientele are seen as sites that provide a somewhat higher percentage of "ordinary" sex. Locations like the larger and more diverse Sonagachi, in contrast, have an elaborate division of sexual labor practices that includes "English" sex. Sonagachi's clientele ranges from daily wage earners to wealthy businessmen who may choose between low-cost prostitutes up through expensive *agrawallis* (high-class prostitutes who claim to be from the central Indian city of Agra). There is no question, however, that the foreign appeal and the local stigma of "English" sex has contributed to this fragmentation and remapping of specific sex market locations in Calcutta.

This fragmentation is not only based on foreign/indigenous or middle-class/working-class codings but also on how well sex workers can "do femininity." Some women deemed beautiful define the boundaries of their bodies by providing only "ordinary" sex. In Kalighat, one sex worker I spoke with in 1993 territoralizes herself in terms of time, bodily access, and practice, "I work between 7 and 10 p.m. only. Because I am so pretty, I don't even take my clothes off. I even hit men that do things that hurt or things I don't approve of [like oral and anal sex] . . . [I do] only ordinary sex." Because this worker is twenty-three and pretty, she embodies Indian notions of youthful beauty. She can exert the power to enforce, therefore, a set of practices that are closer to Indian feminine norms of proper sexuality. She keeps herself modestly clothed, remains comparatively unavailable, and insists that men may only have ordinary, even demure, sex with her during very proscribed hours. If they violate these norms, she punishes them.

In contrast, those women who are seen as dark skinned or who are older cannot easily do the pale youthfulness of hegemonic femininity. Their skin is not "wheat" colored like the young prostitute's and they tend to have, in one sex worker's words, "crossed my age." Because of this they may have to be more willing to violate the norms of ordinary sex. Hence, they may specialize in "special" sex acts for regular clients who pay well.

For instance Renu (a pseudonym), a dark-complexioned woman by Indian standards whom I met in 1993, was saving an impressive Rs. 4,000 (US$131.18) a month in 1993 because of her oral sex specialization. By challenging bhadralok models of social mobility through respectability, then, the increasing demand for "English" sex due to the transnational flow of pornographic videos allows some sex workers like Renu to earn enough to build retirement homes in good neighborhoods. Because of Renu's earning power and consequent respectable retirement plans, she was particularly cautious about participating in my research. "I don't mind being taped. But I don't want photos taken because I want to retire and if they see [the photos of me as a prostitute] where my land is, I won't be allowed to live." She insisted that no pictures be taken in order to protect her ability to cross back over to a respectable life, leaving her prostitute identity behind. Renu's ability to establish a respectable Indian home apart from her work world of "English" sex seems to provide an uncanny parallel to those Indian men who "sullied" themselves by working for the English colonial administration—thereby earning a middle-class income—that in turn afforded them a private household of indigenous respectability. A well-to-do Indian lifestyle, in the inherent irony of (neo)colonialism, may have been and continues to be purchased by some through the wages of supposedly foreignizing practices. Sex workers, who will not perform anything but ordinary sex but know women like Renu in their red light district, will act as go-betweens. "Supposed we get a customer," explains a sex worker, "we tell him that though I may not do it, I can get him somebody who can. So, he sits in my room, drinks and eats, and then I call for the girl and she acts as per his demands. Because he comes to my room and uses it, he pays first my rate; and when that girl comes, she says her rate so that if he agrees, they have the work done. The girl leaves with her payment." This double payment system is one means through which sex workers can earn without directly providing services they find render them less than Indian. Again, it is worth noting the colonial parallel. This "middle man" position also has a long colonial history among some middle-class

Indians who found lucrative ways to have fellow Indians to do what saheb wanted without doing it themselves.

Not every prostitute who specializes in "nonordinary" sex, however, may deploy it as effectively as Renu or those who refer clients to her. Many feel compelled to specialize in this practice that they find repugnant in order to survive as they get older. In this case, "nonordinary" sex becomes a source of serious conflict for prostitutes as it is for some wives, both of whom may not have the economic resources or feminine attributes either to control the sexual practices they perform or to leave prostitution or marriage. One sex worker, Mrs. Das (a pseudonym), whom I spoke to in 1993, insisted that she was not "in the line," as they say. "You see," she explained, "I am married." I asked her why she lived in the red light district. "Because I couldn't find another place to live!" she retorted. She was thirty-nine and dressed with all the conventional markings of a wife. As her landlord intervened: "Although she's married and dresses like a married woman in bangles and sindhur [a crimson streak in her parted hair], her customers are older men who are attracted to her because she isn't good looking and therefore will have to give good service to please them. They are mainly elderly men, all kinds." Mrs. Das presents herself as a patibrata or quintessential good wife, embodying her claim to marital respectability in her dress and adornment. She is thus attempting to mobilize power in her life by taking up this conventional feminine position. Yet this constructed position of wife combined with her middle age and lack of looks does not put her in a position of power with her clients. She must provide the services that older clients demand. Like some wives, she must do as they say to keep their financial support, even if they ask for "English" sex.

Both Renu and Mrs. Das are negotiating an Indian construction of the prostitute/wife divide. Renu constructs this divide in her attempt to move from one (prostitute) to the other (wife; or at least a woman of a good household outside the red light district). Her success will depend on her ability to foreclose her sex worker past, making the distinction as complete as possible. Mrs. Das, on the other hand, tries to live both the sex worker and wife identities simultaneously, even going so far as to obscure her sex work through her proper wifely appearance. In some senses, she uses the wifely identity to gain standing in the red light district and with her clients. Yet her use of old-fashioned feminine power does not serve her well. This is because it calls up in the minds of those around her the restrictions and judgments of "proper femininity" that do not include selling sex. Both women, neverthe-less, are seeking to mobilize a hybrid construction of the prostitute/wife dialectic for their own empowerment in a local market that is increasingly impacted by transnational commodities and practices.

Conclusion

Confrontations are taking place between men and women, middle class and working class, and older and younger generations as to how to mediate the global/local nexus of India in the world. Sexuality is at the center of these postcolonial identity issues. In this essay, I have sought to explore how sexual discourse and practice comprise contested social territory in colonial and postcolonial India. I have discussed how the home and the world dichotomy was deployed to contest social territory in colonial India. The transnational circulation of practices is now complicating and refiguring this dichotomy. The influx of vcr technology and the marital viewing of "English" videos are but one instance of how liberalization is resulting in conflict over increasingly ambiguous boundaries—between private and public femininities, between the national and the foreign, and between male desire and female behavior. This circulation of sexual practices challenges the old gendered nationalist tropes of nation as woman or middle-class honor as feminine purity. "This is kaliyuga [a time of destruction]," mourned a sex worker. "Have you seen the cinemas? Cable TV? I have seen it with my own eyes."

Nationalism in India will continue to construct an imagined community through the exclusion of nonreproductive-oriented sexual practices. Yet, as transnational commodities continue to remap Indian markets, older assumptions regarding the salience of a world/home divide become more problematic.

Notes

I thank the members of Durbar Mahila Samanyaya Committee (Unstoppable Women's Coordination Committee), the organization of sex workers fighting for worker's rights. I am indebted to them for their invaluable insights and experience. I thank Indrani Sinha of Sanlaap for generously providing her knowledge. Rajori Datta Ray's exceptionally insightful interviewing and translations were great blessings. Aloka Mitra's Women's Interlink Foundation provided invaluable research capabilities. I also thank the Society for Community Development for their kindness. I am grateful for comments from Arjun Appadurai, Barbara Ramusack, and others during my presentation of portions of this essay at the American Anthropological Association Meeting in 1997 and at the twenty-eighth Annual Conference on South Asia in 1999. All undocumented quotes in the text are from my interviews and notes taken during my fieldwork research in 1993 and 2001.

1 Smarajit Jana, former director of the Sonagachi HIV Prevention Program and the All India Institute of Hygiene and Public Health Red Light District clinics, interview with the author, 16 July 2001, Calcutta.

2 The sexual discourses produced by foreign invasion have a far longer history in India than suggested by the relatively recent arrival of the British.

3 Trevelyan, the finance member of the governor-general's council, stated in the 1864 legislative council debates that the prostitute was a respectable identity in India (Ballhatchet 1980).

4 As Said (1979: 188) suggests, there has been an "almost uniform association between the Orient and sex." There have been a number of recent studies of how the Western imagination has projected sexualities onto places like Thailand and India (Manderson 1997b; Hyam 1986).

5 Chatterjee is an upper-caste name that often seems as plentiful in Calcutta as Jones is in the United States and Britain.

6 Anonymous, personal communication, West Chester, PA, 25 October, 1997. See also Liechty 1997.

7 Ravikanth R. Reddy, "India: Spurt in Hot Films Screening," *Hindu*, 3 August 2000, online at http://web.lexis-nexis.com/universe/doc.

8 "State to Curb 'Permissive' Culture," *United Press International*, 20 April 1995, online at http://web.lexis-nexis.com/universe/doc.

9 "Asian Marketing," *Asian Wall Street Journal Weekly*, 2 October 2000, online at http://web.lexis-nexis.com/universe/doc.

10 Reddy, India," n.p.

11 I use "sex worker" interchangeably with "prostitute." Relabeling prostitution as "sex work" acknowledges that activity as a form of labor that people engage in to earn a living (cf. Dell 1999).

12 Although beyond the scope of this paper, much could be written here about how AIDS as a "foreign" disease parallels and serves as a metaphor in some Indian nationalist imaginations for the terrible cost to the Indian body politic of having joined the world market as a result of the government's neoliberal development policy.

13 Lohar Kala, Robin Abreu, Kanchan Apte, Anna M. M. Vetticad, Methil Renuka, and Labonita Ghosh, "Girls Night Out," *India Today*, 1 May 2000, online at http://web.lexis-nexis.com/universe/doc.

VINCANNE ADAMS

Moral Orgasm and Productive Sex:

Tantrism Faces Fertility Control in

Lhasa, Tibet (China)

. . .

Tibetan tantric Buddhism has long been devoted to the exploration and particularization of sexual intercourse, focusing on not just the passions but the movement of bodily fluids, the harnessing and control of sexual energies, and the "appropriateness" of sexual relations among the genders. Its more important focus, however, has been the spiritual and moral possibilities of ecstatic states of orgasm. At different historical times and in different lineages of Tibetan Buddhism we find reference to distinctions between what might be called "ordinary" sex and the religious practices of tantric "sexuality" as distinctions that emerge within (local and debated theorizing) on "sex." Still, in Tibet, religious debates had an enormous influence on more widespread cultural ideas about appropriate and inappropriate, healthy and unhealthy, and beneficial and harmful acts of sexual union, no matter where and among whom the acts were pursued.

In what follows I explore the meanings of "sex" in the Tibetan historical context, noting that although practices of intercourse were written about, thought about, condoned, condemned, and in some sense preoccupied Buddhist Tibet, we might also consider how different the meanings of this "sex" were from those that are now also found in contemporary Tibet. The momentous events of the past forty years, most significantly the effort to implement socialist fertility control policies, helped turn sexual practices and norms into secular state possibilities. Folded within the state's efforts to mandate fertility control were efforts to get Tibetans to think in new ways about their sexual acts in relation to class identity, reproduction, and state-directed modernization. These efforts contrasted dramatically with the religious contexts within which Tibetans historically were asked to think about sex. These transformations point, in the contemporary context, to a set of contested meanings of "sex" in and around its moral possibilities. I begin here with the historical religious contexts.

In framing this analysis I work through two kinds of materials. One is historic and derived from textual materials, with additional insights provided on the past by informants with whom I have worked in Lhasa Tibet. The other comes directly from my field research in Tibet that I began in 1993 and is ongoing today. Here I start with an introduction to the Buddhist canonical views of sexual intercourse. I then turn to historical information about the various ways that concerns with sexual activity became visible to Tibetans in an old Tibet. I then pursue the meanings of this historical framing of "sex" by way of the available literature and languages of sex. Finally, I contrast these meanings with contemporary insights about the new meanings of sex that are available in the words and actions of contemporary Tibetans.

Sex in the Buddhist Canon and in Historic Tibet

"[In] dealing with the tantras, it is, in fact, difficult to say where a ritual, whether external or interior, is described in sexual terms, and where a sexual act is expressed in ritual terms" (Kvaerne, cited in Faure 1998: 52).

Bernard Faure points out that despite the enormous amount of attention paid to sexual desire in Buddhism, and despite similar discursive operations, it would be wrong to identify a *scientia sexualis* (Foucault 1978) for the historical Buddhist textual approaches to sexuality. Although similar to European discourses on sexuality in that sex was "simultaneously repressed and celebrated in Buddhism, [it] never treated sex in isolation, but always as an element of general discourses on desire or power . . . Sexuality was perhaps not, as it is in our society, the central, organizing principle around which the notion of the self crystallized" (Faure 1998: 10). Indeed, the very idea of a "self" was parsed quite differently in Buddhist discursive traditions, but more significantly there was nothing one might call a "Buddhist sexuality" that emerged from this set of liturgical concerns. The notion that one has a "sexuality" as a central aspect of the self in relation to a discursive apparatus of governance, scholarship, or even social relations—a concept distinctively rooted in Western history (Weeks 1998)—is not found in historical Tibet, despite the fact that the acts and motivations for sexual intercourse were much written about, struggled with, identified, and explored.

In general, Buddhist concerns about sex were and are ambivalent, a point well made by Faure. Throughout the Buddhist canon we find evidence of both normative prohibitions on sexual acts and sexual relations—in which these are taken as sites for the production of the poison of desire—and the idea that transgression of this prohibition (that is, fulfillment of sexual desire) can be the very key to the highest Buddhist spiritual achievement. Harnessing the passions of sexual desire, when aroused by compassionate motivations is, in some Buddhist teachings, a cause of instantaneous enlightenment.

If Buddhism in general offers ambivalence about sexuality, Tibetan Buddhism takes both ends of this ambivalence to their extremes. Nowhere is this ambivalence more the case than in Tibetan Vajrayana Buddhism, which takes as its most esoteric and efficient method of religious practice the tantric sexual act, while at the same time claiming, in some lineages, that absolute celibacy is necessary to achieve enlightenment. The moral ambivalence that permates "sex" is matched, and perhaps inaugurated by, conflict between different lineages within Tibetan Buddhism over what constitutes morally "correct" sexual union. Whereas it is popularly held that practitioners of the oldest lineage, rNyingma pa, adhere to the idea that properly engaging in tantric sex with living consorts can be productive of spiritual attainment,[1] Gelukpa lineages (the youngest of the Tibetan Buddhist schools) celebrate the symbolic act of sexual union while advocating strict rules of celibacy. In both (and all) lineages, however, the idea that desire is to be avoided is equally matched by concrete ritual techniques for putting one's sexual desires to good use—that is, toward the goal of achieving enlightenment through compassionate bliss.

In Vajrayana, the organs are converted into or recognized as instruments of wisdom and compassion (female and male genitalia, respectively), suggesting the possibility of a union of both within a single being, the *yab-yum* (father-mother).[2] Tantric ritual practices propose a recovery of the gendered elemental components that make up the fleshy body. In acts of orgasm, and in death, it is believed that one can glimpse momentarily the possibility of enlightenment through a "flash" of insight about the state that is both prior to and exceeding the corporeal being. This is believed possible by disciplined techniques for stilling the body's internal "winds." Winds are responsible for movement in the body, as they are outside of it. Winds are aroused by the presence of karma—the effects of deeds from past lives. Not surprisingly, the winds are most strongly aroused by the ongoing presence of desire, and desire in some sense produces the "winds." When united in a ritual context that enables the cessation of all desires, the unity of these "marked" aspects of the person (marked in genitalia, for example) can produce great bliss and the experience of emptiness—an awareness that all things are not without a cause. That is, the bliss is aroused by the recognition that desire itself, and the physical body produced therefrom, are caused by prior conditions. The ritual practices are meant to educate and habituate the body to this set of experiential possibilities.

Faure (1998) offers the following description of the ritual practices: "the perfect union, *prajnaopaya*, can be concretized by the union of a male practitioner with a female partner (the Tibetan *yab-yum*). The Great Bliss (*mahasukha*) that ensues coincides with the realization of Emptiness (called *vajra*; diamond or thunderbolt). During the sexual union, the male practitioner is supposed to meditate "in the forehead or in the sex organ" (Stein 1972: 91). During the preliminary ritual "invocation" of the deity, it is a meditation through which the practitioner sees himself as male (*yab*) united to a goddess (*yum*), or as a female (*yum*) united to a god (*yab*). In the course of the ritual, this mental copulation can be translated into actual coitus with a "wisdom woman" (*vidya*) or "seal" (*mudra*). During the act, the practitioner must concentrate on his or her *bodhicitta*, a term that in Mahayana refers to a psychic and mental state, the "thought of awakening," but that is used here in the more specific sense to designate the semen. The thought of awakening (bodhicitta) is identified with the *bindu*, the "drop," that is, the product of the fusion of the seed (*sukla*, the "white," semen, or *upaya*) with the ovum (*rakta*, the "red," the menses, or *prajna*). The bindu is the egg, the germ, just as the thought of awakening is the germ of a new being. This practice is related to the *coitus reservatus* with a female partner (*mudra*). The trick is to stir this seminal essence without losing it through ejaculation, so that it may ascend through the central artery into the seat of Great Bliss located in the brain. The process, which is said to lead ultimately to the union of Bliss and Emptiness, can be practiced alone during meditation, or with a female partner. Likewise, the term Great Bliss means not only a spiritual state but also "sexual fluid" (Faure 1998: 50).

Explanations of the mechanics of tantric sexuality are meant to be read in the context of practice, in which the practitioner would only learn these meanings after having undertaken vows not only to practice this method of sexual meditation but also to confirm that the purposes for doing so were motivated by the moral possibilities it aroused. In fact, Tibetan liturgical materials point to the many ways in which the "sexual domain" in this

Tibetan tradition is rendered meaningful mainly by its moral imperatives and possibilities. Sex is problematic both because it arouses great desire and because it holds the potential to arouse a great bliss that transcends desire. Thus, whether viewed from the perspective of its prohibitions or its ritual excesses, sex always harbors the potential for arousing great moral outcomes. But if this is what Buddhist literary sources tell us about sexuality, then what can be said about how, historically, the average Tibetan understood sexuality in the context of exposure to these liturgical renderings and the languages that were used to describe these practices, potentials, and meanings?

Sex, Families, and the State

The state in early modern Tibet struggled with tensions between secular and religious forces (Goldstein 1989). One form of political leadership was based on the system of reincarnation, in which the spiritual offspring of former rulers were "found" among young males who were not the product of sexual reproduction by existing rulers. This method of governance obviated the problems (or concerns) found in lineage-based societies of regulating the sexual behaviors of lineage members, because actual sexual reproduction was not the basis for inheritance of power (in many cases, although not all). What this form of leadership did accomplish, however, was to reinforce, far and wide, the idea that "not having ordinary sex" was a legitimate means of reproducing power (Robert 1982). Here, in particular, there is a religious moral basis for this logic: the assumption was that sexuality was a moral concern and the best rulers were not sexual in ordinary ways. Because "ordinary sex" was taken as a sign of existing desires and as the potential cause of escalating rivalry and strife between others (jealousy, attachment, envy, etc.), refraining from ordinary sex made Tibet's rulers appear to be beyond the sins of desire and attachment and therefore suitable for governing (or for taking on other positions, such as that of abbot).[3]

Sexuality was thus historically a state concern insofar as elements within Tibet's historic theocracy embodied the professed idealism of celibacy, in the sense that celibacy was seen as the ultimately virtuous form of "sexual union." Celibacy of Tibet's highest rulers, starting from at least the thirteenth century, was tied to this religious view. This sexual requirement was, however, also a source of complications surrounding the transfer of leadership. In nearly all of the cases of Tibet's theocratic leaders, from the Dalai and Panchen Lamas to the numerous abbots of the great Gelukpa monasteries throughout the three provinces of Tibet, certain powers of the state were vested in lamas who were supposed to remain celibate. The transfer of power from one ruler to the next was thus more a matter of religio-political negotiation than simply of reckoning blood heirs. More important, the sexual purity of the selection team and the "teachers" of these rulers was as important as the sexual purity of the chosen ruler. A transgression of this ideal (and the moral force of retribution for it) was, according to some authors, partly a cause for the theocracy's eventual demise (Goldstein 1989). Indeed, along with many other political and social forces, the sexual transgressions of Reting Rinpoche (regent for the thirteenth Dalai Lama in the first half of the twentieth century) are considered one of the reasons for his inability to provide oral tantric instructions to the fourteenth Dalai Lama, and one reason for the ultimate weakening of the Tibetan religious institutions of governance in the period just prior to China's "peaceful liberation" of Tibet.

In Tibet's other form of political leadership, concerns over the limits to reproduction of the lineage—and therefore with regulating sexual relations within and between lineages—were important. In addition to the religious leaders who were selected at a young age on the basis of their "reincarnate" status, called *trolku*,[4] there were lamas of other lineages within Tibetan Buddhism who acquired their positions as religious and political leaders by birthright (Stein 1972). These positions of political power were more like the system used by the Tibetan ruling elite, the aristocracy, for whom marriage and reproduction were used in strategic government alliances involving rights to land tenure, taxation privileges, and political offices. Aristocratic families were able to transfer the ownership of their property and title to certain government offices to their blood heirs, sometimes with little or no intervention from the religious leaders (Carrasco 1959).

Marriages between elite families were thus often arranged to ensure the continuance of family wealth. However, it was not uncommon for young Tibetan women in other social classes to have sexual relations and even produce children before a formal family-orchestrated betrothal. Autobiographical accounts of Tibetan women attest to the ambiguities surrounding norms for sexual behavior in relation to marriage (Pachen and Donnelley 2000). Moreover, there clearly were large differences between the customs of nomadic Tibetans and of the settled, agricultural elite Tibetans when it came to sexual relations and marriage. Robert Eckvall (1974: 522) writes that in the nomad populations he witnessed from 1926 to 1941, nomadic young people were very sexually active and marital unions were formed on the basis of amorous relations between the youths: "With regard to women, this freedom [in interpersonal relationships] shows in casual directness cosiderable license, and in the fact that virtually all marriages are arranged by the young people themselves, with scant reference to the parents" (1974: 522).

Although "premarital" sex was not uncommon among Tibetans, particularly among nomads, the oral accounts of historical sexual norms among elite families that I collected tell another story. These accounts relate that it was often assumed that when a man and woman began to have sexual relations, they were considered by Tibetan custom to be "married" whether or not the elaborate, time-consuming process of negotiating marriage ceremonies, dowries, and transfers of wealth were complete. However, in estate-holding lineages, great effort was made to ensure that these unions were favorable in terms of status and financial concerns. When a sexual relationship developed between two young persons whose parents did not accept the union (usually because one side considered the other to be of inappropriate social status), the lack of formal betrothal ceremonies was used as a means of terminating the relationship. Thus, in some cases, even though sexual relations between a couple had resulted in the birth of children, the lack of formal marriage that bonded the families to one another could validate a separation between the couple. At the same time, sexual unions that did result in offspring between a couple whose families were positive about the union were considered grounds for calling the couple "married" even before their formal betrothal and marriage, involving both families, was complete.

The ambiguity around these practices of sex and marriage goes some way in explaining the fact that, even today, inquiries about whether or not a woman is having sexual relations with a man are made by posing the question "are you married?" as opposed to "are you having 'sex'?" It also explains the linguistic variety of phrases that today can be glossed as "sex" but also mean "marriage," as I demonstrate below. The ambiguity also led in some cases to morally problematic situations. In premarital unions that were not sanctioned by the families and were thus terminated even if there already were children from the relationship, the breakups worked more often in favor of the males than the females involved. In the cases told to me it was the women who had been abandoned by the young men whose parents rejected them as suitable daughters-in-law. Needless to say, these terminations caused enormous strife and accusations of moral transgression in villages and between families.

Thus sexual discipline did figure into techniques of governance for at least some of the ruling elite. The tasks of ensuring that one's children married "well" and that they preserved the estate within the lineage by producing offspring with other elites or political allies were important in the work of domestic, village, and regional political power holders (*dponpo*). Herein, unrestrained sexual unions potentially posed all sorts of complications to a family's ability to maintain control of wealth and power. However, even successfully controlling the sex of one's offspring so as to ensure the production of suitable heirs was sometimes a morally complicated affair, as when it meant abandoning already-born children, jilting "wives," and creating enmity between families and in communities.

What can be said with some certainty here is that sexual relations in historic Tibet were governed in large part by a Buddhist morality. Lay sexual unions were seen as full of moral risks and celibacy was viewed as morally virtuous. It was not that having "premarital" sex was inherently immoral or that "sex" constituted a misdeed sui generis, but that ordinary sexual relations always held the potential to produce outcomes that were harmful to others and therefore nonvirtuous, even sometimes when carried out under the auspices of creating a formal "marriage." A formal marriage had the potential to render "sex" somewhat more virtuous, but it also opened up the possibility of nonvirtue. These moral valences that render sexual acts virtuous or nonvirtuous were in some sense what I believe gave meaning to sexual union for many Tibetans: the moral possibilities that these acts presented and the moral consequences that emerged therefrom were largely what "sex" was about. Carnal pleasure itself was, I suggest, indexed in terms of the moral possibilities (a message that becomes even more clear in the next section, which explores the historic literary materials and languages of "sex" in an older Tibet).

The Moral Logics of Lay Sex

It is not easy to gain a sense of the everyday cultural attitudes about sex in historic Tibet. Surely there were many different attitudes that were not uniformly shared by all Tibetans, and surely there are realms of sexual meaning and practice that are simply beyond the reach of the historical record (or the ethnographic record, for that matter) (Farquhar 2002). At the same time, we do know that Tibetans in general were exposed to the religious representations that gave at least some very specific meanings to the acts of sexual union. Visual reminders of religious images—notably yab-yum statuary and paintings—depicting tantric states as the embrace of male with female consort were found all over Buddhist Tibet prior to the 1960s. Even after Tibet's participation in the Cultural Revolution, such iconography is found in the monasteries that remained, from the smallest village gompas and wealthy homes to the largest monastic centers in the Tibetan regions' major cities. Pilgrims in Tibet regularly saw this immobile intercourse in the monasteries in their villages, in shrine rooms in their homes, and at centers for religious education to which they traveled on annual pilgrimages.

Beyond the monks and nuns who by some estimates constituted nearly a tenth of the population, many Tibetans were educated in the esoteric religious meanings associated with tantric practices—that is, they received instruction on the meanings and methods of tantric sexuality. Thus, the powerful suggestion of eroticism in these painted, cast, and carved figures was probably, for the average Tibetan, associated with neither what twentieth-century Americans would think of as pornography nor the reverse in the European sense of "high art" that posited the purely sensual as an erotic transcendence of the mundane. Nor surely did all Tibetans necessarily see these images as models of proper sexual engagement for themselves. Insofar as most Tibetans took these images to depict a religious ethic about enlightenment, however, and insofar as the images conveyed to them something about an ethic that was attainable through sexual practices, they cannot be ignored. They surely helped to assign moral meaning to most Tibetans' sensibilities of sex, and this is borne out, once again, in the languages used to describe "sex."

Tibetans had and have an enormous variety of words and phrases to refer to what in English we call "sex," but there is no term that suffices as the equivalent of it exactly. The term 'khrig, for example, glossed as "coitus" or "sexual intercourse," is actually derived from the root verb 'khrig pa meaning to "stick (together)" or "intermingle." Phrases such as 'dod pa spyod (performing lust, or sensual desire, or "sexual embrace") mean literally "the joining of desire." Nye rig pa (knowing intimacy) and nye jungs (intimate pairing) are often used even today as euphemisms for sexual intercourse. Sometimes the referents are more specifically set in relation to religious concepts, as in mi tshangs spyod ("not practicing celibacy" or "performing impurity").

Even here we find moral ambiguity in the terms. Rmongs is glossed as "copulation" but it derives from the root for "delusion"; that is, the use of this term for "sex" implies the potential for immorality. In other contexts, we find the use of the more general term dag' (delight, joy, happiness), implying "sex" as an abbreviated form of dga' dgur spyod pa, meaning to indulge in the making of delight (spyod pa means "a deed or action" and dga' dgur is taken to mean "intercourse," but literally "many delights"). But the use of this term can also imply a potential moral infraction similar to "performing impurity," because the performing of these "deeds" is a cause of karma, and karma is a cause of rebirth. The latter term can also refer to the performance of conjugal rites (in the sense of what Westerners refer to as consummating a marriage, for example) implying an appropriate socio-moral context for such indulgence. However, even here where such actions are considered appropriate socially, there is from the religious perspective the ever-present risk of immorality: because even this sort of sexual union can produce greed, attachment, and desire.

This subtle moral ambiguity of things "sexual" is carried over into the Tibetan words used to describe things associated with "sex acts." For example, *chags* and *chags chu'i*, meaning "love" but also "attachment" or "affection" and also "desire" (an affliction, one of the three "poisons" in Tibetan medicine), is one of the most frequently used in Tibetan glosses of what in English is called "sex." Terms like *chags sems slong ba'*, which literally translates to "giving a mind of desire" and is glossed in contemporary spoken translations as "sexy," in other words indicates "arousing" desire in others but, again, is considered to be of questionable morality. In a religious sense, it would be unvirtuous to arouse the poison of desire in another. Thus another translation of *chags pa* is "lust." The term most commonly used in medical discussions about "sex" in Lhasa today is *chags pa* or *chags spyod*, the latter meaning something more like "copulation" or "fornication" ("the behavior of love"), with all of the potential moral associations, both good and bad, that come from being in a state of "desire" or "attachment." One Tibetan young woman explained to me that the term *chags pa* means "sex" but also "attachment to something, or that something is broken."

Not surprisingly, the contexts in which the terms are used are important for meaning. For example, in some contexts the phrase *skye ba spyod* (performing conception) is used to describe sexual intercourse leading to the production of a fetus, whereas in other contexts it means literally "giving rise to a human" in the sense of the karmic deeds that produce this result. That is, it is not simply sexual behavior that gives rise to a human form but rather a whole series of actions (that produce virtuous and unvirtuous outcomes) that result in rebirth in human form (as opposed to nonhuman forms of life or no rebirth, that is, enlightenment). The lay term for sex in this context is is *phru gu gyab*, literally to "make a baby."

Similarly, the phrase *dbang po gnyis spyor* (literally, the union of two empowerments) is glossed in English as "sex" or "copulation," and the term *spyor ba* (union) itself can also imply the sexual act because it can mean "intermingling" or "making delight." But in other contexts these terms mean simply "to join" or the "esoteric symbolic union of compassion and wisdom" with no implication of sexual relations, tantric or otherwise. The term *gsang spyod* (performing the secret) is used as a euphemism for tantric sex, with the implication of a religious meaning or a secret tantric meaning of what is also referred to as "the union of two organs" or the "intimate pairing." These words can also refer to the "secret" of tantric oral instruction, without reference to "sex" per se. In these contexts, the words used refer to sexual acts that bestow high moral virtue; that is, engaging in these acts, and calling them by these terms, provides the actor or writer/speaker with the opportunity to demonstrate morality and acquire virtue because they imply a kind of sex that is without desire or attachment.

But this meaning is contrasted with many others associated with other terms. By using the same root *dga'* (seen above) the phrase *dga' wa dman pa* is used in religious contexts to mean "sex" or literally "sordid" pleasure, again implying a negative moral judgment about the behaviors of laypersons who are seen by religious teachers to indulge in all of life's pleasures without concern for their morality. This is sex that is full of attachment and desire. Along these lines, even the phrase *khrong pa'i chos*, or the "religion of the village," is found to be a phrase that implies sexual intercourse, suggesting that Tibetans are so preoccupied with the pursuit of ordinary sexual pleasures that it becomes their "true religion."

Finally, the moral ambiguity of terms associated with sex is also seen in the variety of colloquial terms for sexual relations. For example, phrases such as *nyam du bsdad wa* ("going together" or "staying together") as well as *pho mo'i sbrel wa* ("man-woman together, or connection") and *mtshan ma mnyam bsdad* ("genital connection") are meant to imply a morally correct union of two persons (always heterosexual union). Finally, *trugu gyap* ("to make a baby") is translated as "sex" with the implication of producing a life, as opposed to the pursuit of pleasure as in the morally questionable sense of the English term "fornication." Even though these acts are full of the potential for negative karmic results (carried out with desire or selfish interest), they can be seen as the means by which to engage in acts of compassion (to the extent that any marital relations are recognized within Tibetan Buddhism as virtuous, and to the extent that a union for the production of another life can likewise be seen this way).

At the other end of the spectrum, *dgah wa dman-pa*, meaning "low delight" or "sordid pleasure," is also glossed as "sexual pleasure," thus implying a kind of unvirtuous sexuality that is tied to the ordinary "sexual" life of laypersons. At the far extreme, I was told that today a common term for sex was *rgyo wa*, to ravish, implying an act that is morally bereft, vulgar, or obscene, derived from the phrase *rgyo brgyab*, which means literally "to throw" or "fling" or "beat" when put together with *rgyo*, which perhaps is best glossed as the English term "fuck."

There is, it seems, no neutral ground for the signification of the sexual act of intercourse that in English rests not ambivalently but much more neutrally in the biological concept associated with the English term "sex." In the sense that Tibetan culture was predominantly influenced by Buddhist culture (which is not to say that all Tibetans were Buddhist), it is clear that certain religious precepts were found in and throughout much of popular Tibetan culture when it came to things "sexual." Particularly, the moral ambivalence that made it either good or bad, but nothing that was neutrally in-between.

Perhaps the best example of a primary source on the lay views of sexuality is the work of Gedun Chopel (1905–1951), a monk trained in the Gelukpa lineage yet who advocated a more liberal attitude about sexual intercourse than did his monastic contemporaries. In his work Chopel (1992 [1938]) refers to sexual norms that prevailed in at least the urban aristocratic Tibet of his time. In some cases, these norms become visible by his questioning of them. His book *Treatise on Passion* explains various techniques of sexual arousal, penetration, and ecstasy. Jeffrey Hopkins, who translated and edited the treatise, notes in his introduction to the translation that Chopel's stated goal is to help ordinary Tibetans understand that carnal bliss can augment one's progress toward spiritual bliss and enlightenment.

In apparently disregarding the dominant Gelukpa lineage vows of celibacy of his time, Chopel the monk not only experimented widely with many sexual practices and partners but also chastised the clergy and lay public alike for what he considered their hypocritical views regarding sexual relations. He convincingly blurs esoteric and scholarly distinctions between "ordinary sex" and religiously conceived sexual practice (tantric sex) by suggesting that the conventional wisdom (that lay or ordinary sex can only be impure, full of desire and attachment) is as insufficient as the monastic view that celibacy alone enables one to pursue a sexual practice (tantric) that will, because it is pure, bring one to a state of enlightenment.

Chopel enters into this discussion obliquely by way of a discussion of the inequality between the sexes when it comes to standards of sexual behavior. He scorns the double standard held by Tibetans about sexual relations outside of the conjugal union: "There is no difference between men and women with regard to adultery," he writes. But, "if one examines it carefully, men are worse. A king's having a thousand queens is still proclaimed as high-class style. If a woman has a hundred men, she is slandered as if there is nothing comparable. If a king does it alternately with a thousand women, where is there any sense of adultery! Since doing with a wife is not adultery, how could the rich ever be adulterous! An old man of wealth with hair like snow selects and buys a young girl. Being a mere article sold, she is given a price. Alas, women have no protectors!" (183).

Chopel's indictment tells us that adultery was not uncommon, and that it was considered less morally acceptable for women to commit it than for men. His reference is somewhat confusing, however, because he implies that polygyny can be called adultery. Keeping in mind that polyandry was also common in Tibet, Chopel's critique suggests that he is talking about sexual relations outside of these two forms of marriage, although the ambiguity about the relationship between sexual relations and marital bonds is in some sense embedded in his passage. He scorns the idea that wealth can transform extramarital relations into acceptable sexual unions (by way of bride-price), because a wealthy man can purchase the sexual favors of women and call it marriage, but a woman who might engage in sexual relations with many men would be scorned for this. This he considers a hypocrisy on the part of men.

In both cases, he reminds us, adultery was considered morally problematic. "Giving up praising as proper that which is not, giving up the various forms of adultery, and putting a sign of copulation [a child] at the breast of a woman are the respectable ways of the world" (184). Thus, he suggests that the most appropriate sexual unions are those between husband and wife, faithfully, resulting in the conception of a child. He goes on to note that having sex with widows is appropriate but not with wives whose husbands are gone for long periods of time (as this might result in conceiving a child, which would cause great conflict between the father and husband).

At the same time, Chopel advocates a liberal position regarding sex outside of marriage. Expressing sympathy toward the woman who is sexual beyond conjugality, Chopel calls sexual relations an opportunity for gaining virtue, just as he advocates the same for the man who is "virtuously" sexual. "Sex is disclaimed from the mouths of all, but it alone is what is liked [in] the minds of all. . . . It is said in the chapter on practice in the Kalachakra Tantra [one of the most important religious texts for his lineage] that providing a woman for someone who is desirous is the supreme of gifts. If you do not believe me, look there, and it will be evident" (180). He considers prudery toward sex to be unvirtuous because it implies a kind of lying: people like engaging in sex, even if they profess it as unvirtuous. Further, he considers Tibetans' overt conservatism regarding sex—a conservatism consistent with a strong religious praise for celibacy—to be misguided. He notes that all people enjoy the pleasures of sexual union ("it alone is what is liked by all"), yet not all people are allowed the same freedoms of sexual activity because convention prohibits this equality. Chopel's first attack is aimed at the gender bias: an act that a man can do openly and be praised in doing is for a woman only a misdeed. Chopel also attacks celibacy itself: what monks must never do (e.g., have sexual partners or multiple sexual partners) is allowed for non-monastic men, and yet it is precisely the latter who, because they lack spiritual training, do not know how to turn their actions into virtue, and it is precisely the former who do know how to do this.

Chopel recognizes celibacy as virtuous inasmuch as it represents the suppression of the poison of inner desire or attachment, but if celibacy produces so much sexual desire by being forbidden, it is more dangerous than having sex without restraint. As Hopkins writes: "The denial of the inner desires of the human creates craving and 'the sin of craving is greater than that of doing it' " (128). Moreover, insofar as sex can relieve sadness, Chopel argues that it should be seen, again, as a virtuous undertaking: Suffering is inevitable, but "relieving a saddened mind is the divine religion of the excellent. Eventually, it comes down to what is done with the mind" (127). In the end, Chopel writes, "do the deed of passion in the ways that you like it in all its forms, and taste all the forms of pleasure described in the various commentaries. When both [participants] become intoxicated with strong passion due to being well acquainted, trusting, and without qualms, during sex do not refrain from anything; do everything without exception" (132).

Hopkins notes in this introduction that Chopel's "other concern is at the heart of his ethic of love and the *raison d'etre* for [Chopel's] sixty-four arts of passion" (132–33). He states that Chopel is not merely "taking poetic license" by "praising sexual ecstasy as a means for transformation into divinity"; rather, he genuinely thinks of sexual union as inherently spiritual. As Chopel writes: "At the time of pleasure the god and goddess giving rise to bliss actually dwell in the bodies of the male and the female. Therefore, it is said that what would be obstacles to one's life if done [under usual circumstances] are conquered, and power, brilliance, and youth blaze forth. The perception of ugliness and dirtiness is stopped, and one is freed from conceptions of fear and shame. The deeds of body, speech and mind become pure, and it is said that one arrives in a place of extreme pleasure" (96). Recognizing sexual union in this way, Chopel suggests, hastens one on the spiritual path, and tasting the fruits of compassion in this ultracorporeal way forms a basis for great spiritual pursuit.

Unlike the views found in conventional Buddhist texts and translations or interpretations of them (Faure 1998), Chopel advocates the benefits of having sex with many partners as a boon both to procreation (without which, he notes, there would be no practitioners of the *dharma*) and to one's personal effort to achieve enlightenment.[5] In his introduction, Hopkins clarifies the ethnographic placement of Chopel's insights: "As scandalous as the conflation of religions with worldly activities is [for this period of time], Gedun Chopel provides a secular adaptation of high Buddhist ideals—much needed in a culture oriented to states beyond the reach of most practitioners" (132). It is perhaps for this reason that his text circulated widely among the literate public of Tibet in the years up to the 1950s, apparently for its insights about the possibilities of morally affirming ordinary sexual relations.[6]

Thus, even in Chopel we get a sense that "sex" among Tibetans was viewed ambivalently in ways that were formulated largely within Buddhist frameworks: that is, virtuous and unvirtuous. The fact that Chopel feels the need to educate his compatriots about how to make what many consider "unvirtuous sex" virtuous suggests that "ordinary sex" must have been viewed by Tibetans as filled with moral risks—the risk of attachment, of increasing the poison of desire, and of forgoing fortuitous rebirths. The only truly virtuous sex was that associated with religious celibacy, and the opposite of this was endless selfish desire for sexual pleasure. However, we find in Chopel's work the possibility of an "ordinary sex" that can be made into something morally tolerable within the contours of a Buddhist universe. This kind of sexual union was referred to in terms of its social responsibilities and obligations, and its intimacies were ideally seen as driven by compassionate motives because of these social obligations. Sex in the terms that mean "conjugal union," "intimate pairings," or "going together" is not a morally neutral, biological, or physical "sex" as we know it but rather a set of terms defining relationships between persons who are morally bound to one another. This is why many of the terms that are today glossed as "sex" are synonyms for marriage itself. Sexual union that made virtue out of potentially unvirtuous acts by way of marriage turned the pursuit of pleasure into a set of social obligations and outward concern for others. In fact, this was precisely Chopel's strategy: his goal was to bridge the gap between esoteric representations of the most virtuous sexual acts (in tantrism) and the everyday sexual behaviors that tended to be viewed as inherently unvirtuous.

But contexts outside of religion helped generate the meaning of sexual union for Tibetans, and it would be wrong to claim that religion is the only domain that shaped attitudes about sex or its meanings. We have seen that the meanings of sexual practices must also be understood in terms of other institutions, such as reproduction, the family, and the state in historic Tibet, and that these were informed by Buddhist esoteric ideals. If we want to see how the meanings of sex have changed in the contemporary period, then we must also continue to look at those domains that concern reproduction and the state that have an important role in shaping the ideas and ideals of sex. Just as sex wasn't simply about the physical act but rather about the production of virtue or its opposite in historic Tibet, then surely the ways sex was negotiated in matters of the state, in various domains of power, and in families also still needs to be accounted for in a contemporary Tibet in which religion itself has taken on new meanings. Reproduction of the lineage, as much as assurances of paternity of one's offspring, for example, are still matters that concern sexual union. Similarly, the role of the state in negotiating those unions and their meanings is still pronounced and can be explored in its contemporary incarnations. Let us turn, then, to a modern Tibet in which the meanings of sex are negotiated by way of a new socialist form of governance.

Sex in Contemporary Tibet

"There is not love in sex [*chags spyod*] anymore."—comments of a young Tibetan woman in an English-language discussion group cited in Li 2000

Although any number of ruptures in the history of Tibet might be taken to explore transitions in social life and the creation of new meanings of various social behaviors, certainly the most visible today is the rupture produced in the wake of the "peaceful liberation" of Tibet by the Chinese People's Liberation Army in the early 1950s. The social changes brought about by this "liberation" include the steady and progressive programs of state-directed "modernization" that affect nearly every aspect of life among Tibetans, including their practices and attitudes about sexual relations. Talking with a female doctor at the Tibetan medical hospital one day, I brought up the question of sexuality in contemporary Lhasa. The doctor had been writing an article on this topic, she told me; her concern was with the visible increase in the number of young Tibetan women who didn't seem to "care" about their relationships with men. "What do you mean, they don't care?" I asked. "They have sex (*chags pa*) with many men, and they even get pregnant but then they leave that man for another," she explained. "They have relations with one man and then another. They have abortions, and this is bad for their health. Nowadays, if you have sex with someone it doesn't require love. It used to require love between the couple."[7]

What is meant when Tibetans tell us that "there is not love in sex anymore" or that "having sex does not require love"? If "taking care" of oneself means caring about one's relationships to others, or that caring about the endurance of relations made intimate through sexual union is what is lost today, how did this come about? What I pursue in the sections following is the question of rupture and continuity in Tibetan attitudes and meanings of "sexual union." In some sense, it is the disjuncture between these two competing possibilities that renders visible both the historical moral concern and the new set of moral concerns regarding "sex" under socialism.

Modernizing Sex

The programs to "modernize" Tibet that occurred over many different periods of time since "liberation" were not uniform in their expression or meaning. Nor did these varied programs generate uniform responses among Tibetans. Efforts on the part of the Maoist government to teach Tibetans to regulate their sexual behaviors in new ways, however, did produce effects that can be seen in the tensions that are still felt by a number of Tibetan women—tensions that have withstood the changing orders of governance from Mao to Deng Xiaoping and their successors and the radical political reforms ushered in by each. Ironically, if governance in Tibet had previously been legitimized by the moral force of a disciplined sexuality (tantric celibacy), then governance under socialism was also instrumentalized partly by the state's concern with regulating the sexual activities of the population as an ethical project (Sigley 2001). But the moral assignments of "sex" could not have been more different in these two eras.

Maoist rule in Tibet deployed a concept of "sex" that was, I suspect, entirely new to Tibetans. It focused on sex as reproduction in an equation that mapped sexual life in an inverse relationship to the productivity needs of the state. It did so first by way of introducing a morally neutral and biological sex (a sex "created" in the field of population sciences) and then by way of suturing that sex to ideals of secular socialist patriotism. Sex in Maoist Tibet was not just about the moral possibilities invested in the passions of the moment, the intimacies of conjugal ties, the transcendent virtues of remaining celibate, the morality of marital bonds and or premarital obligations, or even about the nonvirtue of lust and selfish delight that could be expressed in and through sexual unions. Rather, through Maoism sex became also potentially about biological reproduction, labor, and productivity needs and the outward show of political allegiance to a socialist state. Sexual virtue was now a secular political project for all Tibetan citizens, and this virtue took shape primarily in and by way of reproductive policies.

From the early 1950s through the mid-1960s, during the first years of socialism, Mao adopted a policy of gradualism in Tibet, slowing the pace of reforms in ways that allowed for more sensitivity to traditional cultural norms (Goldstein 1997; Janes 1995). The Chinese government and intellectual elites had long concerned themselves with the translatability and applicability of Western sciences of sexuality in the Chinese context, beginning in the republican period (Dikötter 1995). The deployments of sexual sciences in China were multiple and varied in their effects, notably being refigured by and between existing conceptualizations of sexual power, potency, virility, and fertility, as well as by popular conceptions of the relationship between erotics and economics (Farquhar 2002; Sigley 2001).

Few of these concerns, however, found their way into the Tibetan plateau in the forms that were seen in the rest of China. Still, Tibetans were introduced to government programs designed to intervene in their fertility in one way or another by at least the mid-1950s. By the late 1950s, Tibetans felt the effects of Mao's rapidly changing policies that would quickly advance socialism. Among these were his pronatalist policies stemming in part from an outgrowth of assumptions that foreign imperialism could only be curtailed by a strong and plentiful internal military made from a large population base from which to recruit solders. As other researchers have shown for other peoples (Schneider and Schneider 1995; Sigley 2001), Tibetans did not fail to recognize that scientific and governmental messages about family size and fertility were indirectly messages about regulating sexual behaviors and about the links between the state and one's ability to behave sexually in ways that resulted in fertility outcomes desired by the state.

Throughout the years of the Great Leap Forward, pronatalism was advanced among Tibetans in ways that encouraged Tibetan women to have many chidren while working harder than ever in labor-intensive jobs smelting iron and building roads. A Tibetan woman laborer in her sixties spoke with me about this one day when she noticed my look of surprise after telling me that she had five children, all of whom had survived their childhood and were still alive today. She said, "We all had many children in those days. It wasn't then like it is today. In those days, Mao asked us to have more children." My surprise was as much over the fact that all five of her children had survived to adulthood as with the fact that she had had five children. She had been working in her village in the southwest region of Tibet (Kham) when the first of her children were born. In her village, as in others, production efforts had shifted to the village industries of "industrialization" (iron smelting). However, she was lucky, she said, because she and her husband and children always found enough food to eat.

I had met other older women who had given birth to many children in the early days after "liberation," but few of them were able to tell me that all of their children had survived. "Mao asked us all to have more children in those days," she repeated. "It is not like today. Now, our children are told to have only one or two babies." I told her she must feel very lucky that all of her children survived childhood and are alive today, and she went on to enumerate by counting on the joints of her fingers, not only how many grandchildren she had but also how many great-grandchildren. She lost count and started again, then said simply, "nearly ten," as she raised both hands in the air signaling her lack of desire to continue counting.

I had met many other women from this generation who recounted more depressing stories of their early reproductive years. Those who started having their children during the Great Leap Forward in 1958 told me most often about the deaths of their children. Miscarriages, stillbirths, and deaths from disease and starvation—all of these were attributed to the burdens of heavy labor during this time and the failed agricultural results of Mao's rapid leap to an industrial model of socialism. Soon after, Tibetans were told to plant wheat (rather than their traditional barley), and because it could not grow well in Tibet's climate many people starved. In many cases, the sicknesses of the women I met were tied to their early reproductive failures, which in turn were a direct result of government policies.[8] In their minds, female bodies were forced to carry the demands of both labor and reproduction under the reckless leadership of the government elite—that is, Mao, the Politburo, and the Tibetans who had taken over leadership of the Autonomous Region on behalf of the ruling party.

What I realized, however, some months after talking with the lucky woman whose five children had survived was how meaningful it was for her to utter that she had more children because Mao had wanted it. Her own sentiments about her reproduction were embedded in a series of reflections about the intentions and desires of the state, for which Mao once stood. Her motivation was not necessarily to please Mao, although for many Tibetans the idea that one could still "displease" Mao himself, even though he was dead, was not uncommon. Rather, she wanted me to know that Mao would not have opposed her having five children. Mao instantiated the modern state and the modern state cared about her fertility and thus her sexual unions.

Things were very different now, she told me. Urban Tibetans were repeatedly subjected to state campaigns aimed at limiting their fertility throughout the 1960s and 1970s, but by the 1980s fertility control, via women, had become one of the single most important concerns of the administration, and this concern was carried forward into 1990s Tibet. Besides government efforts to limit, alter, or eliminate Tibetans's religious behaviors, their efforts to contain, alter, and control the fertility of Tibetan women was seen by many Tibetans as the government's primary reason to be in Tibet. The first step in this process of government-imposed reform involved removing sexuality from the realm of religion and making it an object of socialist and secular morality. To do this, new meanings had to be assigned to sexual unions.

Refiguring Sex

Evidence from government campaigns to change Tibetan fertility suggest an assumption that from the beginning Tibetans had to be shown how "different" their sexuality was from the Han majorities. Unlike the "civilized" Han, Tibetans were depicted in government campaigns as sexually unruly—they were barbarians whose sexual appetites were to be feared. Tales were still told, in Chinese storybooks sold in Tibet, of historical Chinese emperors who appeased the Mongol and Tibetan hordes by sending them a beautiful, white-skinned, frail Chinese princess as a sexual prize in an act of geopolitical diplomacy. The "gift" of a Chinese beauty worked to convey the message that Tibetans could be appealed to by way of appeasing their unlimited sexual appetites and that sending a "civilized" sexual emissary from the Han culture would potentially have the effect of taming these "barbarian" sexual ways.

Images of a "hypersexual" Tibetan whose sexual appetites defined Tibet's "role" in the national landscape suggested that they still needed to be civilized by the same Han majorities who perpetuated this image. Tibetans were taught that their own understandings of sexual morality were a threat to the survival of the Chinese nation. In other words, moral framings for the sexual relations that were articulated in and through Tibetan Buddhism were portrayed as dangerous, leading to a licentiousness and promiscuity (like that imputed to tantrism) at the same time they were taught about the evils of Tibet's theocratic feudalism. This effort included removing from homes, villages, and cities the literature, images, and icons that depicted tantric sexuality. The teachings of tantrism were at first curtailed and then even forbidden during the Cultural Revolution. The institutions of political office by reincarnation were reconfigured as institutions of socialist democracy as opposed to moral and sexual achievements (thus reincarnate celibate lamas were selected by political appointment of the government and many were forced to break their vows of celibacy and take wives). As if to reinforce the perception that the civilizing processes required a new kind of sexuality, monks and nuns were disrobed and forced to marry (that is, forced to break their vows of celibacy), and among nuns who refused this rule of law it was not uncommon for them to suffer imprisonment and rape.

These activities were accompanied by reforms in sexual behaviors that were deployed through reproductive policies. Despite the fact that Tibet was not overpopulated, Tibetans became a target for slowing population growth throughout the 1970s, which culminated in the deployment of China's "one child only" policy in 1979.[9] This too had an impact on sexual relationships. As minorities, Tibetans were allowed more children than were the Han majorities, meaning that at various times they were allowed two in urban areas and more than two in rural families. However, the degree to which such policies were enforced depended on the severity of the directives sent down from Beijing (e.g., deploying quotas) as well as the peculiarities of the officials working in the unit or region whose job it was to monitor fertility. In general, Tibetans were forced to limit their reproduction from that time forward, adhering to policies of forced abortions for women who exceeded government limits and dealing with the embarrassment, fines, and in some cases imprisonment for failing to meet government demands.

Concern with regulating fertility required members of work units both to pay attention to their own sexual behaviors and also to engage in surveillance over the sexual behaviors of their fellow Tibetans. Couples who wanted to engage in sexual relations had to obtain permission to do so by requesting permission to marry from work unit leaders. Communes, and later government work units, designated a female in each unit who was in charge of ensuring that her unit met fertility quotas. Efforts to circumvent this strict policy, or to engage in sex without negotiating marital bonds, were surely plentiful. In some units, efforts to ensure that any such liaisons did not result in reproduction led to the posting of menstrual cycles on bulletin boards. Sexuality here was made into a didactic and biopolitical instrument to teach about the biological link between sexuality and reproduction by way of making the most intimate aspects of women's bodies a public concern. Although it seems likely that elsewhere in China, commune and rural production teams contained the seeds of an eroticism tied to the commune itself (and accounts of contemporary Maoist nostalgia attest to this—e.g., Farquhar 2002), it is not clear that similar sentiments were aroused in Tibetan production units.[10]

Although post-Mao liberalization policies put in place by Deng Xiaoping promised economic reforms and more freedoms to retain and practice traditional culture in places like Tibet, they did little to lighten the burden of reproductive policies. Throughout the late 1980s and 1990s, restrictions on reproduction actually seemed to increase rather than decrease for Tibetans. In late 1990s Tibet, the restrictive birth control policies ensured that in urban work units, Tibetan women were subjected to extreme pressures to have only one child. In rural areas, Tibetan women were often pressured to undergo sterilization after having only two children.

In thinking back over the impact on Tibetans of the history of family planning I realized that my elderly interlocutor's quick response about Mao's allowing her to have five children was perhaps well rehearsed, because now it was considered virtually criminal to give birth to that many children in Tibet. To me, her conversation and that of other women I met in the Tibetan hospital led me to understand that whatever associations Tibetans had with their sexual behaviors in relation to their labor, their productivity, or the state's interest in their reproduction prior to socialism, it was these repressive associations that came to be paramount in their thinking about "sexuality" during their forty years of experience with socialist rule.

In one sense, discourses of reproduction colonized sentiments about sexuality for many Tibetans. The government's refusal to allow couples to have children until the work unit approved their request occasionally led to the dissolution of marriages when policies were violated. Women were told when and how to have sex: the when concerned timing their sexual relations for periods of lowest fertility, and the how was a matter of using effective contraception. Many of these policies continue to be deployed in Tibet in the present day. Women in urban Tibet are today not allowed marriage certificates until they are twenty-two years old, nor are they allowed abortions in public hospitals without proof of a marriage license. What was a family matter was turned into an affair of the modern state; what was a matter of intimate moral possibility was turned into a matter of public medical regulation. In many cases, finding virtue in socialist sex meant the exact opposite of what finding virtue in sexual unions meant under traditional Buddhist ideals.

The message conveyed to Tibetans by way of government policies was that their traditional sexual customs were problematic and that there were other, correct, ways to be sexual in socialist Tibet. Sexual relations configured around the sentimental bond between lovers or spouses, or worse yet around the ideals of a celibate form of sex in tantrism, were at best viewed as "bourgeois" by the Red Guards and party cadres and at worst as counterrevolutionary. Instead, the bond between the state (early on embodied in Mao) and the masses (a sentiment meant to replace sentimental ties between conjugal pairs or lovers) became paramount. In the first step, then, sex was tied to reproduction and dissociated from religion; it was presented as an object of population statistics, an instrument for modernization, and a political and biological "fact of life" (Pigg, this volume). In the second step, sex was "liberated" from reproduction as well and made into an instrument for showing loyalty to the state, with or without reproduction.

Sexual relations were first reinscribed as state concerns and as opportunities to show socialist morality and patriotism. In the early days, before contraception was available, this meant ascribing to sexual behaviors that were guided by the principles of population statistics, which were, in turn, deployed in the service of the socialist state. Later, making sure one was reproductive in ways that met state interests in limited fertility growth was one way to show a commitment to the socialist project (even if inwardly opposed to that project). Indeed it was not really something about which an individual had a choice. Being sexual in reproductively disciplined ways by using birth control and having abortions could be translated by party officials, and work unit monitors, as signs of party loyalty. Whether sincere or not, this process of thinking through one's sexual subjectivity in relation to the state had sequelae: it made it possible for Tibetans to think about their "sexuality" as if it were primarily about reproduction. At the same time, it made it possible for Tibetans to think about their sexual identity as part of that subjectivity. That is, given the state's early efforts to teach women that their sexual relations were a state political concern, it is not surprising that Tibetans, especially women, did eventually learn to look to their "sexuality" in order to demonstrate acquiescence to, or their rejection of, that same state and thus to think about their "sexual identities" in ways that were scripted by the Chinese state. With the introduction of birth control, in particular, it became possible for Tibetans to think about demonstrating their loyalty to state modernization by way of their nonreproductive sex or, in some sense by way of their public sexual image.

The reforms to modernize Tibet thus set in motion two often contradictory forces in regards to "sex": one that tried to secularize and discipline sexuality in the effort to control fertility, and another that increasingly sexualized Tibetan women, teaching them that making themselves more sexually "modern" also made them more "politically conforming." Of course, reproductive policies were and are directly tied to identity politics in modern Tibet. They deliberately intended to transform identities by showing Tibetans (but particularly Tibetan women) how to be sexually "modern." This meant, in part, adopting the view that sex could be "just about 'sex' and, at the same time, just about being a good citizen.

This effort was at least partially successful in that for many Tibetans, women who refused contraception were seen as being traditional and backward (if not politically suspicious), whereas women who embraced contraception and multiple sexual partners prior to marriage considered themselves "modern." In weekly political meetings that Tibetan women were required to attend, messages about the importance of using contraception to limit family size were delivered in between political messages about the importance of following government policies, including economic quotas that were set for work units, new religious restrictions, and new political suspects that they were collectively meant to ferret out and disclose. Among the requirements of the state were that they limit their family size, either by using contraception before they conceived more than one or two children, or by undergoing abortions in the event that they did conceive more than this number.

Among women who had come of age prior to the reforms of socialism, these messages were often met with conflicting concerns about the moral basis of their political conformity. Even young Tibetan women raised in contemporary Tibet voiced concerns over their ability to fulfill the expectations of the state when it came to fertility control measures. Religious considerations over the karmic burdens of killing living beings, for example, were commonly uttered as fears in regard to the use of contraception. The most common outcome of adopting "modern" practices of sexuality were thus in many ways outcomes that were considered undesirable among a fair number of Tibetan women.

One women explained to me that the burden of taking a human life, a life that was one of the hardest for a sentient being to obtain (given how easy it was to be reborn as an animal or a hungry ghost or a hell being), was the worst sort of "sin" (nonvirtue; *dikpa*) she could commit. She knew that according to the socialist program modern women should not care about taking lives through abortions, because what mattered was that they could meet state fertility quotas, work unit regulations, and so on, but it was not easy for her to shake off the Buddhist moral discourse that had governed outcomes of sexual relations. For her, the karmic load of taking a life was more than could be amended for in prayers of blessings in this life, or, as she told me, "the result of killing a sentient being can't be eliminated. It can affect our next life and that is my burden." This woman happened to be in the hospital, recovering from a uterine infection most likely caused by her abortion. She told me she would probably start using contraception, "because it is the most reliable, and I don't want to conceive again and get rid of it because I can't have another child [her work unit disallowed it]. I am doing a lot of sin [*dikpa*] by aborting. In Tibet, we believe this is the biggest sin, to abort, because it is killing a person. . . . People say that when you get an abortion you should not shed tears, but I cried a lot and felt very sad about what I had done. I will [make religious offerings] as a way of praying for the child to get a life in a human form sooner rather than later."

Later, I explored the options for contraception with the woman's doctor and was told that from a Tibetan medical perspective, there weren't any really good choices: "When a man and a woman join, the white element (semen) is meant to flow from the man into the secret place of the women, and not elsewhere. If it goes elsewhere, it can cause diseases." I then asked, "So do you recommend that patients abstain from having sex?" "Not exactly," the doctor answered. "The main thing is that the pills, condoms, IUD, injection [Depo Provera], implant [Norplant] . . . all of these are disruptive to the body. But abortion is the most disruptive. So, we just encourage women to be careful, and to avoid having so many sexual partners, . . . to stay with one man." "But many of these women are already married," I noted. "They are having sexual relations with only one man, but they still must come for abortions." The doctor replied, "Yes. This is another problem," and then carefully scripting the rest of her response to avoid openly criticizing the government, she continued: "Women have to think about the effects these abortions are having on their bodies. They cannot just have one after another . . . then they come in with infections. . . . They must realize that eventually they will have many health problems from this."

From this we can see how a governing strategy articulated through reproductive policies might not just be an instrument for containing the reproduction of the Tibetan population but also an instrument for reeducating the population about the meanings of sex and the appropriate ways of having it. Our conversation continued as I saw an opportunity to ask about sexual norms. I asked whether she or her colleagues had heard of Gedun Chopel. "Of course" she said, "*The Yellow Book*," offering the Chinese name for his reprinted *Treatise on Passion*. "It is banned," her colleague interrupted. "It is a *yellow* book [prohibited]." Uncertain about whether I should pursue the issue further, I took the risk and asked why it was banned. Her colleague took the opportunity to join the conversation:

> It was allowed for a few years, and you can get copies from Beijing, but it is not available here. He [Chopel] was imprisoned by the Tibetan government, you know. Actually, I think his book should be published here. It is banned because it has a lot of religion, but really it is about sex and it is very educational. It should be taught in schools here. It is a good book for sex education because in the countryside they can't imagine about these things, but it really depends on the reader. One point that is really important in the book is that it emphasizes respect between a man and a woman, a husband and wife, and tells why they should respect one another. It explains that this is really the meaning of sex between a man and a woman. Sex without this respect is the basic problem we face today.

Her colleague then joined in: "Yes, now love is not required. Before love was required. Now it is just sex for sex."

In the new state, refraining from sex or having it on terms that were deemed "safe" by the state became the public expression of patriotism in a whole new way that obviated the need for this historic discourse about Buddhist virtue, and yet it was the desire to rekindle such concerns that were most visible among those asked to implement socialist rule. It seems that ordinary sex was still a morally tricky business in the sense that it still challenged Buddhist ethical norms for many Tibetans. The ability to show these concerns was, however, politically tricky. Whether or not an individual actually was politically committed to the socialist modernization project, it was best to be, or appear to be, sexual and reproductive in the political ways mapped out by the state—by the neighborhood fertility monitor; by the public service messages that were posted on work unit walls; or by the lessons all young Tibetans were taught in school about sex, its biological representations, its medical truths, and its demographic consequences. This meant suppressing emotion about abortions and expressing a concern about "mod-

ern" sexual practices in terms of the biological outcomes and the responsibilities of dutiful female citizens.

Thus, concerns about sexuality today focus on the fact that from traditional perspectives, Tibetan youth are not "moral" about their sexuality: they
have sex without love, they abort their unwanted babies and don't worry
about the moral consequences, they have many lovers without concern for
marriage, they think about their sexual unions as if they were simply about
pleasure and being "modern." It is these behaviors that "fit" within the
political script for sexual modernity given by the state, but it is these behaviors that trouble other Tibetans because they seem "immoral," showing
how uneven the effects of moral transformation can be.

Sexuality and the State

That sexuality had always been a contested moral terrain among Tibetans is
without a doubt. But what I have tried to show here is that the terms of this
contestation in 1990s Tibet were in some part new. It was not that socialism
had stripped sex of its moral trappings (although that was in some sense the
goal of a reproductive science). It was rather that the trappings of socialism
were new for Tibetans. For many Tibetan women, these new moralities felt
like no morality at all. These sentiments became evident in the conversations
I had outside of the clinic. Over lunch one day my Tibetan companions
pointed out several Chinese prostitutes among the other diners in the restaurant. These prostitutes, I was told, were probably the "expensive ones" because their patrons were taking them to dine in the middle of the day. One of
my friends quietly leaned over to tell me that "these days, prostitutes are
everywhere in Lhasa," as if I could have somehow not noticed the ubiquity of
their salons on nearly every street in nearly all the new sectors of the city.
This influx of prostitutes was a new phenomenon. Most of the prostitutes
were Chinese, but increasingly Tibetan women were turning to prostitution
as well. Moreover, there were more and more "sex shops" in the city. These
shops openly sold sexual paraphernalia ranging from inflatable dolls and
traditional Chinese aphrodisiacs to skimpy lingerie. My lunch companions
assured me that these shops not only sold sexual paraphernalia but also, if
requested, customers could purchase sex.

This new venue for sex bothered my friend enormously. In the first place,
it was clear to her that many Tibetan men used their services. "Of every ten
Tibetan husbands, eight will be visiting prostitutes," my companion's friend
said, joining in. "What do they like about them?" she asked, and continued,

"Maybe it is their white skin, or their red lips. You know, so many Tibetan women are trying to bleach their skin now, to look more like these women." They went on to note that these prostitutes earned a lot of money. Indeed, I was told, sometimes they came from poor rural provinces outside of Tibet and earned a lot of money in a few years, after which they would leave to start a business for themselves elsewhere in China. Echoing my friends at the Tibetan hospital, my luncheon companion then said, "They have sex just for the money. It is just like having sex for sex, without love (*nying je*: compassion)."

As the conversation continued I realized that what was more frightening to my friend than the presence of these prostitutes was the fact that these women were setting new standards for all Tibetan women. It was not so tragic that some Tibetan girls were turning to prostitution but that the standards for modern sexual behavior that were being set for these women were modeled after what they considered the questionable moral standards of Chinese prostitutes, those who engaged in "sex just for the sake of sex." It was similar to the concerns expressed by the Tibetan doctors: many young Tibetan girls from Lhasa who were not prostitutes per se were still acting as if they were prostitutes by having sex with many men before settling down to monogamous marriage. As my friend explained to me: "It used to be that a woman who had sex with another man was considered married to that man, but these days women have sex and even get pregnant with one man, and then they abort that child and have sexual relations with another man, and on and on like this. It is causing them a lot of problems with their health, having so many abortions like this. They don't seem to care."

The fact that standards of dress and modes of participating in Lhasa's leap to modernity entailed for at least the younger generation the sporting of Beijing fashions that emphasized the bodily contours in different ways than traditional dress, including vast expanses of bare upper torsos and legs in the summer, accentuated breast lines, tight pants or hot pants, and very high heels, and the fact that young women who were not prostitutes wore these fashions as often as they could was disturbing to my friends. They were also bothered by the fact that these women were increasingly visible not only in Lhasa's many new discotheques and karaoke bars but also on the streets in front of the Jokhang and Potala. Their concern was that it seemed to them that these women felt that "nothing" was sacred about these places that would in turn inspire them to wear traditional clothes that covered more of their bodies. I was sympathetic to their perception of the contrast between the contemporary clothes and the traditional Tibetan women's clothing that essentially covered a woman from neck to toes. For my colleagues, these women were not simply a symptom of the Sinification of Tibet; they were a sign of its demoralization.

During this time and even now Lhasa Tibetans were experiencing the radical unsettling of a way of life signified in a shift in standards about "sex," but it was also the shift in meanings of "sex" contained therein that was troubling for them. As a Tibetan man explained in a conversation with a colleague about the "problem of sex" among young women, noting that the terms one might use to describe these different standards and meanings were also in transition: "The term *gshang tshong ma* [literally, "private parts commercial one," or a woman who trades in her private parts] means prostitute," he said, "but for an unmarried woman who sleeps around or has multiple boyfriends but who is not a prostitute in that she is not getting paid for her services . . . a girl's mother might call her a prostitute, *gshang tshong ma*, while arguing with her. Other people might use the term derogatorily for her also. . . . They might say she is *che-mo*, 'bad character.' "

The rise of Chinese prostitution and the public sense that there was a state-sanctioned effort to "pollute" Tibetan culture through the sexual license of rampant prostitution was an attitude I frequently encountered. As my friend explained to me soon after our luncheon conversation: "The government says prostitution is illegal, but they do nothing to stop it in Tibet. Here, the government endorses it. Even the police chief and the army chief have their own special prostitutes." She considered this one of the many strategies deployed from Beijing that was intended to "pollute" Tibet. It was part of the same system of governance that corrupted young Tibetan women into not recognizing the "immorality" of their ways—not recognizing that having "sex" for the sake of "sex" was, for these more conservative onlookers, a sign of moral decay.

Predictably, the Tibetan women who were identified this way rejected the idea that they were being "immoral" by having multiple sexual partners or by having multiple abortions, as is often the case with young women who are sexual in this way. For them, being modern meant embracing sexual activity in modern ways and conforming to Beijing's idea of a modern youthful citizen. For them, this was an inherently moral way of behaving because it conformed to the state's expectations for their modernization. Despite the state's official policy and position that prostitution was illegal, and that women of "easy virtue" were to be castigated, the messages that Tibetans were interpreting from the state's efforts to modernize were that they should advance themselves by being more "modern" in the ways that other Chinese girls were becoming modern, and this meant being more overtly "sexual" in ways that the state authorized and condoned. This did not mean restricting one's sexual activity; on the contrary, it seemed more often to mean increasing it but in ways that conformed with fertility policies and the "appearances" of modernity that were brought into Lhasa on the bodies of young Chinese prostitutes.

Forty years of efforts to both eliminate traces of the old culture and simultaneously target fertility as the means by which Tibetans would become "modern" resulted in a good deal of tension between Tibetans over how to "think" about their sexual and reproductive lives. Singling out "traditions" as a source of trouble and then offering reforms that were seen by many Tibetans as having devastating effects on their society—psychologically, socially, and morally—only made those traditional customs all that much more respectable to many Tibetans. But such sentiments were politically risky and so, not surprisingly, others embraced a different set of possibilities. Some adopted a "modern sexuality"—modeled after the type of Chinese girls who were depicted in magazines and who sold themselves on the streets of Lhasa (and who were bought by Tibetan men)—suggesting to Tibetan women that they could remain politically safe and desirable to their husbands by endorsing these sexual norms. In modern Tibet, sexuality had become meaningful in all of these contradictory ways that layered religious traditionalism and secular state patriotism (not to mention dissent between the genders about appropriate sexual norms) on top of one another and sometimes led to internal confusion about moral propositions and political risks.

Conclusion

A good example of the way that the moral object of sex was configured for contemporary Lhasa Tibetans was made apparent to me in summer 1998 in a story that circulated among them about a young woman who worked many years of her life as a prostitute. Apparently, she was sought by customers from far and wide because of her extraordinary abilities. Her habit was to visualize herself as a *dakini*—a female Buddhist deity-adept. By visualizing herself as such, she dedicated her work to selflessly fulfilling the desires of her male customers—indeed, as I was told, "devoting herself entirely to their happiness and asking for nothing in return." When she died, she underwent what is called a "rainbow body" death, in which the corpse does not decompose but rather gradually shrinks until it disappears entirely into clear light and rainbows. (Buddhist texts say this type of death occurs among practitioners who have accumulated so much virtue that they transcend ordinary rebirth.) What concerned the two Tibetans telling me this story was not the fact of her prostitution (for clearly it had been virtuous), but rather that the government feared the implications of her shrinking body so much that they took it away and disposed of it in an unknown location.

Whether or not the story of the "rainbow body" prostitute is apocryphal or true (a question I cannot answer), its circulation on the streets of Lhasa in the late 1990s suggests something about its ability to resolve a growing set of concerns about the changing moralities and meanings of sex among contemporary Tibetans. At a time when many Tibetans feel that their government has compromised the moral foundations of their society, in part through the introduction of a new set of meanings about "sex" and the attack on its traditional religious possibilities, the story of the rainbow body proposes a resolution. Deep-seated fears about the penetrations of a modern immoral sexuality are assuaged by the possibility that even the basest form of immoral sex (prostitution)—a kind of sex that many Tibetans associate with the regimes of population control and the sciences of demographic transition that were put in place by the socialist government—can be redeemed as virtuous. Such a possibility poses a critique of the government's claims to socialist ethical superiority at the same time that it enables traditionally oriented Tibetans to cope with the changing sexual mores of their time.

Notes

1 See Gyatso (1998) for a more thorough exploration of this in the rNyingma pa lineages.
2 This logic follows partly from the Tibetan soteriological recognition of a union of female and male components in the development of the human embryo itself. The seeds of germination of the human being contain within them the components of male and female (semen and blood) from which the physical body is created. A transmigrating consciousness ignites this fetal mass and enables the male and female components to first form the body's three central channels and, from there, the remaining bodily constituents and its regulatory systems (the humors of wind, bile, and phlegm) (Meyer et al. 1992). The presence of desire in the transmigrating consciousness makes this possible. Desire enacted in past lives creates seeds of desire (based on the law of karma) in the transmigrating consciousness (sems) that sees its copulating parents. These seeds then form the basis of its migration into the fetal mass where it will give rise, by way of winds, to a corporeal being. So long as one acquires the moral baggage of having committed unvirtuous acts—chief among these being unrestrained desire—the more likely one will be reborn, again and again, and never achieve transcendence or Buddhahood. In this view, however, actual sex becomes a moral problem because it is paradigmatic of desire. Desire is

considered a moral flaw, a poison, and an obstacle to achieving enlightenment. Hence the Tibetan Buddhist view of sexuality is that it enables the body to become a moral register and template; the body is considered literally the "flesh and blood" version of the quality of one's spiritual morality from past lives that is ignited with copulation and the enlivening of a fetal mass. Further, the body produced therefrom will be a site for the expression of morality in one's present life, in part, through sexual behavior.

3 Beyond the ruling elite, ordinary sexual relations among subjects of the theocracy was not a "state-level" political concern. Only in cases of lineage-based reincarnations (such as in the Kargyu lineages, which did dominate in some areas) did family-based reproduction become important. At local political levels, concerns invested in marital, reproductive, and therefore sexual acts were focused on such things as adultery, illegitimate children, and inheritance among spouses and offspring (French 1995), but these were adjudicated at local levels not as state concerns. Moreover, French has argued that these adjudications were informed by Buddhist conceptualizations of the law. Marriage, for example, was generally undertaken with formal contracts between spouses' families. Of concern in the contract was that the astrological signs between the spouses were auspiciously matched (requiring the counsel of a lama), that the family make appropriate prostrations to deities who would protect the marriage, and that property was exchanged (38–39). In cases of adultery, adjudication was based on the moral quality and "root" sources of the discord, especially when it could be seen as a cause of further discord leading to more adultery, fighting, divorce, and/or murder (143). The logic derives from religious cosmologies that take as a vow (the commitment against causing dissent) and discord among the *sangha* (community of disciples).

4 Trulku means emanation body, that is, a being who has foretold his or her rebirth and is discovered as a child by his rememberance of episodes from his or her past life or lives.

5 From Chopel (1992: 115, 179): "Alas, I am crazy nowadays, and though those who are not will laugh at me, the experience of bliss is not of little meaning, and the birth of family lineages is not of little meaning. If one can sustain the way of passion from within bliss and emptiness, how can that have little meaning?" . . . "If there were no human beings, how could there be monks and the Buddhist teaching?"

6 Under Chinese rule, Gedun Chopel was identified as a heroic figure (because he flirted with Marxism and wrote critically against religious hierarchy and hypocrisy), but his book on the arts of love was banned by the same rulers because it advocated too much religion.

7 All undocumented quotes are from my notes taken during fieldwork from 1993, 1995, 1998, or 2000.

8 Growths in the uterus and ovaries, irregular bleeding and arthritislike symptoms, as well as heart diseases of various sorts were often attributed to traumas suffered in some cases nearly forty years earlier. Rofel (1999a) presents rich case histories of women "speaking bitterness" about the years before and during the Cultural Revolution. Note that I don't consider that "confessions" in the hospital beds to be of the same sort as those elicited by the state in the "bitterness" campaigns.

9　Greenhalgh 1992. See also Anagnost 1995 for a good discussion of the state's investment in reproductive policy in order to improve the quality of the nation.

10　This is in part because many of the accounts of life in socialist Tibet come from persons whose circumstances may have been extraordinary rather than ordinary (Pachen and Donnelley 2000; Goldstein, Seibenschuh, and Tsering 1997). We do not have many accounts of "ordinary" Tibetan life in the commune period in rural Tibet.

PART 3

Contestations of Liberal Humanism

Forged in Sexual Identity Politics

• • •

In this volume an analytical trajectory found in many essays but highlighted in the final two concerns the negotiation of a morally based liberal humanism in and through the process of making sexual subjects whose resulting identity politics are, in some sense, inspired by new technologies and development efforts devoted to the management of things "sexual." Vinh-Kim Nguyen and Lawrence Cohen both attend to questions of sexual identity politics aroused in part by AIDS development work by nongovernmental organizations (NGOS). Whereas much sexuality literature has critiqued AIDS work for its presumption of uniform and global sexual identities, little has explored the ways in which these debated classifications actually effect sexual behaviors and normativizing processes on the ground in the locales where they have taken root. Moreover, while most of these critiques subscribe to the view that the idea of a "sexual identity" is a modern phenomenon that is associated with Western industrialized settings, few studies question the solidity of this "sexual identities" category itself.

The negotations of liberal humanism aroused by AIDS prevention work often point to a monopolizing tendency in which the moral high ground is claimed for both identities and politics. Risk reduction by way of safe sex education and the formation of political movements around these efforts are as much about authorizing the moral authority of sexual identities identified therein as they are about the moral certainty of health provision articulated in and around scientific "facts." The essays in the final section of this volume demonstrate the fallacy of this presumed moral high ground. What is perceived as a liberating agenda in one geographic location is contested as repressive in another, and even within a specific locale what is adopted by some as an opportunity to escape repressive traditions is for others within the same network of activists or participants a route to exploitation.

In Nguyen's case, we see how attempts in Côte-d'Ivoire (Ivory Coast) to create the physical and moral space for sexual liberalism are brought on the wake of responses by modernization NGOS to AIDS that overtly cultivate a notion of self-conscious "sexual identities." But, he notes, this process should be understood in terms of the history of both the cultural construction of masculinity and the social and economic forces operating in the wake of colonial forms in places such as West Africa. The fashioning of "homosexuality" in Abidjan might be read as the outcome of a colonial process, insofar as homosociality is encoded in Western cultural forms and where the encoding of this identity as "homosexual" often entails identification with the cultural meanings associated with homosexuality in the West. But Nguyen notes, we should also pay attention to the ways that male-male sexual relations, which did exist prior to colonialism, have perhaps been and remain embedded in concerns about economic participation in modernity at the same time that they are sometimes about refashioning the terms of masculinity within this culture. In the "interzone" between globalized NGO development efforts and the local struggles for survival in an economic crisis, the sexual practices of Abidjan men reveal an articulation of local and transnational social relations and discourses of sexual identity.

Cohen's exploration of the kothi wars refers at once to the various contrary meanings generated by the desire to identify the specific homosexual identity groups by NGO workers, leaders of sexual identities movements in India, and academics, and simultaneously to the kinds of limitations these desires place on sexual practices. The attempt to fit the kothi—a term generated by the search for an AIDS target, in this case a male who prefers one sort of homoerotic sex over another—into categories generated by the studies of sexuality in the wake of AIDS and HIV prevention efforts leads to interesting political negotiations over the fact that such categories do not fit with what happens in practice. When Indian men identify themselves in their sexual encounters with other men in relation to these AIDS categories they become wedded to larger transcultural political interests and contests, including Muslim-Hindu identity politics in contemporary India. Cohen notes that recognition means interpellation, and yet he shows that it is in part the misrecognition of gender categories that authorizes an engaged politics of the body and of rights in the international AIDS funding infrastructure of India. The ethical terrain is a return to hallmark debates in AIDS politics, in which who is allowed to name "categories" (authorized by health sciences work) and who gets to claim the identities within those categories is as much an engagement with power in the academy and its writings as it is for those whose identity (betwixt and between categories) is at stake because they are targeted by nationalist concerns.

VINH-KIM NGUYEN

Uses and Pleasures: Sexual Modernity, HIV/AIDS, and Confessional Technologies in a West African Metropolis

• • •

In the wake of the AIDS epidemic, a new version of the "facts of life" has traveled across the globe, disseminated by mass-media campaigns, street theater, and a plethora of awareness-raising techniques. The role of the CD4 lymphocyte, the dangers of unprotected sex, and the viral etiology of this terrible new disease are some of the scientific facts that have been stabilized by an ever-broader network of actors that, as Stacy Pigg points out in this volume, is global in scope. Like others in this volume, I will examine here how the practices that diffuse these "new facts of life" work to constitute new moral objects of sex by focusing on the "forms of life" that spring up on the margins of this global biomedical assemblage.

The terrain for this investigation is the evolving sexual modernity of Francophone West Africa's most important metropolis, the coastal city of Abidjan in the nation of Côte d'Ivoire (Ivory Coast). As a major crossroads of trade and migration since it was established as the French West African hub for a colonial export economy, Abidjan grew into a self-consciously high-modernist metropolis under the stewardship of its first postcolonial president, Félix Houphouët-Boigny. Buoyed by high export prices for coffee and cocoa, the country's major exports, the city's lights glowed brightly in the 1960s and 1970s, attracting migrants from all over West Africa. As a result its population swelled to over two million and a modernist, multiethnic urban culture was created. Social and geographic mobility, exposure to

"Western ways," and the economic empowerment of women provided a fertile ground for new gender roles, a phenomenon that received widespread media attention.

When in the mid to late 1970s export commodity prices collapsed in the wake of the petroleum crisis, the Ivoirian economy fell like a house of cards and everyday life and its popular culture—songs, tabloid commentary, and comic novels—were rife with the modernist tropes of liberated women, anxious men, and dangerous mistresses (Vidal 1979). Consonant with the theses of Michel Foucault (1990, 1984), a discourse of sexuality emerged and iterated concerns about how in the rapidly evolving and modernizing social landscape of Abidjan, an individual was to orient itself to the prevailing moral order in and through sex. This discursive apparatus laid the groundwork for the emergence of a gendered public sphere and allowed sexuality to emerge as an ethical project, making sex available for individual forms of self-fashioning. It was against this landscape of sexual modernity, and after the HIV epidemic had become a major public health problem in the city (De Cock 1989), that issues of sexual behavior became linked to those of sexual identity.

Spurred by funding from development organizations and other international donors with AIDS prevention on their agenda, in 1994 local community groups began to proliferate. Drawing on health education approaches honed in AIDS prevention campaigns in the West, these community groups were vehicles for disseminating AIDS prevention messages that encoded normative, biologized notions of sexuality. These public health messages also worked to further differentiate the sexual public of Abidjan's cultural modernism, showing how local and transnational NGOS functioned as sites of translation.[1] In this essay I will show how the social technologies imported by international NGOS to prevent HIV/AIDS furnished an opportunity for Abidjan's homosocial communities to redefine themselves in light of the "new facts of life."

Transnational and transcultural negotiations were used by Abidjan men and youths to adapt social practices imported by NGOS working with AIDS issues to local circumstances, thus helping to reshape the cultural geography of same-sex relations. These practices advocated sexual openness such as frank depictions of sexual activity in order to foster the adoption of safer sexual practices such as condom use during penetration. They also sought to "give a face" to the epidemic by using confessional technologies (techniques deployed in workshops such as role playing, using open-ended questions, and so on) to encourage Africans diagnosed with HIV to "come out" about their illness and testify. Together, these practices worked to link dissident performances of gender to notions of sexual orientation.

My argument here is that while the "new facts of life" disseminated by AIDS and the response of development agencies may have constituted a moral object of sex, their importance lies more in the effects of the social technologies used to disseminate them. These discursive practices located sexuality within a tactical domain, thus making it available as both substance and objective of the strategies by which individuals sought to position themselves pragmatically within an unraveling postcolonial political economy. The ethical dimension of this process is to be found most clearly in how sexuality became a tactic for self-fashioning.

I will present this argument in three parts. First, there is evidence of a homosocial culture that flourished in the early postcolonial years in Abidjan—the years of the postcolonial economic boom (the Ivoirian "miracle") that preceded the economic crisis of the 1980s. This flourishing culture testifies to the draw exercised by the city's reputation for sexual liberalism and affords a glimpse into how, in the flush of postcolonial modernisms, sexual relations extended beyond questions of reproduction to include forms of self-fashioning produced through performances of gender. In other words, I argue here that this "sexual liberalism" made an almost experimental "playing" of gender roles available as a strategy for fashioning selves.

Second, within the city's heterogeneous social landscape, narratives about individuals make up a "social repertoire" that allows social relations to be negotiated even where kinship networks are weak sources of intelligence or are simply unreliable. Circulating as rumors in the contemporary homosocial community, these narratives allowed the dissemination of sexual imaginaries as well as knowledge about them. With the global economic crisis of the 1970s that ushered in the "crisis years" of the 1980s, awareness of social inequality was heightened even as poverty deepened; as a result, social mobility became a more important basis for negotiating sexual relations and identities. Certainly, social mobility offered the potential for increased material and emotional security, but it also expanded opportunities for new experiences and pleasures. Consequently, this repertoire of narratives took on particular material significance, inserting sex into a variety of discursive practices and, in the process, making it available as a tool for self-fashioning.

Third, in the early 1990s, growing awareness of the seriousness of the AIDS epidemic instigated a response on behalf of international donor institutions that championed "breaking the silence" around sex, as well as the "self-help" and "empowerment" of people living with HIV and AIDS. As NGOS made available an array of social technologies and norms, initially through pedagogical approaches to sexuality and sexual education, these fostered a culture of openness and disclosure around intimate issues. Subsequently the desire to encourage people with HIV to "break the silence" and speak out about their illness created a demand for "testimonials" and the confessional practices for eliciting them. As a result, these confessional technologies conjugated with the narratives and the material effects they produced of existing social networks, and were tactically taken up by individuals to fashion themselves and address a broad range of material needs and desires. Thus AIDS prevention efforts, and the NGO mchanisms through which they were disseminated, allowed homosexual men to organize a quasi public space legitimated by a culture of sexual openness within which "gayness"— in this case, one of many possible narratives of sexual identity—could be cautiously affirmed.

Boubar, Oscar, and the Emergence of the "Milieu"

Abidjan's homosocial scene has, at least since the 1970s, been known as the "milieu."[2] Its history is most often remembered through the story of two nightclubs and of their owners and their patrons. No one recalls exactly how the rivalry between Oscar's and Boubar's establishments developed; but everyone does remember that it developed during the 1970s. For most, the milieu was a question of style. Boubar's was "conservative" and "old school." Boubar's "boys"—an assortment of handsome young men who may or may not have been his lovers—might have always been smartly dressed, *sapé* perhaps,[3] but they were certainly not innovative. Boubar's social circle revolved around his restaurant, laconically known as Boubar's, which served every day for lunch the national dish from his native Senegal, *tiep bo djen* (fish cooked with rice, yams, squash, eggplant, and sweet potato). At night, Boubar's was turned into a disco frequented by men and women from the milieu and also *entraineuses* (women hired by the bar to entice men into the establishment), their patrons, and a diverse cross-section of neighborhood characters.

Oscar, on the other hand, was "trendy." His crowd was considered "hip," relatively outrageous, and prone to hysterics, scandal, and drama. Oscar, unlike Boubar, eventually became somewhat famous because stories about him appeared in the local and international press. He came to Abidjan from Mali in 1969, after failing his baccalaureat exams. Once in Abidjan he developed a network of connections through his job as a hairdresser at the famous La Coupe hair salon in the Plateau district. Oscar's French *patronne* introduced Oscar to her coterie, a mixed group of European socialites and bored housewives who frequented the salon and gossiped while having their hair done. Oscar was a natural confidante.

At a Mardi Gras party in 1978, at the suggestion of one of his clients from the salon, Oscar rounded up some friends and put on a drag show. He and his group were an instant success. The impromptu drag show quickly became a troupe and played to packed and appreciative audiences at private soirées, even in the interior of the country. Within a year, Oscar had found a home for his *copines*—girlfriends—on the rue Pierre et Marie Curie in the nightclub district of zone 4, where he set up a cabaret. The show featured his copines under a string of modernist pseudonyms: Zaza Intercontinentale, Estella Boeing 747, Mercedez Benz 281. Initially frequented by mainly European patrons, Chez Oscar's African clientele grew and soon became a rival to Boubar's as the milieu. The show at Oscar's featured brilliant impersonations of all the "sophisticated ladies" of African cultural life, including the traditional Baoulé singer Allah Thérèse (a favorite of Houphouët), Josephine Baker ("Mon Pays Haïti"), and Miriam Makeba ("Pata-pata") as well as American disco divas Diana Ross and Grace Jones ("La Vie en Rose" and "My Jamaican Guy"). The crowd favorite was, predictably, Oscar's rendering of the queen of Afro-zouk, Ivoirian singer Aïcha Koné ("Africa Liberté").

Oscar's story was the subject of reports in the widely read Paris daily *Libération* in 1983. *Libération*'s front-page story followed on the heels of a feature in *Ivoire-Dimanche* (popularly referred to as *I-D*), the Abidjan weekly that was avidly read for its occasionally provocative—given the assumed prudishness of the literate public—coverage of social life in the capital. The story on Oscar and his troupe was remarkable in that it did not gloss over the homosexuality of Oscar, Zaza, and the others: "To assert that Oscar and his troupe are homosexuals is a line that most Abidjanais would not cross. Startled by the appearance and behaviour of these young boys, certain would swear—often without the least proof—that we are dealing with a band of sexual inverts. We leave each side to its own truth, in order to remind the reader what is certain: we are here in the realm of art" (Mandel 1983). The story was widely read and well received: in an interview following the *Libération* story, Oscar says that his African clientèle grew after the article was published.

That the story passed with little controversy is surprising and attests to a certain "liberalization" at the time of the discursive climate around sexuality. Nine years earlier, in 1974, *I-D* published an interview with a self-avowed lesbian that caused a small scandal. In the interview the young woman explained how she became a lesbian, including rather frank details of her amorous life. The story outraged *I-D's* readers and brought a severe rebuke from the political bureau of Houphouët's ruling party (the PDCI, Côte-d'Ivoire's single party at the time) and an apology from *I-D's* editor. Perhaps *I-D's* Oscar story, by being couched as a theater review, passed scrutiny more easily, or perhaps frank depictions of lesbianism exacerbated male anxieties about the postcolonial economic order. When I interviewed the now-current editor of a major Abidjan daily who was a writer for *I-D* at the time, he attributed the different reception accorded the two stories by noting that "mentalities had evolved" in the nine years that separated them, largely because stories dealing with sexuality had become more commonplace—the inevitable result of the liberalizing effect of the international media.

Some remember the late 1970s and early 1980s as the heyday of the milieu. Oscar's cabaret did not fare well with the deepening economic crisis, and he moved to Libreville in Gabon in the late 1980s. Many visible members of the milieu dropped out of sight. Boubar's restaurant still exists but no longer turns into a nightclub. Indeed, at one point in the late 1980s he got married, had the first of many children, and went on the hadj pilgrimage. He died two years ago. Oscar's cabaret is no more, and though Boubar's restaurant is now run by his wife it is only open for lunch.

When Oscar was interviewed by *Libération* in 1983 he dismissively referred to the common perception throughout Africa that homosexuality was a colonial importation: "It's true that in colonial times it was widespread, but it existed before. You only have to go to the village, it still exists . . . In traditional societies homosexuality is practiced but we don't talk about it!" The ethnographic literature on homosexuality in Africa is equally laconic. E. E. Evans-Pritchard (1970) devoted a study to "sexual inversion" among the Zande and South African historian Patrick Harries (1990) notes that homosexuality among miners scandalized missionaries in the early twentieth century. Michel Leiris (1996), the pioneering French surrealist and ethnographic writer, makes a fleeting reference to African "pederasts" dancing cheek to cheek in a Dakar nightclub in 1929 at the outset of his journal detailing the Dakar-Djibouti expedition. These accounts are, however, silent about whatever homosexual exchanges Europeans may have been engaged in. Oscar came originally from Mali, and a number of other informants have confirmed that, to those who found gender roles in the village (or even in other cities) too restrictive, Abidjan's cosmopolitanism was enticing. What was at stake in those early years was not so much being able to have sex with other men—that was always possible in less urban settings, where sexual license depended more on one's social position than one's gender—but rather being able to play with gender outside of sanctioned roles. For these African moderns, what was at stake in "sex" was performance rather than bodily pleasures or fundamental truths about the self.

The Contemporary Social Geography of Homosocial Relations

Speaking almost twenty years later, my informants reiterated Oscar's perception of Abidjan as a sexual cosmopolis. Curiously enough, those who assert that homosexuality is a purely European colonial import to Africa agree with "queer theorists" (e.g., Sedgewick 1990; Lane 1995) who have argued that homosociality is deeply encoded into Western cultural forms. What is at stake in these arguments, ultimately, is the manner in which masculinity is constructed through culture and, I would argue, social and economic relations. After the economic crisis of the 1980s that turned the Ivoirian "miracle" into a mirage and drove an ever-growing proportion of the population into a spiral of poverty, the role of socioeconomic relations in shaping the trajectories through which sexuality is enacted has become more salient than the modernist quest for self-expression depicted in Oscar's narratives.

"Economic bisexuals" are the emblematic figure of the impact of the economic crisis on the homosocial milieu. I first heard the term used by a young gay man from a wealthy family, Oumar, in reference to one of his lovers, Karim. Karim told me that eventually he would like to marry an African woman with a good education but who was also "house broken"—that is, who would make a good wife and mother, yet his economic circumstances precluded such a move. He had a girlfriend, but at the time preferred seeing men because "with women it's too much of a problem," meaning, he explained, the demands that had to be met. "You have to take women out," he explained, "you have to take care of them, and when you don't, there's always problems." With men it was different, "they take care of you . . . even if they don't give you money, they will buy you a pair of jeans or take you out to dinner."

Born and raised in Abidjan, the child of a large family that lives in one of the modernist apartment blocks in one of the livelier older quarters of the city, Karim explained to me that he was "introduced to the milieu" by a neighbor, whose cross-dressing was the source of local gossip by neighborhood youths. Many neighborhood boys like to go to "Suzanne's" because there was often food and drink there and Suzanne was an almost maternal figure. Although Suzanne has since gone to live in Europe, she is still remembered fondly.

Karim's social circumstances certainly played a role in shaping his sexual trajectory. Although he had obtained the baccalaureat, there were no jobs for "little people" like him who did not have the connections to land a position in the government or in a private firm. Without a job he could not hope to raise a family. Oumar's family was wealthy and, as a result, promised access to the fabled world of the rich, the fact of which Karim must have been aware. Karim's social network was not limited to the milieu because he maintained an active role in a local political group. Should his party win power in upcoming elections, he might be able to get a patronage job through that connection. But it was through the milieu that Karim was introduced to Oumar, which was his first break at getting himself "settled" and in a position to marry and raise children.

The term *yossi* is used by those in the milieu to refer to a masculine man who entertains romantic relationships with both men and women. Significantly, however, the term has a less materialistic connotation than does Oumar's qualification of these bisexuals as "economic" because it does not necessarily impute purely economic motives to relationships between men. Karim's story is typical of how the manner in which many yossis, "economic bisexuals," or "ambiguous" types perceive their entry into the milieu in terms of the potential for acquiring a wealthy benefactor—presumably European but not necessarily so. The desire for a "sugar daddy" is certainly stoked by the neighbourhood *folles* (queens) who skillfully leverage local youths' perceptions of their fabulous networks of wealth and prestige in order to obtain sexual favors. Thus, the term yossi does not so much refer to a sexual proclivity as to versatility in sexual object choice and dexterity when it comes to sexual relations. It also indexes the performative dimension of gender referred to by Oscar when he described the attractions of Abidjan's homosocial scene earlier on in the postcolonial era: yossis act like "real" men and that is what matters.

In contemporary Abidjan, however, this performative dimension is embedded in material circumstances of social relations and the tactics used to navigate them for individual and collective benefit. As Oumar once patiently explained to me, local boys *passent à la casserole* (get broken in) before they ever get introduced to anyone important. Sampling by sexual brokers is of course an important business strategy for brokers because the quality of the networks they entertain—the economic returns that can be expected from them—depends in part on the desirability and performance of the youth they can marshal for introductions. However, sampling can also serve as an apprenticeship. Entry in the milieu also involves frank sexual talk, as well as becoming conversant with a specialized subdialect of *nouchi* that is impenetrable to those outside the milieu. The local folle's acerbic tongue and perceptive reprimands teach the language of dress style and body language. Rumors and gossip—about what is whose "type," what "look" is in with whom, and sexual preferences—impart detailed knowledge of "taste." This knowledge translates into symbolic capital as youth learn how to dress, talk, and act in order to be attractive to "sugar daddies." Oumar's dismissal of bisexuality as "economic," rational, and calculating was, I found, often inaccurate. For many youth, the acquisition of style was desired in terms of being "fashionable" or the pleasure of belonging to a secret community rather than being part of a conscious strategy for "getting" men. Homosexual relations could not be reduced to economic strategy, nor were they simply about experimenting with gender roles. Rather, as forms of self-fashioning they incorporated concerns that were simultaneously those of material and emotional satisfaction, pleasure and desire.

Talking Names around Town: Social Epistemology and
Rumouring Networks

Much of the social knowledge of the milieu comes from the stories people tell about other people: stories that I realized were as much about conveying information as positioning the teller, the listener, and the subject of the story in a broader commentary on social relations. Sex is embedded in a discursive ecology (again, why economy?) that conditions with material consequences the tactics called on by individuals. The incidents I describe below that surrounded the circulation of a European film show how the performative dimension of gender is never just about play and fantasy but, in this context, engages particular economies of desire and the material tactics they inform.

Men of Africa was the talk of the milieu in 2000. This pornographic video had been made earlier that year by French producers who were drawn to Abidjan by the city's reputation for sexual liberalism and by the assumption that actors could be easily and cheaply found there. Once in Abidjan, the producers used the milieu to find a cast of characters who were only too willing to figure in the video once they had been told of the pay (I was quoted fees ranging from $100 to $500 depending on who my informants were) and had been promised that the video would never circulate in Abidjan. Of course, once produced the video did find its way back to Africa: a young man named Dje-dje procured a copy on one of his trips to Paris and brought it back as a trophy. The video stimulated vivid interest, not least because the characters were locals and Abidjan viewers thought they might recognize someone they knew.

I heard countless stories about what happened once the video was "out." I never got to see the video because Dje-dje was very coy and never told me that he had a copy—perhaps he thought I would disapprove. Connoisseurs told me the video was cheesy and "nothing special," but much commentary was offered on the sexual performances and anatomical attributes of the characters. The local circulation of the video did have material consequences, however. One of the characters, I was told, attempted suicide with an overdose of sleeping tablets because he felt that his manhood had been compromised by the video and because his family found out about it. The leading character in the video was quickly nicknamed "la Star." He already had a local reputation as rough trade and sure trouble, but he nonetheless became a hot property that was eagerly sought out for sex by members of the milieu.

Dje-dje, brandishing his video, was first in line, but his tryst with Star turned into a disaster. Star beat him up and was caught with Dje-dje's expensive watch by Dje-dje's then-boyfriend, Théophile, who was returning to the apartment with his three-year-old daughter in tow. Théophile confronted Star in the living room, appealing to him "as a brother" to give back the watch. Star was impervious to reason, however, and left with the watch. Thankfully, the scene with Théophile in the living room was not violent and no one else was hurt. Dje-dje suffered some bruises and a wounded ego (he never told me about the story, and I never asked). Word about the incident quickly got around town, but it didn't seem to diminish Star's desirability: if anything, it enhanced it.

After the story about Dje-dje another story circulated about how Star accepted a proposition from a man named Joseph. After undressing, Star demanded the man give him his mobile phone—a demand that was considered presumptuous because nothing sexual had yet happened. The confrontation once again turned violent, and in the ensuing scuffle Joseph suffered a broken wrist, Joseph's boyfriend received black eye, and Star left with the phone. The bandaged wrist and blackened eye were much commented on afterward. Star subsequently took up with Bruno, a Congolese medical student. This relationship lasted for some months, with Bruno squandering on Star the allowance he got from his parents in Kinshasa for his medical studies. Bruno later failed his qualifying exams, Star disappeared from circulation, and Bruno's reputation suffered as a result.

Indeed, Bruno's name was "spoiled" by what was considered his frivolous behavior. After a while, I found out that during the time he was "keeping"

Star, Bruno was ostensibly "going out" with a wealthier man who had been supporting him, although this man was already himself involved with another young man. One informant laughingly explained to me that it was likely that it was this first protégé who "spoiled" Bruno's name: "Well, you know, it's like when you have two wives, the first wife checks on the second wife 'cause if the second wife's name gets talked around town then it's the first wife who's gonna get grief." Star eventually ended up in prison, although he was released after the 1999 coup when, during an attempt by soldiers to liberate political prisoners held at the Abidjan jail, in the ensuing chaos all six thousand inmates escaped.

In their dizzying array of serial and parallel relationships, these stories—and countless others I collected—depict the random motion of urban life. By espousing homosexuality as an identity and as the pursuit of desire, young men such as Dje-dje released themselves from the social moorings that usually anchor sexual networks. Most Abidjanis look with suspicion on strangers and insist on knowing "who is who" before getting involved. Knowing "who" someone is requires, above all, knowing their family. Because discussions of same-sex desire are not transmitted easily along kinship networks (talk of such things with family can lead to being associated with the milieu) rumoring circulates, in the form of stories, valuable information. Similar to the system of e-mail, stories accumulate and are often broadcast or redirected, giving rise to a plethora of potential misinterpretations that must be navigated carefully by scrutinizing them for their true intent, because at stake is knowing who is who in this social epistemology.

Knowing who is who is also crucial to participating in the informal economy—it allows one to know whom to extend credit to and who can be convinced to buy what. In the city, where poverty makes everyday life precarious, knowing who is who is the key to survival, and as such requires that opinions, gossip, and rumors be collected and weighed against the credibility of the source. Within this set of discursive options, the gender performativity showcased by *Men in Africa* could be inscribed as an economy of desire, transforming sexual performances into material tactics.

Imagining African Masculinities

Rumoring disseminates sexual imaginaries and, when these are conjugated with the inequalities of Abidjan's postcolonial economy, make sex into a powerful technology of the self. I followed one rumor through, a story that concerned a Swiss man who lived in a mansion in Cocody, the wealthy neighborhood across the lagoon from the Plateau. Accompanied by the friends who brought me there I was able to visit his house, and I was surprised to find that the stories had not exaggerated its opulence. From the palm-shaded garden, marble steps led up in to a vast living room, the entrance flanked by two enormous Bambara statues.

The stories about life in the mansion were largely concerned with the nine young men that at one point or another lived there with the Swiss man. The young men all bear a striking resemblance to each other, occasionally leading outsiders to assume they are all brothers. Their dress expresses a certain *loubard* look: baseball caps, jeans, gold chains, and construction boots. The resemblance is not, in fact, familial. Rather, it is a reflection of the Swiss man's adherence to his "type" in his choice of partner. As a result, the expression "potential Swiss" was occasionally used to describe the look of a new face in the milieu. The awareness of the "Swiss type" stems in large part from stories that are told about the benefits of "Swiss patronage."

Although some of the "Swiss boys" no longer live in the mansion, they all retain a bedroom on the ground floor. One of my informants, Kouadio, left after the Swiss man paid for his studies and set up a small electronics business that gave him an independent income that was enough to marry. Kouadio still returns for regular visits. The contrast between the similarity of the "look" and the difference in character and aspirations belies the structuring power of, in this case, "Swiss" imaginings of African masculinity.

The patronage of the Swiss man is rumored to be generous—private schooling that is paid for (and often squandered), decadent group trips to the Middle East, and even cars. Many stories focus on one of the young men, Yaya, who is said to have masterminded an armed robbery. The victim of the robbery was the Swiss man himself, who was dispossessed of his Mercedes and a significant amount of cash. However, although Yaya was later arrested at a police roadblock driving the car, his patron came and bailed him out of jail. A few years later, Yaya took the Mercedes while drunk, packed it with friends, and had a severe road accident in which several were killed. The Swiss man then had to fly back from Zurich to pay the hospital bills. This story was told to me by Kouadio, who after the accident had to front the money so that the hospital would agree to treat the injured. The mercenary "what's in it for me" attitude displayed by the older boys, of which Yaya was one, was in striking contrast to the vulnerability of the younger boys. How much of this difference, I wondered, could be attributed to their long "Swiss" apprenticeship?

The "tastes" of wealthier men—and the constructions of African masculinity that underlie them—are disseminated as gossip through the milieu, which in turn shapes the way young men present themselves and construct their own masculinity. The projections of masculinity that disenfranchised youths appropriate and reflect back in a quest for economic and emotional resources are not limited to culturally encoded manifestations of desire on the part of wealthier men. For others such as Kouadio, who despite marrying continued to travel the far reaches of the townships in search of young men, sex was also about placing one's identity as an African man attracted to other African men, a complex equation of desire not easily reduced to active/passive or masculine/feminine stereotypes. Kouadio, absorbed by his own issues of identity, and the Swiss man, who was shielded by wealth, were unaware of the power rumoring networks had to project their own desires and make their fantasies come true.

Karim's story, described earlier, of his "recruitment" into the milieu identifies the role of drag queens in signaling the existence of minority sexualities in Abidjan's pullulating townships. However, as the stories of Karim and the Swiss acolytes indicate, what is at stake for these youths is a complex concatenation of material, emotional, and sexual concerns rather than a straightforward quest to subvert the "traditional" gender roles that Oscar and others who migrated to Abidjan in the 1970s found so confining. Within the broader environment of rumor and gossip, young men such as Karim are able to make use of the stories that occur within an economy of discursive practices that produce knowledge about individuals.

These stories show how rumors transmit along, and solidify, social networks, as well as being effective strategies for disseminating information important for survival. These networks are material in that they can be mobilized for economic survival in the city and also that they are concrete, "mappable" trajectories and constitute a social epistemology, which refers to the ways of knowing and navigating social worlds that take hold in this labile urban environment. It is the stuff of what Hebdige (1981) has called "subcultures," stuff whose materiality can be observed in the way that subjects fashion themselves, present themselves to others, and trace particular trajectories in an uncertain world.

Nodes and Networks: Nongovernmental Organizations and AIDS

When Abidjan emerged as the epicenter of the West African HIV epidemic in the late 1980s, its (not unrelated) economic importance and "modernity" made it a logical place for international organizations to pioneer funding local community groups to implement grassroots AIDS prevention programs. While most of these community groups were young, having been created in response to the drive of large international funding organizations to strengthen "civil society" throughout developing countries in the 1990s, in many respects their genealogy can be traced to colonial voluntary associations. According to the anthropologists who studied the urban realities of colonial modernity, these voluntary associations were a form of "urban kinship" bricolage of "traditional" kinship relations, moral economies, and "modern" forms of social organization.

It is in the space cleared by some of these postcolonial voluntary associations that a quasi-public homosocial sphere is to be found. A few, like the Association des Travesties de Côte-d'Ivoire (ATCI), are legally incorporated and make no bones about their sexual affinities. Others are informal associations of friends and acquaintances who will occasionally organize evening get-togethers or dances, collecting money to rent a dance hall or for purchasing food that they will cook together. In between are organizations and associations whose raison-d'être is unrelated to the issue of sexual orientation, but that have nonetheless become informal meeting places for exchanging stories and knowledge about the city's differentiated sexual terrain. Such organizations include sports clubs, religious groups, and political associations; for example, an impromptu gym in Abobo township, a Buddhist worship club, or the neighborhood youth wing of one of the major political parties. These are not meeting places in the sense of "cruising grounds" where people meet for sex. Rather, they are spaces of complicity where issues of sexuality—including homosexuality—are discussed. They are also informal sites of self-help, where a shared interest like politics, body building, or worship allows the development of solidarity. In these spaces, the discourse of homosexuality is not one about sexual desire. Rather, it emerges as a strategy within a broader calculus of pleasure that conjures material, emotional, and physical pleasures.

While these associations forged urban kinship relations and informal friendship circles, they also acted as nodes within diverse social networks, allowing practices imported by "foreign" agencies to be taken up and disseminated, their objectives and products refashioned according to local agendas. The association Positive Nation is one example of a group whose purpose is ostensibly unrelated to homosexuality, but where the diffusion of practices meant to foster sexual openness and "empower" people with HIV/AIDS led it to develop as a quasi homosocial sphere where sexuality became linked to identity rather than social mobility.

Positive Nation first came to my attention in 1995 when I came across their colorful and slickly produced AIDS prevention pamphlets. The pamphlet contained cartoon figures to illustrate condom use, some of which showed two men while others showed a man and a woman. The sexual explicitness of the educational materials mirrored those of French AIDS organizations. Curious about the source of the educational materials, I became acquainted with the organization and its members. The organization, I learned, was founded in 1993 by two young men, Christophe and Kouamé, who had briefly been lovers before becoming friends. At the time, few people were interested in HIV/AIDS, believing that it was "a disease of poor people, drug addicts, and Western homosexuals." Further, it was felt that it was the responsibility of the state to deal with such public health matters, and the state itself did not seem to think that AIDS was a problem. However, Chistophe and Kouamé, who had lost friends to AIDS, wanted to combat these views.

As I gradually learned more about the organization's two young founders, it became clear to me that Positive Nation represented an attempt to organize a homosocial space that was not just about getting sex. That, Christophe explained to me, was easy enough—in large part due to the difficult economic circumstances the local youths found themselves in. As a result, he explained, there is no shortage of what he called "economic bisexuals," the attractive, masculine young men who look to relationships with other men as a strategy for survival. While these men are referred to using the term described earlier as yossi, their lovers are *woubis*.[4]

Although Christophe would not be called a *woubi*—"*il n'est pas folle!*" (Christophe is no queen) one of his boyfriends once growled at me when I asked—he lived out his homosexuality through a woubi-centered network. Woubis are popular figures in the neighborhoods where they live: their houses are open to local youths who can count on having meals there when there is not enough at home and occasionally might even be treated to a beer at the local *maquis*. Woubis had money because they had jobs, which they had gotten like everyone else in Abidjan, through contacts. As a result, many neighborhood youths seek out their patronage, much in the same way described earlier when Karim sought out a relationship with Suzanne. These young men have little in the way of economic resources because they come from large families where they are increasingly marginalized when they are unable to contribute financially to the household. "Hanging out" with woubis promises access to wealthier homosexual men.

Such access is not granted easily, however. Christophe told me that these neighborhood youths had to demonstrate that they could be trusted not to "steal at the first opportunity" and could be counted on to perform errands. The visibility of woubis as presumed homosexuals ensured that the youths who courted them were not homophobic and presumably homophilic. Some of the youths were sexually curious, and when sex was consummated they graduated to the category of yossi. Some woubis functioned as informal dating services, introducing attractive yossis to shyer men who were uncomfortable in public.

After a few years, when he reached his mid-twenties, Christophe tired of socializing with woubis. He had never been interested in them sexually and their antics and "carryings-on" tired him. "They're all drama queens" he told me, adding that he had realized that their "introductions" were less than disinterested. Indeed, he was expected to return the favor in the form of reciprocal introductions to an imagined circle of wealthy, preferably European, men who would shower the youths with gifts, a portion of which would return to the woubi who had originally set up the introductions. He added that he was tired of being used as a "stepping stone" and of being "constantly hit up for loans by little queens who don't know how to manage their money."

Of course, the woubi network was not the only way to meet men. Christophe could always make propositions in the random contacts of everyday life: butcher boys at the market, car washers, peddlers, shopkeepers. However, perhaps because these men hadn't been checked out beforehand by a neighborhood woubi, or perhaps because Christophe just "didn't know how to pick them," these encounters often turned into disasters. After a few such disasters, he would turn to more reliable sources—making use of the "social epistemology" of the milieu—before returning to more spontaneous, and more sexually exciting, strategies.

For Christophe, the founding of Positive Nation allowed his engagement with the milieu to gradually broaden beyond meeting men for sex. The organization was modeled on a French AIDS activist group that had taken highly visible actions in France, and had itself been inspired by an earlier American gay and AIDS activist group. Once the group was founded, its rhetoric of openness around sexuality as a strategy for combating AIDS easily attracted funding—from international agencies that found its culture of sexual openness "refreshing" and "adapted" to the needs of AIDS prevention work—as well as a broad cross-section of recruits.

Kouamé's charisma played an important role in drawing other men, although of undetermined sexuality, to the organization. The first time I interviewed Kouamé in 1996, he had come home from work for lunch and was

on the balcony of an apartment he shared with friends, busily peeling potatoes in the sweltering heat for a quick meal of *steak frites*. Unlike Christophe, Kouamé is brimmingly self-confident, a handsome man whose burly
frame, "in-charge" demeanor, and air of financial ease earns him the respect
that is accorded to "big men" in his neighborhood. In the neighborhood, he
is described as *en forme* (in shape) or simply *le gros* (the big one). Kouamé
"knew" he was attracted to men ever since he was a child growing up in a
poor neighborhood of Abidjan. His first relationship, at age fifteen, was with
a French man he met in a park. The man brought him home and eventually
took him in, paying for his education and then sending him to university in
France in 1992, seven years after they first met. Their sexual relationship was
extremely brief—Kouamé refers to his man, who has since died, as his "tu-
tor." Kouamé loved his stay in France, a country where "the government
respects people," but he returned to Abidjan to be "home" after he finished
his studies.

Kouamé then moved in with a Dutch man he met on his return from
France in 1994, and took a job in a Lebanese-run import-export firm. At this
point, at age twenty-five, he told his family he was homosexual, which was
greeted with general indifference. His sisters, who "adore" him, only adored
him more, and two of his brothers, who never liked him anyway, decided
they liked him less for it. His parents ascribed his announcement to his
European stay and decided to wait for the phase to pass and for him to marry
and have children. Kouamé often showed up at the family compound with
various boyfriends in tow; they were always well received, and treated like
family friends.

Kouamé is the youngest son of a large matrilineal family. His parents and
three of his sisters live in the *cours commune* (shared compound) where he
grew up. This compound is close to where he was born, a village that has
since become incorporated into the townships that sprawl around Abidjan.
Kouamé's parents are now quite elderly, and his mother is paralyzed on her
right side from a stroke. His two brothers have "modern" jobs: one is a
policeman and the other is a nurse. His mother's illness is a constant source
of tension between Kouamé and his family. While Kouamé paid for modern
medicines for her, his brothers and sisters have insisted on treating her with
traditional medicines, thereby crystallizing the conflict with his siblings over
his authority within the family. Advocating the use of modern medicine and
a modern approach to treating his mother's disability is Kouamé's way of
demonstrating that he could have a role in the family even though he would
not have children and was, therefore, refusing a fundamental responsibility.

After a while, I realized that Kouamé's fury at his family's insistence on traditional medicines betrayed his anger at his family's refusal of his "modernity" that the insistence on traditional medicines implied.

In the city, Kouamé's charismatic personality rapidly earned him a place at the center of a vast constellation of friends, acquaintances, fans, and hangers-on. The relationship with Hans, who Kouamé characterizes as "the love of my life," did not, however, survive the ups and downs of Kouamé's tumultuous flirtations, seductions, and affairs with the succession of young men who were attracted to him. In spite of these relationships he wanted to settle down with an African man. A few months after his break-up with Hans, and after a succession of rowdy affairs with African boys, Kouamé told me that he "wasn't interested" in local boys anymore. They are "all the same": either "they're just with you for financial gain" and not "truly" gay, or they are "silly queens," of whom one tires easily. Needless to say, by then he had launched into a new project.

Bored with his day job at the import-export firm, Kouamé opened a maquis in the city's zone 4 nightlife district. The maquis was a stall perched on the side of a busy road, with low tables and chairs spilling out onto the street. Inside the simple wood structure with its sand floor were a few tables and a bar. Behind the bar was a simple kitchen that produced Ivoirian favorites such as grilled chicken, fried plantain, peanut sauce, and fried potatoes. Kouamé's addition to the traditional Ivoirian recipes was a chili-pepper and palm oil paste enriched with mashed garlic, briefly earning the bar the nickname "Mapouka-Piment."[5] Consonant with his relentless good humor, charisma, and high profile in the milieu (with a push from his succession of dramatic affairs and with their scandalous behaviors) the maquis became a focal point for the milieu. The maquis was also frequented by Liberian refugees who appreciated the generous sampling of American rhythm and blues music that Kouamé enjoyed listening to while he cooked. The Liberians always ordered the same thing, and as a result, the Mapouka-Piment eventually became known as "One-Chicken."

In those years when Kouamé ran One-Chicken all night and worked in the office by day, I often wondered when he slept. The evenings spent at One-Chicken often degenerated into long nights at tawdry zouk bars, raucous karaoke clubs, and "Lebanese" (techno) nightclubs. By then Kouamé had moved out of Hans's apartment and into another on the twelfth floor of one of the blocks of modernist highrises built in the 1970s in the 220 Logements quarter of Adjamé township. As a housewarming present, Hans had given Kouamé a small poodle ("Kwa-kwa"), thus increasing his notoriety in the neighborhood. He moved there with a clutch of young men, including cousins from the village sent to live with him while they went to school, a succession of youths he had "adopted" in his neighborhood encounters, and two nephews. None of these young men were homosexual, but they enjoyed accompanying Kouamé on his evenings out and they clearly worshipped him. One of his nephews went on to graduate as an officer from military college, and he still comes to stay with his uncle whenever he is on leave.

Despite being on the twelfth floor without a functioning elevator, Kouamé's apartment was the hub of a lively social scene. The various youths that congregated there were readily pressed into service in preparing evening meals under Kouamé's supervision. During the meal, programs on television were the focus of attention and the object of much loud commentary and gossip. The crowd favorites were the Brazilian and Mexican soap operas that preceded the evening news, second only to appearances of the nation's first lady on the news program, which were regularly greeted by loud shrieks and sarcastic commentary regarding her hair, her skin color ("if she uses any more skin lightener she'll peel"), and the self-serving nature of her good deeds. The social life at Kouamé's place quietened down after the coup in 1999, however—business was not so good and he had to cut down on expenses. With less food to go around, visitors couldn't count on getting a meal there and they dropped by less frequently as a result.

By then Kouamé's homosocial network and his business connections had converged around Positive Nation. The young men who revolved around Kouamé and his apartment were inevitably invited to Positive Nation meetings, and vice versa. Positive Nation, with its institutional track record built up over the years of the AIDS epidemic, was able to access capital that other start-up businesses could never dream of obtaining from tight-fisted Ivoirian banks. Kouamé applied his business acumen to starting up "revenue-generating" activities for the organization—first a small shop, then a restaurant and café. The success of these enterprises was largely due to Kouamé's managerial skills and flair for mobilizing his vast social network to generate a clientèle; however, the ability of the NGO to obtain investment for what were not quite purely commercial ventures doubtlessly played a role.

Positive Nation's café has gradually come to replace One-Chicken on the local scene, and it has become an important intersection of homosocial and AIDS activist social networks. The rhetoric of openness about sexuality that has been the hallmark of Positive Nation (as seen by their explicit educational materials) has meant that the organization and the meeting spaces that its activities create have instilled a culture of sexual openness that has made it easier for members such as Christophe and Kouamé to be open about their sexual preferences, and for others such as Karim to access these networks. As a node in these social networks, the organization is also a focal point for the transmission of knowledge about the social worlds that intersect there. Within the space of NGOS such as Positive Nation, AIDS had been somewhat of a social leveler, bringing together wealthy, middle-class, and poor Ivoirians in the same social space, much as religion might. As a result, the NGO allows knowledge about different social worlds to flow where they might otherwise not.

In addition to the impact of these mechanical juxtapositions, the NGO and the discourses for which it serves as a vehicle have shaped the trajectories of its members as they partake and mobilize these social epistemologies and use them to negotiate social relations, as we have seen in the stories of Christophe and Kouamé. In this quasi public social sphere, practices of self-fashioning have circulated as part of the international toolkit for addressing the AIDS epidemic. International agencies, trumpeting an agenda that sought to address the ravages of the HIV epidemic through "negotiated sex," "empowerment," and "greater involvement of people living with HIV and AIDS" enrolled Positive Nation in interventions and workshops that stressed sexual openness and creating enabling environments for people with HIV to come out about their diagnosis and reinforce prevention efforts by testifying publicly about being HIV positive in order to "give a face" to the epidemic. This agenda was not limited to rhetoric, however, as powerful techniques were used to train members in the latest HIV prevention techniques: peer-to-peer interventions, "sexual health training," and eliciting testimonials of HIV positive people about their illness. These techniques—role playing, demonstrations, open-ended questions—were essentially social technologies or portable mechanisms for creating standardized forms of "telling the self" and, through them, fashioning the self. As a result, Positive Nation's members became fluent in the sexual culture of post-1960s America and Europe.

The narratives that have been elicited by Positive Nation, whether they are the coming-out stories these individuals tell each other or the stories of illness solicited by the AIDS industry, hybridized with the rumors that allow tellers and listeners to position themselves in a shifting and precarious social landscape. Being able to tell the self and tell about others—both confessing and rumoring—juxtaposes older problematizations of sexuality and gender as performance with newer, more Western forms where these are linked to sexual identity. Sex is no longer about what one does but rather what one is. In Abidjan's kaleidoscopic world that juxtaposes wealth and poverty, modernist hopes and Third World despair, these confessional technologies artic-ulate with local epistemologies and materialist tactics to define the uses of pleasure.

I have argued here that sexuality is more a product of the tactics that are used to assuage desire—for pleasure, beauty, or material security—than a preexisting essence. The emphasis on recounting illness experience—and disclosure about sex—concatenates as an iterative practice of telling the self that produces identity—whether the sexual identity of homosexual men such as Kouamé and Christophe or the biological identity of the HIV positive members of Positive Nation. By the time I collected Christophe's and Kou-amé's stories they had already been fashioned into a familiar "coming-out" narrative, whose soteriological themes of dawning awareness, self-discovery, and self-realization mirrored those of the HIV positive members of Positive Nation. These were, of course, not "just-so" stories—rather, their telling had material effects and, ultimately, biological ones. Several of the young people who joined Positive Nation out of more tactical concerns eventually took the rhetoric of getting tested seriously enough to undergo HIV testing them-selves, only to find out that they were themselves HIV positive. Among those so afflicted were Christophe and Kouamé.

Conclusion

Early accounts of Abidjan's homosocial milieu show how the city's reputa-tion for sexual liberalism encouraged experimentation with alternative no-tions of gender and, as a result, highlight its playful and performative dimen-sions. In contrast, a consideration of today's homosexual milieu in Abidjan shows that discursive practices—narratives of "coming out," rumors, and gossip—cannot be isolated from the way in which individuals come to experi-ence themselves as sexual subjects. The way in which people imagine them-selves and their sexuality—as a true, "inner identity" that is "uncovered" at key points in time, sometimes simply as sexual or romantic fantasy, or as a dream of being emotionally and materially taken care of—structures their rapport with the social world around them and helps to construct both social and sexual networks.

Rumors are a key element in the construction of these networks. Rumor-ing is neither frivolous gossip nor a "hidden transcript" (Scott 1990) that allows people to quietly criticize those in power. Pleasure and power are key elements of rumoring, but in an urban setting they are important sources of knowledge. The cheek-to-jowl social inequality of the city means that getting food into one's stomach, or perhaps even getting rich, is just a story away—a story that can net a sugar daddy, or a good scam, or a business secret, or a miraculous cure, or simply where one might have dinner. As I have shown, the NGOs introduced confessional technologies that conjugated with the narratives and the material effects they produced on existing social networks. These confessional technologies were tactically taken up by individuals to fashion themselves and to address a broad range of material needs and desires. The AIDS prevention efforts, and the NGO mechanisms through which they were disseminated, allowed homosexual men to organize a quasi public space, legitimated by a culture of sexual openness, within which "gayness" could be cautiously affirmed.

Those NGOs such as Positive Nation are also nodes in these networks. Certainly, the AIDS industry's advocacy of sexual openness allowed men like Christophe and Kouamé to imagine NGOs as quasi public spheres within which their sexuality could be expressed. This expression included the aesthetic dimension of desire—the search for an ideal partner either in looks, sexual practices, or identity. In addition, for others, these spaces offered the opportunity of accessing social networks where material gain could be found. For men like Karim, economic and sexual desire are indistinguishable, and homosocial spaces offer opportunities for bettering their condition through the agile use of the technologies of the self they could find there. For these men, the aesthetic dimension of sexuality was materialist—fashioning one's sexuality and one's story in such a way as to be able better to confront the material and emotional hardships of a city and a world struck by deepening poverty and the increasingly elusive dreams of wealth and ease.

Notes

I am grateful to Vincanne Adams, Pierre Sean Brotherton, Bob White, and the two anonymous reviewers whose comments greatly improved this paper.

1   See Fisher 1997 for a descriptive review of the anthropology of NGOS. Fassin 1994 and Pigg 2001b offer more critical approaches to AIDS and NGOS. For a more general critique of the role of NGOS and humanitarians, see Appadurai 2000; Pandolfi 2002; and Rabinow 2001.

2   The story of Boubar, Oscar, and the "scene" in the late 1970s and 1980s was pieced together from my interviews with informants, as well as from the work of Claudine Vidal (1979) and Vidal and Marc Le Pape (1984). I am particularly grateful to Vidal and Le Pape for forwarding to me certain difficult-to-find publications, including Kader 1976; Paulus 1983; and Mandel 1982. All other undocumented quotes in this essay are from my interviews with informants conducted in 1999–2003.

3   The term derives from the acronym for Société des Ambienceurs et des Personnes

Élégantes, an urban club that started as a social-intellectual group but later became a male fashion and elegance club that introduced stylish European fashion to colonial Brazzaville.

4 The distinction is explored in the 1998 documentary *Woubi chéri*, which was written and directed by Philip Brooks and Laurent Bocahut (Dominant 7 Productions/la Sept ARTE, Paris).

5 *Mapouka* is a traditional Ivoirian dance that is noted for its rhythmic shaking of the buttocks. The conjugation with *piment* (hot pepper) connotes a rather spicier version of the dance, which was the subject of some controversy at the time. Purists decried the new improvisations of the dance as pornographic, while modernists pointed out that the updated dance had made a name for Abidjan in the African dance world.

LAWRENCE COHEN

The Kothi Wars: AIDS Cosmopolitanism and the Morality of Classification

· · ·

In the summer of 2001, police in the north Indian city of Lucknow arrested several men who worked as outreach workers for a nongovernmental organization (NGO) called Bharosa Trust. Bharosa was organized to conduct what in the AIDS world is known as prevention research and to provide AIDS prevention information and counseling to males who have sex with other males. The offices of Bharosa and of its affiliate NGO (and, in effect, patron), Naz Foundation International (NFI) were raided, outreach material including a dildo used for condom-wearing demonstrations was confiscated, and various accusations against Bharosa and NFI were released to the press.[1] The police attacked the work of the two groups as a front for "gay clubs," and further alleged that NFI's prominent organizer, Shivananda Khan, might be allied to the Pakistani secret spy network, the infamous ISI. Activists and lawyers from a broad spectrum of progressive NGOS in India and abroad began planning a critical response to what was widely seen as homophobic, predatory, and in India relatively unprecedented state action.

The issue of how to name the beneficiary of these welfare organizations quickly came to the fore in several such planning meetings. Was Bharosa targeting gays or the more general and less stigmatized category of "men who have sex with men" (MSM)? Given the terms of the police accusation, the question seemed far from academic. But resistance to "gay" men as Bharosa's target population was not simply a matter of prudence or realpolitik. Like other NGOS supported by Khan's NFI, Bharosa subscribed to what Khan termed the "*kothi* concept." Kothi (also transliterated as koti) was for the NFI-sponsored family of NGOS an indigenous gender category for a

"feminized" identification within nonelite (and thus nongay) networks of
~~M S M S. Many of these N G O S rejected identification with "gays,"~~ and the police
charge that Bharosa was a front for gay clubs was taken by them among other
things as a gross misreading of N F I commitments.

Not all fellow travelers who wanted to support the Bharosa outreach
workers were aware of or committed to the need for the distinction. But the
apparent high stakes dividing gay from kothi camps within the A I D S N G O
universe of discourse and linking kothi to M S M long preceded the 2001
response to the Lucknow affair. Over the subsequent months, these distinctions and linkages would be invoked in numerous ways. For some participants in post-Lucknow meetings and actions and in the conversations that
swirled around them the stakes boiled down to the rivalry between Khan and
his fellow activist, the Mumbai (Bombay) journalist Ashok Row Kavi. Row
Kavi was accused of instigating the arrests in the first place, and of utilizing
his much discussed connections to leaders in the Hindu Right organization
the Vishva Hindu Parishad (V H P) to accuse Khan of I S I links. Khan was
accused of failing to protect local activists—the men arrested and vilified in
Lucknow—in service of his overextended global ambitions and of blaming
his failures on the easy target of the ever politically incorrect Row Kavi.

Things grew ugly, though for the many activists, funders, and bureaucrats
who knew both men the accusations were familiar. The context: two competing networks of identification, capital, and surveillance had consolidated in
urban South Asia in the 1990s through state, bilateral, and N G O-funded
efforts to constitute culturally appropriate A I D S prevention interventions for
men who have sex with men. Each offered their various auditors a distinctive
mapping of local categories of desire, comportment, and practice, a distinctive ethic of how to "empower" men to reduce their risk of H I V infection,
and—more unexpectedly—a distinctive form of moralizing against cosmopolitan inauthenticity. Each was dominated by a charismatic, visionary, and
controversial activist, one initially based in London (Khan) and the other
primarily in Mumbai (Row Kavi). In the late 1990s, the conflict between
these two networks escalated into an often heated series of contests over the
authenticity and historicity of the identities gay and kothi, so much so that
the police action in Lucknow could be read on either side as less about the
state than about "vested interests" promoting the wrong category.

Borrowed by internationally funded fieldworkers from the language of
Chennai (Madras) *alis* (transgender communities also known in Hindi as
hijras and in English as eunuchs), the word kothi came to refer to men who
act or identify in some way as women, who repeatedly enact a desire to be

penetrated by a real man (the so-called *panthi*), and who are sometimes sex workers. One network cast kothi and panthi as the dominant nonelite forms of South Asian male desire for another male, framed these as embodying "gendered" as opposed to "sexual" norms, and utilized a systematic "kothi-panthi model" as the core of any future interpellation of msms for preventive health. Gay men within these terms were an elite minority with different needs, not rooted in local communities, and aids interventions targeting the majority of msms were to lie elsewhere. The other network located multiple subtypes of kothis within a complex grid of identifications and practices that included gay men and refused gender as the dominant structuring axis defining men's desire for sex with men. The elite other is rather that of the foreign NGO (i.e., the British-born Khan) that can "discover" authentic Indian culture and impose it on the natives and that can imagine a universe where sexuality and gender are analytically distinct. Both networks articulated their work as a stand against the inauthenticity of a category ("gay" or "kothi") promoted by what we might term AIDS cosmopolitanism, an imagined formation of dislocated agents using the economically fortified social enterprise of AIDS prevention to support its own covert projects.

Here Come the Kothis

My sense that there was a story worth telling emerged during a 1999 conference on South Asian masculinities organized by anthropologist Sanjay Srivastava in Melbourne, Australia. Gayatri Reddy, another anthropologist then completing her Ph.D. at Emory University, presented a paper concerning kothi and panthi, words that she effectively argued were more salient than straight or gay in organizing male homosociality and its imaginable breaks for many of the nonelite men in the southern Indian city of Hyderabad.[2] At the same conference, several activist-researchers from the Bandhu Social Welfare Society, an HIV/AIDS group supported in part by NFI and with a mandate to work with MSMs in Dhaka, Bangladesh, gave a paper summarizing studies their fieldworkers had carried out.[3] The research followed NFI's model in carefully mapping sexual place and massaging it for its other languages. Like Reddy, the Bangladeshi activists found that a "Western" straight/gay binarism (Sedgwick 1990) was irrelevant to the situations of most men and that the alternative opposition of choice was kothi/panthi.

Faced with a vibrant kothi-panthi concept extending from Hyderabad to Dhaka, we all were left to conclude that such words demonstrated a pan–South Asian cultural frame, that they were central to a contextualized AIDS prevention practice, and that what political scientist Dennis Altman (1996, 1997, 2001) and others have described as the globalization of the cosmopolitan category of the gay through translocal circuits of signs, space, bodies, capital, viruses, and governance was far from totalizing or complete. Whether subjugated or just different, the cultural logic of kothi and panthi under the necessary gaze of the AIDS enterprise was in 1999 asserting itself.

These were both excellent pieces of research, within their distinct scholarly versus activist frames. But I was curious about the truths demanded of them that threatened to reduce the complexity of Reddy's analysis or the deep groundedness of the Bandhu project to the black box of a counterbinarism. I had lived and worked for a number of years in Varanasi (Banaras), in north India and more or less halfway between Hyderabad and Dhaka; more recently I had done fieldwork in Lucknow itself as well as in Delhi and Mumbai. In years of conversations with numerous men who had sex with men, no one in my memory ever uttered the words kothi or panthi until the mid-1990s. And more than words were at issue: for although I knew numerous men who might fit what kothi and panthi seemed to denote, I also knew many others in similar social locations for whom neither such an oppositional frame nor the cosmopolitan frame of the gay would have offered a useful entrée to a conversation nor, necessarily, to effective AIDS prevention.

Now I was a foreigner, and Hindi was a fourth language, and Varanasi where most of my time had been is small in comparison to Hyderabad or Dhaka. Was the apparent absence of the nominated kothi merely a matter of my own limitations as an India scholar? Was provincial Varanasi simply out of the loop? Or, even granted one or both of these provisos, might there be more to the invocation of kothi/panthi, and to its materialization of a social landscape, by the time it had become an instantiating gesture at international conferences? The last is my presumption. The problem, it turns out, has vexed many others, and indeed there is no space of innocence such as my conference story presumes: the politics of the kothi, in particular, have become controversial, and every position (including studied neutrality) is already spoken for.[4]

She Has Science

When I returned from the conference, I called up a friend from Varanasi to ask him if there were kothis or panthis there.[5] V. was an old lover who had watched me mutate over the years since we first met, from naïf to libertine to yet another academic from elsewhere with dreams of studying sex to confront AIDS. More recently he married a former roommate of mine and now has a green card and travels back and forth between Varanasi and a series of nonunion jobs in Boston. When I returned to Varanasi in 1993 with a grant to study AIDS and MSMS and began to hang out "for research" in places I used to frequent for less complicated purposes, V. was disappointed. At the time I had a new American boyfriend. "I know what she has that we don't," V. said, referring to the boyfriend. "She has *science*." This was in Hindi, with "science" in English. "You know, we meet someone, you and I, and we have fun and fall in love and then we are separated and we hurt. But you dry your tears and write a book." Got it? "That's science."

I denied everything, but went on to write two articles on Varanasi and homosex in which friends, neighbors, and tricks appeared in altered form. In one of them V. became "Guddu" (1995b). Now, on the phone to Boston, I was calling him into being as Guddu once again. No one in the Varanasi parks, I said, had spoken of the sexual world divided into two, into kothis versus panthis or anything like that. Some men, the kinds he as a younger man used to disparage as low class and refer to as Number Sixes or *jankha* (effeminate), would act like hijras or vamps—do *lachak mathak* (swivel their waist and hips), call each other girlfriend (*saheli*), and do dance gigs for weddings or caste gatherings of men—and distinguish themselves from *siddhesade log*, ordinary men, straight men, their boyfriends, husbands, or customers. Were the folks that you called Number Sixes, who I called jankhas and should have just called girlfriends, I wondered aloud, the same folks people are now calling kothis?

I thought of A. He was a Varanasi neighbor who became Ashok, to his girlfriends Anita, in the same article where V. became Guddu. To Guddu, A. was a real Number Six, an itinerant soap factory worker and local sex worker from a family of tailors. A. never believed me when I wanted to go dancing with the girlfriends: you're too *siddhesada*, he said, too straight. You can be my husband. Here was something like kothi panthi, splayed out in this case along axes of class, race, and nation.

But other guys, sometimes with no more money, were neither girlfriends nor siddhesade log. They came to the park for *dosti*, friendship; for *khel masti*, for fooling around, literally intoxicating or lusty play; and sometimes for *pyar mohabbat*, for love. Nor were they "gay," like some other men that V. and I knew, middle-class men who had a job in Varanasi but whose families inevitably lived elsewhere. Whatever pyar mohabbat was, it differed radically from the love and the duties between a husband and a wife: it implied only the identification of the desiring gaze, *nazar*, and was incoherent in other words. In another essay—published the same year I organized these multiple frames of friendship, gendered and penetrative identification, and love along two axes—an axis of difference structured around the figure of penetration and an axis of sameness structured around the figure of play. Pyar mohabbat, I suggested, might be thought of as the juncture where penetration and play collapse into one another (1995a).

But times change, and the most artful of synchronic models lose their relevance. Gay groups have appeared in large cities, films are attacked as lesbian and anti-Hindu, AIDS and its signifiers and institutional apparatuses are a ubiquitous presence, and hijras are winning municipal and state elections. Was there a new language of kothi and panthi in the parks, at street corners at night, or among friends? V. said that some guys did call each other kothi sometimes, but not a lot. Anticipating my next question, he said he thought it meant guys who liked to fuck. "*To* fuck [*karna*]?" I said. "Not *karvana* [to be fucked]?" He paused. It had been six years since my "science" gig had cut that close to friendships; I had long since changed direction in what I asked about, and I had stopped doing research in the city of my old haunts. V. had moved to my hometown, and he knew some other variant of science well in working for Bread and Circus, a well-known organic supermarket. Although the chain promoted Indian spices and freeze-dried curries, V. would be let go about a month after our conversation on the day he became eligible for health benefits. There was a familiarity in my again wanting to know what his words meant, and how they worked, and where they mapped onto people and gestures and parts.

Finally, over the phone, on the penetrability of the kothi: "No."

Hijra Nation

In Melbourne, both Reddy and the Bandhu researchers had noted that kothi and panthi were hijra words that had become more widely adopted. The coming of the kothi is one of multiple public cultural sites framing Indian neoliberalism that iterate hijra difference. In at least one case—the number of films featuring hijras as protagonists (*Tamana, Daira, Darmiyaan*) in the new middlebrow cinema funded and shown by Rupert Murdoch's Star TV and its successors—we might read this proliferation as fulfilling the requirements of emergent neoliberal mediascapes for particularly located scenes of abjection. In a second site, the endless series of U.S. or European features on Indian exotica (by the BBC, ABC, and so forth) that are then circulated globally, hijras are similarly deployed as local signs of a liberal condition. The BBC was particularly interested in following the story of Bombay loan agents hiring hijras to coerce debtors to pay up, and the story has become a repeated affirmation of Indian sameness and difference within the current global order of debt and repayment.[6]

The 1990s and since have witnessed an outpouring of scholarly attention and particularly a saturation of political rhetoric, regarding the figure of the hijra. All of this attention may displace an earlier account of hijra difference generated by colonial administrative and excolonial anthropological attention: that of authentic hijra thirdness versus inauthentic *zenana* crossdressing. Hijras in the context of anthropological and other patronizing interpellation have often distinguished their *asli*, or authentic, practices of nomination and gender from the *nakli* or *kharab*, counterfeit or bad, practices of others seemingly like them (Cohen 1995b). Classically, although not in all instances, asli hijras lacked male genitals while nakli hijras had not yet had the operation. The common accusatory term for these nakli others in many settings has been *zenana* (Ibbetson, MacLagen, and Rose 1911; Lynton and Rajan 1974; Nanda 1990), usually translated from the Urdu as female or effeminate (Sangaji 1983 [1899]). Anthropologist Serena Nanda cites Ibbetson's 1911 anthropological survey of castes and tribes, in which hijras interviewed attacked zenanas as being male prostitutes who harm the reputations of hijras and take business from real (female) prostitutes. Three quarters of a century later, one of Nanda's hijra interlocutors told her:

These other people, who imitate us, they are real men, with wives and children. They come to join us only for the purpose of making a living. How do we know what a person is when he comes to join us? Just recently there was a case in our group. This man's name was Hari. He was the father of four children and he dressed up as a woman and put on a woman's hairstyle. He behaved like a hijra and danced at people's houses, disguised as a hijra. One day we caught him red-handed. We beat him up bodily and handed him over to the police. . . .

One time, when I myself left my group after a quarrel, out of desperation I also joined a group of these zenana and went out to dance and sing with them. One day we went to dance for a family where a man had a son after having five daughters. We came to the house and one of the imposters said, "I will dance today, give me the ankle bells." So she started dancing, and while she was dancing her skirt flew up and all the people said, "This is not a hijra, this is a man." They chased us away and we lost all respect. I also lost respect. So I thought to myself, I am so different from them, like the earth and the sky." (1990: 11–12)

In my essay based on conversations both with hijras and with A. and her girlfriends (Cohen 1995b) I argued that the distinction between asli and nakli third gender was mobile, often tied more to a hijra's commitment to her hijra guru and sisters than to the presence of an operated or intersexed body. At the same time I tried to reread asli/nakli from the perspective of the nonhijra girlfriends. People on both sides of the imaginary line between hijras and sahelis deployed a powerful sense of the true and the counterfeit in speaking of a sexed/gendered body and its history, however varied the particular mapping of authenticity.

The kothi would—like the zenana and the Varanasi saheli—appear to offer a challenge to hijra authenticity by using a counterfeit thirdness to claim the hijras' well-known rights (*jajman*) in births, weddings, and small merchants' petty cash. Indeed Khan in his creation of the kothi-panthi concept has attempted to keep the concepts kothi and hijra absolutely distinct, reiterating hijra and kothi difference in the service of a model for AIDS prevention. But the creation of the kothi sets up a new border—between kothi and gay, to which asli/nakli appears displaced. Hijra and kothi, in this context, appear to collapse into one another.

American linguist Kira Hall is a well-known scholar of hijra language and a leading presence in debates over queer language and performativity more generally. Hall's early work stressed the active agency of hijra self-making through language. For example, in 1994 she wrote: "Their use of language in particular reflects a lifestyle that is constantly self-defining: they study, imitate, and parody dichotomous constructions of gender in an effort to gender themselves. Not only do they switch between feminine and masculine morphological forms in their everyday discourses, they also employ a mixture of conversational styles variously associated with either femininity or masculinity." At the same time, Hall was careful to extend this performative agency to non-hijras, women and men: "I suggest that linguistic negotiations of gender, although perhaps particularly overt in the Hindi-speaking hijra community, are not unique to alternative identities; rather, women and men of all communities manipulate culture expectations of feminine and masculine speech in order to establish varying discursive positions" (1994).

Intriguingly, in work done later, in 2001, Hall appears to abandon the effort to join groups through their parallel performative strategies and to now accentuate hijra difference. To do this she extends the domain of hijra language to "kotis" and chooses an NGO field site where the linguistic difference between kothis and the anglophone "upper-middle class gay community" is exemplified:

> Language practices that characterize the emergent urban gay and lesbian community contrast sharply with those of the hijras or kotis,[7] transgender communities that claim an indigenous lineage dating back to the eunuchs of the medieval Mughal courts. Tensions between the newer gay community and the long-standing hijra and koti communities materialize in language choice, with the upper-middle class gay community embracing English as an index of progressive sexuality and the comparatively lower class hijra and koti communities employing a variety they call "Farsi" as a marker of indigenous sexuality. The latter variety, structurally consistent with Hindi yet unintelligible to Hindi speakers, is characterized by distinctive intonational patterns and an extensive alternative lexicon. Although Koti/Hijra Farsi is unrelated to Persian Farsi, its speakers conceptualize it as the language of the Mughals, employing it in the construction of an historically authentic sexual identity. When gay-identified and koti-identified Hindi speakers come together, as in the nongovernmental organization where I conducted my fieldwork, conversational interaction reveals much about local ideologies regarding the relationship between sexual identity, class, and language. Both groups find Hindi at times inadequate for the expression of same-sex desire, switching into either English or Farsi to distinguish themselves as gay or koti (2001).

Hall's discussion of hijra Farsi is of great importance in opening up a field of language ideology and in moving beyond the ahistorical treatment of "gender" in her earlier work.[8] My interest here is in the inclusion of kothis as a long-standing and distinct "community" linked to hijras. Kothis have arrived, at least in one Delhi NGO, and they make powerful claims of corporeality and continuity on visiting academics. Although invisible in earlier academic work, they are suddenly a presence and one that refuses any account of a recent origin. And they appear congruent with hijras.

The translatability of hijra language in Reddy's Hyderabad is not surprising. Hijras, as Harriet Lynton and Mohini Rajan (1974) document, were until the middle of the twentieth century still a relatively valued part of courtly life in the Deccan capital. Some have in fact argued for a Telegu etymology for kothi (Row Kavi 2000, contextualized below); Telegu is one of the dominant languages of the Hyderabad region. But one of the Bandhu researchers from

Dhaka acknowledged that the term kothi was not commonly used five years previously. "Most men did not know the word then," he said. The Dhaka researchers, like other affiliates of the NGO Naz Foundation International (including the Delhi NGO where Hall worked), had been trained to look for kothis. "Do you think," I asked, "that there are now more kothis because of the influence of your research project?" "No," the Bandhu researcher answered, "it is because of the movement of hijras. They can move easily across borders, and they have brought the kothi concept to Bangladesh from India."

Thus there are at least two articulations of transnational flow here, that of NGO governance and that of hijra supranationalism. Each is overdetermined. Contemporary hijra leaders in India entertain a reflexive practice of citizenship in which hijras uniquely address the problem of political lack at the core of postcolonial nationalism. When in the waning years of the Cold War the USSR auditioned several Indians as possible cosmonauts, a widely circulated news item in India reported on the offer from a prominent hijra association of a hijra as India's contribution to the space race. The first animal, the first man, and the first woman in space have already been claimed, went the logic of the offer. India would gain little honor from yet another man in space and Rakesh Sharma's space flight would be revealed as the political sop that it was. But a hijra in space: only India was uniquely qualified to secure this first. The offer, although legible primarily as a joke, hailed hijras not only as citizens of the nation but as exemplary cynosures for it.

The genital mark or cut as a ticket or passport, as a signature of difference and loss that marks specific rights (*jajman*) in spaces, institutions, and communities but that can be forged by false hijras, is a ubiquitous feature of hijra claims to citizenship. Hijras sometimes refer to their wound as an "all-India pass" that enables them to board trains and buses without the formalities of tickets. Because many men say that looking at the site of a hijra's operation would unman them, making them impotent and virtual hijras themselves, hijras are unlikely to be challenged by conductors less than eager to have them pull up their saris and expose themselves.

During the late 1990s the wound as marker of citizenship took on an expanded reference when several hijras were elected to municipal and state office (Cohen forthcoming). Although strategically crafted by local kingmakers as attacks on opponents, these contests built on the cut as the guarantor of hijra asceticism and, in a Parsonian sense, their modernity: "We are eunuchs," hijra candidate Madhu Tiwari in U.P.'s Haidergarh district offered after dancing for each crowd. "We have no caste, gender or religious bias. Our philosophy cuts across all kinds of people. We also have no family."[9]

The immediate context to the promise/joke of the hijra as both citizen and leader is the ubiquitous reverse formulation, which achieved intensified publicity in the early 1990s, of the citizen and leader as hijra. Most famously in the speeches of regional Hindutva (pro-Hindu) party Shiv Sena leader Bal Thackeray, and widely circulated on cassette and video, right-wing politicians attacked centrist opponents and their supporters as pro-Muslim and therefore impotent: hijra, *napunsak, namard.*[10] Drawing on earlier and ongoing genres of political insult (Kumar 1988; Cohen 1995a), the hijra attack became a regularized feature of public political speech marking political difference.[11] Hijras contesting elections inverted the hijra attack to frame themselves against ordinary politicians, and in so doing utilized the distinction between asli and nakli hijras: "'I am not going to win. But I will surely tell people that they should choose the real eunuch instead of these politically impotent people,' Tiwari said."

In the kothi wars the contest over gender's counterfeit is again recast. The new and dominant formulation is that of the distinction between hijras and kothis on the one side, and Westernized gay men on the other. As with Nanda's account of the nakli interloper, accusations fly and the police are called in.

Queer Planet

Hijras have always had a complex relation to the emergence of the cosmopolitan category of the homosexual. In both colonial and national-era sexological and anthropological compendiums of what Rudi Bleys (1995) has termed "the geography of perversion," hijras have served as the sine qua non of Indic queerness. Richard Burton's (1956 [1895]) famous articulation of a "Sotadic Zone" of tropical excess girdling the earth where the vice of pederasty was tolerated is narratively centered on his explorations in a Karachi brothel of eunuchs and boys. The question of possible categorical distinction between the two groups of sex workers—the substantive core of the kothi concept—was seldom taken up by the colonial literature or its heirs. Hijras rather than "boy prostitutes" were progressively reified as the body in the category. In more recent omnibuses like David Greenberg's *The Construction of Homosexuality* (1988), the identification is repeated.

As urban Indian activists in the metropolises looked to diasporic South Asian gay and lesbian groups in the 1980s in constructing local models of association, hijras were by and large formally ignored. Not only were activists generally elite anglophones and hijras by and large poor, socially marginal, and often Muslim or lower caste, but hijras also threatened to stigmatize a fledgling social movement. Many men allying with "gay groups" throughout the 1990s in Delhi, Mumbai, Bangalore, and elsewhere told me, in describing their identification, that they struggled not to be seen and attacked as being a hijra by family and society. "Hijra" in this sense occupied a larger semantic space than the associations of those formally received into the hijra community and referred to a generalized position of masculine abjection including impotent men and other men "like that" presumed to desire being anally penetrated.

Thus until the late 1990s outreach efforts to link politically with hijra leaders by this emergent activist cohort were few. In Delhi, lawyer and activist Siddharth Gautam returned from graduate studies at Yale determined to unite different queers under a common banner: it was, not coincidentally, the moment of American queer politics and Yale was one of its academic centers. Gautam eventually died of leukemia and his memory and vision have become enshrined, but several Delhi activists recall the strong resistance to his project of helping to bring queer women, men, and hijras together. Gautam's vision was criticized as American naiveté. A story I heard a few times in 1993 and 1997 described a gay party to which Gautam had invited some hijras, who turned out to be thieves and made off with the host's property. Friends of Gautam, on the other hand, recall visits with hijra leaders in Old Delhi where they learned about the robust and multilayered forms of kinship, care, and community that hijras and their longtime neighbors had developed.

White American transgender activist Anne Ogborn read Nanda's book on hijras and saw them as potential allies and models for a radical tansgender movement that appropriated surgical technology from medical gatekeepers and defined transgender not in hegemonic binary terms but through distinct and (to nontransgenders) esoteric language and powerful religion. Ogborn went to India in 1993 for a well-advertised conference in Delhi on alternate sexualities but was surprised and angered that no hijras were invited. Given the disparities in a common language or culture, such a project would have appeared impossible to its organizers (which included Khan, with Row Kavi and myself in attendance), or at best tokenism. After Gautam's death, few were taking it on. In the evenings after conference sessions, when male and female conference attendees split up for gender-assigned events, Ogborn had no particularly welcoming place to go. Some attendees read her anger (and my presence) as neocolonial; others took her to a slum not far from the conference venue where she met a wretchedly poor group of hijras who eventually admitted her as a member. On Ogborn's second trip, more-powerful hijras became interested in working with her and in establishing a hijra presence in North America, and she returned to San Francisco to set up a community.

In early 1990s Mumbai, the relation between gays, other MSMS, and hijras was more complex than in the other Indian metropolises given the presence of the film industry and its relationship with hijras and other trans-gender performers, layered through the historical contingencies of theatrical forms like the Maharashtrian *tamasha* and the Marathi theater (Hansen 2001; Rege 1998). Many men in elite, high-middle-class, and nonanglo-phone "service class" friendship and party networks worked or socialized in various strata of the Bombay film and emerging television industries. Class and religious difference were far more explicit and present in everyday social discourse than among Delhi's more segregated elites, and points not only of distinction but of relationship between differently positioned hijras and men were multiple. Hijras were never part of the Bombay Dost collective, the group virtually headed by Row Kavi that put out India's first "gay" publication, but several Dost members had worked with hijras or recruited them for film projects.

This relation grew even more complex as NGOS in the early 1990s funded by foundation and bilateral monies began investing in AIDS prevention tar-geting MSMS. As NGO-disseminated AIDS capital began to enter the world of the new gay groups, these groups grew, fissioned, and spun-off trusts and rivals in response to money and the accusations and competition that accompanied it. Hijra-gay connections, as all relations with stakes in these new sodalities, were remade. Large dance and sex parties, more than occasionally funded through AIDS prevention projects ostensibly as safe-sex workshops, were competitively developed by promoters tied to the proliferation of gay- and MSM-focused AIDS groups. Funding for AIDS could secure a venue and security; promoters often charged high admission fees and made a lot of money. An accusation I heard several times in 1994 was that one party promoter had attacked a rival by paying hijras to disrupt the latter's party. The presence of hijras threatened to give the promoter a down-market reputation, and their "distasteful" songs and dances drew unwanted media and police attention to attendees. Gautam's dream of queer spaces linking gays and hijras was thus being achieved in unanticipated form.

By the mid-1990s, an expansive group of Indian gay-themed media outlets, primarily utilizing the Internet and in intensified conversation with young persons identifying as diasporic Asians (in the United Kingdom) or South Asians (in North America) as well as various non–South Asian enthusiasts, was constructing a new relation to hijra space as carnival utopia. Discussions and reports of hijra festivals in the south and west of India where thousands of ordinary "working-class men" would gather and either assent to or seek sexual relations with any cross-dressed man were frequent on the web. Such reports could be tied to a more general growth of elite accounts of desire for a consolidating category of "working-class" or "straight" men. Against the consolidating divide between gays and hijras/kothis, through the logic of the counterfeit, the emergence of an urban gay male and queer space primarily through virtual encounter claimed the hijras as part of a proliferating recognition of identifications and pleasures.

Kothi as "Black Box"

The 1994 Mumbai debate over the relation between AIDS funding and the promotion of for-profit gay parties and the fissioning and conflicts it spawned demonstrated the shape of things to come. On one side in numerous accounts of these conflicts was the Bombay Dost collective and its most public member, Row Kavi. Row Kavi was controversial not only because he was unrelentingly featured in national and international media as "India's first out gay man" but also as he had a history of outrageous pronouncements about women, Christianity, and Islam and was rumored to be a "communalist" of the Hindu Right. On the other side were a variety of promoters and activists with ties to Khan and what was then still the Naz Foundation (United Kingdom). Committed to supporting projects in Asian "homelands" to identify culturally appropriate languages and identities in the service of effective AIDS prevention, Khan became a magnet for people distressed with Row Kavi's politics or who were looking for money for their own projects. At some point Khan split off from the parent group he founded, thereafter forming NFI and devoting himself full time to setting up affiliate AIDS research and prevention groups throughout South and Central Asia.

The kothi concept became popularized in part through Khan's intervention in the south Indian city of Chennai (Madras). The Chennai-based head of Sahodaran, an NFI affiliate, was Sunil Menon, whom I interviewed in 2000 in San Francisco where he was doing a training course in prevention research design at the Center for AIDS Prevention Studies (CAPS) of the University of California, San Francisco. When I had met Menon in Chennai earlier the same year, he told me he was the first in the AIDS world to comment on kothis. I asked him in the interview to talk about how he first met kothis and why the use of the word spread.

Menon is a polymath. His family, British-era nobility, is from the state of Kerala, although he grew up in Madras. Menon initially wanted to be a wildlife biologist but there was no program in the city; his father suggested anthropology as he could study primates. So Menon did his undergraduate training, studied nonhuman primate species, and went on to do a Masters in anthropology. The graduate course consisted primarily of urban ethnography, with people. Meanwhile, he was getting involved in other fields, including choreographing shows for the exploding fashion industry—a major site of foreign investment and interest and an emerging social space that became central to gay life in the 1990s—as well as volunteering within the emerging AIDS NGO world.

Madras was the first site of the making of Indian AIDS: the periodic testing of female sex workers in the city, along with the testing of foreign and primarily African students across India, led to several women testing positive for antibodies to HIV in late 1984 and to the emergence of prostitutes and an imagined category of loose women more generally as the dominant risk group within the discourse and organization of AIDS prevention resources. Official wisdom among legislatures and bureaucrats at this time, and to a significant extent throughout the subsequent fifteen years, was that India lacked "homosexuals." Shifting alliances of new and emerging Indian gay groups, traveling AIDS experts who were often themselves gay- or queer-identified, and diasporic South Asian queer and AIDS prevention organizations argued for prevention research and resources targeting the more politically and epidemiologically viable category of MSM. We can thus redefine AIDS cosmopolitanism as the field of these new articulations and their effects. Funders and planners from North American, Western European, and Australasian bilateral agencies; from WHO, UNAIDS, and other multilateral institutions; and from the large private foundations circulated and cultivated leaders among the new gay/AIDS activists. Research centers like CAPS in San Francisco sought out activists and sympathetic physicians and health researchers, offering retraining in basic epidemiology and behavioral modification interventions. Internationalist lesbian and gay NGOs sent emissaries from Europe and the United States and gathered information on the state's compliance with rights and prevention agendas.

Robert Oostvogels, a European anthropologist working for WHO, was doing sex research in several Indian cities and met Menon. Impressed by

Menon's anthropology background, Oostvogels hired him and a second young man to work as fieldworkers, mappers of MSM space in Madras. Particularly, local idiom, was part of what they were encouraged to produce. The second field worker, Menon told me, was a young man who had worked in the canteen at the Madras airport, where his older male coworkers (many of whom in all probability lived in or near the canteen) regularly used him for sex. Although few men who had sex with men then saw the growing equation of AIDS and female prostitution as in any way implicating them, in the version of the story I transcribed the young man somehow ended up in search of refuge at the new AIDS prevention NGO where Menon worked and from where they were recruited.

The two did research in Panagal Park in the middle-class neighborhood of T. Nagar, where young male hustlers from elsewhere, who sometimes called themselves *dangas*, hung out. Menon's employers were interested in the nominated dangas, but apparently were disappointed that few specifications in language of the dangas' clients emerged from the fieldwork. Later, Menon said, he and his colleague started working on Marina Beach, the broad seafront that faces the city. Because there were army and navy bases not far from the northern end of the beach, near the Coomb River estuary, many young hustlers and *alis* (hijras)[12] cruised the area looking for military men who would pay for "discharge." Many young men who were beach habitués did the tough femme bit like the park dangas but called themselves kothis, a word they sometimes said came from the alis. The kothis, unlike the dangas, had a word for the men who patronized them, panthis.

Oostvogels was excited by this binarism and Menon was invited to Berlin for the International AIDS conference, where he presented a paper on kothi-panthi. The paper brought him in contact with many players in the global AIDS world, including Shivananda Khan. Menon then worked for some other projects, thus experiencing the power and money politics of the new AIDS enterprise and slowly learning his way within them. Eventually, Khan helped Menon organize a much broader program of research and intervention; a new NGO, Sahodaran, became closely linked to NFI and to the growing number of other Naz affiliates, such as Bandhu in Dhaka. The kothi concept, taken from the language of poor male sex workers in one part of the city but not another, became the basis for a much more extensive series of interventions in Chennai. Through the network of NFI, its affiliates, and their funders, the "kothi-panthi framework" became important in AIDS prevention research and intervention with MSMs throughout South Asia and its diaspora, as well as an accepted and recognizable feature of "Indian culture" cited by knowledgeable experts. In Bruno Latour's (1987) sense, the kothi concept—both the term and the binary supporting it—were being enclosed into a "black box," becoming an unquestioned and unquestionable fact. Or, indeed, they became more than unquestionable: black boxes for Latour do not merely mime reality but engender it. Kothis were not only a matter for experts but were an emergent reality in streets and slums.

Pragmatic Visionary

"Shivananda Khan"—the Hindu ascetic "Shivananda" joined to the Muslim "Khan"—is an unusual name. Khan was born in Britain and given the name Duncan. He once told me the story of his renaming. As I remember the story, Khan was walking along Mumbai's Chowpatty Beach when he saw a boy in the water who looked to be drowning. Relatively few people in India can swim. He dove in and saved the boy's life. A sadhu, a Hindu holy man, saw him and as Khan relates gave him the new name Shivananda. This is a powerful account resonating with mythic origins: Duncan Khan, Eastern and Western, black and white, is reformed by an itinerant ascetic within an alternate, truer hybridity: renouncer and saver of lives, Muslim and Hindu, encompassing the nation, indeed all of Asia, bearer of the true all-India pass. When the Special Branch of the government of India began to investigate Khan as a possible spy for Pakistan (leading to the events of 2001 that I discuss below) both the state and newspapers covering the case refused the new name and saw it as a screen for the covert actions of one D. G. Khan.

Khan has lived up to the mythic quality of his rebirth. In his emergence as an activst he moved from creating identity-based Asian queer groups— in a very specifically British setting of migration, diaspora, racism in the Thatcher years, and the problem of culture—to setting up AIDS prevention resources and designing and implementing prevention research. Naz began by developing a variety of AIDS prevention and support resources for Asians, primarily South Asians in London, and grew. Khan and his colleagues created informational resources and interventions in a variety of languages: Gujarati, Urdu, Punjabi, Hindi, and Bengali, among others. The project of translation immediately raised challenges: one was not as much translating universal concepts and identifications as reframing specific practices and rhetorics of desire, pleasure, and identification. Khan began to look for partners to explore what it meant to live and enjoy and be at new sorts of risk as an Asian, an Indian, a Muslim, a Hindu, and so forth.

When I first met Khan, he had hooked up with an equally larger-than-life activist—the writer-philosopher Giti Thadani who was engaged in a massive project of photographing ancient and medieval temples and ruins and re-reading early Vedic scripture in search of traces of nonpatriarchal cosmogonies and forms. Both were radically self-made persons and recognized as much in each other. Khan supported Thadani's archival work for some time, seeing in it a critical non-Western genealogy of relation, subject, object, and sex. I recall a remarkable conversation on Thadani's Delhi rooftop in 1993 with Shiv, Giti, and a younger local activist, Alok, who along with friends had started a "gay group" of middle-class young men looking for a social life beyond the parks and as an alternative to the elite parties where some felt uncomfortable. Both Thadani and Khan shared a mutual commitment to promoting what they termed a nonpenetrative sexuality, which they saw as a critical alternative to patriarchy, homophobia, and even AIDS. Alok listened patiently but with increasing alarm as Giti brilliantly worked through tantric ideas of the internalized phallus and the earlier Vedic primordial logics of the twin; as Shiv explained the impossibility of an adequate AIDS prevention without rethinking the penetration imperative; and as both linked penetration to patriarchal violence in their own histories or in those of others they cared for. Disturbed, I rehashed a "third wave" feminist critique of Andrea Dworkin even as I heard myself sounding American and academic. Finally, Alok finally blurted out: "But I *like* to be fucked!"

Khan and Thadani both went their separate and successful ways, and the project of translation eventually led Khan away from the universalizing gay not through a particular feminist rejection of penetration but its redeployment as the kothi-panthi framework. Through Naz Delhi and other Naz spinoffs, and later through NFI, which he came increasingly to center in Lucknow, Khan succeeded in disseminating a focused message: kothi/panthi maps far more effectively onto the practice and body politics of most men who have sex with men or hijras than does "gay" or the too-vague MSM category itself. The impact of his "framework" has been radically to separate prevention targeting "gay men" from the far larger group of men who have sex with men. (Affiliates of NFI following Khan later doubly redefined MSM as, first, "males who have sex with males," emphasizing the involvement of children and youth, and, second, as MSWM, "men who have sex with women and men," to emphasize the limited usefulness of the homosexual/heterosexual binarism.) Kothi-panthi has become identified as "best practice" disease prevention by UNAIDS and other global AIDS funding brokerages. Although not a public figure like Row Kavi, Khan is ubiquitous behind the scenes in the Asian AIDS world.

Abstracted, Khan's practice involves delineating specific behavioral forms, indexing these forms to language or to its absence, and looking for commonalities to reach a workable model of a distinctively South Asian grid of sexual norms. Norms indexed to language on this alternative grid form the entry point for behavioral intervention: implicit is a cultural and economic caesura between Western and Asian reference. Thus, the "kothi" or "kothi-panthi" framework emerges as the product of a lengthy series of experimental practices of sex and language research that threw up alternatives to the gay to determine which if any had the capacity to anchor an alternative grid. Language cannot encompass behavior, which always exceeds its specification. Kothis do not act like the word demands. But language does enable the beginnings of a conversation. To intervene is to move beyond translation.

Khan summarized the state of his thinking in an October 2000 essay in NFI's newsletter, *Pukaar.*

> We should really be talking about male to male sexual behaviors rather than specifically men who have sex with men. . . . In South Asia . . . [for] a majority of males involved in male to male sex, MSM is not about a sexual identity but most often a behavior arising from a feminine gender identification, or a perceived "manly" discharge need. Such behaviors are not contextualised within a heterosexual-homosexual oppositional paradigm.
>
> It appears that a significant level of MSM behaviors in the region is contextualised within a gendered framework—where a feminised gender performance frames the *kothi.*
>
> This gendered framework is constructed within a *kothi/panthi* dynamic, where the *kothi* perceives himself and his desire for other males in the context of gender roles in South Asia, i.e., the "penetrated" partner. *Kothis* construct their social roles, mannerisms and behaviors in ways which attract what they call *panthis*—"real men", identifying as feminised males. In this context *kothis* are usually the visible MSM in a range of public environments and neighborhoods, but *panthis* are not, for they could potentially be any "manly" male.
>
> These "real" men do not see themselves as homosexuals or less masculine because of their sexual involvement with *kothis.* . . .
>
> *Kothis* see any male that is sexually penetrated as another *kothi*, whether they identify as gay, bisexual, or whatever. To *kothi*-identified males such identities represent a form of "closetness." . . .
>
> In a culture that excludes females from public spaces, that socially polices females and controls their access by males, and where sexual behaviors are

based on gender identification rather than sexual identity, it is possible that for many "manly" males, sexual access will be with *kothis,* or those deemed less "manly", i.e. young males and adolescents. (2000)

For most men, here the "panthis," sexual activity with other men and with women is not a free-floating domain of sex but more specifically "discharge." The idea of discharge surfaced when international funders early on imported the "African model" of AIDS prevention and its focus on truck drivers as critical vectors of spread. Many research groups were interviewing drivers by the early 1990s and reporting that these men explained condomless sex with women or boys as a need to discharge the heat built up in driving a hot engine for hours or days at a time.

The turn with AIDS to cultural explanations of such semen-expulsive reason radically reworked the sometimes tortured ethnological terrain of "semen-loss anxiety." Before AIDS, the prevailing wisdom among many elite or non-Indian social scientists and psychiatrists working in India was that most men internalized humoral and substantivist "traditional" medical imperatives to retain semen. Fears of semen loss were understood as a broadly transhistorical phenomenon leading in extreme cases to a "culture-bound syndrome." To lose semen was to lose strength and manhood, from the millennia-old emergence of classical Ayurveda and Yoga to the present.[13] For anthropologists like the British psychiatrist G. Morris Carstairs (1975), semen-loss anxiety was, along with the tolerance of hijras, the sine qua non of an abject Indian masculinity in which oriental despot fathers produced a defensive refusal by young sons to enter into oedipal contest, leading in adulthood to an exquisitely vulnerable masculinity and the normalization of male homosexuality. With attention focused on truck drivers in the late 1980s and early 1990s "Indian men" suddenly veered from being pathologically semen-retentive to pathologically semen-expulsive in the social scientific imaginary.

A lengthy engagement with Carstairs is beyond the scope of this essay (see Cohen 1997, 1998: 161–71, 1999), but I mention his work here because, along with the later and similar argument of Sudhir Kakar (1978), it remains the dominant psychoanalytic effort in India to ground what AIDS cosmopolitans will come to insist on as the cultural ground of kothi-panthi distinction. Such studies are easily dismissed because of their crudity, their unquestioned acceptance of a model of family structure with less empirical grounding than their authors presume, their deep homophobia, and in the case of Carstairs, a fairly nasty and in hindsight racialized cultural psychopathology.

The multiple studies convincingly regrounding the narrative of Indian masculinity as feminized or split between aggression and passivity within a colonial dynamic could be cited here (Nandy 1983; Luhrmann 1996), but however convincing the dominant postcolonial critique may be at offering a possible genealogy for elite and middle-class anxiety and lack, the reduction of kothi-panthi to colonial politics and their sequelae is as incomplete an account as the culture and personality anthropology that Carstairs and Kakar offer.

Khan offers a third explanation, functionalist and hydraulic. Extreme patriarchy renders women unavailable. Panthi desire is the routinization of what the early sexologists called pseudohomosexuality and Freud (1949) in the *Three Essays on the Theory of Sexuality* termed contingent inversion. For the male migrant workers I interviewed in Delhi in 1993, convenience and access were offered as reasons for homosex. A dominant mapping of desire over the life course, of which I heard variants in several cities, was that adolescent boys and girls often "played" with same-sex partners but with marriage this physical side of friendship lessened or ceased. Conversely, the persistence of same-sex play was occasionally framed as a morally ambivalent continuation of youthful friendship, a kind of disease of nostalgia. In the terms of my earlier biaxial model, the threat of penetration is lessened by reading it along the axis of play.

But the very use of the language of past contingency as a rhetoric to locate present homosex suggests that hydraulic narratives point both to structural conditions of sexual separation and to something rather different. Havelock Ellis (1942 [1936]: 82–88) long ago noted this limit to contingency explanation. Khan offers a more interesting argument in moving from the adequacy of a hijra language of the panthi to a more complicated reading of nonkothi homosex: "Beside the *kothi* frameworks, there is another dynamic of male to male sexual behaviors, which because of a shame-based culture, cannot be readily accessed. This includes [intra]-family male to male sex, sex between friends, sex in male only spaces. Such behaviors are not identity-based where desire is based on same-biological sex, but rather on immediacy, 'body heat' and felt 'discharge' needs. Such behaviors could be significantly high since there is a limited social construction of heterosexuality" (2000).

Here Indian difference (the anthropologically dutiful "shame-based culture") is offered less as an analytic problem and more as an admission of the limits to survey research and what Kath Weston (1993) has criticized as "ethnocartography." Khan's insight—that if one acknowledges the limits to heterosexual prohibition, neither gay/straight nor kothi/panthi are sufficient as models—is based on the extensive research he has conducted or sponsored over the course of more than a decade. Why, then, the persistence of the kothi at the center of the NFI model?

To assert the centrality of the kothi to South Asian homosex offers a positive formulation as opposed to the absence of speech girding sex between relatives and between friends. The kothi offers her presence as a means of entry not only to the secret sex of the panthi but to the unspeakable regions of shame: "*Kothis* by their very number, 'nature' and practices have access to a broad range of other males whom they access for sex, and can be seen as an entry point to the dominant framework of men who have sex with males in Bangladesh and India" (Khan 2000). Kothis are to the public like panthis are to the secret—literally the "entry point" for public health penetration through and beyond them to the regions of shame.

The presence of kothis, their positive location in a linguistic system of positions, can not be taken as a guarantee of behavior: "This does not mean that *kothis* do not penetrate or that *panthis* are not penetrated. They do, but these behaviors are seen as crossing the gender and are considered even more shameful. They are kept even more secret. And while *kothis* have a term for such behaviors—*do parathas, double-deckers, dubla,* and so on, generally such individuals are looked upon with scorn. A *panthi* who is penetrated is called a *gupt* [secret] *kothi.*" (Khan 2000). Panthi shame appears here like the loquacity of Foucault's Victorians: unlike familial shame it generates an iterative chain of signifiers. It is not clear in Khan's discussion whether kothi and panthi transgressions are equally shameful: the sense is that kothis expect their panthis to act like men, reminiscent of anthropologist Don Kulick's (1998) discussion of poor Brazilian *travesti* in Salvador, who get their sex—polymorphously—from customers but get their gender from their boyfriends. The dialectic of shame and disclosure is only operative in the latter relationships: kothi and panthi transgressions, in other words, may not be nearly as shameful in the context of commerce as in the context of care.

The Mother and the Monk

If Khan's understanding of the kothi recognizes the importance of how they get gender, Row Kavi's understanding recognizes how they get sex. Kulick's account of travestis mentioned above suggests that despite their performance of penetrated femininity and its enactment with boyfriends, with clients, and with other lovers their sex is far more polymorphous. Row Kavi's criticism of the kothi concept lies in its apparent insistence on active panthi versus passive kothi and the inclusion of all exceptions under the logic of shame. The presumption of a shame-based culture is the kind of anthropologism that Row Kavi argues is to be expected of a neocolonial diasporic enterprise like NFI. Row Kavi, of course, adopts his own anthropologisms in the service of an authentic Hindu homosexuality: the postcolonial condition comes with anthropologists on all sides.

Row Kavi and Khan come from radically different worlds, like poles of a Salman Rushdie plot in their respective Bombay film/Hindu/national and working-class British/Muslim/diasporic backgrounds. Both of their remarkable projects—Row Kavi's efforts to create gay legitimacy, publicity, and community in Bombay and Khan's to move beyond white British identifications and assumptions in building queer and then AIDS-prevention resources and spaces for U.K. Asians—quickly grew into complexly and distinctly global projects. Both sets of efforts attracted accolades and both received criticism. Row Kavi first attracted widespread foreign publicity when a gay *New York Times* reporter based in India featured him in a story on that paper's front page. He quickly became a notorious celebrity within the novel cosmopolitan mediascape of "liberalizing" India, arguably less for his exquisitely public gay identification than for his infamous recalling on a Murdoch-station television talk show of an alliterative insult he once levied as a younger man against Mahatma Gandhi. Behind some of the publicity of that event lay a concern by certain progressives in Delhi and abroad that Row Kavi was an important ally of the Hindu Right. Such concerns were not immaterial—Row Kavi has himself as an ex-monk had a close relation to some in the Vishva Hindu Parishad (VHP)—but they are selective in their reading of his complex political affiliations and they refuse his deep critique of the sufficiency of liberalism and developmentalist understandings of sexual health.

Like Giti Thadani in Delhi, Row Kavi has structured a monumental history, in Nietzsche's sense, of an Indian homoeroticism alienated through successive capitulations. Whereas Thadani in the early 1990s posited an indigenous matriarchal culture eroded through Brahmanic phallogocentrism, Islamic iconoclasm, and Western orientalism, Row Kavi has focused on the latter two moments as critical losses. Part of a gay recognition for Row Kavi is the refusal of its exteriority as a gift of Western modernity to be acquired through a process of personal and national development. There is no need, therefore, for the production of multiple grids of surveillance, Indian versus Western. Row Kavi in his presentations since the late 1990s draws a large Venn diagram with a series of interlocking circles surrounding an empty center. Each circle represents a particular social formation, some "identity" based and some only based on "behavior." Research on AIDS expands the number of circles and AIDS politics links them together and creates greater regions of overlap. Overlap implies communication and translation, as well as access for health initiatives. There are roughly four quadrants to the diagram—gay-identified MSMS; sex workers; unidentified MSMS; and transgendered hijras and multiple kothi subtypes—but overlap and not axial distance characterizes the relations between them.

Overlap makes conversation possible, and conversation leads to recognition and harm reduction. None of these ideas are foreign to the NFI model, which in fact is exemplary in its rationalized professionalism and garners international acclaim as "best practice" AIDS prevention. But the NFI multiplication of grids—kothi/panthi, gay male, hijra—refuses recognition as a common dynamic. Recognition for Row Kavi and Hamsafar, the AIDS NGO he built out of Bombay Dost, is central to how Row Kavi links gay, AIDS, and civic politics. Recognition implies an interpellation: the question is what kind of political and social assemblage hails one. For Row Kavi, recognition by the Indian state is critical. Although he has attacked the NFI network as betraying a neocolonial desire for foreign recognition, he mobilizes similar types of internationalist symbolic capital: the Elizabeth Taylor Foundation, global AIDS conferences, American gay media, the International Gay and Lesbian Human Rights Commission, the Berkeley anthropologist Cohen. But this capital shores up claims for recognition by the state and its constituent elites. Row Kavi long worked to have both Bombay Dost and Humsafar registered as official organizations and to link the latter directly to the Municipal Corporation of Mumbai, not only to ensure the legal access to foreign NGO funds but to demand state hailing: interpellate this!

As new gay groups appeared across India through the 1990s, claiming both Bombay Dost and diasporic groups like San Francisco Bay Area Trikone as templates, Row Kavi counseled them to register appropriately as charitable trusts before publishing, organizing, or researching—a process that could take months to years. But the incentives of the new AIDS capital—and arguably, of the disease itself—worked on a different time frame. Row Kavi's admonitions were seen by some as efforts by him to keep the new AIDS money to himself. As Khan began recruiting group after group to join the London-based NFI umbrella, Row Kavi warned of dire consequences if groups structured themselves as foreign or global and not civic or national. Obviously, by then he was in competition with NFI, and the latter's funds, scale, and professionalism were more attractive than an assemblage linked to Row Kavi's controversial persona. His calling Mahatma Gandhi a bastard on television had cemented his publicity as dangerously illiberal.

One cannot but note the empty center in the diagram of circles—the lack that the multiplication of sexual types covers over. Here I betray, through and around my long friendship with Row Kavi, my own anxiety and anger with illiberal politics. This whole for Row Kavi is structured as a vision of a culturally polymorphous and accommodating Hindu tradition, an assertion of the modernity of that tradition and its ability to encompass the gay, and a politics of group formation through identification with the modernity of that tradition. It is recognition through encompassment, here by the (Hindu) sexual nation rather than NFI's globally located assertion of a pan–South Asian but anti-Western "construct."

Row Kavi's specific response to the kothi concept has shifted as kothis emerged in cities like Mumbai as a new social fact. The HIV/AIDS counseling and referral center for gay men that he and others set up several years ago, Humsafar, has shifted from a counseling center and meeting place identified with the English-speaking middle-class men that founded it to a more broad-based outreach program where underclass, working-class, and "service-class" (clerks and petty bourgeois) men along with a few non-English speaking lesbians and hijras, congregate. Many of these people identify themselves in a number of contexts as kothis. Language—the lack of access to English—unites the group more than explicit class, gender, or sexual identification. Perhaps the heightened liability of vernacular identification under a neoliberal economy helps explain Hall's insight that the hijra/zenana divide has been supplanted and replaced by a new kothi/gay split. The shift is similar to one that has occurred among the various NFI-affiliated groups like Chennai's Sahodaran.

The period from 1997 to 2000 saw a dramatic shift in the social constitution of all of these NGO spaces. Whether at Row Kavi's Humsafar or at the NFI affiliates, kothis appeared. Whatever and wherever kothis were before this time, these NGO kothis represented a distinct and still emergent social moment. Initially they were recruited by middle-class outreach workers to replace themselves, to help fulfill funders' mandates for more and better sexual truth. Second-generation research called for more quantitative data collection requiring larger numbers of fieldworkers. These were men the first generation of outreach workers had met in the parks or other cruising sites and trusted; or they were visitors to the drop-in centers who didn't fit in with the English-speaking crowd but hung on. They brought friends with them, increasingly, and English-speaking attendance began to drop off. In Mumbai, a set of new and younger anglophone gay groups emerged around this time and marked their distance from Humsafar and Row Kavi. When Row Kavi received funding for a weekly STD clinic to be held at the Humsafar center, the number of Marathi, Hindi, and Gujarati speaking young men swelled. More and more of these men were beginning to know themselves as kothis.

Row Kavi has been tirelessly involved in both the clinic and other HIV work elsewhere in the city. Despite national and international infamy, he is a beloved figure and a mother for many younger men. But there are limits to the mother love. Despite Humsafar's eventual inclusion of kothis within the ring of circles, Row Kavi has persisted in attacking the kothi concept in various media as being little more than a Telegu slur meaning "dancing monkey": the language is different than Khan's cool professionalism. Many young non-anglophone men who were allied with a formerly "gay" group, Udaan (initially modeled after Bombay Dost and claiming Ashok as patron), shifted allegiance to NFI and Khan. Udaan became an explicitly kothi group, and some members along with others set up an Internet group called koti-world.

Not surprisingly, the Internet has become what one might call both an interpellative and a performative matrix for the kothi wars, eliciting identifications and countermoves. In an interview with a U.S.-based gay Internet news service, Row Kavi argued that "there was this mumbo-jumbo by this London 'expert' about 'frameworks of male-male sex in South Asia reflecting indigenous identities and patterns, different from that assumed to exist in the West. Local patterns of male-male sex are not an exclusive practice of a few homosexual men, but part of the general sexual practices of a significant number of males in south Asia.' This is the exact quote. You'll observe it is similar to Burton's imaginary 'sodatic crescent!'" The Burton reference, probably emerging out of earlier conversations with me, challenges Khan as suggesting that in effect all men in the tropics are addicted to the vice. Row Kavi continued:

> This fellow recently held a hush-hush conference where "only Kothi identified (passive homosexuals) men" were invited to Calcutta. The disgusting thing was when my friend, Joe Thomas, a reputed social activist in Hong Kong, put it on the international website of Sea-Aids, he was warned not to. A Westerner "penetrating India" is a very good example of a metaphorical meaning here.

The lack of transparency was so blatant that the whole show was wrongly held under "Male Reproductive Sexual Health." Among the participants was a person who outed harmless school teachers in a small town; a shop lifter who beats up and mugs poor queens and assorted characters. This was sponsored by international organizations like UNAIDS, who got conned into this with various slick ways.[14]

The conference in question, organized by NFI in Calcutta with outside funders present, had led to angry letters from Row Kavi alleging that delegates from Humsafar were invited late or not at all, while those from NFI affiliates were flown in, and that the nomination of "kothi" was cover for a selective politics of favoring NFI affiliates, cutting other groups like Humsafar out of access to international funding. Row Kavi's allegations appear stretched, to say the least, but certainly part of the stakes was a mutual sense of competing organizations being evaluated by largely foreign auditors: thus Row Kavi's framing of Khan as the new Burton in his own appeal to an American auditor. Elsewhere in the interview Row Kavi attacks Khan for being an elitist "Anglo-Indian," that is, of mixed Indian and British origins.

In his subsequent comments in the interview, Row Kavi offers a very different sense of the politics of the dominant binarism as he understand it, not kothi-panthi but "gay men" versus MSM: "Now we all know about the problem between gay men and men-who-have-sex-with-men (MSM). But MSM are in the same category as female sex workers; their negotiating power to use condoms is as bad as that of female CSWs. You need to educate the fuckers, not the fuckees." "Fucker" and "fuckee" here are not literally applied: the point seems to be that "gay men" are in positions of power and knowledge regarding HIV but their sexual partners, the MSM, have limited access to either.

Let me clarify this point because it is important. For both Khan and Row Kavi, "gay men" are an elite category. In Row Kavi's understanding, and I would add for many elite anglophone men whether or not they identify as gay, the object of desire of a typical middle-class or elite man who likes men is an ordinary working-class or service-class man, by definition not gay given his linguistic and class position. These men form a group of sexually available types in the understanding and experience of elites, from "masseurs" passed among friends or found near Andheri train station at night to "drivers" and "Maharajs" (Brahman cooks, frequently from Rajasthan) to other "vernac queens" who are awed by the language and privilege of gays and who must be protected from their tricks. For the Ashok, to protect nonelite MSMS is to make them gay, to put them in the position of power. To reify their current position in the glorification of the kothi is a trick: "So obviously, the name of the game is to always 'use' the helpless. This way you retain the power without empowering the target group. This game is becoming so obvious that most gay men in India are now very wary of these Western-style activists seeing India as the 'exotic other.' This fellow is always mentioning something called 'South Asia,' which is another construct of the West."

Of course, the ultimate stakes are that Khan, like myself and other category brokers, gets to hold on to the position of the "fucker" by standing both inside and outside Row Kavi's world in a way that Ashok, no matter how well traveled, can not invert. However contradictory his refusal of the kothi, the ultimate stakes for Row Kavi are tied to Khan's apparent effort to leave no other position worth mentioning. As he states in his interview with the Internet news service: "Damn it! A 'South Asian construct' is about as real as a 'European construct.' I mean, an Italian doesn't think of sex the same way that a Swede or a German does. A Pathan tribesmen from Pakistan would be scandalized to think he is equated to a Tamil or a Bengali. Yet this fool from London puts them all into one huge tureen; as if it's a convenient little term paper he is doing. I mean Sir Richard did the same anyway with his shabby translation of the Kama Sutra."

Kothi Electronica

These complex and (from the outside) vitriolic exchanges are broadcast on several e-mail lists identified as queer and South Asian, and they generate responses from all over the world. One reader queried the list about Row Kavi: why is he, as a senior kothi, not more responsible? A response came that these slinging insults—which, again, Khan himself has stayed away from—are part of "kothi speak," the language of Bombay queens wherever they may reside. Row Kavi—up front, exaggerated, unfair, and provocative—had become the biggest kothi of them all.

The density of these electronic spaces and the sheer number of the letters that pass across them make any comprehensive treatment impossible. Geographer Chandra Balachandran has written on the centrality of virtual space to South Asian queer organizing and identification, and like other writers on the Internet he has noted the easy intimacy and easy violence that can emerge. Kothi enters the lists in several dominant ways: as a debate over the morality of classification; as an accusatory field against elements of one or the other NGO formation and its sources of capital, political support, and information; or, particularly on koti-world, as an effort by those kothis with some English and electronic access to constitute a broader kothi counter-cosmopolitanism.

Thus Goda Bai, a leader of Udaan and an informal moderator of koti-world, writes: "I am happy that our people have also started communicating thru net. This is really great. Inform all your friends who come across you to register on this site for any help etc." And a trickle of koti-identified letters did come. Far more common, however, were long missives on the category from nonkothis, in most cases affiliated with an NGO on one side or the other, as shown in the following two excerpted letters. Both are from persons identified with the competing networks, Khan's and Row Kavi's respectively.

From: Alok Srivastava
Date: Tue Jun 19, 2001
Subject: Response to Goda's comment

First let me apologise to Goda for taking this discussion in the way where the organisers of this group did not mean to take it. . . . I must say, since my interest in being in this group is only that I am a keen observer and student of gender and sexuality, it will be unfair for me to stay here for long. I can't even claim to be working for either "koti" or "gay" people. . . . I must warn that I tend to rub "gay" men the wrong way, because I challenge some of the things that they claim. I am surprised to find myself on the right side of Kotis though. . . .

Let's first talk about the fluidity of the Indian Culture, whether it is the religious scene or the sexual one. Let's talk about fluidity in general. Is it not how nature intended things to be?

The whole problem with the "gay" identity and it being borrowed from the west is that it is rooted in the mistaken Western belief that men are basically attracted only to women and that sexual attraction for other men occurs at best as a deviation. . . .

Take the Indian situation on the other hand. Sexual attraction towards other men is not only accepted as a nature of man, but in limited sense even expected of men in the traditional Indian concept of "masculinity" (this acceptance is in tacit form at the community level and more verbal at the peer level). It even has names such as "masti" (you don't have to be gay to do that). This is what gives Indian men fluidity in expressing their sexual feelings. This fluidity may not be enough, but has great scope to be worked upon. . . .

The west is a society divided on the basis of sexuality. While we are a society divided on the lines of gender. There are strict differences between men and women here. Likewise, men are also divided on the lines of whether they relate with masculine identity or the feminine identity (Remember traditional identities like chakka, hijra, mehra, homo, etc.). . . . Indian men do not relate to a sexual identity but only to gender identities. Even if you try to inject a sexual identity it will be changed to a gender one. . . .

And haven't Indian men made their choice [?] Most men who wish to express their sexuality for other men are wary of joining the "gay" community. They may use that space but relating with it is a totally different thing. . . .

"Gay" activists have tried for so long to implant the "gay" identity in India, but to no avail. It is one thing to pump in lakhs of Rupees in India and force an MSM or other such identity, but quite another thing to make people relate to it. . . . Can you imagine how absurd and meaningless it would sound for a non-English speaking Indian man to tell his family, "main 'gay' hoon"!

In response, the following message appeared:

From: Integration <pawan.>
Date: Wed Jun 20, 2001 3:39 am
Subject: Response to Goda's comment
Dear Alok

A pretty good line of argument. But honestly quite inapplicable. I actually find it quite laughable that "gay activists" have been "pumping lakhs of money from abroad or wherever" to "implant" the gay identity in India, on Indian men. I don't know how many gay activists you have worked with or come across, but as far as I know, when it comes to working day in and day out, it doesn't matter to activists whether the person across them is using "gay" as a gender or a sexual identity. That word acts more as a symbol of what the person might be feeling, desiring or fearing. Which turns out to be very often the same as a person who may be using the term "koti" or some other term or very often no term at all. . . . I do agree that one has to escape the trap of looking at things with preconceived notions. Which is what I don't think you have been doing.[15]

Goda Bai then responds to both letters, first taking on the volume of Alok's discourse: "Dear Alok, Thanks for your mail. Please also understand that kotis are not much educated. Your mail seems to be too long. I have read but other kotis on the net . . .??? With love, Goda." Pawan, writing from the other side, is attacked by many kothis. Goda points out that without a specific identity one lacks entitlement and thus access to foreign NGO funds—words bring money: "I think you are not aware of the difference between a koti and a gay. It is totally different. For purpose few Gay masiah ["messiahs," i.e., Row Kavi] would have included Gay and Koti in the same context and must have excluded bi-sexuals from the so called circles of sexual identities which is wrong. For few people it is like when the funds come for Hijras—all are Hijras. If it comes for Gays all are gays and so on. . . . We kotis do not want to be counted as Gays. . . . We all are happy with each other and have understood the concept well and [are] happy with what we are."

AIDS Cosmopolitanism

I began working with the new gay groups in 1993: I soon found myself on the Bombay Dost advisory board and excerpted in Naz's journal *Pukaar*. Khan, who began building organizations in the crucible of race relations of Thatcher's London, was acutely aware of the politics of race and location in deploying my work but pragmatic in utilizing all comers to achieve his goal of defining a culturally appropriate Asian model. He was articulate and well-funded and in the years that I knew him became far more well-funded. Row Kavi was then coming into his own on the international stage and beginning to attract funds: the Bombay Dost collective was redefining itself into an AIDS research platform. Khan sought out Row Kavi as he had Thadani and others, but Row Kavi was looking for a funder and not a patron. Each man created client relationships with leaders of new gay groups; Khan both more aggressively and successfully. These relations succeeded when as in Lucknow and Dhaka local gay leaders were not globally oriented AIDS professionals and needed NFI for a pedagogy into the new funding, and later as in Mumbai and Pune with kothi groups emerging in the shadow of Row Kavi looking for independent access to funding and, increasingly, to recognition. They sometimes failed when as in Delhi, Colombo, and Chennai local leaders were professionals less dependent on NFI and less committed to all of Khan's pan-Asian vision.

Khan in his own way was as high-risk a figure as Row Kavi, and like the latter attracted scores of rumors. According to new reports in summer 2001, agencies within the government of India had been paying close attention to Khan as part of a broader series of efforts to follow NGO money that might be linked to Pakistan's secret service, the ISI. Khan was Muslim and British, regularly traveled to Bangladesh and Central Asia, and worked in Lucknow—in particular with a gay group dominated by Muslim activists whose activities apparently included protests over the anti-Muslim impact of the popular Hindi film *Gadar.* In July, five members of the Lucknow organization were arrested and their offices were ransacked: the one Hindu among the leadership—a retired army colonel living with his family in the suburbs—was spared, although he went into hiding. The arrests used the antisodomitical and antipandering articles of the Indian penal code, based according to all jurists interviewed in the press on extraordinarily flimsy charges, and reports circulated of the scandalous quality of the safe sex literature found in the NGO office (along with the dildo, taken into custody). Most newspapers reported the successful breaking of a "sex ring" and several alluded to the possibility of a Pakistan connection. In some circles, Row Kavi, on his own or in cahoots with the colonel, was seen as responsible for the accusations. Row Kavi offered his own theories of internal dissent within the NFI umbrella.

Many NGO leaders (including Row Kavi) united in protesting the arrests. At stake were liberal freedoms of association and modern developmentalist practices of welfare. But also at stake were the concerns of state bodies regarding the difficulties of imagining sovereignty under conditions that Michael Hardt and Antonio Negri (2000), among others, in the Clinton era characterized as a radical new immanence of flexible and dislocated global "empire," concerns legible in terms of a global Islamic conspiracy and the free-floating monies that supported it. Flexibility was doubled as conspiracy, development as terrorism. The subsequent post–9/11 politics of total war further legitimated the proliferation of such doubles.

AIDS stands at the crux of these stakes, a vehicle generating the global flow of developmental capital to previously marginal associations and challenging the moralizing state while threatening the linked diminution of both sovereignty and sexual reason. Australian political scientist Dennis Altman, the most well known of analysts of globalization, AIDS, and the gay, has chronicled the global spread of American gay institutions through the historical conjuncture of neoliberalism and AIDS and their reconfiguration into an Asian gay assemblage of identifications, institutions, and capital that itself "globalizes." I want to read this terrain as AIDS cosmopolitanism, and I have told a story of the kothi to suggest its fractured and contested quality and the importance of a decentered moralizing critique to debates over the category. I began my thinking about the kothi wars in some despair—knowing many of the activists and clients as colleagues and a few as friends—and in frustration with the ongoing chain of accusations. But here I would end on a different note, with a different question. What kind of ethics and what kind of care are possible and likely under contingent instances of particular global conjunctures? "Care" in an arc of queer work has become both the unit of analysis and the proffered redemption of a new anthropology of the relation (see, in particular, Borneman 1997). I am wary of only foregrounding the modernity of witchcraft and of the accusation in terms of new economies of entitlement and scarcity and new magics of capital and debt. The category is perhaps a critical site of the ethical, of efforts amid the competing networks variously described here and the limits they constitute to imagine and remake relations of care.

The kothi wars are experienced by many within them simultaneously as class warfare and a family feud, save when the police arrive, and I wonder at the nature of the accusation as an utterance in such context. Over the summer of the Lucknow arrests, attacks on Pawan on the koti-world list continued. At some point NFI-friendly gays intervened to ask Goda Bai if the Humsafar-identified Pawan had really intended an attack on kothi identity or autonomy. Goda replied that they had missed the point of the fight: "This is sisterly talks between Pawan and me. We love and argue with each other and this is real love." Against elites positioned as friends offering her a cosmopolitan reinterpretation of an elite positioned as an enemy, Goda Bai offers a different idiom in which to read contestation, difference, and the possibility of something else in exciting but sometimes difficult and, as AIDS spreads in Mumbai, sometimes tragic times. The logic of the new cosmopolitan is not as obvious or necessary as Goda's friends may think.

Notes

So many thanks are due that most must be deferred until I write the book. Central to this particular piece were the insights of Vincanne Adams, Paola Bacchetta, Veena Das, Maria Ekstrand, Kira Hall, Saleem Kidwai, Caitrin Lynch, Ramesh Menon, Sunil Menon, Rakesh Modi, Donald Moore, Stephen Murray, Anne Ogborn, Aihwa Ong, Geeta Patel, Stacy Leigh Pigg, Paul Rabinow, Raka Ray, Gayatri Reddy, Lisa Rofel, Vimal Shankar, Sanjay Srivastava, Giti Thadani, and Ruth Vanita. But of course it is to the extraordinary activists Shivananda Khan and Ashok Row Kavi that I owe both thanks and necessary apologies. Over many years both men have been unfailingly generous to me with time and argument. Although I met them, over a decade ago now, as an interviewer in search of an interviewee, other strands of relationship blossomed. Given their consistent opposition to one another, at some point I found it too hard to maintain close friendships in good faith with both, and because I had been working far more closely with Ashok, and in fact had been refashioned as a gay man by his example, I made a choice. The double difficulty that ensued, the loss of Shiv's wisdom and ever-present critique and the challenge of Ashok's intimacy with the Hindu Right, have marked my life and work since. I have tried as much as I am capable of personally and positionally to be fair to both men and to the networks of activists and health workers affiliated with each, recognizing of course that such fairness is in itself a privilege and form of power. As V. once told me, long ago, my *pyar mohabbat*, my true love, is science. I hope I have been somewhat unfaithful.

1 Naz Foundation International is usually abbreviated as Naz, not NFI. However, there are several organizations with the name, spinoffs of the original Naz serving British Asians that Khan was instrumental in founding but no longer controls, including a prominent but largely distinct Naz in Delhi, and thus I use NFI to avoid confusion. NFI has offered different kinds of support, not necessarily fiscal, to the various local NGOS I frame as being part of its network.

2 See Reddy 1999. The subject of her conference paper will be expanded and detailed in her forthcoming book.

3 Bandhu was aided by NFI in obtaining funding from the Ford Foundation, NORAD, and other grantors to support this research.

4 Mine no less than others: I have known well several critical players in the kothi wars, including Khan, Sunil Menon, and Ashok Row Kavi. Ashok in particular is a close friend; his strong criticism of the "kothi concept" colored my early exposure to the word and thus our relationship presents particular problems of bias.

5 Whether with friends, fellow conference attendees, or strangers, conversations like this one were neither recorded nor immediately transcribed, and are recollected with all attendant biases. I write and reconstruct within a network, and I hesitate to restrict anthropologizing to formalized encounters at its margins. This use of the network is informed by Riles 2000. In this essay, the only exception to informally reconstituted comments are those of Sunil Menon, which I put together from formal interview notes.

6 "Indians Lure Eunuchs to Recover Missing Millions," *Herald-Sun*, 8 January 2001, 29–30.

7 The English orthography is worth close attention here as elsewhere: the appearance of both koti and kothi in the literature may attest to the South Indian origins of the current usage or to the similar Hindi word *kotha* (prostitute's apartment), but primarily to an ongoing process of securing a set of conventions for appropriate representation.

8 None of the existing English-language literature on hijras takes up seriously the question of Farsi (Lynton and Rajan 1974; Nanda 1990; Sharma 1989; Vyas and Shingala 1987), and thus is a testimony to Hall's anthropological linguistics, to the novelty of a reflexive language ideology among hijras in the late 1990s, or to both.

9 Quoted in Sutapa Mukerjee, "Flamboyant Indian Eunuch Takes on Chief Minister in State Polls," wire report, Agence France-Presse, April 2002.

10 For example: "The BJP has been pretty frazzled by Thackeray's acidic comments over its governance. What has rankled severely is the Sena chief's description of the Prime Minister and the Home Minister as 'namards' (eunuchs)," (Sujata Anandan, "Quit if You Differ with Us, BJB to Sena Chief," *Hindustan Times*, 2 March 2001, n.p.).

11 See Manuel 1993 for a relevant discussion of the Hindutva deployment of "cassette culture" and the transformation of the quality of public political speech.

12 *Ali* is used in Tamil, the primary language of Chennai today. Alis and hijras are the same thing, or so say the alis and hijras I have talked with in different parts of India. Alis/hijras move, and the terms are used fluidly. Some scholars of Tamil language have split and parceled out the joint Hindu and Muslim genealogy of the contemporary ali/hijra, making the Tamil alis the authentic heirs to Hindu transgender and the Hindu/Urdu hijras the heirs to Islamic and Central Asian courtly practice. See Ulrike Niklas, "The Mystery of the Threshold: 'Ali' of Southern India," *Kolam* 1, 2000, at http://www.uni-koeln.de/phil-fak/indologie/kolam/kolam1/alieng.html. But while the forthcoming work of both Gayatri Reddy and Lucinda Ramberg addresses the complex relation between local "Hindu" and "Muslim" practice and specific transgender nominations, the logic of some pronouncements that Tamil is to Hindu as Hindi/Urdu is to Muslim is unfortunate.

13 As Akhil Gupta 1998 demonstrates for the hybrid agronomic and ecological reasoning of Uttar Pradesh farmers, such humoral and substantivist frames are mutually imbricated with "modern" and "developmentalist" forms of material reason. In the case of the reason, practice, and need constituting discharge, semen has been reworked over a century of sociopolitical movements of somatic discipline (as the extensive work of Joseph Alter [1992, 1997] has shown) and several decades of family planning incentive and coercion. In contemporary literature and political rhetoric, discharge often marks the distinction between the disciplined but increasingly illegible national body of the citizen and the romance of the postdisciplinary "Hindu" and "neofeudal" bodies (Cohen 1995a). In work in progress, I term the legitimacy of discharge the political secret.

14 "India's Pioneer: Ashok Row Kavi," interview by Perry Brass, 3 May 1999, online at http://gaytoday.com/garchive/interview/050399in.htm.

15 Personal e-mail correspondence.

REFERENCES

• • •

Abramson, Paul R., and Steven D. Pinkerton. 1995. "Introduction: Nature, Nurture, and In-Between." In *Sexual Nature/Sexual Culture*, ed. Paul R. Abramson and Steven D. Pinkerton. 1–14. Chicago: University of Chicago Press.

Adams, Vincanne. 1998. *Doctors for Democracy: Health Professionals in the Nepal Revolution*. Cambridge: Cambridge University Press.

———. 2003. "Randomized Controlled Crime: Postcolonial Sciences in Alternative Medicine Research." *Social Studies of Science* 32 (5/6): 659–90.

Agamben, Giorgio. 1998. *Homo Sacer: Sovereign Power and Bare Life*. Trans. Daniel Heller-Roazen. Stanford: Stanford University Press.

Aggleton, Peter. 2001. "Beliefs, Desires, and HIV/AIDS Prevention." Paper presented at Belief Systems and the Place of Desire, third conference of the International Association for the Study of Sex, Culture, and Society, University of Melbourne.

Agrafiotis, D., P. Pantzsou, E. Ioannidis, A. Doumas, C. Tselepi, and A. Antonopoulou. 1990. "Knowledge, Attitudes, Beliefs, and Practices in Relation to HIV Infection and AIDS: The Case of the City of Athens, Greece." Unpublished manuscript, Department of Sociology, Athens School of Public Health.

Ahlberg, Beth Maina. 1991. *Women, Sexuality, and the Changing Social Order: The Impact of Government Policies on Reproductive Behavior in Kenya*. Philadelphia: Gordon and Breach.

———. 1994. "Is There a Distinct African Sexuality? A Critical Response to Caldwell." *Africa* 64 (2): 220–41.

All India Institute of Hygiene and Public Health. 1992. "Report of the Community Based Survey of Sexually Transmitted Diseases, HIV Infection and Sexual Behaviour among Sex Workers in Calcutta, India." Department of Epidemiology, All India Institute of Hygiene and Public Health, Calcutta.

Allman, Jean, and Victoria Tashjian. 2000. *"I Will Not Eat Stone": A Woman's History of Colonial Asante*. Portsmouth: Heinemann.

Alloula, Malek. 1986. *The Colonial Harem*. Minneapolis: University of Minnesota Press.

Alonso, Ana Maria, and Maria Teresa Koreck. 1989. "Silences: 'Hispanics,' AIDS, and Sexual Practices." *Differences: A Journal of Feminist Cultural Studies* 1 (1): 101–24.

Alter, Joseph S. 1992. *The Wrestler's Body: Identity and Ideology in North India*. Berkeley: University of California Press.

——. 1997. "Seminal Truth: A Modern Science of Male Celibacy in North India." *Medical Anthropology Quarterly* 11 (3): 275–98.

Altman, Dennis. 1996. "On Global Queering." *Australian Humanities Review* 2. http://www.lib.latrobe.edu.au/AHR/archive/Issue-July-1996/altman.html.

——. 1997. "Global Gaze/Global Gays." *Gay and Lesbian Quarterly* 3 (4): 417–36.

——. 2001. *Global Sex*. Chicago: University of Chicago Press.

Anagnost, Ann. 1995. "A Surfeit of Bodies: Population and the Rationality of the State in Post-Mao China." In *Conceiving the New World Order: The Global Politics of Reproduction*, ed. Faye D. Ginsburg and Rayna Rapp. 22–41. Berkeley: University of California Press.

Anderson, Benedict. 1987. "The State and Minorities in Indonesia." In *Tribal Groups and Ethnic Minorities in Southeast Asia, Cultural Survival*, ed. Jason Clay. 73–81. Cambridge: Cultural Survival Inc.

——. 1999. "Nationalism Today and in the Future." *Indonesia* 67: 1–11.

Anderson, Warwick. 2003. *The Cultivation of Whiteness: Science, Health, and Racial Destiny in Australia*. Melbourne: Melbourne University Press.

Antonov, A. I., and V. M. Medkov. 1987. *Vtoror Rebenok*. Moscow: Mysl'.

Antonov, A. I., and S. A. Sorokin. 2002. *Sud'ba sem'i v Rossii XXI veka*. Moscow: Graal Publishing House.

Appadurai, Arjun. 1996. *Modernity at Large: Cultural Dimensions of Globalization*. Minneapolis: University of Minnesota Press.

——. 2000. "Grassroots Research and the Globalisation of the Imagination. *Public Culture* 12 (1): 1–21.

Apostolopoulou, Sophia. 1994. "Population Policy and Low Birth Rate in Greece." *Planned Parenthood in Europe* 23 (2): 14.

Arce, Alberto, and Norman Long. 2000. *Anthropology, Development, and Modernities: Exploring Discourses, Counter-Tendencies, and Violence*. London: Routledge.

Aristotle. 1947. "Nicomachean Ethics." Trans. (from the ancient Greek) W. D. Ross. In *Introduction to Aristotle*, ed. Richard McKeon. 308–543. New York: Modern Library.

Arnold, Marlene Sue. 1985. "Childbirth among Rural Greek Women in Crete: Use of Popular, Folk and Cosmopolitan Medical Systems." Ph.D. diss., University of Pennsylvania.

Asdar Ali, Kamran. 2002. "Faulty Deployments: Persuading Women and Constructing Choice in Egypt." *Comparative Studies in Society and History* 44 (2): 370–94.

Attwood, Lynne. 1990. *The New Soviet Man and Woman: Sex Role Socialization in the USSR*. London: Macmillan, in association with the Centre for Russian and East European Studies, Birmingham.

Babasyan, Natalya. 1999. "Freedom or 'Life': Secular and Russian Orthodox Organizations Unite in a Struggle against Reproductive Freedom for Women." *Izvestia*, 26 February. Reprinted in *Current Digest of the Post-Soviet Press* 51 (12): 4–6.

Ballhatchet, Kenneth. 1980. *Race, Sex, and Class under the Raj*. New York: St. Martin's Press.

Bandyopadhyay, Sandip. 1989. "The 'Fallen' and Noncooperation." *Manushi* 53: 18–21.

Banerjee, Sumanta. 1989. *The Parlour and the Streets: Elite and Popular Culture in Nineteenth-Century Calcutta.* Calcutta: Seagull Books.

——. 1990. "Marginalization of Women's Popular Culture in Nineteenth-Century Bengal." In *Recasting Women: Essays in Colonial History,* ed. Kumkum Sangari and Sudesh Vaid. 127–79. New Brunswick: Rutgers University Press.

Barber, Karin. 1997. "Introduction." In *Readings in African Popular Culture,* ed. Karin Barber. Bloomington: Indiana University Press.

Barroso, Carmen, and Sonia Côrrea. 1995. "Public Servants, Professionals, Feminists: The Politics of Contraceptive Research in Brazil." In *Conceiving the New World Order: The Global Politics of Reproduction,* ed. Faye D. Ginsburg and Rayna Rapp. 292–306. Berkeley: University of California Press.

Bastian, Misty L. 2000. "Young Converts: Christian Missions, Gender, and Youth in Onitsha, Nigeria, 1880–1929." *Anthropological Quarterly* 73 (3): 145–58.

Bennett, Linda. 1999. "Indonesian Youth and HIV/AIDS." *Development Bulletin* 52: 54–57.

——. 2002. "Modernity, Desire, and Courtship: The Evolution of Premarital Relationships in Mataram, Eastern Indonesia." In *Coming of Age in Southeast Asia,* ed. Lenore Manderson and Pranee Liamputtong. 96–112. Richmond: Curzon Press.

Berg, Marc, and Stefan Timmermans. 2000. "Orders and Their Others: On the Constitution of Universalities in Medical Work." *Configurations* 8: 31–61.

Bharadwaj, Aditya. 2000. "How Some Indian Baby Makers Are Made: Media, Narratives, and Assisted Conception in India." *Anthropology and Medicine* 7 (1): 63–78.

——. 2002. "Conception Politics: Medical Egos, Media Spotlights, and the Contest over Test-Tube Firsts in India." In *Infertility around the Globe: New Thinking on Childlessness, Gender, and Reproductive Technologies,* ed. Marcia C. Inhorn and Frank van Balen. 315–33. Berkeley: University of California Press.

Birken, Lawrence. 1988. *Consuming Desire: Sexual Science and the Emergence of a Culture of Abundance, 1871–1914.* Ithaca: Cornell University Press.

Blackburn, Susan, and Sharon Bissell. 1997. "Marriageable Age: Political Debates on Early Marriage in Twentieth-Century Indonesia." *Indonesia* 63: 107–42.

Bleys, Rudi. 1995. *The Geography of Perversion: Male-to-Male Sexual Behavior outside the West and the Ethnographic Imagination, 1750–1918.* New York: New York University Press.

Blum, Richard, and Eva Blum. 1965. *Health and Healing in Rural Greece: A Study of Three Communities.* Stanford: Stanford University Press.

Boellstorff, Tom. 1999. "The Perfect Path: Gay Men, Marriage, Indonesia." *Gay and Lesbian Quarterly* 5 (4): 475–510.

Bond, George, and Joan Vincent. 1997. "AIDS in Uganda: The First Decade." In *AIDS in Africa and the Caribbean,* ed. George Bond, John Kreniske, Ida Susser, and Joan Vincent. 85–98. Boulder: Westview Press.

Borneman, John. 1996. "Until Death Do us Part: Marriage/Death in Anthropological Discourse." *American Ethnologist* 23 (2): 215–38.

——. 1997. "Caring and Being Cared for: Displacing Marriage, Kinship, Gender, and Sexuality." *International Social Science Journal* 49 (4): 573–84.

Bourdieu, Pierre. 1977 [1972]. *Outline of a Theory of Practice*. Trans. Richard Nice. Cambridge: Cambridge University Press.

Bowker, Geoffery C., and Susan Leigh Star. 1999. *Sorting Things Out: Classification and Its Consequences*. Cambridge: MIT Press.

Brandt, Allan. 1987 [1985]. *No Magic Bullet: A Social History of Venereal Disease in the United States since 1880*, 2nd ed. New York: Oxford University Press.

Brenner, Suzanne. 1998. *The Domestication of Desire: Women, Wealth, and Modernity in Java*. Princeton: Princeton University Press.

——. 1999. "On the Public Intimacy of the New Order: Images of Women in the Popular Indonesian Print Media." *Indonesia* 67: 13–38.

Bristow, Joseph. 1997. *Sexuality*. London: Routledge.

Brown, Helen Gurley. 2000. "Don't Give Up on Sex after 60." *Newsweek* (May 29): 55.

Brown, Paula, and Georgina Buchbinder. 1976. "Introduction." In *Man and Woman in the New Guinea Highlands*, ed. Paula Brown and Georgina Buchbinder. New York: American Anthropological Association.

Burke, Timothy. 1996. *Lifebuoy Men, Lux Women: Commodification, Consumption, and Cleanliness in Modern Zimbabwe*. Durham: Duke University Press.

Burton, Richard. 1956 [1885]. "Terminal Essay." In *Homosexuality: A Cross-Cultural Approach*, ed. Donald Webster Cory. 207–47. New York: Julian Press.

Butler, Judith. 1989. *Gender Trouble: Feminism and the Subversion of Identity*. New York: Routledge.

Butt, Leslie. 1999. "Measurements, Morality, and the Politics of 'Normal' Infant Growth." *Journal of Medical Humanities* 20 (2): 81–100.

——. 2001a. "An 'Epidemic of Runaway Wives': Discourses by Dani Men on Sex and Marriage in Highlands Irian Jaya, Indonesia." *Crossroads* 15 (1): 55–87.

——. 2001b. " 'KB Kills': Political Violence, Birth Control, and the Baliem Valley Dani." *Asia-Pacific Journal of Anthropology* 2 (1): 63–88.

Butt, L., G. Numbery, and J. Morin. 2002. "The Smokescreen of Culture; AIDS and the Indigenous in Papua, Indonesia." *Pacific Health Dialog* 9(2): 283–89.

Cáceres, Carlos F. 2000. "Afterword. The Production of Knowledge on Sexuality in the AIDS Era: Some Issues, Opportunities, and Challenges." In *Framing the Sexual Subject: The Politics of Gender, Sexuality, and Power*, ed. Richard Parker, Regina Maria Barbosa, and Peter Aggleton. 241–60. Berkeley: University of California Press.

Callon, Michel. 1991. "Technoeconomic Networks and Irreversibility." In *A Sociology of Monsters: Essays on Power, Technology, and Domination*, ed. John Law. 132–61. London: Routledge.

Campbell, John. 1964. *Honour, Family, and Patronage: A Study of Institutions and Moral Values in a Greek Mountain Community*. Oxford: Oxford University Press.

Caplan, Patricia. 1987. *The Cultural Construction of Sexuality*. London: Routledge.

Carrasco, Pedro. 1959. *Land and Polity in Tibet*. Trans. Jeffrey Hopkins. Seattle: University of Washington Press.

Carstairs, G. M. 1956. *The Twice-Born: A Study of a Community of High-Caste Hindus*. London: Hogarth Press.

CEDPA (Centre for Development and Population Activities) Nepal Field Office and

SCF/US (Save the Children/United States). 1997. "Talking Together: Integrating STD/SIDS in a Reproductive Health Context—a Facilitator Guide for the Training of Community Health Workers." Kathmandu, Nepal: CEDPA/SCF.

Chakrabarty, Dipesh. 1994. "The Difference-Deferral of a Colonial Modernity: Public Debates on Domesticity in British Bengal." In *Subaltern Studies VIII: Essays in Honour of Ranajit Guha*, ed. David Arnold and David Hardiman. 50–88. New York: Oxford University Press.

———. 2000. *Provincializing Europe: Postcolonial Thought and Historical Difference*. Princeton: Princeton University Press.

Chatterjee, Indrani. 1990. "Refracted Reality: The 1935 Calcutta Police Survey of Prostitutes." *Manushi* 57: 26–36.

Chatterjee, Partha. 1989."Colonialism, Nationalism, and Colonialized Women: The Contest in India." *American Ethnologist* 16 (4): 622–33.

Chatterjee, Ratnabali. 1993. "Prostitution in Nineteenth-Century Bengal: Construction of Class and Gender." *Social Scientist* 21 (9–11): 159–72.

Chopel, Gedun. 1992 [1938]. *Tibetan Arts of Love: Sex, Orgasm, and Spiritual Healing* (written by Gedun Chopel, introduced and translated by Jeffrey Hopkins, based on the text *Treatise on Passion*, written by Gedun Chopel). Ithaca: Snow Lion Publications.

Clark, Jeffrey. 1997. "State of Desire: Transformations in Huli Sexuality." In *Sites of Desire, Economies of Pleasure: Sexualities in Asia and the Pacific*, ed. Lenore Manderson and Margaret Jolly. 191–211. Chicago: University of Chicago Press.

Clarke, Adele E. 1998. *Disciplining Reproduction: Modernity, American Life Sciences, and the "Problem of Sex."* Berkeley: University of California Press.

Clarke, Adele E., and Theresa Montini. 1993. "The Many Faces of RU486." *Science, Technology, and Human Values* 18 (1): 42–78.

Cleland, John, and Benoit Ferry, eds. 1994. *Sexual Behaviour and AIDS in the Developing World*. London: Taylor and Francis, in association with the World Health Organization.

Cohen, David W. 1986. *Towards a Reconstructed Past: Historical Texts from Busoga, Uganda*. Oxford: Oxford University Press.

Cohen, Lawrence. 1995a. "Holi in Banaras and the Mahaland of Modernity." *Gay and Lesbian Quarterly* 2 (4): 399–424.

———. 1995b. "The Pleasures of Castration: The Postoperative Status of Hijras, Jankhas, and Academics." In *Sexual Nature, Sexual Culture*, ed. Paul R. Abramson and Steven D. Pinkerton. 276–304. Chicago: University of Chicago Press.

———. 1997. "Semen, Irony, and the Atom Bomb." *Medical Anthropology Quarterly* 11 (3): 301–3.

———. 1998. *No Aging in India: Alzheimer's, the Bad Family, and Other Modern Things*. Berkeley: University of California Press.

———. 1999. "The History of Semen: Notes on a Culture-Bound Syndrome." In *Medicine and the History of the Body*, ed. Shigehisa Kuriyama. 113–38. Tokyo: Ishiyaku EuroAmerica.

———. Forthcoming. "Operability: Surgery at the Margin of the State." In *The State at Its Margins*, ed. Veena Das and Deborah Poole. Santa Fe: School of American Research.

Collier, Jane, Michelle Z. Rosaldo, and Sylvia Yanagisako. 1997. "Is There a Family? New Anthropological Views." In *The Gender/Sexuality Reader*, ed. Roger N. Lancaster and Micaela di Leonardo. 71–81. London: Routledge.

Comaroff, Jean. 1982. "Medicine: Symbol and Ideology." In *The Problem of Medical Knowledge: Examining the Social Construction of Medicine*, ed. Peter Wright and Andrew Treacher. 49–68. Edinburgh: Edinburgh University Press.

———. 1991. *Of Revelation and Revolution: Christianity, Colonialism, and Consciousness in South Africa*. Chicago: University of Chicago Press.

———. 1993. "The Diseased Heart of Africa: Medicine, Colonialism, and the Black Body." In *Knowledge, Power, and Practice: The Anthropology of Medicine and Everyday Life*, ed. Shirley Lindenbaum and Margaret Lock. 305–29. Berkeley: University of California Press.

Comninos, Anthony C. 1988. "Greece." In *International Handbook on Abortion*, ed. Paul Sachdev. 207–15. New York: Greenport Press.

Connell, R. W. 1987. *Gender and Power*. Palo Alto: Stanford University Press.

Connell, R. W., and G. W. Dowsett. 1992. "'The Unclean Motion of the Generative Parts': Frameworks in Western Thought on Sexuality." In *Rethinking Sex: Social Theory and Sexuality Research*, ed. R. W. Connell and G. W. Dowsett. 49–75. Philadelphia: Temple University Press.

Connelly, Matthew. 2003. "Population Control Is History: New Perspectives on the International Campaign to Limit Population Growth." *Comparative Studies in Society and History* 45 (1): 122–47.

Cornwall, Andrea. 2002. "Body Mapping: Bridging the Gap between Biomedical Messages, Popular Knowledge, and Lived Experience." In *Realizing Rights: Transforming Approaches to Sexual and Reproductive Well-Being*, ed. Andrea Cornwall and Alice Welbourn. 219–34. London: Zed.

Cornwall, Andrea, and Alice Welbourne, eds. 2002. *Realizing Rights: Transforming Approaches to Sexual and Reproductive Well-Being*. London: Zed.

Crawford, Robert. 1980. "Healthism and the Medicalization of Everyday Life." *International Journal of Health Services* 19 (3): 365–88.

Creatsas, George. 1994. "Women and AIDS." Panel presented at the fifth Panhellenic Conference on AIDS and Sexually Transmitted Diseases, Athens, 11–13 February.

Cushman, Thomas. 1995. *Notes from Underground: Rock Music Counterculture in Russia*. Albany: State University of New York Press.

Das, Veena. 1993. "National Honor and Practical Kinship: Unwanted Women and Children." In *Conceiving the New World Order: The Global Politics of Reproduction*, ed. Faye D. Ginsburg and Rayna Rapp. 212–33. Berkeley. University of California Press.

Davis, Paula Jean. 2000. "On the Sexuality of 'Town Women' in Kampala." *Africa Today* 47 (3/4): 29–60.

D'Cunha, Jean. 1991. *The Legalization of Prostitution: A Sociological Inquiry into the Laws Relating to Prostitution in India and the West*. Bangalore: Wordmakers.

De Cock K. M., A. Porter, K. Odehouri, B. Barrere, J. Moreau, L. Diaby. 1989. "Rapid Emergence of AIDS in Abidjan, Ivory Coast." *Lancet* 2 (8660): 408–11.

Delaney, Carol. 1991. *The Seed and the Soil: Gender and Cosmology in Turkish Village Society*. Berkeley: University of California Press.

Dell, Heather. 1999. "Hierarchies of Femininity: Sex Workers, Feminists, and the Nation." Ph.D. diss., Duke University.

D'Emilio, John. 1997. "Capitalism and Gay Identity." In *The Gender/Sexuality Reader*, ed. Roger N. Lancaster and Micaela di Leonardo. 169–78. London: Routledge.

Derné, Steve. 1992. "Beyond Institutional and Impulsive Conceptions of Self: Family Structure and the Socially Anchored Real Self." *Ethos* 20 (3): 259–88.

de Zalduondo, Barbara O. 1990. "Prostitution Viewed Cross-Culturally: Toward Recontextualizing Sex Work in AIDS Intervention Research." *The Journal of Sex Research* 33: 223–48.

Diamandouros, Nikiforos. 1993. "Politics and Culture in Greece, 1974–91." In *Greece, 1981–89: The Populist Decade*, ed. Richard Clogg. 1–25. London: Macmillan.

Dikötter, Frank. 1995. *Sex, Culture, and Modernity in China: Medical Science and the Construction of Sexual Identities in the Early Republican Period*. Honolulu: University of Hawaii Press.

di Leonardo, Micaela. 1991. *Gender at the Crossroads of Knowledge: Feminist Anthropology in the Postmodern Era*. Berkeley: University of California Press.

Dilger, Hansjörg. 2003. "Sexuality, AIDS, and the Lures of Modernity: Reflexivity and Morality among Young People in Rural Tanzania." *Medical Anthropology* 22 (1): 23–52.

Dixon-Mueller, Ruth. 1993. "The Sexuality Connection in Reproductive Health." *Studies in Family Planning* 24 (5): 269–82.

Donham, Donald L. 1999. "Freeing South Africa: The 'Modernization' of Male-Male Sexuality in Soweto." *Cultural Anthropology* 13 (1): 3–21.

Donzelot, Jacques. 1979. *The Policing of Families*. New York: Pantheon Books.

Dorkofiki, Irini. 1985. "Amvlosis: O Afanismós tou Yénous" [Abortion: The annihilation of the race]. Athens: Ellinikí Evroëkdhotikí.

Dubisch, Jill, [ed.] 1986. *Gender and Power in Rural Greece*. Princeton: Princeton University Press.

——. 1993. "'Foreign Chickens' and Other Outsiders: Gender and Community in Greece." *American Ethnologist* 20 (2): 272–87.

——. 1995. *In a Different Place: Pilgrimage, Gender, and Politics at a Greek Island Shrine*. Princeton: Princeton University Press.

du Boulay, Juliet. 1974. *Portrait of a Greek Mountain Village*. Oxford: Clarendon Press.

——. 1986. "Women: Images of Their Nature and Destiny in Rural Greece." In *Gender and Power in Rural Greece*, ed. Jill Dubisch. 139–68. Princeton: Princeton University Press.

Duden, Barbara. 1990. *The Woman beneath the Skin: A Doctor's Patients in Eighteenth-Century Germany*. Cambridge: Harvard University Press.

Dureau, Christine. 2001. "Mutual Goals? Family Planning in Simbo, Western Solomon Islands." In *Borders of Being: Citizenship, Fertility, Sexuality in Asia and the Pacific*, ed. Margaret Jolly and Kalpana Ram. 232–61. Ann Arbor: University of Michigan Press.

Durham, Deborah. 2000. "Youth and the Social Imagination in Africa: Introduction to Parts 1 and 2." *Anthropological Quarterly* 73 (3): 113–20.

Eckvall, Robert B. 1974. "Tibetan Nomadic Pastoralists: Environment, Personality, and Ethos." *Proceedings of the American Philosophical Society* 118 (6): 519–37.

Ellis, Havelock. 1932 [1929]. "Preface." In *The Sexual life of Savages in North-Western Melanesia: An Ethnographic Account of Courtship, Marriage, and Family Life among the Natives of the Trobriand Islands, British New Guinea*, by Bronislaw Malinowski. London: George Routledge and Sons, Ltd.

——. 1942 [1936]. *Studies in the Psychology of Sex*. Vol. 4. 3rd ed. New York: Random House.

Elliston, Deborah. 1995. "Erotic Anthropology: 'Ritualized Homosexuality' in Melanesia and Beyond." *American Ethnologist* 22 (4): 848–67.

Emke-Poulopoulou, Ira. 1994. *To Dhimografikó* [Demographics]. Athens: Ellin.

Escobar, Arturo. 1995. *Encountering Development: The Making and Unmaking of the Third World*. Princeton: Princeton University Press.

Evans, Sara. 1979. *Personal Politics: The Roots of Women's Liberation in the Civil Rights Movement and the New Left*. New York: Vintage Books.

Evans-Pritchard, E. E. 1970. "Sexual Inversion among the Azande." *American Anthropologist* 72 (6): 1428–34.

Fabian, Johannes. 1978. "Popular Culture in Africa: Findings and Conjectures." *Africa* 48 (4): 315–34.

——. 1983. *Time and the Other: How Anthropology Makes Its Object*. New York: Columbia University Press.

Fallers, Lloyd. 1957. "Some Determinants of Marriage Stability in Busoga: A Reformulation of Gluckman's Hypothesis." *Africa* 27: 106–23.

——. 1965. *Bantu Bureaucracy: A Century of Political Evolution among the Basoga of Uganda*. Chicago: University of Chicago Press.

——. 1969. *Law without Precedent: Legal Ideas in Action in the Courts of Colonial Busoga*. Chicago: University of Chicago Press.

Family Planning Association of Greece (FPAG). 1993 "Conclusions of the Seminar on Women and Family Planning." Cultural Centre of the Municipality of Athens, 11 December.

——. n.d. "What Do You Know about Contraception?" Athens: FPAG.

Fanon, Frantz. 1967. *Black Skin, White Masks*. New York: Grove Press.

Farmer, Paul, Margaret Connors, and Janine Simmons, eds. 1996. *Women, Poverty and AIDS: Sex, Drugs, and Structural Violence*. Monroe, Maine: Common Courage Press.

Farquhar, Judith. 2002. *Appetites: Food and Sex in Postcolonial China*. Durham: Duke University Press.

Fassin, Didier. 1994. "Le domaine privé de la santé publique: Pouvoir, politique et sida au Congo." *Annales Histoire, Sciences Sociales* 49 (4): 745–76.

Faure, Bernard. 1998. *The Red Thread: Buddhist Approaches to Sexuality*. Princeton: Princeton University Press.

Fausto-Sterling, Anne. 1985. *Myths of Gender: Biological Theories about Women and Men*. New York: Basic Books.

——. 2000. *Sexing the Body: Gender Politics and the Construction of Sexuality*. New York: Basic Books.

Ferguson, James. 1991. *The Anti-Politics Machine: "Development," Depoliticization, and Bureaucratic Power in Lesotho*. Cambridge: Cambridge University Press.

————. 1999. *Expectations of Modernity: Myths and Meanings of Urban Life on the Zambian Copperbelt.* Berkeley: University of California Press.

Ferzacca, Steve. 2002. "Governing Bodies in New Order Indonesia." In *New Directions in Medical Anthropology*, ed. Margaret Lock and Mark Nichter. 35–67. London: Routledge.

Field, Deborah Ann. 1996. "Communist Morality and Meanings of Private Life in Post-Stalinist Russia." Ph.D. diss., University of Michigan.

Field, Mark G. 1995. "The Health Crisis in the Former Soviet Union: A Report from the 'Post-War' Zone." *Social Science and Medicine* 41 (11): 1469–78.

Findlay, Eileen J. Suárez. 1999. *Imposing Decency: The Politics of Sexuality and Race in Puerto Rico, 1870–1920.* Durham: Duke University Press.

Fisher, William. 1997. "Doing Good? The Politics and Antipolitics of NGO Practices." *Annual Review of Anthropology* 26: 439–64.

Fletcher, Ruth. 1995. "Silences: Irish Women and Abortion." *Feminist Review* 50: 44–66.

Fordham, Graham. 2001. "Moral Panic and the Construction of National Order: HIV/AIDS Risk Groups and Moral Boundaries in the Creation of Modern Thailand." *Critique of Anthropology* 21 (3): 259–316.

Foucault, Michel. 1978. *The History of Sexuality. Vol. 1: An Introduction.* Trans. Robert Hurley. New York: Random House.

————. 1984. *Histoire de la sexualité. Vol. 3: Le souci de soi.* Paris: Gallimard.

————. 1990. *The History of Sexuality, Vol. 2: The Use of Pleasure.* Transl. Robert Hurley, New York: Vintage Books.

Franklin, Sarah. 1997. *Embodied Progress: A Cultural Account of Assisted Conception.* London: Routledge.

French, Rebecca Redwood. 1995. *The Golden Yoke: The Legal Cosmology of Buddhist Tibet.* Ithaca: Cornell University Press.

Freud, Sigmund. 1949. *Three Essays on the Theory of Sexuality.* Trans. James Strachey. London: Imago.

Friedl, Ernestine. 1967. "The Position of Women: Appearance and Reality." *Anthropological Quarterly* 40 (3): 97–108.

Fritz, Kathy. 1998. "Women, Power, and HIV Risk in Rural Mbale District, Uganda." Ph.D. diss., Yale University.

Früstück, Sabine. 2000. "Managing the Truth of Sex in Imperial Japan." *Journal of Asian Studies* 59 (2): 332–58.

Fuglesang, Minou. 1994. "Veils and Videos: Female Youth Culture on the Kenyan Coast." Ph.D. diss., Stockholm University.

Gagnon, John. 1990. "The Implicit and Explicit Use of the Scripting Perspective in Sex Research." *Annual Review of Sex Research* 1: 1–43.

Gal, Susan, and Gail Kligman. 2000. *The Politics of Gender after Socialism.* Princeton: Princeton University Press.

Gardner, Katy. 1997. "Mixed Messages: Contested 'Development' and the 'Plantation Rehabilitation Project.'" In *Discourses of Development: Anthropological Perspectives*, ed. R. D. Grillo and R. L. Stirrat. 133–56. Oxford: Berg.

Georges, Eugenia. 1996a. "Abortion Policy and Practice in Greece." *Social Science and Medicine* 42 (4): 509–19.

——. 1996b. "Fetal Ultrasound Imaging and the Production of Authoritative Knowledge in Greece." *Medical Anthropology Quarterly* 10 (2): 157–75.

Ghosh, Durba. 1994. "Prostitution, Sanitation, and Soldiers: The Contagious Diseases Acts of India, 1864–1888." Masters' thesis, University of Wisconsin at Madison.

Giblin, James. 1999. "Family Life, Indigenous Culture, and Christianity." In *East African Expressions of Christianity*, ed. Thomas Spear and James Currey. 302–23. London: Oxford.

Giddens, Anthony. 1991. *Modernity and Self Identity: Self and Society in the Late Modern Age*. Stanford: Stanford University Press.

Gilligan, Carol. 1982. *In a Different Voice: Psychological Theory and Women's Development*. Cambridge: Harvard University Press.

Gilmore, David, ed. 1987. *Honor and Shame and the Unity of the Mediterranean*. Washington, D.C.: American Anthropological Association.

Ginsburg, Faye D. 1989. *Contested Lives: The Abortion Debate in an American Community*. Berkeley: University of California Press.

Ginsburg, Faye, and Rayna Rapp, eds. 1995. *Conceiving the New World Order: The Global Politics of Reproduction*. Berkeley: University of California Press.

Goldstein, Melvyn. 1989. *A History of Modern Tibet: The Demise of the Lamaist State, 1913–1951*. Berkeley: University of California Press.

——. 1997. *The Snow Lion and the Dragon: China, Tibet, and the Dalai Lama*. Berkeley: University of California Press.

Goldstein, Melyn, Edward Seibenschuh, and Tashi Tsering. 1997. *The Struggle for Modern Tibet*. New York: M. E. Sharpe.

Good, Bryon. 1994. *Medicine, Rationality, and Experience: An Anthropological Perspective*. Cambridge: Cambridge University Press.

Gould, Stephen Jay. 1998. *Rock of Ages: Science and Religion in the Fullness of Life*. New York: Ballantine.

Greenberg, David F. 1988. *The Construction of Homosexuality*. Chicago: University of Chicago Press.

Greenhalgh, Susan. 1992. "Controlling Births and Bodies in Village China." *American Ethnologist* 21 (1): 3–30.

——. 1996. "The Social Construction of Population Science: An Intellectual, Institutional, and Political History of Twentieth-Century Demography." *Comparative Studies in Society and History* 38 (1): 26–66.

Gupta, Akhil. 1995. "Blurred Boundaries: The Discourse of Corruption, the Culture of Politics, and the Imagined State." *American Ethnologist* 22 (2): 375–402.

——. 1998. *Postcolonial Developments: Agriculture in the Making of Modern India*. Durham: Duke University Press.

Gupta, Jyotsna Agnihotri. 2000. "Riddled with Secrecy and Unethical Practices: Assisted Reproduction in India." In *Bodies of Technology: Women's Involvement with Reproductive Medicine*, ed. Ann R. Saetnan, Nelly Oudshoorn, and Marta Kirejczyk. 239–53. Columbus: Ohio State University Press.

Gyatso, Janet. 1998. *Apparitions of the Self: The Secret Autobiographies of a Tibetan Visionary*. Princeton: Princeton University Press.

Hacking, Ian. 1999. *The Social Construciton of What?* Cambridge, Mass: Harvard University Press.

Halkias, Alexandra. 1998. "Give Birth for Greece! Abortion and Nation in Letters to the Editor of the Mainstream Greek Press." *Journal of Modern Greek Studies* 16: 111–38.

Hall, Kira. 1994. "Coquettish Cursers and Foul-Mouthed Flirts: Shifting Gender Positions in the Discourse of Hindi-Speaking Hijras." Paper presented at Stanford University.

——. 2001. "Language Choice and Sexual Identity in New Delhi." Paper presented at Stanford University.

Hall, Lesley. 2000. "The Sexual Body." In *Medicine in the Twentieth Century*, ed. Roger Cooter and John Pickstone. 261–75. Amsterdam: Harwood.

Halperin, David M. 1998. "Forgetting Foucault: Acts, Identities, and the History of Sexuality." *Representations* 63: 93–120.

Hansen, Karen Tranberg. 1992. "Introduction: Domesticity in Africa." In *African Encounters with Domesticity*, ed. Karen Tranberg Hansen. 1–36. New Brunswick: Rutgers University Press.

Hansen, Karen Tranberg, ed. 1992. *African Encounters with Domesticity.* New Brunswick: Rutgers University Press.

Hansen, Kathryn. 2001. "Theatrical Transvestism in the Parsi, Gujarati, and Marathi Theatres (1850–1940)." *South Asia* 24: 59–73.

Haraway, Donna. 1997. *Modest_Witness@Second_Millenium:FemaleMan_MeetsOncoMouse: Feminism and Technoscience.* London and New York: Routledge.

——. 1998. *How Like a Leaf: An Interview with Thyrza Nichols Goodeve.* London: Routledge.

Harding, Sandra G. 1993. "Introduction: Eurocentric Scientific Illiteracy—A Challenge for the World Community." In *The Racial Economy of Science: Toward a Democratic Future*, ed. Sandra G. Harding. 1–22. Bloomington: Indiana University Press.

——. 1998. *Is Science Multicultural? Postcolonialisms, Feminisms, and Epistemologies.* Bloomington: Indiana State University.

Hardt, Michael, and Antonio Negri. 2000. *Empire.* Cambridge: Harvard University Press.

Harries, Patrick. 1990. "The Symbolism of Sex: Cultural Identity in the Early Witwatersrand Gold Mines." *Cahiers d'etudes africaines* 30 (4): 451–74, 539.

Hartmann, Betsy. 1995 [1987]. *Reproductive Rights and Wrongs: The Global Politics of Population Control.* Rev. Ed. Boston: South End Press.

Hartono, Djoko, H. Rumdiarti, and Erni Djohan. 1999. *Akses Terhadap Pelayanan Kesehatan Reproduksi: Studi Kasus di Kabupaten Jayawijaya, Irian Jaya* [Access to Reproductive Health Services: A Case Study from Jayawijaya Regency, Irian Jaya]. Jakarta: PPT-LIPI.

Harvey, David. 1989. *The Condition of Postmodernity: An Enquiry into the Origins of Cultural Change.* Cambridge: Blackwell.

Heald, Suzette. 1999. *Manhood and Morality: Sex, Violence, and Ritual in Gisu Society.* London: Routledge.

Hebdige, Dick. 1981. *Subculture: The Meaning of Style.* London: Routledge.

Heider, Karl. 1970. *The Dugum Dani*. Chicago: Aldine.

——. 1972. "The Grand Valley Dani Pig Feast: A Ritual of Passage and Intensification." *Oceania* 42 (3): 169–97.

——. 1976. "Grand Valley Dani Sexuality: A Low Intensity System." *Man* 11 (2): 188–201.

Herdt, Gilbert H. 1980. *Guardians of the Flutes: Idioms of Masculinity*. New York: McGraw-Hill.

——. 1984. *Ritualized Homosexuality in Melanesia*. Berkeley: University of California Press.

——. 1999. *Sambia Sexual Culture: Essays from the Field*. Chicago: University of Chicago Press.

Herzfeld, Michael. 1983. "Semantic Slippage and Moral Fall: The Rhetoric of Chastity in Rural Greek Society." *Journal of Modern Greek Studies* 1 (1): 161–72.

——. 1985. *The Poetics of Manhood: Contest and Identity in a Cretan Mountain Village*. Princeton: Princeton University Press.

——. 1986. "Within and Without: The Category of 'Female' in the Ethnography of Modern Greece." In *Gender and Power in Rural Greece*, ed. Jill Dubish. 215–33. Princeton: Princeton University Press.

——. 1991. "Silence, Submission, and Subversion: Toward a Poetics of Womanhood." In *Contested Identities: Gender and Kinship in Modern Greece*, ed. Peter Loizos and Evthymios Papataxiarchis. 79–97. Princeton: Princeton University Press.

——. 1997. *Cultural Intimacy: Social Poetics in the Nation-State*. London: Routledge.

Hess, David J. 1997. *Science Studies: An Advanced Introduction*. New York: New York University Press.

Hirschon, Renée. 1978. "Open Body/Closed Space: The Transformation of Female Sexuality." In *Defining Females: The Nature of Women in Society*, ed. Shirley Ardener. 66–88. New York: John Wiley and Sons.

Hoad, Neville. 1999. "Between the White Man's Burden and the White Man's Disease: Tracking Lesbian and Gay Rights in Southern Africa." Special issue, "Thinking Sexuality Transnationally," *Gay and Lesbian Quarterly* 5 (4): 559–84.

Hodgson, Dorothy L., and Sheryl A. McCurdy. 2001. "Introduction: 'Wicked' Women and the Reconfiguration of Gender in Africa." In *"Wicked" Women and the Reconfiguration of Gender in Africa*, ed. Dorothy L. Hodgson and Sheryl A. McCurdy. 1–24. Portsmouth, N.H.: Heinemann.

Horn, David. 1994. *Social Bodies: Science, Reproduction, and Italian Modernity*. Princeton: Princeton University Press.

Hull, Terence, Erling Sulisyaningsih, and Gavin Jones. 1999. *Prostitution in Indonesia: Its History and Evolution*. Jakarta: Pustaka Sinar Harapan.

Hull, Terence, Djoko Hartono, H. Rumdiarti, and Erni Djohan. 1999. "Culture and Reproductive Health in Irian Jaya: An Exploratory Study." *Development Bulletin* 48: 30–32.

Hunt, Nancy Rose. 1997. " 'Le bébé en brousse.': European Women, African Birth Spacing, and Colonial Intervention in Breast-Feeding in the Belgian Congo." In *Tensions of Empire: Colonial Cultures in a Bourgeois World*, ed. Frederick Cooper and Ann Laura Stoler. 287–321. Berkeley: University of California Press.

——. 1999. *A Colonial Lexicon of Birth Ritual, Medicalization, and Mobility in the Congo.* Durham: Duke University Press.

Hyam, Ronald. 1986. "Empire and Sexual Opportunity." *Journal of Imperial and Commonwealth History* 14 (2): 34–89.

Ibbetson, D. C. J., M. E. MacLagen, and H. A. Rose. 1911. *A Glossary of the Tribes and Castes of the Panjab and North-West Frontier Province.* Lahore: Civil and Military Gazette Press.

Ingkokusumo, Gunawan. 2000. "Sakit Salah Jalan: Sexually Transmitted Illness: Perception, and Health Seeking Behavior among the Dani Men." Master's thesis, University of Amsterdam.

Iossifides, Marina. 1991. "Sisters in Christ: Metaphors of Kinship among Greek Nuns." In *Contested Identitities: Gender and Kinship in Modern Greece,* ed. Peter Loizos and Evythymios Papataxiarchis. 135–55. Princeton: Princeton University Press.

Irvine, Janice M. 1995. *Sexuality Education across Cultures: Working with Differences.* San Francisco: Jossey-Bass Publishers.

——. 2002. *Talk about Sex: The Battles over Sex Education in the United States.* Berkeley: University of California Press.

Jackson, Peter A. 1997a. "Kathoey⟩⟨Gay⟩⟨Man: The Historical Emergence of Gay Male Identity in Thailand." In *Sites of Desire, Economies of Pleasure: Sexualities in Asia and the Pacific,* ed. Lenore Manderson and Margaret Jolly. 166–90. Chicago: University of Chicago Press.

——. 1997b. "Thai Research on Male Homosexuality and Transgenderism and the Cultural Limits of Foucaultian Analysis." *Journal of the History of Sexuality* 8(1): 52–85.

Janes, Craig. 1995. "The Transformations of Tibetan Medicine." *Medical Anthropology Quarterly* 9 (1): 6–39.

Jeater, Diana. 1993. *Marriage, Perversion, and Power: The Construction of Moral Discourse in Southern Rhodesia, 1894–1930.* New York: Oxford University Press.

Jennaway, Megan. 2002. "Inflatable Bodies and the Breath of Life: Courtship and Desire among Young Women in Rural North Bali." In *Coming of Age in South and Southeast Asia,* ed. Lenore Manderson and Pranee Liamputtong. 75–95. Richmond: Curzon Press.

Jolly, Margaret, and Kalapana Ram, eds. 2001. *Borders of Being: Citizenship, Fertility, and Sexuality in Asia and the Pacific.* Ann Arbor: University of Michigan Press.

Jordanova, Ludmilla. 1989. *Sexual Visions: Images of Gender in Science and Medicine Between the Eighteenth and Twentieth Centuries.* Madison: University of Wisconsin Press.

——. 1995. "Interrogating the Concept of Reproduction in the Eighteenth Century." In *Conceiving the New World Order: The Politics of Reproduction,* ed. Faye D. Ginsburg and Rayna Rapp. Pp. 369–86. Berkeley: University of California Press.

Kader, A. 1976. "Hommes et femmes: Mœurs particulières." *Ivoire-Dimanche* 61 (8 February): 14–18.

Kakar, Sudhir. 1978. *The Inner World: A Psycho-Analytic Study of Childhood and Society in India.* Delhi: Oxford University Press.

Kalema Report. 1965. *Report of the Commission on Marriage, Divorce, and the Status of Women.* Kampala, Uganda: Ministry of Justice.

Katz, Jonathan Ned. 1990. "The Invention of Heterosexuality." *Socialist Review* 20(1): 7–33.

Kaufert, Patricia, and John D. O'Neil. 1993. "Analysis of a Dialogue on Risks in Childbirth: Clinicians, Epidemiologists, and Inuit Women." In *Knowledge, Power, and Practice: The Anthropology of Medicine and Everyday Life*, ed. Shirley Lindenbaum and Margaret Lock. Pp. 32–54. Berkeley: University of California Press.

Kayunga, Sallie Simba. 1994. "Islamic Fundamentalism in Uganda: A Case Study of the Tabligh Youth Movement." In *Uganda: Studies in Living Conditions, Popular Movements, and Constitutionalism*, ed. Mahmood Mamdani. Kampala, Uganda: Centre for Basic Research.

Keck, Margaret E., and Kathryn Sikkik. 1998. *Activists beyond Borders: Advocacy Networks in International Politics*. Ithaca: Cornell University Press.

Keller, Evlyn Fox. 1995. *Secrets of Life, Secrets of Death: Essays on Language, Gender, and Science*. London: Routledge.

Kelly, John D. 1997. "Gaze and Grasp: Plantations, Desires, Indentured Indians, and Colonial Law in Fiji." In *Sites of Desire, Economies of Pleasure: Sexualities in Asia and the Pacific*, ed. Lenore Manderson and Margaret Jolly. 72–98. Chicago: University of Chicago Press.

Kelsky, Karen. 1996. "Flirting with the Foreign: Interracial Sex in Japan's International Age." In *Local/Global: Cultural Production and the Transnational Imaginary*, ed. Rob Wilson and Wimal Dissanayake. 173–92. Durham: Duke University Press.

——. 1999. "Gender, Modernity, and Eroticized Internationalism in Japan." *Cultural Anthropology* 14 (2): 229–25.

Kennedy, Robinette. 1986. "Women's Friendships on Crete: A Psychological Perspective." In *Gender and Power in Rural Greece*, ed. Jill Dubisch. 121–38. Princeton: Princeton University Press.

Ketting, Evert. 1995. "Editorial: Dealing with Infertility." *Planned Parenthood in Europe* 24 (1): 1.

Khan, Shivananda. 2000. [Untitled essay.] *Naz ki Pukaar*. (October): n. p.

Kharkhordin, Oleg. 1999. *The Collective and the Individual in Russia: A Study of Practices*. Berkeley: University of California Press.

Kinsman John, Stella Nyanzi, and Robert Pool. 2000. "Socializing Influences and the Value of Sex: The Experience of Adolescent School Girls in Rural Masaka, Uganda." *Culture, Health, and Sexuality* 2 (2): 151–66.

Kligman, Gail. 1998. *The Politics of Duplicity: Controlling Reproduction in Ceausescu's Romania*. Berkeley: University of California Press.

Kleinman, Arthur. 1995. *Writing at the Margin: Discourse between Anthropology and Medicine*. Berkeley: University of California Press.

Knauft, Bruce. 1997. "Gender Identity, Political Economy, and Modernity in Melanesia and Amazonia." *Journal of the Royal Anthropological Institute* 3: 233–59.

Kon, Igor Semenovich. 1995. *The Sexual Revolution in Russia: From the Age of the Czars to Today*. New York: Free Press.

Konde-Lule, Joseph, Nelson Sewankambo, and Martina Morris. 1997. "Adolescent Sexual Networking and HIV Transmission in Rural Uganda." *Health Transition Review* 7: 89–100.

Kuhn, Thomas S. 1962. *The Structure of Scientific Revolutions*. Chicago: University of Chicago Press.

Kulick, Don. 1998. *Travesti: Sex, Gender, and Culture among Brazilian Transgendered Prostitutes*. Chicago: University of Chicago Press.

Kumar, Nita. 1988. *The Artisans of Banaras: Popular Culture and Identity, 1880–1986*. Princeton: Princeton University Press.

La Fontaine, Jean. 1977. "The Power of Rights." *Man* 12: 421–37.

Lancaster, Roger N. 1995. " 'That We Should All Turn Queer?' Homosexual Stigma in the Making of Manhood and the Breaking of a Revolution in Nicaragua." In *Conceiving Sexuality: Approaches to Sex Research in a Postmodern World*, ed. Richard G. Parker and John H. Gagnon. 135–56. London: Routledge.

Lane, Christopher. 1995. *The Ruling Passion: British Colonial Allegory and the Paradox of Homosexual Desire*. Durham: Duke University Press.

Laqueur, Thomas W. 1989. *Making Sex: Body and Gender from the Greeks to Freud*. Cambridge: Harvard University Press.

Larkin, Brian. 1997. "Indian Films and Nigerian Lovers: Media and the Creation of Parallel Modernities." *Africa* 67 (3): 406–39.

Larvie, Sean Patrick. 1999. "Queerness and the Spector of Brazilian National Ruin." Special issue, "Thinking Sexuality Transnationally," *Gay and Lesbian Quarterly* 5 (4): 527–58.

Latour, Bruno. 1986. "Visualization and Cognition: Thinking with the Eyes and Hands." *Knowledge and Society: Studies in the Sociology of Culture Past and Present* 6: 1–40.

——. 1987. *Science in Action: How to Follow Scientists and Engineers through Society*. Cambridge: Harvard University Press.

——. 1993. *We Have Never Been Modern*. Trans. Catherine Porter. Cambridge: Harvard University Press.

——. 1999. *Pandora's Hope: Essays on the Reality of Science Studies*. Cambridge: Harvard University Press.

Latour, Bruno, and Steve Woolgar. 1986 [1979]. *Laboratory Life: The Construction of Scientific Facts*. Princeton: Princeton University Press.

Lazanas, 1994. "Women and AIDS." Paper presented at the Fifth Panhellenic Conference on AIDS and Sexually Transmitted Diseases, Athens, 11–13, February.

Lefkarites, Mary P. 1992. "The Sociocultural Implications of Modernizing Childbirth among Greek Women on the Island of Rhodes." *Medical Anthropology* 13: 385–412.

Le Pape, Marc, and Claudine Vidal. 1984. "Libéralisme et vécus sexuels à Abidjan." *Cahiers internationaux de sociologie* 16: 111–18.

Levine, Philippa. 1993. "Venereal Disease, Prostitution, and the Politics of Empire: The Case of British India." *Journal of the History of Sexuality* 4 (4): 579–602.

——. 1997. "Modernity, Medicine, and Colonialism: The Contagious Diseases Ordinances in Hong Kong and the Straits Settlements." *positions* 6 (3): 675–705.

Li, Tania M. 1999. "Compromising Power: Development, Culture, and Rule in Indonesia. *Cultural Anthropology* 14 (3): 1–28.

Liechty, Mark. 1997. " 'This Kind of *Love* I Don't Like Too Much': Women, Pornography, and Consumer Sexuality in Kathmandu." Presented at the annual meeting of the American Anthropological Association, Washington, D.C., November.

———. 1998. "The Social Practice of Cinema and Video-Viewing in Kathmandu." *Studies in Nepali History and Society* 3 (1): 87–126.

Lock, Margaret, and Mark Nichter. 2002. "Introduction." In *New Directions in Medical Anthropology*, ed. Margaret Lock and Mark Nichter. 1–34. London: Routledge.

Luhrmann, T. M. 1996. *The Good Parsi: The Fate of a Colonial Elite in a Postcolonial Society.* Cambridge: Harvard University Press.

Lykouropoulos, Giorgos. 1994. "To toúnel tis aghápis" [The tunnel of love]. *01* (5): 72–74.

Lynton, Harriet Ronken, and Mohini Rajan. 1974. *The Days of the Beloved*. Berkeley: University of California Press.

Lyons, Maryinez. 1997. "The Point of View: Perspectives on AIDS." In *AIDS in Africa and the Caribbean*, ed. George Bond, John Kreniske, Ida Susser, and Joan Vincent. 131–148. Oxford: Westview Press.

———. 1999. "Medicine and Mortality: A Review of Responses to Sexually Transmitted Diseases in Uganda in the Twentieth Century." In *Histories of Sexually Transmitted Diseases and HIV/AIDS in Sub-Saharan Africa*, ed. Philip W. Setel, Milton Lewis, and Maryinez Lyons. Westport, Conn.: Greenwood Press.

MacCormack, Carol P., and Marilyn Strathern. 1979. *Nature, Culture, and Gender*. Cambridge: Cambridge University Press.

Mair, Lucy. 1969. *African Marriage and Social Change*. London: Cass.

Manalansan, Martin F. IV. 1997. "In the Shadows of Stonewall: Examining Gay Transnational Politics and the Diasporic Dilemma." In *The Politics of Culture in the Shadow of Capital*, ed. Lisa Lowe and David Lloyd. 485–505. Durham: Duke University Press.

Mandel, Jean-Jacques. 1983. "L'Afrique de l'an 2000?" *Libération* (11 January): 24–25.

Manderson, Lenore. 1997a. "Colonial Desires: Sexuality, Race, and Gender in British Malaya." *Journal of the History of Sexuality* 7 (3): 372–88.

———. 1997b. "Parables of Imperialism and Fantasies of the Exotic: Western Representations of Thailand—Place and Sex." In *Sites of Desire, Economies of Pleasure: Sexualities in Asia and the Pacific*, ed. Lenore Manderson and Margaret Jolly. 123–44. Chicago: University of Chicago Press.

Manderson, Lenore, Linda Rae Bennett, and Michelle Sheldrake. 1999. "Sex, Social Institutions, and Social Structure: Anthropological Contributions to the Study of Sexuality." *Annual Review of Sex Research* 10: 184–209.

Manderson, Lenore, and Margaret Jolly, eds. 1997. *Sites of Desire, Economies of Pleasure: Sexualities in Asia and the Pacific*. Chicago: University of Chicago Press.

Mani, Lata. 1987. "Contentious Traditions: The Debate on Sati in Colonial India." *Cultural Critique* 7: 119–56.

———. 1990. "Cultural Theory, Colonial Texts: Reading Eyewitness Accounts of Widow Burning." In *Cultural Studies*, ed. Lawrence Grossberg, Cary Nelson, and Paula A. Treichler. 392–408. London: Routledge.

Manuel, Peter. 1997. *Cassette Culture: Popular Music and Technology in North India*. Chicago: University of Chicago Press.

Margaritidou, Vaso, and Liz Mestheneou. 1991. "Aksiologísi ton ipiresíon ikogeniakóu programmatismóu" [Valuation of family planning services]. Athens: Ekdhosi Eterías Ikoyeniakóu Programmatismóu.

Margaritidou, Vaso, and Elizabeth Mesteneos. 1992. "The Family Planning Centres in Greece." *International Journal of Health Sciences* 3 (1): 25–31.

Marks, Lara. 1997. "A Cage of Ovulating Females: History and the Early Oral Contraceptive Pill Clinical Trials." In *Molecularizing Biology and Medicine: New Practices and Alliances*, ed. Soraya de Chadarevian and Harmke Kamminga. 221–47. Amsterdam: Harwood Academic Press.

Martin, Emily. 1986. *The Woman in the Body: A Cultural Analysis of Reproduction*. Boston: Beacon Press.

———. 1994. *Flexible Bodies: Tracking Immunity in American Culture from the Days of Polio to the Age of AIDS*. Boston: Beacon Press.

Massey, Doreen B. 1994. *Space, Place, and Gender*. Minneapolis: University of Minnesota Press.

McCulloch, Jock. 2000. *Black Peril, White Virtue: Sexual Crime in Southern Rhodesia, 1902–1935*. Bloomington: Indiana University Press.

McIntosh, Mary. 1981. "The Homosexual Role." In *The Making of the Modern Homosexual*, ed. Kenneth Plummer. 30–44. Totowa, N.J.: Barnes and Noble.

McKinley, Michelle. 2003. "Planning Other Families: Negotiating Population and Identity Politics in the Peruvian Amazon." *Identities* 10: 31–58.

Medvedeva, Irina, and Tat'iana Shishova. 2000. "Demograficheskaia voina protiv Rossii." *Nash Sovremennik* 1: n.p.

Meyer, Fernand et al. 1992. *Introduction to the Illustrated Medical Thangkas*. London: Serindia Publications.

Mitchell, Lisa M., and Eugenia Georges. 1997. "Cross-Cultural Cyborgs: Greek and Canadian Women's Discourses on Fetal Ultrasound." *Feminist Studies* 23 (2): 373–401.

Molodtsova, Viktoria. 1999. "Seks: Razvrashchenie vmeste prosveshcheniia." In *Rossiiskaya gazeta*, p. 8. Reprinted in *CDPSP* 51 (24): 14–15.

Moore, Donald. 1999. "The Crucible of Cultural Politics: Reworking 'Development' in Zimbabwe's Western Highlands." *American Ethnologist* 26 (3): 654–89.

Moore, Henrietta. 1987. *Feminism and Anthropology*. Minneapolis: University of Minnesota Press.

Morris, Henry F. 1967. "Marriage Law in Uganda: Sixty Years of Attempted Reform." In *Family Law in Asia and Africa*, ed. J. Anderson. New York: Praeger.

Morris, Rosalind C. 1994. "Three Sexes and Four Sexualities: Redressing the Discourses on Gender and Sexuality in Contemporary Thailand." *Positions* 2 (1): 15–43.

———. 1995. "All Made Up: Performance Theory and the New Anthropology of Sex and Gender." *Annual Reviews in Anthropology* 24 :567–92.

Morsy, Soheir A. 1993. "Bodies of Choice: Norplant Experimental Trials on Egyptian Women." In *Norplant under Her Skin*, ed. Barbara Mintzes, Anita Hardon, and Jannemike Hanhart. The Netherlands: Eburon Publishers.

———. 1995. "Deadly Reproduction among Egyptian Women: Maternal Mortality and the Medicalization of Population Control." In *Conceiving the New World Order: The Global Politics of Reproduction*, ed. Faye D. Ginsburg and Rayna Rapp. 162–76. Berkeley: University of California Press.

Mort, Frank. 2000 [1987]. *Dangerous Sexualities: Medico-Moral Politics in England since 1830*. London: Routledge.

Mote, Octavianus, and Danilyn Rutherford. 2001. "From Irian Jaya to Papua: The Limits of Primordialism in Indonesia's Troubled East." *Indonesia* 72: 115–40.

Mukerjee, Sutapa. 2002. "Flamboyant Indian Eunuch Takes on Chief Minister in State Polls." Wire report. Agence France-Presse, April 6.

Murray, Alison J. 2001. *Pink Fits: Sex, Subcultures, and Discourses in the Asia-Pacific*. Clayton: Monash Asia Institute, Monash University Press.

Murray, Stephen O., and Will Roscoe. 1998. "Preface: 'All Very Confusing.'" In *Boy-Wives and Female Husbands: Studies of African Homosexualities*, ed. Stephen O. Murray and Will Roscoe. xi. New York: St. Martin's Press.

Musere, Jonathan. 1990. *African Sleeping Sickness: Political Ecology, Colonialism, and Control in Uganda*. Lewiston, N.Y.: E. Mellen Press.

Musisi, Nakanyike. 2002. "Politics of Perception or Perception as Politics? Colonial and Missionary Representations of Baganda Women, 1900–1945." In *Women in African Colonial Histories*, ed. Jean Allman, Susan Geiger, and Nakanyike Musisi. 95–115. Bloomington: University of Indiana Press.

Mutongi, Kenda. 2000. "'Dear Dolly's' Advice: Representations of Youth, Courtship, and Sexualities in Africa, 1960–1980." *International Journal of African Historical Studies* 33 (1): 1–25.

Nair, Janaki. 1993. "From Devadasi Reform to SITA: Reforming Sex Work in Mysore State, 1892–1937." *National Law School Journal* (feminism and law edition) 1: 82–94.

——. 1996. *Women and Law in Colonial India*. New Delhi: Kali for Women.

Nanda, Serena. 1990. *Neither Man nor Woman: The Hijras of India*. Belmont: Wadsworth.

Nandy, Ashis. 1983. *The Intimate Enemy. Loss and Recovery of Self under Colonialism*. Delhi: Oxford University Press.

Narayan, Uma. 1997. "Contesting Cultures: 'Westernization,' Respect for Cultures and Third-World Feminists." In *The Second Wave: A Reader in Feminist Theory*, ed. Linda Nicholson, 396–414. NY: Routledge.

Naziri, Despina. 1991. "The Triviality of Abortion in Greece." *Planned Parenthood in Europe* 20 (2): 12–14.

Newberry, Janice, and Steve Ferzacca. 1999. "It Takes a Village to Make the State: Reproduction in New Order Indonesia." Paper presented at the annual meeting of the American Anthropological Association Annual, Chicago, November.

Nguyen, Vinh-Kim. 1996. "Illness, Epidemiology, and Visibility: An Anthropological Account of the Emergence of a Community-Based Response to the AIDS Epidemic in Côte d'Ivoire." Master's degree research paper, McGill University.

Niklas, Ulrike. n.d. "The Mystery of the Threshold: 'Ali' of Southern India." *Kolam* 1. http://www.uni-koeln.de/phil-fak/indologie/kolam/kolam1/alieng.html .

Noddings, Nel. 1984. *Caring: A Feminine Approach to Ethics and Moral Education*. Berkeley: University of California Press.

Oaks, Laury. 2001. *Smoking and Pregnancy: The Politics of Fetal Protection*. New Brunswick: Rutgers University Press.

Obbo, Christine. 1993. "HIV Transmission through Social and Geographical Networks in Uganda." *Social Science and Medicine* 36 (7): 949–55.

O'Brien, Denise. 1969. "The Economics of Dani Marriage." Ph.D. diss., Yale University.

Oetomo, Dede. 2000. "Masculinity in Indonesia: Genders, Sexualities, and Identities in a Changing Society." In *Framing the Sexual Subject: The Politics of Gender, Sexuality, and Power,* ed. Richard Parker, Regina Maria Barbosa, and Peter Aggleton. 46–59. Berkeley: University of California Press.

Oldenburgh, Veena Talwar. 1990. "Lifestyle as Resistance: The Case of the Courtesans of Lucknow." *Feminist Studies* 16 (2): 259–87.

O'Neil, John D., and Patricia Kaufert. 1995. "Irnitakpunga! Sex Determination and the Inuit Struggle for Birthing Rights in Northern Canada." In *Conceiving the New World Order: The Global Politics of Reproduction,* ed. Faye D. Ginsburg and Rayna Rapp. 59–77. Berkeley: University of California Press.

Orley, John H. 1970. *Culture and Mental Illness: A Study from Uganda.* Nairobi: East African Publishing House.

Ortner, Sherry B., and Harriet Whitehead, eds. 1981. *Sexual Meanings: The Cultural Construction of Gender and Sexuality.* Cambridge: Cambridge University Press.

Oudshoorn, Nelly. 1994. *Beyond the Natural Body: An Archaeology of Sex Hormones.* London: Routledge.

Pachen, Ani, and Adelaide Donnelley. 2000. *Sorrow Mountain.* New York: Bantam Doubleday Dell.

Packard, Randall, and Paul Epstein. 1991. "Epidemiologists, Social Scientists, and the Structure of Medical Research on AIDS in Africa." *Social Science and Medicine* 33 (7): 771–94.

Padgug, Robert A. 1979. "Sexual Matters: On Conceptualising Sexuality in History." *Radical History Review* 20 (spring/summer): 3–23.

Pandolfi, Mariella. 2001. "L'industrie humanitaire: Une souveraineté mouvante et supra-coloniale: Réflexion sur l'expériences des Balkans." *Multitudes* 3 (autumn): 97–105.

Papataxiarchis, Evthymios. 1991. "Friends of the Heart: Male Commensal Solidarity, Gender, and Kinship in Aegean Greece." In *Contested Identities: Gender and Kinship in Modern Greece,* ed. Peter Loïzos and Evthymios Papataxiarchis. 156–79. Princeton: Princeton University Press.

Parikh, Shanti A. 2001. "Desire, Romance, and Regulation: Adolescent Sexuality in Uganda's Time of AIDS." Ph.D. diss., Yale University.

——. 2003a. "Sugar Daddies and Sexual Citizenship in Uganda: Rethinking Third Wave Feminism." *Black Renaissance/Renaissance Noire* 5 (2): n.p.

——. 2003b. "'Don't Tell Your Sister or Anyone that You Love Me': Considering the Effects of Adult Regulation on Adolescent Sexual Subjectivities in Uganda's Time of AIDS." In *Gender, Sexuality, and HIV/AIDS: Research and Intervention in Africa,* ed. Britt Pinkowsky Tersbøl. 53–84. Copenhagen: Institute of Public Health, University of Copenhagen.

Parker, Andrew, Mary Russo, Doris Sommer, and Patricia Yaeger. 1992. "Introduction." In *Nationalisms and Sexualities,* ed. Andrew Parker, Mary Russo, Doris Sommer, and Patricia Yaeger. 1–18. London: Routledge.

Parker, Richard G. 1987. "Acquired Immune Deficiency Syndrome in Urban Brazil." *Medical Anthropology Quarterly* I (2): 155–72.

——. 1991. *Bodies, Pleasures, and Passions: Sexual Culture in Contemporary Brazil*. Boston: Beacon Press.

——. 1992. "Sexual Diversity, Cultural Analysis, and AIDS Education in Brazil." In *The Time of AIDS: Social Analysis, Theory, and Method*, ed. Gilbert Herdt and Shirley Lindenbaum. 225–42. Newbury Park: Sage Publications.

——. 1996. "Empowerment, Commodity Mobilization, and Social Change in the Face of HIV/AIDS." *AIDS* 10 (supplement) 28–31.

Parker, Richard, Regina Maria Barbosa, and Peter Aggleton. 2000. "Introduction: Framing the Sexual Subject." In *Framing the Sexual Subject: the Politics of Gender, Sexuality and Power*, ed. Richard Parker, Regina Maria Barbosa and Peter Aggleton. 1–28. Berkeley: University of California Press.

Parsons, Susan F. 1987. "Feminism and the Logic of Morality: A Consideration of Alternatives." In *Ethics: A Feminist Reader*, ed. Elizabeth Frazer, Jennifer Hornsby, and Sabina Lovibond. 380–412. Oxford: Blackwell.

Patton, Cindy. 1985. *Sex and Germs: The Politics of AIDS*. Boston: South End Press.

——. 1990. *Inventing AIDS*. London: Routledge.

——. 1995. *Fatal Advice: How Safe-Sex Education Went Wrong*. Durham: Duke University Press.

——. 1996. "Queer Peregrinations." In *Challenging Boundaries: Global Flows, Territorial Identities*, ed. Michael J. Shapiro and Hayward R. Alker. 363–82. Minneapolis: University of Minneapolis Press.

——. 1997. "From Nation to Family: Containing African AIDS." In *The Gender/Sexuality Reader: Culture, History, Political Economy*, ed. Roger Lancaster and Micaela di Leonardo. 279–90. London: Routledge.

Paulus. 1982. "Oscar, imitateur d'Aïcha Koné." *Ivoire-Dimanche* 611 (24 October): 43–45.

Pavert, Jan ver der. 1986. "Ima Wusan: A Purification Ritual among the Dani of West Irian." *UNITAS* 59 (1): 5–154.

Paxson, Heather. 1997. "Demographics and Diaspora, Gender and Geneaology: Anthropological Notes on Greek Population Policy." *South European Society and Politics* 2 (2): 34–56.

——. 2002. "Rationalizing Sex: Making Modern Lovers in Urban Greece." *American Ethnologist* 29 (2): 307–34.

Petchesky, Rosalind P. 2000. "Sexual Rights: Inventing a Concept, Mapping an International Practice." In *Framing the Sexual Subject: The Politics of Gender, Sexuality, and Power*, ed. Richard Parker, Regina Maria Barbosa, and Peter Aggleton. 81–103. Berkeley: University of California Press.

Peters, Hermann. 1975. "Some Observations on the Social and Religious Life of a Dani Group." *Irian: Bulletin of Irian Jaya Development* 4 (2): 1–197.

Petersen, Alan R., and Deborah Lupton. 1996. *The New Public Health: Health and Self in the Age of Risk*. St. Leonards, NSW, Australia: Allen and Unwin.

Pickering, H., M. Okongo, K. Bwanika, B. Nnalusiba, and J. Whitworth. 1996. "Sexual Mixing Patterns in Uganda: Small-Time Urban/Rural Traders." *AIDS* 10 (5): 533–36.

Pigg, Stacy Leigh. 1992. "Inventing Social Categories through Place: Social Representations and Development in Nepal." *Comparative Studies in Society and History* 34 (3): 491–513.

——. 1996. "The Credible and the Credulous: The Question of 'Villagers' Beliefs' in Nepal." *Cultural Anthropology* 11 (2): 160–201.

——. 1997. "'Found in Most Traditional Societies': Traditional Medical Practitioners between Culture and Development." In *International Development and the Social Sciences: Essays on the History and Politics of Knowledge*, ed. Frederick Cooper and Randall Packard. 259–90. Berkeley: University of California Press.

——. 2001. "Languages of Sex and AIDS in Nepal: Notes on the Social Production of Commensurability." *Cultural Anthropology* 16 (4): 481–541.

——. 2001b. "Les politiques de développement et les politiques de la santé: les contradictions de la prévention du sida au Népal." Special issue: "Économie politique féministe," ed. Marie-France Labrecque. *Anthropologie et Sociétés* 25 (1): 43–62.

——. 2002. "Too Bold, Too Hot: Crossing 'Culture' in AIDS Prevention in Nepal." In *New Horizons in Medical Anthropology: Essays in Honor of Charles Leslie*, ed. Mark Nichter and Margaret Lock. 58–80. London: Routledge.

Pigg, Stacy Leigh, and Linnet Pike. 2001. "Knowledges, Attitudes, Beliefs, and Practices: The Social Shadow of AIDS Prevention in Nepal." Special issue: "Sexual Sites, Seminal Attitudes: Sexualities, Masculinities and Culture in South Asia," ed. Sanjay Srivastava. *South Asia* 24: 177–95.

Pitch, Tamar. 1992. "Decriminalization of Legalization? The Abortion Debate in Italy." In *The Criminalization of a Woman's Body*, ed. Clarice Feinman. 27–40. New York: Harrington Park Press.

Porter, Roy, and Lesley Hall. 1995. *The Facts of Life: The Creation of Sexual Knowledge in Britain, 1650–1950*. New Haven: Yale University Press.

Povinelli, Elizabeth, and George Chauncey. 1999. "Thinking Sexuality Transnationally: An Introduction." *Gay and Lesbian Quarterly* 5 (4): 439–50.

Prakash, Gyan. 1999. *Another Reason: Science and the Imagination of Modern India*. Princeton: Princeton University Press.

Probyn, Elspeth. 1999. "Bloody Metaphors and Other Allegories of the Ordinary." In *Between Woman and Nation: Nationalisms, Transnational Feminisms, and the State*, ed. Caren Kaplan, Norma Alarcon, and Minoo Moallem. 47–62. Durham: Duke University Press.

Rabinow, Paul. 1996. "Artificiality and Enlightenment: From Sociobiology to Biosociality." In *Essays on the Anthropology of Reason*. 91–111. Princeton: Princeton University Press.

——. 2002. "Midst Anthropology's Problems." *Cultural Anthropology* 17 (2): 135–50.

Ragoné, Helena, and France Winddance Twine. 2000. *Ideologies and Technologies of Motherhood: Race, Class, Sexuality, Nationalism*. London: Routledge.

Ram, Kalpana. 1998a. "Uneven Modernities and Ambivalent Sexualities: Women's Constructions of Puberty in Coastal Kanykumari, Tamilnadu." In *A Question of Silence? The Sexual Economies of Modern India*, ed. Mary E. John and Janaki Nair. 269–303. New Delhi: Kali for Women.

——. 1998b. "Maternity and the Story of Enlightenment in the Colonies: Tamil Coastal Women, South India." In *Maternities and Modernities: Colonial and Postcolonial Expe-*

riences in Asia and the Pacific, ed. Kalpana Ram and Margaret Jolly. 114–43. Cambridge: Cambridge University Press.

——. 2001. "Rationalizing Fecund Bodies: Family Planning Policy and the Modern Indian State." In Borders of Being: Citizenship, Fertility, and Sexuality in Asia and the Pacific, ed. Margaret Jolly and Kalpana Ram. 82–117. Ann Arbor: University of Michigan Press.

Rapp, Rayna. 1988. "Chromosomes and Communication: The Discourse of Genetic Counselling." Medical Anthropology Quarterly 2 (2): 143–57.

Ratcliff, Kathryn Strother. 1989. "Introduction." In Healing Technology: Feminist Perspectives, ed. Kathryn Ratcliff, Myra Marx Ferree, Gail O. Mellow et al. Ann Arbor: University of Michigan Press.

Reddy, Gayatri. 1999. "Crossing 'Lines' of Subjectivity: The Negotiation of Sexual Identity in Hyderabad, India." Paper presented at Deakin University Conference on Sexualities, Masculinities and Culture in South Asia.

——. 2001. " 'You Don't Need Genitals for Politics': 'Diva Citizenship' and the Rights of 'Eunuchs' in Contemporary India." Paper presented at Belief Systems and the Place of Desire, Third Conference of the International Association for the Study of Sex, Culture and Society. University of Melbourne, 2001.

Reed, Adam. 1997. "Contested Images and Common Strategies: Early Colonial Sexual Politics in the Massim." In Sites of Desire, Economies of Pleasure: Sexualities in Asia and the Pacific, ed. Lenore Manderson and Margaret Jolly. 48–71. Chicago: University of Chicago Press.

Rege, Sharmila. 1998. "Hegemonic Appropriation of Sexuality: The Case of the Lavani Performers of Maharashtra." Contributions to Indian Sociology 29 (1–2): 23–38.

Reiter, Rayna Rapp. 1975. Toward An Anthropology of Women. New York: Monthly Review Press.

Remmenick, Larissa I. 1991. "Epidemiology and Determinants of Induced Abortion in the USSR." Social Science and Medicine 33 (7): 841–48.

Riles, Annelise. 2000. The Network Inside Out. Ann Arbor: University of Michigan Press.

Rival, Laura, Don Slater, and Daniel Miller. 1998. "Sex and Sociality: Comparative Ethnography of Sexual Objectification." Theory, Culture and Society 15 (3–4): 295–321.

Rivkin-Fish, Michele. 1999. "Sexuality Education in Russia: Defining Pleasure and Danger for a Fledgling Democratic Society." Social Science and Medicine 49: 801–14.

——. 2000. "Health Development Meets the End of State Socialism: Visions of Democratization, Women's Health, and Social Well-Being for Contemporary Russia." Culture, Medicine, and Psychiatry 24: 77–100.

——. 2003. "Anthropology, Demography, and the Search for a Critical Analysis of Fertility: Insights from Russia." American Anthropologist 105 (2): 289–301.

Robbins, Bruce. 1998. "Comparative Cosmopolitanisms." In Cosmopolitics: Thinking and Feeling beyond the Nation, ed. Pheng Cheah and Bruce Robbins. 246–64. Minneapolis: University of Minnesota Press.

Robert, Paul. 1982. Tibetan Symbolic World. Chicago: University of Chicago Press.

Robinson, Kathryn. 1998. "Love and Sex in an Indonesian Mining Town." In Gender and Power in Affluent Asia, ed. Krishna Sen and Maila Stivens. 63–86. London: Routledge.

Rofel, Lisa. 1999a. *Other Modernities: Gendered Yearnings in China after Socialism.* Berkeley: University of California Press.

——. 1999b. "Qualities of Desire: Imagining Gay Identities in China." Special issue, "Thinking Sexuality Transnationally." *Gay and Lesbian Quarterly* 5 (4): 451–74.

Rosaldo, Michelle Zimbalist, and Louise Lamphere, eds. 1974. *Woman, Culture, and Society.* Stanford: Stanford University Press.

Rosario, Vernon A. 1997. *The Erotic Imagination: French Histories of Perversity.* Oxford: Oxford University Press.

Roscoe, John. 1911. *The Baganda: An Account of their Native Customs and Beliefs.* London: Macmillan.

——. 1915. *The Northern Bantu, an Account of Some Central African Tribes of the Uganda Protectorate.* London: F. Cass.

Ross, Ellen, and Rayna Rapp. 1997. "Sex and Society: A Research Note from Social History and Anthropology." In *The Gender/Sexuality Reader,* ed. Roger N. Lancaster and Micaela di Leonardo. 153–68. London: Routledge.

Row Kavi, Ashok. 2000. "Emerging LGBT Identities in India and the World." Paper presented at Samabhavana Society Inaugural Meeting, February 26–27, J.J. Nursing Association Retreat, Mumbai, India.

Rubin, Gayle. 1975. "The Traffic in Women." In *Toward an Anthropology of Women,* ed. Rayna R. Reiter. 157–210. New York: Monthly Review Press.

——. 1984. "Thinking Sex: Notes for a Radical Theory of the Politics of Sexuality." In *Pleasure and Danger: Exploring Female Sexuality,* ed. Carole S. Vance. 267–319. Boston: Routledge and Kegan Paul.

Rutherford, Blair, and Rinse Nyamuda. 2000. "Learning about Power: Development and Marginality in an Adult Literacy Center for Farm Workers in Zimbabwe." *American Ethnologist* 27 (4): 839–54.

Said, Edward. W. 1979. *Orientalism.* New York: Vintage Books.

Sangaji, S. 1983 [1899]. *Dictionary Urdu-English, Based on Shakespear* [sic] *and the Best Modern Authorities.* New Delhi: J. Jetley.

Scheier, Rachel. 2003. " 'Aunts' Who Used to Join Couples on Their Wedding Nights, Now Dispense Health Advice." *Boston Globe,* 28 October.

Scheper-Hughes, Nancy, and Margaret Lock. 1991. "The Message in the Bottle: Illness and the Micropolitics of Resistance." *Journal of Psychohistory* 18 (4): 409–32.

Schneider, Jane, and Peter Schneider. 1995. "Coitus Interruptus and Family Respectability in Catholic Europe." In *Conceiving the New World Order: The Global Politics of Reproduction,* ed. Faye D. Ginsburg and Rayna Rapp. 177–94. Berkeley: University of California Press.

Schoepf, Brooke Grundfest. 1997. "AIDS, Gender, and Sexuality during Africa's Economic Crisis." In *African Feminism: The Politics of Survival in Sub-Saharan Africa,* ed. Gwendolyn Mikell. 310–32. Philadelphia: University of Pennsylvania Press.

Scott, James C. 1998. *Seeing like a State.* New Haven: Yale University Press.

——. 1990. *Domination and the Arts of Resistance.* New Haven: Yale University Press.

Sedgwick, Eve Kosofsky. 1990. *Epistemology of the Closet.* Berkeley: University of California Press.

Setel, Philip W. 1999. *A Plague of Paradoxes: AIDS, Culture, and Demography in Northern Tanzania*. Chicago: University of Chicago Press.

Shapin, Steven, and Simon Schaffer. 1985. *Leviathan and the Air-Pump: Hobbes, Boyle, and the Experimental Life*, including a translation of Thomas Hobbes's "Dialogus Physicus de Natura Aeris" by Simon Schaffer. Princeton: Princeton University Press.

Sharma, Satish Kumar. 1989. *Hijras, the Labelled Deviants*. New Delhi: Gian.

Sharpless, John. 1997. "Population Science, Private Foundations, and Development Aid: The Transformation of Demographic Knowledge in the United States, 1945–1965." In *International Development and the Social Sciences: Essays on the History and Politics of Knowledge*, ed. Frederick Copper and Randall Packard. 176–202. Berkeley: University of California Press.

Sigley, Gary. 2001. "Keep It in the Family: Government, Marriage, and Sex in Contemporary China." In *Borders of Being: Citizenship, Fertility, and Sexuality in Asia and the Pacific*, ed. Margaret Jolly and Kalpana Ram. 118–53. Ann Arbor: University of Michigan Press.

Sivaramakrishnan, K. 2000. "Crafting the Public Sphere in the Forests of West Bengal: Democracy, Development, and Political Action." *American Ethnologist* 27 (2): 431–61.

Smith, Daniel Jordan. 2000. " 'These Girls Today Na War-O': Premarital Sexuality and Modern Identity in Southeastern Nigeria." *Africa Today* 473 (3/4): 99–120.

Solomon, Susan Gross. 1992. "The Demographic Argument in Soviet Debates over the Legalization of Abortion in the 1920s." *Cahiers du Monde Russe et Sovietique* 33 (1): 59–82.

Somerville, Siobhan. 1997. "Scientific Racism and the Invention of the Homosexual Body." In *The Gender/Sexuality Reader: Culture, History, and Political Economy*, ed. Roger N. Lancaster and Micaela di Leonardo. 37–52. London: Routledge.

Spear, Thomas, and Isaria Kimambo, eds. 1999. *East African Expressions of Christianity*. Oxford: James Currey.

Sperber, Dan. 1985. *On Anthropological Knowledge*. Cambridge: Cambridge University Press.

Srivastava, Sanjay. 2001. "Non-Ghandian Sexuality, Commodity Cultures, and a 'Happy Married Life': The Cultures of Masculinity and Heterosexuality in India." Special issue: "Sexual Sites, Seminal Attitudes: Sexualities, Masculinities, and Culture in South Asia," ed. Sanjay Srivastava. *South Asia* 24: 225–249.

Stambach, Amy. 2000. *Lessons from Mount Kilimanjaro: Schooling, Community, and Gender in East Africa*. London: Routledge.

Star, Susan Leigh. 1991. "Power, Technologies, and the Phenomenology of Conventions: On Being Allergic to Onion." In *A Sociology of Monsters: Essays on Power, Technology and Domination*, ed. John Law. 26–56. London: Routledge.

Stein, R. A. 1972. *Tibetan Civilization*. Stanford: Stanford University Press.

Stewart, Kearsley. 2000. "Toward a Historical Perspective on Sexuality in Uganda: The Reproductive Lifeline Technique for Grandmothers and Their Daughters." *Africa Today* 47 (3/4): 123–48.

Stocking, George W. 1987. *Victorian Anthropology*. New York: Free Press; Collier Macmillan.

Stoler, Ann L. 1992. "Sexual Affronts and Racial Frontiers: European Identities and the Cultural Politics of Exclusion on Colonial Southeast Asia." *Comparative Studies in Society and History* 34 (3): 514–51.

——. 1997a. "Educating Desire in Colonial Southeast Asia: Foucault, Freud, and Imperial Sexualities." In *Sites of Desire, Economies of Pleasure: Sexualities in Asia and the Pacific*, ed. Lenore Manderson and Margaret Jolly. 27–47. Chicago: University of Chicago Press.

——. 1997b. "Carnal Knowledge and Imperial Power: Gender, Race, and Marginality in Colonial Asia." In *The Gender/Sexuality Reader: Culture, History, and Political Economy*, ed. Roger N. Lancaster and Micaela di Leonardo. 13–36. London: Routledge.

——. 2002. *Carnal Knowledge and Imperial Power: Race and the Intimate in Colonial Rule*. Berkeley: University of California Press.

Strathern, Marilyn. 1988. *The Gender of the Gift: Problems with Women and Problems with Society in Melanesia*. Berkeley: University of California Press.

Summers, Carol. 2002. *Colonial Lessons: Africans' Education in Southern Rhodesia, 1918–1940*. Portsmouth, N.H.: Heinemann.

Sunindyo, S. 1998. "When the Earth is Female and the Nation Is Mother: Gender, the Armed Forces and Nationalism in Indonesia." *Feminist Review* 58: 1–21.

Suryakusama, Julia I. 1996. "The State and Sexuality in New Order Indonesia." In *Fantasizing the Feminine in Indonesia*, ed. Laurie J. Sears. 92–119. Durham: Duke University Press.

Sutton, David. 1994. "Tradition and Modernity: Kalymnian Constructions of Identity and Otherness." *Journal of Modern Greek Studies* 12: 239–60.

Symeonidou, Haris. 1990. *Aposchólisi ke gonimótita ton yinekón stin periohí tis protévousas* [Occupation and Fertility of Women in Great Athens]. Athens: Ethnikó Kéndro Kionikón Erevnón.

——. 1994. "Fertility: Trends and Projections." Paper presented at "Contemporary Demographic Trends and Family Planning in Greece," sponsored by the Family Planning Association of Greece, Athens, 21 January.

Tan, Michael L. 1995. "From Bakla to Gay: Shifting Identities and Sexual Behaviors in the Philipines." In *Conceiving Sexuality: Approaches to Sex Research in a Postmodern World*, ed. Richard G. Parker and John H. Gagnon. 85–96. London: Routledge.

Terto, Veriano Jr. 2000. "Male Sexuality and Seropositivity: The Construction of Social Identities in Brazil." In *Framing the Sexual Subject: the Politics of Gender, Sexuality, and Power*, ed. Richard Parker, Regina Maria Barbosa, and Peter Aggleton. 60–80. Berkeley: University of California Press.

Thomas, Lynn M. 2003. *Politics of the Womb: Women, Reproduction, and the State in Kenya*. Berkeley: University of California Press.

Thompson, Mary S. 2000. "Family Planning or Reproductive Health? Interpreting Policy and Providing Family Planning Services in Highland Chiapas, Mexico." In *Contraception across Cultures: Technologies, Choices, Constraints*, ed. Andrew Russell, Elisa J. Sobo, and Mary S. Thompson. 221–43. Oxford: Berg Press.

Tsalicoglou, Fotini. 1995. "A New Disease in Greek Society: AIDS and the Representation of 'Otherness.' " *Journal of Modern Greek Studies* 13 (1): 83–97.

Tsing, Anna. 2000. "On the Global Situation." *Cultural Anthropology* 15 (3): 327–60.

UNAIDS. 2000. "Uganda: Epidemiological Fact Sheet on HIV/AIDS and Sexually Transmitted Infections." Geneva: World Health Organization.

Utomo, Dwisteyani. 2002. "Sexual Values and Early Experiences among Young People." In *Coming of Age in South and Southeast Asia*, ed., Lenore Manderson and Pranee Liamputtong. 207–26. Richmond: Curzon Press.

Valaoras, Vasilios, and Dimitri Trichopoulos. 1970. "Abortion in Greece." In *Abortion in a Changing World*, vol. 1, ed. Robert Hall. 284–90. New York: Columbia University Press.

Vance, Carole S. 1984. "Pleasure and Danger: Toward a Politics of Sexuality." In *Pleasure and Danger: Exploring Female Sexuality*, ed. Carole S. Vance. 1–27. Boston: Routledge and Kegan Paul.

———. 1991. "Anthropology Rediscovers Sexuality: A Theoretical Comment." *Social Science and Medicine* 33: 867–84.

Vasil'chenko, G. C. 1990. *Spravochnik seksopatologiia*. Moscow: Meditsina.

Vatsyayana. 1963. *Kamasutra*, trans. S. C. Upadhyaya. Bombay: D. B. Taraporevala.

Vaughan, Megan. 1991. *Curing Their Ills: Colonial Power and African Illness*. Cambridge: Polity Press.

———. 1992. "Syphilis in Colonial East and Central Africa: The Social Construction of an Epidemic." In *Epidemics and Ideas: Essays on the Historical Perception of Pestilence*, ed. Terence Ranger and Paul Slack. 269–302. Cambridge: Cambridge University Press.

Vidal, Claudine. 1979. "L'argent fini, l'amour est envolé. . . ." *L'Homme* 19 (3–4): 1–18.

Vishnevskii, A. G. 1996. "Konservativnaia revoliutsiia v SSSR." *Mir Rossii* 5 (4): 3–66.

———. 1999a. *Serb i rubl': Konservativnaia modernizatsiia v SSSR*. Moscow: OGI.

———, ed. 1999b. *Naselenie Rossii 1998*. Moscow: Institute Narodnokhoziaistvennogo prognozirovaniia RAN Tsentr demografii i ekologii cheloveka.

Vornik, B. M. 1994. *Seksologiia: entsiklopedicheskii spravochnik po seksologii i smezhnym oblstiam*. Minsk: "Belaruskaia entsyklapedyia" imeni Petrusia Brovki.

Vyas, M. D., and Yogesh Shingala. 1987. *The Life Style of the Eunuchs*. New Delhi: Anmol.

Waldby, C. Susan Kippax, and J. Crawford. 1993. "Cordon Sanitaire: 'Clean and Unclean' Women in the AIDS Discourse of Young Men." In *AIDS: Facing the Second Decade*, ed. Peter Aggleton, Peter Davies, and Graham Hart. 29–40. Philadelphia: Falmer Press.

Walkowitz, Judith R. 1980. *Prostitution and Victorian Society: Women, Class, and the State*. Cambridge: Cambridge University Press.

Ward, Martha C. 1991. "Cupid's Touch: The Lessons of the Family Planning Movement for the AIDS Epidemic." *The Journal of Sex Research* 28 (2): 289–305.

———. 1995. "Early Childbearing: What Is the Problem? and Who Owns it?" In *Conceiving the New World Order: The Global Politics of Reproduction*, ed. Faye D. Ginsburg and Rayna Rapp. 140–61. Berkeley: University of California Press.

Wardlow, Holly. 2001. " 'Prostitution,' 'Sex Work,' and 'Passenger Women': When Sexualities Don't Correspond to Stereotypes." Paper presented at "Belief Systems and the Place of Desire," third conference of the International Association for the Study of Sex, Culture, and Society, University of Melbourne.

——. 2002. "Giving Birth to Gonolia: 'Culture' and Sexually Transmitted Disease among the Huli of Papua New Guinea." *Medical Anthropology Quarterly* 16 (2): 151–75.

Weeks, Jeffery. 1989 [1981]. *Sex, Politics, and Society: The Regulation of Sexuality since 1800.* 2nd. ed. London: Longman.

——. 1998. "The Sexual Citizen." *Theory, Culture, and Society* 15 (3–4): 35–52.

——. 2000. "Sexuality and History Revisited." In *Making Sexual History.* 125–41. Cambridge, Eng.: Polity Press.

Weston, Kath. 1993. "Lesbian/Gay Studies in the House of Anthropology." *Annual Review of Anthropology* 22: 339–67.

——. 1996. *Render Me, Gender Me: Lesbians Talk Sex, Class, Color, Nation, Studmuffins.* New York: Columbia University Press.

White, Luise. 1990. *The Comforts of Home: Prostitution in Colonial Nairobi.* Chicago: University of Chicago Press.

Wieringa, Saskia. 1998. "Sexual Metaphors in the Change from Sukarno's Old Order to Suharto's New Order in Indonesia." *Review of Indonesian and Malay Affairs* 32 (2): 143–73.

Wilt, Judith. 1990. *Abortion, Choice, and Contemporary Fiction: The Armageddon of the Maternal Instinct.* Chicago: University of Chicago Press.

Wolf, Eric. 1982. *Europe and the People without History.* Berkeley: University of California Press.

Woost, Michael. 1993. "Nationalizing the Local Past in Sri Lanka: Histories of Nation and Development in a Sinhalese Village." *American Ethnologist* 20 (3): 502–21.

Yanagisako, Sylvia J., and Carol L. Delaney, eds. 1995. *Naturalizing Power. Essays in Feminist Cultural Analysis.* New York: Rouledge.

Yoder, P. Stanley. 1997. "Negotiating Relevance: Belief, Knowledge, and Practice in International Health." *Medical Anthropology Quarterly* 11 (2): 131–46.

Yurchak, Alexei. 1997. "The Cynical Reason of Late Socialism: Power, Pretense, and the Anecdote." *Public Culture* 9: 161–88.

Zinovieff, Sofka. 1991. "Hunters and Hunted: Kamaki and the Ambiguities of Sexual Predation in a Greek Town." In *Contested Identities: Gender and Kinship in Modern Greece,* ed. Peter Loizos and Evthymios Papataxiarchis. 203–20. Princeton: Princeton University Press.

Zola, Erving. 1976. "Medicine as an Institution of Social Control." In *The Cultural Crisis of Modern Medicine,* ed. John Ehrenreich. 80–100. New York: Monthly Review.

CONTRIBUTORS

· · ·

VINCANNE ADAMS is a professor of Anthropology in the Department of Anthropology, History, and Social Medicine at the University of California at San Francisco. She has published several books on modernity and change in Inner Asia, including *Tigers of the Snow and Other Virtual Sherpas* and *Doctors for Democracy*, and has been conducting fieldwork since 1993 on women's experience of modernity in Tibet.

LESLIE BUTT is an assistant professor of Pacific and Asian Studies at the University of Victoria. She conducted fieldwork in West Papua (Irian Jaya) in 1994–1995, 2000, 2001, and 2003. Her research among the Dani focuses on the intersections between politics, reproduction, sexuality, and AIDS. Most recently, she has studied the impact of sex work on parenting among young Dani women.

LAWRENCE COHEN is an associate professor of Anthropology and South and Southeast Asian Studies at the University of California at Berkeley and is the author of *No Aging in India: Alzheimer's, the Bad Family, and Other Modern Things*. He is currently completing a book titled "India Tonight: Homosex and the Political Secret."

HEATHER S. DELL teaches feminist theories and international women's issues in the Women's Studies Program at the University of Illinois at Springfield. Her research focuses on the sex worker rights movement in Kolkata.

VINH-KIM NGUYEN is an HIV clinician and medical anthropologist in Montréal and has worked since 1994 with community-based groups in West Africa on the issue of expanding access to treatment for HIV. He teaches at McGill University and his clinical practice is at the Clinique l'Actuel.

SHANTI A. PARIKH is an assistant professor of Anthropology and African and Afro-American Studies at Washington University in St. Louis. Her research focuses on the politics of sexual and reproductive health within the context of HIV/AIDS and STDs; the globalization of romance and erotica; and the growth in global inequalities. She has written articles on the age of consent law in Uganda; sugar daddies and sexual citizenship; love letters; and effects of HIV prevention messages on youth. She is currently completing her manuscript "Regulating Romance: Sexuality, Globalization, and HIV/AIDS in Uganda."

HEATHER PAXSON received a Ph.D. in anthropology from Stanford University in 1998. The author of *Making Modern Mothers: Ethics and Family Planning in Urban Greece*, she teaches Anthropology and Gender Studies at the Massachusetts Institute of Technology.

STACY LEIGH PIGG is an associate professor of Anthropology at Simon Fraser University and editor of *Medical Anthropology: Cross-Cultural Studies in Health and Illness*. Her interests lie at the intersection of medical anthropology and the study of postcolonial cultural relations, with a focus on the negotiation of differing frameworks of meaning as this occurs under conditions of social inequality. Her recent research traces the construction of AIDS as a public problem in Nepal.

MICHELE RIVKIN-FISH received a Ph.D. from Princeton University and is currently an assistant professor of Anthropology at the University of Kentucky. She has been conducting research in Russia since 1993, and has recently completed a book, *Women's Health in Post-Soviet Russia: The Politics of Intervention*.

INDEX

• • •

Gandhi, Mahatma, 199, 291, 293
Gautam, Siddarth, 280–81
Gender: performativity, 68, 247, 251, 255, 264, 276; proficiency, 110, 120
Gender norms, 97–99, 109; ethics and, 99
Gender studies, 4–5, 7
Genital transformation, female external. *See* Pulling, labia
Globalization, 10–11, 30 n.12, 60; and gay identities, 272; and intimacy, 11
Great Leap Forward, 224, 225; and female burden, 225
Gshang tshong ma, 235

Habitus, 110, 121
Health, maternal and child. *See* Reproductive
Healthism, 96, 121
Heteronormativity, 174; and development discourse, 183
Hijras, 270, 284, 292–93, 299, 303 n.12; and class difference, 280; and "Farsi" language use, 276–77, 302 n.8; gender authenticity, 275–76, 279; and Indic queer identity, 279; and internet organizing, 282; and neoliberal mediscapes, 274–75, and performative agency, 276; and postcolonial citizenship, 278–79; and the transgender movement, 280–81; and the *zenana* label, 275–76, 293
Hirschfield, Magnus, 63 n.14
HIV corridor, notion of, 129
HIV/AIDS, 125, 129–30, 143, 148, 245, 301; blame for, 142; fear of, 127, 123–24 n.13, 154–55 n.5; as a foreign deviance, 197, 206 n.12, 259; in Greece, 123 n.9, n.12; politics, 242–43; and sexual identity, 246, 264; as social leveler, 264
HIV/AIDS prevention, 19, 30 n.8, 31 n.17, 125–28, 137, 140–42, 148, 153–54, 185 n.9, 282; in Africa, 43–45; and "being modern," 112; as collective endeavour, 60, 96; and confessional technologies,

246–48, 264–66; discourse, 34 n.28, 197, 283; and gender, 47–48; and global flows of capital, 300; in Greece, 112–15; and hijras, 281; in India, 242, 283; and liberal humanism, 241; limited to risk reduction, 143; moral dimension of, 270; in Nepal, 39–40, 45–50, 62 n.5; and "new facts of life," 245; and NGOS, 246, 257–58, 269–71, 281–82, 299–300; and objective neutrality, 45, 47; and openness, 45–46, 248, 260; and the problem of translation, 285–86, 292; religious involvement in, 150–52; and translocal cultural logics, 271–72, 284, 288
Homosexuality, 7, 80, 113; as cosmopolitan category, 279; fashioning of, 242; and gay rights movement, 36 n.34, 63 n.13, 270–71; versus the MSM category, 283; and the Mumbai film industry, 281–82; research on African, 250; ritual, 6; and strategies of pleasure, 258; as Western import, 156 n.13, 250–51. *See also* Same-sex relations
Homosocial culture, 247; and the Abidjan "milieu," 248–60; categories in, 271; and economic access, 259, 265; performative dimension of, 252; and rumoring networks, 253–57; and specialized language, 253; and voluntary associations, 258–64
Hopkins, Jeffrey, 218, 220–21
Houphouët-Boigny, Felix, 245, 249–50
Huaroni people, 8
Huli people, 52
Human, liberal, 241
Human rights, 13
Human sexual constitution, theory of, 81–85; and biological determinism, 83–85; and gender differences, 81–85; and "normalcy," 81, 83–85; and sexual rhythm, 82

Identity: Greek national, 97; "modern" women's, 121–22 n.1; reproductive, 67;

"foreignization" of, 188, 198, 201, 203, 205; and loyalty to socialist state, 230
Norplant, 173, 231

Obote, Milton, 144, 149, 155 n.5
Ogborn, Anne, 280–81
Oostvogels, Robert, 283–84
Orientalism, 166; and projected sexualities, 206 n.4

Panthi, 271–72, 274, 284, 286–88
Papandreou, Andreas, 117
Patibrata, 192–93, 204
Pendatang, 164–65, 169, 177, 179, 181; and citizenship, 171, and family planning, 173; and racist ideology, 176
Pentecostal revivals, 150–51
Pleasure, sexual, 126, 139; commercializing, 128; dangerous consequences of, 143; silence about, 126; Tibetan term for, 217
Politics, identity, 36 n.4, 160, 241; and authenticity, 271; and conflicting allegiances, 281–82; and class, 295–96, 298–99; gay, 63 n.13, 242, 270–301; and internet communication, 282, 294, 296–99; and modernity, 293; Muslim-Hindu, 242; overlap as key to, 292; and power, 295; and reproductive policy, 230
Polyandry, 219
Polygamy, 31 n.17, 134
Polygyny, 166, 170, 174, 183, 219
Population management, 32 n.20, 121, 172; and eugenics, 12; in Maoist China, 223. *See also* Fertility control
Pornography, 160, 188; videos, 193, 195–96
Positive Nation, 258–66; and rhetoric of openness, 263
Prajnaopaya, 210
Pregnancy, medical model of, 119
Pronatalism: in Greece, 106; in Maoist China, 224; in Soviet Union, 71, 93 n.1
Prostitution, 18, 206 n.3, 206 n.11; and

AIDS prevention, 283–84; and charitable work, 200; and class identities, 193; and demoralization of Tibet, 235; and economic resources, 204; and "foreignization" or colonization, 189–92, 199, 201; as label, 157 n.19; and "middle-man" position, 203–4; and modernization, 235–36; and moral redemption, 237; and personal identity, 203; and "rainbow body" story, 236–37; and sexual standards, 234–36; specialization and, 202–4; symbolizing nation's boundaries, 187–91, 204; in Tibet, 233–37; and wife hybrid, 204–5
Public health, 60; colonial, 31 n.17, 149; discourse, 53, 126, 153–54, 170, 246–47; programs, 43, 45–46; racism in, 176
Pulling, labia, 133–34, 138, 149–50, 156 n.16, 158 n.26; commodification of, 138–40; modern form of, 139; as symbol of tradition, 148
Purdah, 191
Pyar mohabbat, 273–74

Queer theory, 5, 7, 251

Racial difference, 181; and legitimation of violence, 183
Racism: and healthcare delivery, 176–77, 185 n.10; and Papuan separatist violence, 185 n.13; and sexual ideology and regulation, 175–76
Reddy, Gayatri, 271–72, 274, 277
Reincarnation, transfers of political power and, 211–12
Representation: limits of, 9; of sexual norms, 165–66
Reproductive health, 13, 40–41, 62 n.3; differential access to, 177; indigenous understandings of, 42; medicalization of, 126; programs, 41, 148, 152; women's, 71. *See also* Sexual health
Reproductive technologies, new, 107
Reting Rinpoche, 212

. . .

Library of Congress Cataloging-in-Publication Data

Sex in development : science, sexuality, and morality in global

perspective / Vincanne Adams and Stacy Leigh Pigg, eds.

p. cm.

Includes bibliographical references and index.

ISBN 0-8223-3479-8 (cloth: alk. paper)

ISBN 0-8223-3491-7 (pbk. : alk. paper)

1. Sex—Developing countries. 2. Sex customs—Developing

countries. 3. Sexual ethics—Developing countries. I. Adams,

Vincanne, 1959– II. Pigg. Stacy Leigh, 1960–

HQ18.D44S49 2005

306.7'09172'4—dc22

2004025372